AMERICANS AT WAR

AMERICANS AT WAR

Society, Culture, and the Homefront

VOLUME 3: 1901–1945

John P. Resch, Editor in Chief

MACMILLAN REFERENCE USA
An imprint of Thomson Gale, a part of The Thomson Corporation

THOMSON

GALE

Detroit • New York • San Francisco • San Diego • New Haven, Conn. • Waterville, Maine • London • Munich

THOMSON

★ ™

GALE

Americans at War: Culture, Society, and the Homefront

John P. Resch, Editor in Chief

LIBRARY OF CONGRESS CATALOGING-IN-PUBLICATION DATA

Americans at war : society, culture, and the homefront/John P. Resch, Editor in Chief.
   p. cm.
     Includes bibliographical references and index.
     ISBN 0-02-865806-X (set hardcover : alk. paper)—ISBN 0-02-865807-8 (v. 1)—
     ISBN 0-02-865808-6 (v. 2)—ISBN 0-02-865809-4 (v. 3)—ISBN 0-02-865810-8
     (v. 4)—ISBN 0-02-865993-7 (e-book)
     1. United States—History, Military. 2. United States—Social conditions.
     3. United States—Social life and customs. 4. War and society—United
     States—History. I. Resch, John Phillips

E181.A453 2005
973—dc22
                                      2004017314

This title is also available as an e-book.
ISBN 0-02-865993-7
Contact your Thomson Gale sales representative for ordering information.

Printed in the United States of America
10 9 8 7 6 5 4 3 2 1

TABLE OF CONTENTS

VOLUME 2: 1816–1900

VOLUME 4: 1946–PRESENT

CONTRIBUTORS

Daniel W. Aldridge, III
Davidson College
    African Americans (Freed People)
    Douglass, Frederick

John K. Alexander
University of Cincinnati
    Sons of Liberty

Donna Alvah
St. Lawrence University
    Military Families
    Vietnam Veterans
    Women's Rights and Feminism, 1946–Present

Angelo T. Angelis
Hunter College
    Revolution and Radical Reform

Janis Appier
University of Tennessee
    Catt, Carrie Chapman

Marie L. Aquila
Ball State University's Indiana Academy of Science,
    Mathematics, and Humanities
    Music, World War II

Robert A. Arlt
Independent Scholar
    Jefferson, Thomas

Stephen V. Ash
University of Tennessee at Knoxville
    Occupation of the South

Jeanie Attie
Long Island University
    United States Sanitary Commission

Allan W. Austin
College Misericordia
    Japanese Americans, World War II
    Tokyo Rose

Jean Harvey Baker
Goucher College
    Lincoln, Mary Todd
    Women's Suffrage Movement

James M. Banner, Jr.
Washington, D.C.
Federalist Party
Hartford Convention

Lance Banning
Independent Scholar
Jeffersonian Republican Party
Madison, James

J. L. Bell
Independent Scholar
Boston Massacre: Pamphlets and Propaganda
Boston Tea Party: Politicizing Ordinary People
Hewes, George Robert Twelves

Richard J. Bell
Harvard University
Republican Womanhood

Scott H. Bennett
Georgian Court University
Dissent in World War I and World War II

Chad Berry
Maryville College
Regional Migration, World War I and World War
II

Michael E. Birdwell
Tennessee Technological University
York, Alvin Cullum

Mary W. Blanchard
Independent Scholar
Visual Arts, World War I

Larry I. Bland
Marshall Museum VMI
Marshall, George C.

Rose Blue
Independent Scholar
Age of Westward Expansion
Cochran, Jackie
Compromise of 1850
Confederate States of America
Davis, Angela
Ford, Henry
Hiroshima Guilt
Kirkpatrick, Jeanne
Madison, Dolley
New York City Draft Riots
Pirates and the Barbary War
United Nations

David Bogen
Emerson College
Iran-Contra Affair

Mark Boulton
University of Tennessee
Allies, Images of
Peace Movements, 1898–1945
Propaganda, 1898–1945
Wayne, John

Terry Bouton
University of Maryland
Civil Liberties: Kentucky and Virginia Resolutions

Charlene M. Boyer Lewis
Kalamazoo College
Recreation and Social Life

Patricia Bradley
Temple University
Slavery and the Homefront, 1775–1783

Stuart D. Brandes
Independent Scholar
Financing, World War I
Financing, World War II

Dewey A. Browder
Austin Peay State University
Berlin as Symbol

Margaret Lynn Brown
Brevard College
Civilian Conservation Corps (CCC)

Mary Lynn McCree Bryan
Duke University
Addams, Jane

Lisa M. Budreau
St. Anthony's College, Oxford University
Armistice Day
Gold Star Mothers Pilgrimage
Monuments, Cemeteries, Spanish American War
Monuments, Cemeteries, World War I

Stephanie M. H. Camp
University of Washington
Slavery

D'Ann Campbell
United States Coast Guard Academy
Equal Rights Amendment (ERA) and Drafting
Women

Feminism
Women and World War I
Women and World War II
Women Integrated into the Military

Nicholas J. Capasso
DeCordova Museum and Sculpture Park
Vietnam Veterans Memorial

Lewis H. Carlson
Independent Scholar
Red Scare

John Whiteclay Chambers II
Rutgers University
Wilson, Woodrow

Paul A. Cimbala
Fordham University
Civil War Veterans
Freedmen's Bureau

J. Ransom Clark
Muskingum College
CIA and Espionage

John E. Clark, Jr.
Independent Scholar
Railroads

Craig T. Cobane
Culver-Stockton College
Atomic Energy Commission
Star Wars
Terrorism, Fears of
Think Tanks

David G. Coleman
Miller Center of Public Affairs, University of Virginia
Kennedy, John Fitzgerald

Susan G. Contente
Independent Scholar
Clothing, World War I and World War II

Conrad C. Crane
United States Army War College
Mitchell, Billy
Stewart, Jimmy

Robert E. Cray, Jr.
Montclair State University
Politics and Expressions of Patriotism

Lynda Lasswell Crist
Rice University
Davis, Jefferson

Wayne Cutler
University of Tennessee
Polk, James K.

Ginger R. Davis
Independent Scholar
Vietnamese and Hmong Refugees
Who Served in Vietnam?

Michael Davis
Independent Scholar
Adams, John
Common Sense
Olympics and Cold War

Mary A. DeCredico
United States Naval Academy
Chesnut, Mary Boykin

James X. Dempsey
Center for Democracy & Technology
Civil Liberties, 1945–Present

Victor G. Devinatz
Illinois State University
Labor, 1946–Present

Jose O. Diaz
Ohio State University
Davis, Varina Howell

Jonathan M. DiCicco
Rutgers, The State University of New Jersey
Disarmament and Arms Control, 1898–1945

Ricky Dobbs
Texas A & M - Commerce
Texas, Republic of

Michael B. Dougan
Arkansas State University
Black Codes
Civil Liberties, Civil War

Robert C. Doyle
Franciscan University of Steubenville
Prisons and Prisoners of War, 1815–1900

James D. Drake
Metropolitan State College
King Philip's War, Legacy of

Mara Drogan
University of Albany, SUNY
Arms Control Debate

Christopher M. Duncan
University of Dayton
Anti-Federalists

Sylvia Engdahl
Independent Scholar
Space Race

Thomas I. Faith
George Washington University
Roosevelt, Eleanor

Victoria A. Farrar-Myers
University of Texas at Arlington
Bush, George H.W.
Bush, George W.

Elizabeth Faue
Wayne State University
Veterans Benefits

Ilene Rose Feinman
California State University, Monterey Bay
Peace Movements, 1946–Present

Daniel Feller
University of Tennessee
Jackson, Andrew

Michael D. Fellman
Simon Fraser University
Lee, Robert E.

Phyllis F. Field
Ohio University
Political Parties

Gayle V. Fischer
Salem State College
Clothing

Thomas Fleming
Independent Scholar
Hamilton, Alexander

Justin Florence
Harvard University
Quasi-War and the Rise of Political Parties

Ernest Freeberg
University of Tennessee
Civil Liberties, World War I
Journalism, Spanish American War

Richard M. Fried
University of Illinois at Chicago
McCarthyism

Tim Alan Garrison
Portland State University
Indian Removal and Response

Edith B. Gelles
Stanford University
Adams, Abigail

Nancy Gentile Ford
Bloomsburg University of Pennsylvania
Americanization
Labor, World War I
Mobilization for War

Delia Gillis
Central Missouri State University
Education
Powell, Colin
Refugees

Andrew D. Glassberg
University of Missouri—St. Louis
Military Bases

David T. Gleeson
University of Charleston
Immigrants and Immigration
Lost Cause

Rebecca Goetz
Harvard University
Galloway, Grace: Diary of a Loyalist

Eliga H. Gould
University of New Hampshire
Peace of Paris, 1763

Lewis L. Gould
University of Texas, emeritus
Great Society
Johnson, Lyndon Baines
1968 Upheaval

Charles D. Grear
Texas Christian University
Blockade, Civil War

Emily Greenwald
Historical Research Associates, Inc. (Missoula, MT)
Dawes Severalty Act

Beth Griech-Polelle
Bowling Green State University
Holocaust, American Response to

David Grimsted
University of Maryland
Violence

Ricardo Griswold del Castillo
San Diego State University
Guadalupe Hidalgo, Treaty of

Michael J. Guasco
Davidson College
Bacon's Rebellion

Allen C. Guelzo
Gettysburg College
Lincoln, Abraham

Joan R. Gundersen
University of Pittsburgh
Brown, Charlotte: Diary of a Nurse
Camp Followers: War and Women
Drinker, Elizabeth

Michael W. Hail
Morehead State University
Poor Relief, 1815–1900
States and Nation Building, 1775–1783

Jeremy L. Hall
Independent Scholar
States and Nation Building, 1775–1783

John Earl Haynes
Library of Congress
Rosenberg, Hiss, Oppenheimer Cases

Sam W. Haynes
University of Texas at Arlington
Manifest Destiny

Kenneth J. Heineman
Ohio University
Americanism vs. Godless Communism
Communism and Anticommunism

Jan Kenneth Herman
Bureau of Medicine and Surgery, Wash DC
Medicine, World War II

Donald R. Hickey
Wayne State College
Embargo
War of 1812

Sarah Hilgendorff List
Independent Historian
Ku Klux Klan
Segregation, Racial, 1815–1900
Whitman, Walt

Sylvia D. Hoffert
University of North Carolina at Chapel Hill
Woman's Rights Movement

Leonne M. Hudson
Kent State University
Food Shortages

Darren Hughes
University of Tennessee
Motion Pictures during World Wars I and II

Jean M. Humez
University of Massachusetts, Boston
Tubman, Harriet

R. Douglas Hurt
Iowa State University
Farming

Samuel C. Hyde, Jr.
Southeastern Louisiana University
Sharecropping and Tenant Farming

Christina Jarvis
State University of New York at Fredonia
Visual Arts, World War II
World War II, Images of

Laura S. Jensen
University of Massachusetts
Veterans' Benefits

Richard Jensen
Independent Scholar
9–11

Herbert A. Johnson
University of South Carolina Law School
Supreme Court
Supreme Court and War Powers

Adam Jones
Center for Research and Teaching in Economics (CIDE), Mexico City
Latinos in the Military, 1946–Present

Steven Jones
Brown University
Nuclear Freeze Movement
Weapons of Mass Destruction

John P. Kaminski
University of Wisconsin, Madison
Washington, George

Angela Frye Keaton
University of Tennessee
Civil Liberties, World War II

Jennifer D. Keene
Chapman University
American Legion
Bonus March
Demobilization
Profiteering

Richard Kirkendall
University of Washington
Truman, Harry S.
Truman Doctrine

Wendy Kozol
Oberlin College
Photojournalism

Gregory Kupsky
University of Tennessee
Prisoner of War Camps, United States

Stanford J. Layton
Weber State University
Homestead Act

Jama Lazerow
Wheelock College
Black Power/Black Panthers

James S. Leamon
Bates College
Armed Conflicts in America, 1587-1815
Loyalists
Shays's and Whiskey Rebellions

Daniel B. Lee
Pennsylvania State University
Television, 1946–Present

Edward Lengel
Independent Scholar
Memoirs, Autobiographies

Neil W. Lerner
Davidson College
Music, Civil War
Music, Musicians, and the War on Terrorism
Music, World War I

J. E. Lighter
University of Tennessee
Literature, World War I
Literature, World War II

Blanche M. G. Linden
Independent Scholar
Anthony, Susan B.
Friedan, Betty

Judy Barrett Litoff
Bryant College
Rosie the Riveter
Women, Employment of

Ellen M. Litwicki
State University of New York at Fredonia
Fourth of July
Memorial (Decoration) Day

M. Philip Lucas
Cornell College
Elections, Presidential: The Civil War

Ralph E. Luker
Independent Historian
Churches, Mainstream
Civil Rights Movement
Jackson, Jesse Louis
King, Martin Luther, Jr.
Nonviolence

Michael Lynch
Cornell University
Iran-Contra Affair

John Majewski
University of California
Financing the War

John W. Malsberger
Muhlenberg College
Cuban Missile Crisis
Kissinger, Henry
Nixon, Richard M.

Anthony Maravillas
Independent Scholar
Tet, Impact of

Rosemary Bryant Mariner
Center for the Study of War and Society
    Conscription, World War II
    National Guard

Norman Markowitz
Rutgers University
    Higher Education
    Labor, World War II

John F. Marszalek
Mississippi State University
    Sherman's March to the Sea

James Marten
Marquette University
    Children and the Civil War

Cathy Matson
University of Delaware
    Continental Congresses

Holly A. Mayer
Duquesne University
    Generals' Wives: Martha Washington, Catharine
        Greene, Lucy Knox

Paul T. McCartney
University of Richmond
    Neo-isolationism
    Triumphalism
    War Powers Act

Richard B. McCaslin
High Point University
    Johnson, Andrew

Michael A. McDonnell
University of Sydney
    Republicanism and War

Gordon B. McKinney
Berea College
    Peace Movements

John R. McKivigan
Indiana University- Purdue University at Indianapolis
    Abolitionists

Sally G. McMillen
Davidson College
    Civil War and Industrial and Technological
        Advances
    Civil War and Its Impact on Sexual Attitudes on
        the Homefront

    Dix, Dorothea
    Family Life
    Stanton, Elizabeth Cady

Daniel T. Miller
Historical Solutions LLC, Indiana
    Alien and Sedition Laws
    Hamilton's Reports

Laura M. Miller
Vanderbilt University
    Arnold, Benedict
    Du Bois, W.E.B.
    Grant, Ulysses S.
    Hemingway, Ernest
    Jackson, Thomas J. (Stonewall)

Randall M. Miller
St. Joseph's University
    Religion, Civil War

D. E. "Gene" Mills Jr.
Florida State University
    Churches, Evangelical, 1946–Present

Curtis Miner
State Museum of Pennsylvania
    Levittown

Susan Moeller
Philip Merrill College of Journalism
    Photography, Civil War
    Photography, World War I
    Photography, World War II

Edwin E. Moise
Clemson University
    Pentagon Papers

John Morello
DeVry University
    Antiwar Movement
    Drugs and Vietnam
    Grunts
    Music, Vietnam Era
    My Lai
    Selective Service

Michael A. Morrison
Purdue University
    Kansas Nebraska Act

James C. Mott
Independent Scholar
    Holocaust Guilt
    Politics and Elections

Malcolm Muir, Jr.
Austin Peay State University
MacArthur, Douglas

Brigitte L. Nacos
Columbia University
Hostage Crisis, 1979–1981

Corinne J. Naden
Independent Scholar
Age of Westward Expansion
Cochran, Jackie
Compromise of 1850
Confederate States of America
Davis, Angela
Ford, Henry
Hiroshima Guilt
Kirkpatrick, Jeanne
Madison, Dolley
New York City Draft Riots
Pirates and the Barbary War
United Nations

June Namias
Independent Historian
Rowlandson, Mary

Michael S. Neiberg
United States Air Force Academy
ROTC
Volunteer Army and Professionalism

John Nerone
University of Illinois, Urbana–Champaign
Newspapers and Magazines

Thomas M. Nichols
Naval War College
Preemptive War
Preventive War

Travis Nygard
University of Pittsburgh
Visual Arts, Civil War and the West

Greg O'Brien
University of Southern Mississippi
Jamestown: Legacy of the Massacre of 1622
Legacies of Indian Warfare
Native Americans: Images in Popular Culture

Christopher J. Olsen
Indiana State University
Secession

Russell Olwell
Eastern Michigan University
Manhattan Project

William L. O'Neill
Rutgers University
Roosevelt, Franklin Delano

Stephen R. Ortiz
University of Florida
Hoover, Herbert
Veterans of Foreign Wars

Victoria E. Ott
University of Tennessee
Widows and Orphans
Women on the Homefront

Matthew M. Oyos
Radford University
Roosevelt, Theodore

Chester J. Pach, Jr.
Ohio University
Eisenhower, Dwight D.
Korea, Impact of
Nitze, Paul
Nonalignment
Patriotism
Reagan, Ronald

Richard Panchyk
Independent Historian
Clinton, William Jefferson
Conscription, World War I
Flags
Fort William Henry Massacre, Cultural Legacy
Homeland Security
Men on the Home Front, Civil War
Monuments, Cemeteries, World War II
Rationing
War, Impact on Ethnic Groups
Washington's Farewell Address

Melinda Lee Pash
Independent Historian
African Americans, World War I
American Indians, World War I and World War II
National Anthem
Sexual Behavior

Sidney L. Pash
Fayetteville State University
Economy, World War I
Economy, World War II

Isolationism
McKinley, William
New Deal
Pearl Harbor Investigation
Public Opinion

Edward Piacentino
High Point University
Humor, Political

Jim Piecuch
Clarion University
Commonwealth Men
Federalist Papers
Stamp Act Congress

S. W. Pope
University of Lincoln, UK
Sports, World War I
Sports, World War II

Charles B. Potter
Independent Scholar
Cooper, James Fenimore
The Spy: First American War Novel
Wyoming Valley Conflict

Caren Prommersberger
Independent Scholar
Conscription, World War I
Fort William Henry Massacre, Cultural Legacy
Monuments, Cemeteries, World War II

Luca Prono
ABC-Clio
Painters and Patriotism, Late 18th and Early 19th
     Centuries
Popular Culture and Cold War
"Who Lost China" Debate

Sarah J. Purcell
Grinnell College
Battle of New Orleans
Bunker Hill Monument
Lafayette's Tour
Memory and Early Histories of the Revolution
Montgomery, Richard

Richard J. Regan
Fordham University
Just-War Debate

John P. Resch
University of New Hampshire—Manchester

Constitution: Creating a Republic
Paine, Thomas
Religion and Revolution
Revolutionary War Veterans

Jason S. Ridler
Royal Military College of Canada
H-Bomb, Decision to Build

Edward Rielly
Saint Joseph's College of Maine
Fiction and Memoirs, Vietnam

Stuart I. Rochester
Office of the Secretary of Defense
POW, MIA

John B. Romeiser
University of Tennessee
Journalism, World War II

Frank A. Salamone
Iona College
Civil War and Industrial and Technological
     Advances
Civil War and Its Impact on Sexual Attitudes on
     the Homefront
Gays, Civil Rights for, 1946–Present
Journalism, World War I
Multiculturalism and Cold War
Race and Military
Teenagers, 1946–Present

Walter L. Sargent
University of Minnesota
Association Test
Mobilization, War for Independence

Alfred Saucedo
University of Chicago
Enemy, Images of

Gregory L. Schneider
Emporia State University
Goldwater, Barry
John Birch Society

Nancy Schurr
University of Tennessee, Knoxville
Medicine and Health

Larry Schweikart
University of Dayton
Aerospace Industry

Ben H. Severance
University of Tennessee, Knoxville
Reconstruction

John Y. Simon
Southern Illinois University Carbondale
Gettysburg Address

Philip L. Simpson
Brevard Community College
Cold War Novels and Movies
Literature

Gerald L. Sittser
Whitworth College
Religion, World War II

Sheila L. Skemp
University of Mississippi
Franklin, Benjamin

David Sloan
Morehead State College
Poor Relief, 1816–1900

Fred H. Smith
Davidson College
Economic Change and Industrialization

John David Smith
North Carolina State
Emancipation Proclamation

Mark M. Smith
University of South Carolina
Stono Rebellion

André B. Sobocinski
Bureau of Medicine and Surgery, Washington, D.C.
Medicine, World War I

Richard C. Spicer
Boston University
Music and the Revolution

Kathryn St. Clair Ellis
University of Tennessee, Knoxville
GI Bill of Rights

Ian K. Steele
University of Western Ontario
European Invasion of Indian North America,
1513–1765

Stephen K. Stein
University of Memphis
Israel and the United States

Christopher H. Sterling
George Washington University
Radio and Power of Broadcasting

Margaret D. Stock
United States Military Academy
Al-Qaida and Taliban
Supreme Court, 1815–1900

Brian D. Stokes
Camden County College
States' Rights, Theory of

Amy H. Sturgis
Belmont University
Monroe, James
Monroe's Tour of New England

Kirsten D. Sword
Georgetown University
Families at War

James Lance Taylor
University of San Francisco
Slavery in America

Athan Theoharis
Marquette University
Federal Bureau of Investigations (FBI)

Rod Timanus
Independent Scholar
Alamo

Lorett Treese
Bryn Mawr College Library
Valley Forge

A. Bowdoin Van Riper
Southern Polytechnic State University
Civil Defense, 1946–Present

John R. Vile
Middle Tennessee State University
Articles of Confederation
Constitution: Bill of Rights
Constitutional Amendments and Changes

Jonathan E. Vincent
University of Kentucky
Red Badge of Courage

Michael Wala
Ruhr-Universität Bochum, Historisches Institut
Containment and Détente

Matthew C. Ward
University of Dundee, Scotland
French and Indian War, Legacy of
Mobilization, French and Indian War

Matt Wasniewski
University of Maryland
Cold War Mobilization
Military-Industrial Complex
NSC #68

Cindy Weinstein
California Institute of Technology
Uncle Tom's Cabin

Patricia Weiss Fagen
Georgetown University
Human Rights

Douglas L. Wheeler
University of New Hampshire
Espionage and Spies

George White, Jr.
University of Tennessee, Knoxville
African Americans, World War II
Imperialism

Stephen J. Whitfield
Brandeis University
Arts as Weapon

Robert C. Williams
Davidson College
Greeley, Horace

Tony Williams
Southern Illinois University, Carbondale
Vietnam Films

Clyde N. Wilson
University of South Carolina
Calhoun, John Caldwell

Mark R. Wilson
University of North Carolina at Charlotte
Business and Finance
Labor and Labor Movements
Preparedness

Meghan Kate Winchell
Independent Scholar
USO

Mitchell Yockelson
United States National Archives and Records
Administration
Red Cross, American
Veterans of Foreign Wars

Ronald Young
Georgia Southern University
Declaration of Independence
Foreign Aid, 1946–Present
Latinos, World War I and World War II
Urbanization

Rosemarie Zagarri
George Mason University
Sampson, Deborah
Warren, Mercy Otis

Stephen Zunes
University of San Francisco
Muslims, Stereotypes and Fears of

PREFACE

Preparation for war, war itself, and the legacy of war are among the most important forces shaping American society and culture. Nevertheless, the study of war is often treated as if the only topics of importance were battles and campaigns, results measured in territory, and reputations gained or lost. This four-volume reference set, *Americans at War*, provides students with a different perspective by examining the profound effect of war upon American society, culture, and national identity. The 395 articles in this set, written by leading academic and independent scholars, cover a wide range of topics. We hope that these articles, focused on the effect of war upon society, will provide new insights into the nation's history and character, and will serve as a resource for further study of America's past and for charting the nation's future.

Volume 1 covers the longest period, 1500 to 1815, especially the era beginning in 1607 with the first permanent English settlement at Jamestown. Between 1607 and 1700, apart from frontier skirmishes, raids, and ambushes, colonists from South Carolina through New England were engaged in over a score of declared wars, rebellions, and insurrections. In the eighteenth century Americans were at war more than at peace. Between 1700 and 1800 Americans engaged in seventeen separate conflicts and rebellions, including the 1739 uprising of slaves at Stono, South Carolina, and the Revolutionary War, 1775–1783. Between 1798 and 1825 the United States was at war with Barbary pirates, Seminole Indians, and in the "Second War of Independence," 1812–1815, with Great Britain and Canada.

The articles in this volume examine how those wars, especially the Revolutionary War, influenced American literature, art, and music; affected the role of women; shaped the economy; and challenged the institution of slavery. Articles also examine how dissent and rebellion contributed to America's creed of liberty and the formation of its Constitution. Some articles focus on the effects of war in forming and reinforcing American racial attitudes towards Indians and blacks. Others discuss the effect of war upon civil liberties, such as freedom of speech and politics. The memory of America's wars helped to define the nation's culture and identity through patriotic celebrations, monuments, and memorials, and by honoring Revolutionary war veterans. Wars also reinforced the religious view that the nation was a beacon to the world's suffering and repressed.

The articles in Volume 2, 1816 to 1900, examine how wars in the nineteenth century shaped American society, culture, and identity while the United States changed from a small, nearly homogeneous, agricultural country into a continental, multicultural, industrial nation. American literature and art, the role of women, industry and technology, race relations, popular culture, political parties, and the Constitution were influenced by those wars, especially the Civil War (1861–1865). Protests against the institution of slavery and the spread of slavery affected the nation's expansion westward. The coming of the Civil War changed American politics through the formation of new parties.

In many ways, the Civil War was America's second revolution, fought to preserve and advance the founding principles of the nation. When Lincoln spoke of a "new birth of freedom" at Gettysburg, he addressed the meaning and vitality of America's most cherished ideals and values—values that were tested and refined by that war. Prior to the Civil War women sought equal rights and Abolitionists fought to end the institution of slavery. Whereas women did not secure their rights after the war, Constitutional amendments ended slavery and redefined the rights of citizenship that later generations struggled to achieve.

The Civil War also resolved the Constitutional issue of whether the states had the right to secede from the Union. The South clung to its image of the war as a "Lost Cause" that had impoverished the region and undermined its way of life. One legacy of defeat was the restoration of racial subjugation through "Black Codes," sharecropping, and the Ku Klux Klan. For both North and South, the Civil War became a source for literature, art, music, and public celebrations to memorialize their concepts of conflict and to honor their own veterans. Although the Civil War preserved the Union, society and culture remained divided.

The articles in Volume 3, 1901 to 1945, examine how America's rise as an imperial and then a world power shaped American society, culture, and identity. During this period the United States engaged in four significant overseas wars, the Spanish American War (1898), the Philippine Insurrection (1899–1902), the First World War (1917–1918), and the Second World War (1941–1945). American literature and art, the role of women, industry and technology, race and ethnic relations, popular culture, political parties, and the power of government were profoundly affected by those wars. The First World War produced a mass migration of blacks from the South to northern cities to work in defense industries. Hostility toward the enemy produced public discrimination against citizens with German ancestors. A "Red Scare," meaning the fear of Communist subversion and restriction of civil liberties by our government, followed the Russian Revolution in 1917. Americans became increasingly suspicious of aliens and dissenters. While seeking world peace through treaties promoting disarmament and renouncing war in the 1930s, America turned its back on the League of Nations and aggression in Asia and Europe.

When World War II began in Europe in 1939, the United States remained neutral. Nevertheless, the nation began to prepare for war, which was declared after Pearl Harbor was attacked by Japan. World War II reshaped American society. Massive defense spending and the mobilization of young men and women for military service ended the Great Depression, which had begun in 1929. As a result of defense orders, big business prospered and labor union membership soared during the war years. America achieved a full employment economy during this conflict and this required a large number of women to enter the work force to increase defense production. It also spurred the massive migration of many Americans, especially African Americans, to cities in the North and West. The war effort reinvigorated movements to end racial discrimination and gender inequity. Many of the articles examine the legacy of that war in a wide range of areas that include the expansion of the federal government over the economy and the life of the average citizen as well as fashion, sports, veterans' organizations, medicine, gender roles, race relations, movies, music, patriotic celebrations, veterans, civil liberties, and war widows and orphans.

Volume 4's articles cover 1946 to 2004 and examine how the Cold War (1946–1991) and the War on Terror have formed American society, culture, and identity. For nearly fifty years, United States and its allies contested the Communist Bloc led by the Soviet Union. The "cold" part of the Cold War involved an elaborate worldwide network of alliances and military bases, an arms race to produce nuclear weapons, and the means to deliver those weapons to destroy whole civilizations. The fall of the Berlin Wall in 1989 and collapse of the Soviet Union in 1991 left the United States as the only superpower on the globe. The years after 1991 appeared to begin a new era of peace as fear of a cataclysmic war began to fade. However, since September 11, 2001 a new threat, terrorism, has again led America to an unprecedented form of war that is both foreign and domestic. Homeland security has become a feature of war in the twenty-first century.

The articles in this volume reflect the new role of America after World War II. Unlike the generation following World War I, Americans could not return to isolationism. National Defense became the nation's priority. Safeguarding the nation against subversion and aggression affected all parts of American society, culture and identity. Anticommunism following World War II produced a second Red Scare that again tested the limits of civil liberties and introduced a new term, "McCarthyism." In 1954 Congress amended the Pledge of Allegiance, adding "under God" to the description of "one nation" to underscore the difference between "godless communism" and the religious foundation of American democracy.

An arms race with the Soviet Union contributed to the growth of the federal government, fueled spending on education, and created a significant defense industry. In his farewell address in 1961 President Eisenhower warned of a "military-industrial complex." Films and novels about experiences in World War II, the Korean War, and especially the Vietnam War revealed the traumatic effects of combat on soldiers and their families. During the Vietnam War television brought the images of combat into American homes.

Defeating Fascism and Nazi racialism in World War II energized efforts to close the gap between American ideals of equality and opportunity and social practices that involved racial, gender, and sexual discrimination. During the late 1950s, 1960s, and early 1970s, anti-war and anti-establishment protests as well as the civil rights, feminist, and black power movements, challenged cultural conventions and roiled American society. These conflicts changed American literature and art, gender and race relations, popular culture, the entertainment industry, political parties, and the Constitution. The articles in this volume examine those changes as legacies of the Cold War and America's conflicts since World War II. They also explore the impact of the War on Terror on American citizens through the Homeland Security Act, the implications of the concepts of "just wars" and "preemptive war" on American society, culture, and identity as a nation.

All of the articles in these four volumes are written for the general reader and are supplemented with aids to make the material accessible. A Topic Outline assists readers who wish to focus on a particular issue, such as civil liberties, that appears in all volumes. Additional text appears as sidebars to further illustrate or elaborate portions of articles. A select bibliography follows each article for readers who wish to study the subject further. A general chronology of events from 1500 to 2004 will assist readers in placing the articles they are reading in a larger historical context. An Index will lead readers to

specific subjects. A Glossary defines key terms that might not be clear to younger readers. The editors hope that *Americans at War* will not only assist students and researchers in obtaining information, but will also encourage additional reading about the effect of war upon American society, culture, and identity.

Americans at War is the product of 234 authors and the editorial board. I thank all of the contributors for their fine work and outstanding scholarship. In particular, I wish to express gratitude and admiration to my associate editors for their thoughtful, timely, and untiring work on this project. Sally G. McMillen, Babcock Professor of History at Davidson College, edited Volume 2. Professor G. Kurt Piehler, Director, Center for the Study of War and Society, University of Tennessee, edited Volume 3. Professor D'Ann Campbell, Dean of Academics, U.S. Coast Guard Academy, and Professor Richard Jensen, Independent Scholar, edited Volume 4. I wish to thank Hélène Potter, senior editor at Macmillan Library Reference. She brought this editorial team together early in the process and has provided support, guidance, and encouragement to transform a concept into reality.

I also thank Oona Schmid at Macmillan, who recognized the need for a reference set on the effects of war upon American society and initiated the project. I hope that she, although no longer at Macmillan, feels the satisfaction of seeing her vision come true. The editors thank Anthony Aiello, who was our first project editor and who is also a contributor to the set. Finally, we wish to extend our deep appreciation and thanks to Kristin Hart, our project editor, who assisted us through the final stages of producing the set. Her attention to detail, responsiveness, clarity, and helpfulness were invaluable in the completion of the project. Finally, I thank the Humanities Center at the University of New Hampshire–Durham for its grant of a Senior Faculty Research Fellowship which helped to provide the time for me to devote to this project, and for support from the University of New Hampshire–Manchester.

John P. Resch
Editor-In-Chief
Editor, Volume 1
Professor of History
University of New Hampshire–Manchester

AMERICA'S RISE AS WORLD POWER, 1890–1945

The relationship of the United States to the world was transformed between 1898 and 1945. The articles in this volume examine how America's rise as an imperial, and then a world, power have shaped American society, culture, and identity. As a result of four overseas wars—the Spanish American War (1898), the Philippine Insurrection (1899–1902), the First World War (1917–1918), and the Second World War (1941–1945)—the United States emerged as a preeminent global power. American literature and art, the role of women, industry and technology, race and ethnic relations, popular culture, political parties, and the power of government were profoundly affected by those wars. Intervention abroad entailed a dramatic shift in the size, organization, and structure of the U.S. military. It also meant a significant expansion of the influence of the federal government over the economy and the average citizen. Furthermore, America's rise as a world power created tension between protecting civil liberties and restricting them to protect national security.

THE SPANISH AMERICAN WAR

In 1898, the United States possessed a modern steel battleship navy that had been recently built to replace Civil War era sailing ships and ironclads. But it maintained only a small regular army that was deployed principally at scattered outposts in the American West. As required by the United States Constitution and federal law, each state continued to maintain militia units, but these citizen soldiers were often ill-equipped and poorly trained. Frequently state militia were used by the nation's governors to suppress labor strikes or intervene in cases of domestic disturbance. In sharp contrast, most major European powers used conscription to build vast land armies with a significant portion of the male population serving in the reserves after compulsory military service.

America's decision to go to war with Spain in 1898 marked a significant departure from American foreign policy. Why did Americans decide to fight the fading colonial power that controlled Cuba? The American business community had made substantial investments in the island's sugar industry and wanted them protected. But crude economic interest was not the only reason the United States entered the conflict; many Americans felt a genuine sympathy for the Cuban people's struggle against Spanish colonialism. Moreover, the press often wrote provocative stories that highlighted the harsh abuses Spanish officials directed not only at Cubans, but at some Americans. The mysterious sinking of the U.S. battleship *Maine* in Havana Harbor triggered the march to war. Although most evidence points to its having been sunk as a result of an internal explosion, many Americans blamed Spain for the destruction of the ship and cried out, "Remember the Maine, To Hell with Spain."

As they had in past conflicts, Americans flocked to join the U.S. Volunteers and fight for the duration. Few of the volunteers ever got a chance to fight; instead most spent their time battling disease and the heat in Tampa Bay. The U.S. Navy ensured a quick overwhelming victory in the conflict, which lasted only three months. American naval forces easily sank Spanish fleets in Manila Bay, Philippines and Santiago Bay, Cuba. In the case of Guam, Spanish forces surrendered there without even putting up a fight. The regular army did most of the fighting in this "splendid little war" although one unit of U.S. Volunteers, lead by Colonel Leonard Wood and Lieutenant Colonel Theodore Roosevelt, did manage to join the fight in the outskirts of Santiago at the Battle of San Juan Hill.

The United States entered the Spanish American War with the intention of liberating the Cubans from Spanish colonialism. Cuba was granted independence, but the United States placed limits on its new sovereignty and until the 1930s, through the Platt Amendment, reserved the right to intervene. Two other Spanish possessions, Guam in the Pacific and Puerto Rico, were also annexed by the peace treaty and still remain part of the United States.

THE PHILIPPINE INSURRECTION

Despite the desire of many Filipinos, the United States did not grant the Philippines independence, but annexed that former Spanish colony. This decision provoked America's first Asian war. Initially, the United States fought a conventional war against Filipino rebels and prevailed on the battlefield. To continue the struggle, Filipino leaders switched to guerilla tactics. President Theodore Roosevelt proclaimed the end of the insurrection in 1902; however, fighting continued on some parts of the archipelago until the eve of the First World War.

The war in the Philippines provoked significant public opposition. In 1900, the Democratic nominee for president, William Jennings Bryan, ran on a platform that urged America not to obtain overseas colonies. Moreover, several journalist accounts provoked public outrage in several cases where the U.S. military abused innocent Filipinos.

Although the United States won a quick and decisive victory against Spain and ultimately prevailed in the

Philippines, both conflicts provoked serious debates over the effectiveness of the army. Logistically, the War Department strained to supply troops deployed in Florida and Cuba. Many soldiers became ill and in some cases even died because of "embalmed" beef. More soldiers died in the Spanish American War from disease than from enemy bullets. As a result, a series of major structural changes were made to the organization of the War Department, including the creation of the army's first general staff. Also, under the 1903 Dick Act and the National Defense Act of 1916, the federal government provided funds to the states to improve the military readiness of the militia and make it into the army's principal reserve force.

THE FIRST WORLD WAR

In contrast to the beginning of the Spanish American War, the United States entered the First World War only after a prolonged debate. Conflict in Europe began in August, 1914, but the U.S. Congress did not declare war until April, 1917. As late as 1916, President Woodrow Wilson ran for reelection under the slogan, "He Kept Us Out of War." A small but influential peace movement urged the Wilson Administration to avoid war and mediate the conflict. Most German Americans, as well as many Irish Americans, did not want the United States to enter this conflict on the side of Britain and France. Many recently-arrived European immigrants came to America to escape forced military service and Europe's war. Those on the left, especially the Socialist Party under Eugene Debs and the Industrial Workers of the World, condemned this conflict as a capitalist's war.

Despite significant opposition, America eventually did enter the war against Germany and the Austro-Hungarian Empire. Many national political and economic leaders were of English descent and felt strong cultural ties to Great Britain. Americans were appalled by the decision of Germany to invade neutral Belgium in 1914. As a result of an effective British blockade of German ports, trade ties with that nation diminished. In sharp contrast, the American economy boomed as defense orders from Britain, France, Russia, and Italy poured in. To cut off trade to Britain and France, the Germans launched submarine attacks against merchant shipping that on several occasions led to the sinking of passenger ships, most notably the *Lusitania* in 1915. Wilson viewed these attacks as a violation of the laws of war and demanded that Germany avoid sinking passenger ships and ensure that merchant vessels received warning before they were sunk. In 1915 and 1916 the German Government on several occasions bowed to Wilson's demands, but in early 1917 Germany decided to unleash its U-Boats against all ships (enemy and neutral). This led Wilson to seek a declaration of war from Congress in April, 1917.

America's entry into war led to an unprecedented expansion of federal power. For the first time, the United States raised a conscript army to fight a war, jettisoning the century-old system of U.S. Volunteers. Under the direction of Bernard Baruch, the War Industries Board made crucial decisions regarding the management of the economy, especially industrial production and the allocation of scarce resources. For the duration of the conflict, the railroad industry was nationalized. Through the Committee on Public Information, the United States actively sought to shape public opinion through an organized propaganda campaign that involved newsreels, posters, pamphlets, and public speakers. Criticism of the war effort became a federal criminal offense and several dissenters, most notably Eugene Debs, were imprisoned because of their antiwar efforts. Americans were encouraged to support the war effort by voluntarily conserving food and other products, by buying war bonds, and by informing on potential spies and traitors.

Despite this centralization of power in the hands of the federal government, the pace of mobilization remained slow and uneven. Even with conscription, the United States proved unable to send a large army to France until the spring of 1918. The American commander of the American Expeditionary force, General John J. Pershing, resisted calls by the French to break up American units and integrate them into French and British armies. Instead, the Americans fought as a unified force and played an important role in stopping the German offenses in the spring of 1918. In the summer and fall of 1918, American forces contributed to French and British victories that led to the military defeat of German forces in the fall of 1918. In November, 1918, the German high command realized the war was lost and the German Kaiser abdicated the throne.

Even before the Armistice of November 11, 1918, President Woodrow Wilson had outlined in his "Fourteen Points" a vision for a new world order. In January, 1918, Wilson had called for national self-determination to be a guiding principle in determining European boundaries and explicitly declared U.S. support for granting independence to Poland and to many of the subject peoples of the Austro-Hungarian Empire. He affirmed the right of Belgian neutrality and the need to disarm a defeated Germany. Wilson also stressed the importance of establishing a new international organization that would preserve world peace through collective security. In urging the creation of the League of Nations, Wilson urged Americans to embrace internationalism and abandon political isolationism.

The First World War produced an ambiguous outcome. Although the United States, France, Great Britain, Italy, and Japan had prevailed against Germany, the success of the Bolshevik Revolution of 1917 meant the emergence of the world's first communist regime, the Soviet Union. Immediately after the Armistice of 1918, revolutions broke out in other parts of Europe, including Germany. Although these revolutionary movements were suppressed, many Americans feared revolution could break out at home; and this led to a continued climate of suppression during the "Red Scare" of 1919 and 1920. Veterans of the war often protested in the 1920s and 1930s that the federal government failed to provide adequate benefits for them. Even the memorialization of the conflict provoked controversy during the interwar years, especially the decision to maintain overseas cemeteries for the American war dead.

Woodrow Wilson was the first sitting president to travel to Europe and personally led the American delegation to negotiate the final peace treaty at Paris in 1919. Although he made a number of compromises with European leaders, especially regarding the application of self-determination, he did manage to get support for the creation of the League of Nations. When he returned home, Wilson proved unable to convince the U.S. Senate to ratify the Treaty of Versailles and join the League of Nations. Although a majority of senators supported the League, there remained significant concerns over limiting American sovereignty, especially regarding congressional authority to make war.

As a result of the First World War, the United States emerged with enormous economic power. The prolonged war bankrupted the major European powers and they remained indebted to the United States for war loans. The United States insisted that former Allies repay their debt in full (only Finland succeeded) and in turn accepted French and British plans to make Germany pay reparations to cover the cost of the war. The United States never joined the League of Nations, but it did continue to promote international disarmament. Two conferences held in Washington in the early 1920s led to significant reduction in the naval forces of the United States, Great Britain, Japan, France, and Italy. The United States joined other nations in signing the Kellogg-Briand Pact in 1928 to outlaw wars of aggression.

THE SECOND WORLD WAR

In the 1930s, Japan, Italy, and Germany sought territorial expansion through war or the threat of invasion. In 1931, Japan attacked Manchuria and succeeded in wresting control of that region from China despite the condemnation of the League of the Nations and the administration of Herbert Hoover. Soon after Adolf Hitler and Nazis came to power in 1933, they began to violate the terms of the Treaty of Versailles by rearming Germany and moving troops into the Rhineland region.

In 1935, Italy invaded Ethiopia and the economic sanctions imposed by the League failed to halt this aggression. In 1938, Germany annexed Austria and, with consent of Britain and France, large portions of Czechoslovakia. Not until Hitler seized all of Czechoslovakia in 1939 did Britain and France make clear their decision to oppose any further German expansion. On September 1, 1939 Hitler invaded Poland and both Britain and France declared war against Germany.

The United States remained neutral in the opening months of the war. Only after the fall of France in 1940 did the administration of Franklin D. Roosevelt (FDR) decisively move to help Great Britain by providing material aid, initially in the form of overage destroyers. Over the course of 1940 and 1941 President Roosevelt not only sped up American rearmament, but also made the case to the American public for the need to increase support for Britain even at the risk of war. In the Pacific, the United States condemned Japanese aggression and offered moral support and some limited aid to China. The decision by Japan in 1940 to sign the Tripartite Pact hardened American attitudes toward that Asian power. Economic sanctions, including a progressively more stringent oil embargo, were established after Japan began to send military forces to occupy French Indochina in 1940 and 1941.

Not all Americans supported the decision of the United States to escalate American involvement in the affairs of Europe and Asia. Isolationists continued to oppose many of the efforts by the Roosevelt Administration to challenge Nazi Germany and Imperial Japan. Even many internationalists who advocated all-out aid to Britain and the Soviet Union wanted to avoid war. The Japanese attack on Pearl Harbor on December 7, 1941 galvanized public opinion in support of entering the Second World War. Pearl Harbor, combined with Germany's declaration of war against the United States a few days later, ended many of the bitter divisions that existed regarding FDR's foreign and military policies.

The Second World War has many parallels with the earlier world war. Again, the United States resorted to conscription. As in the First World War, the federal government actively managed the economy, especially the allocation of resources. In contrast to its position during the First World War, the United States in 1941 emerged as the preeminent "Arsenal of Democracy," producing the necessary tools of war not only to arm the 15 million men and women who served in the armed forces, but also supplying many of the war needs of Great Britain, the Soviet Union, China, and the other Allies. The Second World War was truly a global war, for the United States and Americans forces were deployed on all the continents of the world except Antarctica in an effort to fight the Axis Powers of Germany, Japan, and Italy.

The Second World War profoundly reshaped American society. Massive defense spending and the mobilization of young men and women for military service ended the Great Depression. As a result of defense orders, big business prospered and labor union membership soared during the war years. America achieved a full-employment economy during the conflict and this required large numbers of women to enter the work force to maintain defense production. It also spurred the massive migration of many Americans, especially African Americans, to cities in the North and West with large defense factories. To finance the massive cost of the war, the federal government resorted to borrowing both from large investors and, through defense bonds, from average citizens.

Americans were unified during the Second World War, especially when threatened by a potential Axis victory in the dark days of 1942 and early 1943. Whereas it was often termed the "Good War," there remained significant divisions within society. For instance, Jim Crow segregation continued to be the norm in the South and in the U.S. military. White Americans in places like Detroit and Los Angeles sparked riots when they attacked minority communities. Although Japanese Americans posed no security risk, the federal government placed those living on the West Coast in internment camps.

The United States won a stunning victory in the Second World War, but one that could not have been achieved without Allies. For instance, in the European Theater, the bulk of the German Army between June, 1941 and May, 1945 fought the army of the Soviet Union. The United States and Great Britain did not open a Second Front against Germany until the D-Day landing of June 1944 in Normandy, France. In the Pacific, the Japanese had the bulk of their army deployed in China. The ability of the United States to defeat the Japanese Navy, beginning with the Battle of Midway, proved pivotal in ensuring Allied victory in the Pacific.

Victory in Europe (May 8, 1945) and over Japan (August 14, 1945) was cause for celebration for Americans. But the world had been changed by the Second World War and the United States did not retreat into isolationism. As a result of the Manhattan Project, the United States remained until 1949 the only country that possessed an atomic weapon. With little dissent, the public supported the America's entrance into the United Nations organization and remained committed to maintaining occupation forces in Japan and Germany. The United States did reduce the size of its military forces, but it never fully demobilized its military because of the Cold War that began shortly after the Second World War ended.

G. Kurt Piehler

This systematic outline provides a general overview of the conceptual scheme of *Americans at War,* listing the titles of each entry in each volume. Because the section headings are not mutually exclusive, certain entries in *Americans at War* are listed in more than one section.

VOLUME 1: 1500–1815

AMERICAN REVOLUTION
Association Test
Boston Massacre: Pamphlets and Propaganda
Boston Tea Party: Politicizing Ordinary People
Common Sense
Commonwealth Men
Continental Congresses
Declaration of Independence
Loyalists
Peace of Paris, 1763
Republicanism and War
Revolution and Radical Reform
Sons of Liberty
Stamp Act Congress
States and Nation Building, 1775–1783

BIOGRAPHY
Adams, Abigail
Adams, John
Arnold, Benedict
Cooper, James Fenimore
Drinker, Elizabeth
Franklin, Benjamin
Hamilton, Alexander
Hewes, George Robert Twelves
Jackson, Andrew
Jefferson, Thomas
Madison, Dolley
Madison, James
Monroe, James
Montgomery, Richard
Paine, Thomas
Rowlandson, Mary
Sampson, Deborah
Warren, Mercy Otis
Washington, George

CONSTITUTION
Alien and Sedition Laws
Anti-Federalists
Articles of Confederation
Civil Liberties: Kentucky and Virginia Resolutions
Constitution: Bill of Rights
Constitution: Creating a Republic
Federalist Papers
Hartford Convention
Shays and Whiskey Rebellions

Demobilization
Financing, World War I
Financing, World War II
Labor, World War I
Labor, World War II
National Guard
Preparedness
Prisoner of War Camps, United States
Rationing
Red Cross, American
Rosie the Riveter
USO
Women, Employment of

MUSIC
Music, World War I
Music, World War II
National Anthem

PATRIOTISM AND NATIONAL IDENTITY
Americanization
American Legion
Armistice Day
GI Bill of Rights
Holocaust, American Response to
Monuments, Cemeteries, Spanish American War
Monuments, Cemeteries, World War I
Monuments, Cemeteries, World War II
National Anthem
Patriotism
Rosie the Riveter
Veterans of Foreign Wars

POLITICS
Bonus March
Civilian Conservation Corps (CCC)
Conscription, World War I
Conscription, World War II
Disarmament and Arms Control, 1898–1945
Gold Star Mothers Pilgrimage
GI Bill of Rights
Imperialism
Isolationism
New Deal
Pearl Harbor Investigation
Preparedness
United Nations

PRIMARY SOURCE DOCUMENTS
Advice to the Unemployed in the Great Depression
Against the Declaration of War
America's War Aims: The Fourteen Points
Bracero Agreement
Dedicating the Tomb of the Unknown Soldier

Excerpt from "The War in Its Effect upon Women"
Executive Order 8802
Executive Order 9066
Executive Order 9835
Green Light Letter
Lend-Lease Act
Lusitania Note
Neutrality Act
Franklin D. Roosevelt's Fireside Chat on the Bank
    Crisis
Franklin D. Roosevelt's First Inaugural Address
Sedition Act of 1918
Selective Service Act
Servicemen's Readjustment Act of 1944
"Over There"
Wilson Asks Congress for War
Women and the Changing Times
Women Working in World War II
Zimmermann Telegraph

RACE AND ETHNICITY
Americanization
African Americans, World War I
African Americans, World War II
American Indians, World War I and World War II
Japanese Americans, World War II
Latinos, World War I and World War II
Refugees
War, Impact on Ethnic Groups

RELIGION
Holocaust, American Response to
Religion, World War II

SCIENCE AND MEDICINE
Manhattan Project
Medicine, World War I
Medicine, World War II

VETERANS
American Legion
Armistice Day
Bonus March
GI Bill of Rights
Veterans Benefits
Veterans of Foreign Wars

VISUAL ARTS
Motion Pictures, World War I and World War II
Photography, World War I
Photography, World War II
Visual Arts, World War I
Visual Arts, World War II

RELIGION
Churches, Evangelical, 1946–Present
Churches, Mainstream
Just-War Debate
Muslims, Stereotypes and Fears of

SCIENCE
Atomic Energy Commission
H-Bomb, Decision to Build
Higher Education
Space Race
Star Wars

VETERANS
Drugs and Vietnam
Grunts
POW, MIA
Vietnam Veterans
Vietnam Veterans Memorial

VISUAL ARTS
Arts as Weapon
Films, Vietnam
Photojournalism
World War II, Images of

CHRONOLOGY

Subjects marked in **bold** can be found within *Americans at War*, either in the main body or in the Primary Source Documents in the appendix.

Date	President	Event
1434		Beginning of African Slave Trade by Portuguese.
1494		Line of Demarcation dividing North and South America between Spain and Portugal.
1500–1542		Spanish and Portuguese exploration and conquests in North and South America. Few Spanish and Portuguese migrate to America. Their officials, soldiers, and priests rule native tribes. Plantations established. **Beginning of the decline of the native population** from 20 million to about 2 million due largely to disease.
1517		Beginning of the Protestant Reformation. Martin Luther posts his ninety-five theses challenging the authority of the Roman Catholic Church.
1519–1522		Hernando Cortez conquers the Aztecs in Mexico.
1529		Henry VIII of England separates from the Roman Catholic Church to create the Church of England.
1520s		**Slaves imported from Africa** in large numbers to work on sugar plantations in the West Indies.
1530–1533		Francisco Pizzaro and *Conquistadores* defeat Inca civilization on the Western coast of South America, now the countries of Peru and Chile.
1539–1542		Hernando de Soto expedition from Florida to the Mississippi.
1540		Silver deposits discovered in Peru and Mexico. Mined by Indians.
		The Society of Jesus, Jesuits, formed by Ignatius of Loyola. Missioners sent throughout the world to convert people to Christianity, including many sent among the Indian tribes of North America.

Date	President	Event
1540–1542		Francisco Vásquez de Coronado explores the Southwest of what would become the United States.
1541		John Calvin and his Protestant followers take control of Geneva, Switzerland.
1542		Juan Rodriquez Cabrillo explores what would become the California coast.
1555		Peace of Augsburg ends religious wars in the Habsburg Empire and divides the land between Protestants and Catholics.
1564		French Calvinists known as Huguenots establish settlement at Fort Caroline in Florida. The fort is destroyed by Spanish in 1564 and most settlers killed.
1565		Queen Elizabeth I of England encourages colonization of Ireland by English Protestants.
August 24, 1572		St. Bartholomew's Day Massacre in Paris, which began a killing spree of Huguenots by Catholic mobs. Massacres and religious warfare in France follows, leaving 70,000 to 100,000 Huguenots dead.
1584		Richard Haklute publishes *A Discourse Concerning Western Planting,* a report on his voyage to America with Sir Walter Raleigh. Report encouraged English settlement to claim land for Protestantism, expand English trade, and to a find productive work for the unemployed.
1588		Founding of the English colony at Roanoke, Virginia by Sir Walter Raleigh. When the supply ship returns three years later the colony is found mysteriously abandoned and the whereabouts of the settlers unknown. All that is left is the message "Croatoan" on a post, the meaning of which is unclear.
		Defeat of the Spanish Armada by the English. End of Spanish effort to conquer England and restore the Catholic Church.
1598		Edict of Nantes ends religious persecution in France; Huguenots are granted religious rights, which are revoked in 1685.
1603		James I becomes King of England. Favors colonization in America.
1605		French colony established at Port Royal in what is now Nova Scotia, Canada.
1606		Virginia Company of Jamestown and Virginia Company of Plymouth created as joint-stock companies to finance and promote English colonization of America.
1607		**Jamestown** founded—first permanent English colony in North America.

Date	President	Event
1608		Quebec founded by Samuel de Champlain for fur trading. Becomes the capital of New France or Canada.
1608–1609		John Smith becomes head of **Jamestown** colony. Colony suffers from disease, starvation and attacks by Indians.
1609		Henry Hudson explores what is now the New York region and Hudson valley on behalf of the Dutch.
1610		Decision made to abandon **Jamestown**; colonists return when relief ships arrive bringing supplies and settlers.
1614		Lutheran refugees from Amsterdam, Holland, establish a trading post in what is now Albany, New York.
1616		John Rolf and Pocahontas visit England to promote tobacco sales and settlement.
1619		First African **slaves** arrive at **Jamestown.**
1620		Pilgrims land at Plymouth. The day before landing they sign the Mayflower Compact, often described as America' first constitution.
1622		**Massacre of 350 settlers at Jamestown** led by Opechancanough.
1624		Jamestown company disbanded. Virginia becomes a Royal Colony.
1626		Dutch purchase Manhattan Island from Indians; establish New Amsterdam.
1630		Puritans led by John Winthrop settle in what becomes Boston, Massachusetts.
1632		Maryland chartered by Charles I to be refuge for English Catholics.
1635		Roger Williams banished from the Massachusetts Bay Colony, establishes Rhode Island.
1636–1637		Pequot War, the first serious armed conflict between Native Americans and settlers, takes place in New England.
1637		Anne Hutchinson excommunicated.
1642		Beginning of English Civil War between supporters of Charles I and Parliament led by Oliver Cromwell.
1649		Charles I beheaded; England becomes a republic under Oliver Cromwell.
1660		Monarchy restored under Charles II. Navigation Act demands colonial tobacco shipped to England for tax.
1660–1688		England establishes six colonies, including Pennsylvania by Quakers and Carolina by Barbadian planters who receive charter in 1663.

Date	President	Event
1664		Dutch colony surrenders to English. New Amsterdam becomes New York.
1675–1676		**King Philip's War** in New England; 10,000 Indians die.
1676		**Bacon's rebellion.** Uprising in Virginia by settlers to overthrow government that prevents them from seizing Indian land.
1688		Glorious Revolution in England. James II deposed and Parliament's power increased.
1688–1689		John Locke produces his *Second Treatise on Government* professing that individuals have inalienable rights of life, liberty and property.
1692		Salem Witch Trials. By the end, nineteen accused witches had been hung, one was crushed to death, and seventeen more died in prison.
1702–1713		Queen Anne's War—A series of raids by the French and their Indian allies upon New Englanders, including the raid on Deerfield, Massachusetts.
1711–1713		The Tuscarora War—War between Carolina settlers and Tuscarora Indians.
1715–1716		Yamasee War—War between Carolina settlers and Yamasee Indians and their allies in Florida.
1730s–1740s		The religious revival led by Jonathan Edwards and George Whitefield, called the Great Awakening, sweeps through the colonies.
1739		**Stono Rebellion,** slave uprising in Stono, South Carolina.
1739–1743		The War of Jenkins Ear—War between England and Spain on the Georgia-Florida border. Named after Robert Jenkins who lost his ear.
1744–1748		King George's War—War between England and France on American soil. Louisburg on Cape Breton is captured by New England troops, stiking a blow to the French.
1754–1763		**French and Indian War**—Conflict for empire. France is defeated and its lands, especially Canada, become part of the British empire.
1763		Pontiac's War—Indian attacks on English posts and settlers in the Great Lakes region.
1765		**Stamp Act** Passed by Parliament; American protest and resistance to the Stamp Act; **"Sons of Liberty"** formed in Boston.
October 1765		**Stamp Act Congress** approves Resolutions upholding rights as Englishmen.

Date	President	Event
1766		Protest against the **Stamp Act** is successful and the act is repealed.
		Parliament passes the Declaratory Act proclaiming full authority over the American colonies.
1767		Townshend duties passed by Parliament; protests result.
1768		Riots in Boston against the Townshend Duties; British Troops sent to Boston.
1770		**Boston Massacre.**
December 16, 1773		**Boston Tea Party.** English tea is destroyed in Boston harbor by the "Sons of Liberty" in reaction to Britain's Tea Act of 1773.
1774		Britain places Massachusetts under military rule—Parliament approves four laws to quell the Massachusetts rebellion. Laws branded by colonists as the Intolerable Acts.
September 5, 1774		First **Continental Congress** meets in Philadelphia to organize colonial protest and resistance.
October 25, 1774		Edenton, North Carolina tea party by local women protesting British imports. Fifty-one local women met and openly declared "We, the aforesaid Ladys will not promote ye wear of any manufacturer from England until such time that all acts which tend to enslave our Native country shall be repealed."
April 19, 1775		Battles of Lexington and Concord. Beginning of the War for Independence.
January 1776		**Thomas Paine** publishes *Common Sense*. Argues for American independence and formation of a republican form of government; rejected European style monarchy and aristocracy.
July 4, 1776		**Declaration of Independence.**
1776		Virginia creates the first state constitution. It includes a Bill of Rights. Other states follow by making their own constitutions.
1777		Vermont outlaws **slavery**.
November 15, 1777		**Articles of Confederation** agreed to by the **Continental Congress**. Creates the United States as an alliance of independent states.
1778		France allies with the United States after the Americans defeat the British at Saratoga in 1777.
1779		Spain declares war on Great Britain.
October 19, 1781		Cornwallis defeated at Yorktown; last major battle of the Revolutionary War and peace negotiations begin.
1783		**Peace of Paris.** American Independence recognized.

Date	President	Event
1787		**Shays's rebellion** in Massachusetts. National government under the **Articles of Confederation** shaken.
May 14, 1787		Constitutional convention gathers in Philadelphia. Proposes to replace the **Articles of Confederation** with a new constitution.
1788		**Constitution** adopted.
1789	**George Washington, 1789–1797**	French Revolution begins.
		French Assembly adopts the *Rights of Man* declaration written by **Thomas Paine.**
April 30, 1789		**George Washington** inaugurated as first president of the United States.
1790		First federal census undertaken.
1791		Bill of Rights—First Ten Amendments added to the **Constitution.**
1792		French Republic proclaimed.
1793		Eli Whitney invents cotton gin.
January 21, 1793		French King, Louis XVI tried and executed; French Revolution takes radical turn.
1794		United States and Great Britain agree to blockade France. Beginning of American **quasi-war** with France.
		Whiskey rebellion in western Pennsylvania. **George Washington** and **Alexander Hamilton** send the militia to put down the protesters against the tax on whiskey.
		"Mad" Anthony Wayne defeats Indians at "Fallen Timbers" near Detroit.
September 26, 1796		**Washington's Farewell Address.**
1797	**John Adams, 1797–1801**	
1798–1800		**Quasi-War** with England and France. Military mobilization proposed. **Alien and Sedition laws** passed to curtail freedom of speech because of threat of war and subversion. **James Madison** and **Thomas Jefferson** respond with the **Kentucky and Virginia Resolutions** proclaiming the right of states to void federal laws that violate individual or states' rights.
1801	**Thomas Jefferson, 1801–1809**	John Marshall appointed Chief Justice of the **Supreme Court** (1801–1835). Generally considered one of the principal architects of American government and cultural values.
1801		**Thomas Jefferson** inaugurated. Peaceful transfer of power between two opposing political parties, Federalists and Democratic Republicans. Beginning of wars with **Barbary pirates** (1801–1805; 1815).

Date	President	Event
		Great Revival begins, Cane Ridge, Kentucky.
1803–1815		Napoleonic Wars. War between France and England in Europe and the Western Hemisphere. American ships and men seized by both countries.
April 30, 1803		American purchase of Louisiana territory from France.
1804–1806		Lewis and Clark Expedition to Pacific.
1808		African Slave traded to the United States prohibited.
1809	James Madison, 1809–1817	
1812–1815		**War with England.** Washington, D.C. occupied by the British and burned.
September 14, 1814		Francis Scott Key composes poem, "Star-Spangled Banner."
1815		**Andrew Jackson's** victory at New Orleans.
		Hartford Convention. New England protest against the war with England. Demands changes in the **Constitution** to weaken Congress's power to declare war. Some New England states threaten **to secede** from the Union if federal power is not reduced.
1816–1826		Outburst of American nationalism and **patriotism.**
1817	James Monroe, 1817–1825	**Monroe's tour of New England** and beginning of **Bunker Hill monument.**
1818		Passage of the **Revolutionary War Pension Act** to honor and reward veterans.
1820s		Expansion of factory towns and creation of new mill cities in New England.
1820		**Missouri Compromise.**
1820–1861		Expansion of the market economy in the North and South. Northern manufacturing, commerce, and farming; Southern farming, plantations, and export of cotton. Wage labor in the North; Wage and slave labor in the South.
1822		Discovery of Denmark Vesey's slave conspiracy for a rebellion in Charleston, South Carolina.
1823		**Monroe Doctrine** proclaimed in 1823.
1824–1825		**Lafayette's tour of the United States.**
1825	John Adams, 1825–1829	Completion of the Erie Canal connecting Buffalo with New York City. Part of the "Transportation Revolution" that binds the nation by roads, canals, and later **railroads.**
1826		Second Bank chartered. National Road completed.

Date	President	Event
		James Fenimore Cooper publishes *The Last of the Mohicans,* a tale about the French and Indian War, 1754–1763. Beginning of an American literature.
July 4, 1826		Death of John Adams and Thomas Jefferson. Viewed as a time of reflection on the Revolution.
1828		First railroad completed, the Baltimore and Ohio.
1829	Andrew Jackson, 1829–1837	
1830		Religious revival, "Second Great Awakening," begins in western New York.
		Indian Removal Act; relocate Indians in Georgia.
1831		*Cherokee Nation v. Georgia Supreme Court* decision.
		Nat Turner slave uprising in Virginia.
1832		William Lloyd Garrison founds the abolitionist newspaper, *The Liberator.*
1833		Garrison and Abolitionists create the American Anti-Slavery society to end the institution of slavery.
		Nullification Crisis in South Carolina; South Carolina votes to nullify federal law on tariffs.
1834		Mobs attack abolitionists in New York City. Race riot in Philadelphia. Female mill workers at Lowell, Massachusetts strike and again in 1836.
1836		Ralph Waldo Emerson publishes *Nature,* first major work on transcendentalism. Part of the effort to create an American literature.
March 6, 1836		Defeat of Americans at Alamo by General Santa Anna.
1837	Martin Van Buren, 1837–1841	
1838		Cherokee Indians forcibly removed from Georgia to Oklahoma; thousands die along the "trail of tears" before arriving.
1840s		Famine in Ireland and failed revolution in Germany in 1848 result in surge of Irish and German immigrants to the United States.
1840		Liberty Party formed. Opposes the spread of slavery to the territories. Receives less than one percent of the popular vote.
1841	William Henry Harrison, 1841; John Tyler, 1841–1845	
1844		Margaret Fuller publishes *Woman in the Nineteenth Century,* which examines the role of women and argues for equal rights for women.

Date	President	Event
1845	James Polk, 1845–1849	Proclamation of **Manifest Destiny** by the United States. Americans feel it is their mission and part of God's plan to spread democracy throughout the continent.
		United States **annexes Texas,** which permits **slavery.**
		Frederick Douglass publishes *Narrative of the Life of Frederick Douglass,* a powerful autobiography that further inspires the **Abolitionist** movement.
1846		United States declares war with Mexico. Anti-war protests divide the nation.
		Wilmot Proviso. Proposal for popular sovereignty to prohibit **slavery** in territories won from Mexico approved by the House of Representatives but defeated in the Senate.
June 10, 1846		Bear Flag Revolt in California. "Bear Flaggers" raise the grizzly bear flag and officially declare the territory free from Mexican rule. The bear flag becomes the official flag of California.
June 15, 1846		U.S. and Great Britain settle Oregon border. The 49th parallel is determined to be the border between Great Britain and the United States, with the exception of Vancouver Island.
1847		Brigham Young leads Mormons to Great Salt Lake, Utah.
1848		**Treaty of Guadalupe Hidalgo** ends war with Mexico and results in the United States acquiring California and what is now the U.S. southwest.
		Free Soil Party formed; opposes the spread of the slave institution. Absorbs the Liberty Party.
		Gold discovered in California, leading to California gold rush of 1849.
July 19, 1848		**Women's Rights Movement** convenes in Seneca Falls, New York. Demands equal rights under the law, including the right to vote.
1849	Zachary Taylor, 1849–1850	Henry David Thoreau publishes *Walden,* an account of man and nature and part of the new American literary genre.
1850	Millard Fillmore, 1850–1853	**Compromise of 1850.** Intended to resolve the conflict over the spread of **slavery**; California admitted as a free state (prohibited slavery). Fugitive slave law strengthens recovery of runaway slaves in the North.
1851		Herman Melville publishes *Moby-Dick,* a novel that has become an American classic.

Date	President	Event
1852		Harriet Beecher Stowe publishes *Uncle Tom's Cabin*. The novel attacks the institution of **slavery** and increases tension between the North and South.
1853	**Franklin Pierce, 1853–1857**	American or "Know Nothing" party formed. The party is composed of nativists, people who oppose immigration, Catholics, and citizenship for blacks. Members, when asked about their organizations were suppose to reply they knew nothing, hence the name of the party.
		Gadsden Purchase adds territory in Southwest.
1854		**Kansas-Nebraska Act** opens the west to the possibility of slavery.
		Republican Party formed to oppose the **Kansas-Nebraska Act**. Absorbs the Free Soil Party.
1856		"Bleeding Kansas" erupts as northerners and southerners fight over future of **slavery** in territory.
1857	**James Buchanan, 1857–1861**	Dred Scott case. **Supreme court** declares that the **Constitution** does not apply to free blacks and that it allows slave owners to take their property (slaves) to any state or territory.
1858		**Lincoln**-Douglas debates in Illinois for Senate seat.
October 16, 1859		John Brown's raid on Harpers Ferry, Virginia. His intent is to arm slaves and to lead a slave uprising. He is captured and later hanged.
1860		**Abraham Lincoln** elected president with 40 percent of the popular vote. South Carolina votes to **secede** from the Union.
1861	**Abraham Lincoln, 1861–1865**	**Confederacy** formed by **seceded** states. Fort Sumter at tacked and **Abraham Lincoln** calls out militia to end rebellion. Civil War begins.
		Harriet Jacob publishes *Incidents in the Life of a Slave Girl*, describing the life of a female under **slavery**.
1862		Bloody battles at Shiloh and Antietam.
		Homestead Act passed by Congress.
January 1, 1863		**Emancipation Proclamation** by Abraham Lincoln, ending **slavery** in territory conquered by northern troops.
July 1863		Battles at Gettysburg and Vicksburg turn the tide toward the Union.
September 2, 1864		Atlanta falls. After several weeks of preparation General **Sherman begins his march to the sea.**
1865	**Andrew Johnson, 1865–1869**	Congress establishes **Freedmen's Bureau** to assist former slaves. South enacts **Black Codes** to suppress blacks.
		Thirteenth Amendment to **Constitution** ratified, abolishing **slavery**.

Date	President	Event
April 9, 1865		End of Civil War at Appomattox Courthouse. Six days later **Abraham Lincoln** is assassinated.
1866		Founding of Equal Rights Association to seek woman's suffrage.
		Formation of the Grand Army of the Republic composed of veterans of the Union Army. To become an organization for **veterans' benefits.**
		Ku Klux Klan organized as the "Invisible Empire of the South."
1868		**Fourteenth Amendment** added to **Constitution,** ensuring all male citizens equal protection of the laws and due process of law.
1869	**Ulysses S. Grant, 1869–1877**	Woman's suffrage groups split in two over tactics and issue of black male suffrage; will reunite in 1890.
		Territory of Wyoming allows women to vote.
May 10, 1869		Completion of transcontinental **railroad** in Promontory, Utah.
1870		**Fifteenth Amendment** added to **Constitution,** guaranteeing the right to vote to males regardless of race or color.
1870–1871		Franco-Prussian War.
1876		Westward migration increases conflicts with Indians. Custer defeated at Little Bighorn.
1877	**Rutherford B. Hayes, 1877–1881**	Troops withdrawn from the South. Disputed election of 1876 resolved and Rutherford B. Hayes was determined to have won 185 electoral votes to Samuel Tilden's 184. **Reconstruction** ended.
1881	**James Garfield, 1881; Chester Arthur, 1881–1885**	Helen Hunt Jackson publishes *A Century of Dishonor*—documents the mistreatment of American Indians.
1882		Chinese Exclusion Act passed by Congress.
1885	**Grover Cleveland, 1885–1889**	
1887		**Dawes Severalty Act,** which dissolves Indian tribes and turns tribal lands into private property for Indians—an effort to Americanize Indians.
1888		Edward Bellamy publishes *Looking Backward*—a critical assessment of American capitalism and endorsement of more cooperative society.
1889	**Benjamin Harris, 1889–1893**	
1890		Formation of the National American Woman's Suffrage Association, uniting the two groups working for woman's suffrage.

Date	President	Event
		Jacob Riis publishes *How the Other Half Lives*, an exposé aided by photographs of squalor and exploitation of New York's **immigrants** and poor.
1890–1904		Ex-confederate states pass laws prohibiting Blacks from voting. "Jim Crow" laws enforce **racial segregation.**
December 29, 1890		Battle of Wounded Knee marking last major conflict between Native Americans and federal troops in West.
1893	**Grover Cleveland, 1893–1897**	
1895		Booker T. Washington's "Atlanta Compromise."
		Stephen Crane published *Red Badge of Courage,* a novel giving psychological insights into combat during the Civil War.
1896		*Plessy v. Ferguson* ruling by the **Supreme Court** that **segregation**—"separate but equal"—is constitutional.
1897	**William McKinley, 1897–1901**	
1898		Spanish-American War.
1899–1902		American-Filipino War. Insurrection against American rule.
1900		United States becoming one of the world's leading industrial powers.
1900–1914		**Immigration** averages one million people a year. Many from Eastern and Southern Europe, including Jews and Catholics.
1901	**Theodore Roosevelt, 1901–1909**	
1903		United States acquires the Panama Canal Zone. Construction on canal begins.
December 17, 1903		First powered flight. The age of air transportation and warfare begins.
1904		President **Theodore Roosevelt** issues his "corollary" to the **Monroe Doctrine.**
1904–1917		Progressives expand the regulatory powers of the national government.
1905		The Industrial Workers of the World (IWW) founded.
1908		**Henry Ford** produces the Model T.
		Race riot in Springfield, Illinois.
1909	**William H. Taft, 1909–1913**	National Association for the Advancement of Colored People (NAACP) founded to fight racial discrimination and to secure **civil rights.**

Date	President	Event
1913	**Woodrow Wilson, 1913–1921**	
1914–1918		World War I in Europe.
1914–1917		Unites States remains neutral about the war in Europe.
1917		Russian Revolution begins. Communists under Lenin seize power.
April 6, 1917		United States declares war on Germany in April. **Draft begins.** Security Espionage Act. President Wilson creates the Committee on Public Information (CPI). Over 400,000 blacks serve in armed forces.
1918		**Sedition Act.** Eugene V. Debs, head of the IWW, jailed.
November 11, 1918		World War I concludes. A total of 112,000 American soldiers killed.
1919		**Peace of Paris.** Congress rejects American membership in the League of Nations.
		Widespread labor strikes.
		Race riot in Chicago.
1919–1920		**Red Scare.** Campaign to suppress communists, radicals and socialists. Federal raids to round up aliens.
1920s		Rise of a consumer society; mass marketing and advertising; expansion of highways and automobile travel, and entertainment industry, particularly **movies.**
1920		Marcus Garvey, a Black Nationalist, calls for blacks to create a separate nation within the United States.
		Nineteenth Amendment to the **Constitution** ratified giving women the right to vote.
		Election of Warren G. Harding on the pledge to return America to "normalcy," meaning returning to the pre-World War I society.
		Census reports a majority of Americans live in cities.
1921	**Warren Harding, 1921–1923**	
1922		Benito Mussolini becomes Fascist dictator of Italy.
		United States along with four other great powers agree to limit the size of their navies.
1923	**Calvin Coolidge, 1923–1929**	Adolf Hitler and his Nazi party attempt to overthrow the government in Bavaria. Hitler imprisoned and writes *Mein Kampf*
April 18, 1923		Yankee Stadium opens. Part of era of mass public **sports** in baseball and college football.
1924		**Ku Klux Klan** achieves a membership of nearly 4 million people.

Date	President	Event
		America **aids European recovery** with the Dawes Plan.
1924–1926		Joseph Stalin rises to power in the Soviet Union.
1925		Hitler rebuilds Nazi party.
		Scopes trial in Tennessee.
1926		**Ernest Hemingway** publishes *The Sun Also Rises* about the "Lost Generation."
1928		Kellogg-Briand Pact. International agreement not to use war as means to fulfill national policies.
1929	**Herbert Hoover, 1929–1933**	Eric Maria Remarque publishes *All Quiet on the West ern Front,* a powerful anti-war **novel**. Made into a popular **film** in 1930.
		Ernest Hemingway publishes *A Farewell to Arms,* another anti-war **novel**.
October 29, 1929		Stock Market crash.
1929–1932		Economic depression spreads through United States and Europe. Unemployment in the United States rises to 25 percent of the work force.
1931		Japan invades Manchuria.
1932		World War I veterans march on Washington. "Bonus Army" dispersed by troops.
		Franklin Roosevelt elected president.
1933	**Franklin D. Roosevelt, 1933–1945**	**Roosevelt's inaugural address** declares that Americans have "nothing to fear but fear itself."
		Adolf Hitler becomes Chancellor of Germany.
1933–1935		First **New Deal**. Prohibition repealed. "Alphabet" measures implemented such as the Agricultural Adjustment Act (AAA), **Civilian Conservation Corps (CCC)**, and Tennessee Valley Authority (TVA). Banking and stock market regulated.
1935		Italy invades Ethiopia.
		Congress passes first of **Neutrality Acts** aimed at keeping the United States out of war.
1935–1937		Second **New Deal**. Social Security Act passed. National Labor Relations Acts (Wagner Act) strengthens unions. Rural Electrification Act brings power to rural America. Works Progress Administration (WPA) provides employment for workers, artists, and performers.
1936		Civil war in Spain. Germany and the Soviet Union aid combatants.
		Germany and Italy agree to form an alliance as "Axis Powers."
1937		Japan invades China.

Date	President	Event
		Neutrality Acts strengthened.
1937–1938		Recovery of the American economy halted. Unemployment approaches 1932 levels.
October 5, 1937		Roosevelt gives his "Quarantine Speech" urging peace-loving countries to unite against aggressors.
1938		Germany occupies part of Czechoslovakia following Munich agreement.
1939		Congress rejects Wagner-Rogers bill to increase **immigration** quotas to allow 20,000 Jewish children in Germany to enter the United States.
September 1, 1939		Germany invades Poland. World War II begins in Europe.
1940		Congress passes the **first peace-time draft.** American rearmament begins.
June 1940		Germany defeats France. Battle of Britain begins.
1941		**Franklin D. Roosevelt** announces the "Four Freedoms."
		Roosevelt proposes that America become the "arsenal for democracy." Congress passes "**Lend-Lease**" legislation to provide arms to Britain.
		Roosevelt creates the Fair Employment Practices Commission (FEPC) to ensure nondiscrimination in industries receiving federal contracts.
		Roosevelt and Winston Churchill agree on the "Atlantic Charter" to create a new world organization to ensure collective security.
December 7, 1941		Japans attacks **Pearl Harbor.** United States declares war. Germany and Italy, allies of Japan, declare war on the United States.
1942–1945		Economic depression begun in 1929 ends. About 15,000,000 people in the armed services. Military remains racially segregated.
1942		Roosevelt signs **Executive Order 9066** authorizing **internment of Japanese** on the west coast for reasons of national security.
		Roosevelt creates the Office of War Information (OWI) to oversee **propaganda** and censorship affecting the war.
		Congress of Racial Equality (CORE) formed to secure **civil rights** for blacks.
1943		Many blacks move north. Black employment in defense industries increases. Race riot in Detroit.
1944		Gunnar Myrdal publishes *The American Dilemma* analyzing the depth of racism in America.

Date	President	Event
		Bretton Woods agreement creates a new economic organization for the world.
		GI Bill passed.
June 6, 1944		D-Day. Allied forces land in Normandy.
December 18, 1944		**Supreme Court** declares **internment of Japanese** constitutional in *Korematsu v. United States.*
1945	**Harry Truman, 1945–1953**	Yalta and Potsdam agreements by allies to divide Germany and reestablish governments in Easter Europe. A source of conflict during the **Cold War.**
May 7, 1945		Germany surrenders unconditionally. One day later is V-E Day, Victory in Europe.
August 6 and 9, 1945		United States drops **atomic bombs** on Hiroshima and Nagasaki. Japan surrenders within days.
September 2, 1945		V-J Day, Victory over Japan.
November 1945		Nuremberg trial of Nazi leaders.
December 1945		**United Nations** established.
1946		Baruch plan for international control of atomic power approved by the **United Nations.**
		Atomic Energy Commission created. RAND (Research and Development) "think tank" established.
		Winston Churchill delivers his "iron curtain" speech in Fulton, Missouri.
1947		Beginning of "**Cold War.**" **Truman Doctrine** National Security Act passes creating the Defense Department, National Security Council, and **CIA.** George Kennan outlines the policy of "containment." President Truman issues **Executive Order 9835** to remove "security risks" from government.
		Marshall Plan approved.
		British colonialism ends in India. Pakistan created. New countries emerge as decolonization occurs elsewhere in the world.
		House Un-American Activities Committee conducts hearings to reveal communist influence in the movie and entertainment industry.
		Postwar baby boom peaks at nearly 27 million births. Suburbs expand. **Levittown,** the beginning of mass housing developments.
1948		Soviet Union blockades West Berlin. Berlin airlift begins.
		State of **Israel** created. **Israel** repels attacks.
		Truman issues Executive Order 9981 desegregating the armed forces.

Date	President	Event
1949		**Communists** under Mao Zedong take control of China.
		Soviet Union detonates its first **atomic bomb.**
		North Atlantic Treaty Organization (NATO) formed for mutual security against a Soviet invasion of Western Europe.
		George Orwell publishes *1984*—prophesizes the triumph of totalitarianism.
		Major League Baseball integrated.
1950s		Beginning in the late 1940s the "new look" return to women's **fashion. Television** replaces radio as the principal source of home entertainment.
		Employment of married mothers outside of the home increases.
1950		**NSC #68,** a top secret policy approved by the National Security Council, which approves use of covert force and encouraging "captive nations" to revolt against Soviet rule. Places the United States on a **quasi-war** footing.
		Julius and Ethel Rosenberg arrested for treason. Both executed in 1953.
		Passage of the McCarran Internal Security Act.
1950–1953		Korean War.
1950–1954		"**McCarthyism.**" **Civil liberties** challenged. 1954 Senate censors Senator Joseph McCarthy.
1951		European Coal and Steel Community formed. Beginning of what would become the European Economic Community (known as the Common Market, and later the European Union.
April 1951		Truman removes **General McArthur** from command in Korea.
1952		Election of **Dwight D. Eisenhower** as president. First Republican in 20 years.
1953	**Dwight D. Eisenhower, 1953–1961**	East Germans rise up against Soviet rule. Suppressed by force.
March 5, 1953		Soviet dictator, Joseph Stalin, dies.
1954		French defeated at Dien Bien Phu. French Indochina divided into Laos, Cambodia and Vietnam.
		Historian David Potter publishes *People of Plenty*, describing the rise of American consumer economy and expansion of the middle class.
		Congress adds "under God" to the Pledge of Allegiance.
		Elvis Presley tops the **music** charts.

Date	President	Event
May 17, 1954		*Brown v. Board of Education.* **Supreme Court** rules that **segregation** in schools is unconstitutional.
1955		Movie *The Blackboard Jungle* warns of social decay caused by youth gangs and rock 'n roll **music.**
December 1, 1955		Rosa Parks refuses to give up her seat on a Montgomery bus. Boycott begins to end **segregation** on the city buses. **Civil rights movement** intensifies. **Martin Luther King, Jr.** and the Southern Christian Leadership Conference emerge as leaders.
1956		Passage of the Highway Act authorizing construction of the interstate highway system to improve American defense and promote commerce.
		Congress approves adding "In God We Trust" to the nation's motto.
		Supreme Court declares **segregation** on public buses unconstitutional.
		Hungarian uprising against **Communist** regime suppressed.
September 1957		Federal troops enforce integration of Little Rock, Arkansas, high school.
October 4, 1957		Soviet Union launches Sputnik, the **first space satellite.** Soviet leadership in missile technology and delivery of atomic weapons feared. Sales of bomb shelters increase in United States.
1958		National Defense Education Act passed to improve the teaching of mathematics and science.
1959		Fidel Castro leads revolution in Cuba. Establishes a **communist** regime.
1960		Young Americans for Freedom (YAF) formed—College activists favoring aggressive American actions to defeat **communism** and to reduce "big government" at home.
1960–1963		Increased **civil rights** activism—sit ins and "freedom rides."
1961	**John F. Kennedy, 1961–1963**	President **John F. Kennedy** increases American aid to South Vietnam against communist insurgents.
		Construction of the **Berlin Wall.**
January 7, 1961		**President Eisenhower's** farewell speech. Warns of the dangers of a "**military-industrial complex**" dominating American economy and society.
April 17, 1961		**CIA** supports attack on Cuba by exiles defeated at the "Bay of Pigs."

Date	President	Event
1962		Students for a Democratic Society (SDS) formed in response to YAF. Young activists against racial discrimination and social injustices. Becomes part of the "New Left." Beliefs expressed in its "**Port Huron Statement.**"
October 1962		**Cuban missile crisis.**
1963	**Lyndon B. Johnson, 1963–1969**	**Betty Friedan** publishes *The Feminine Mystique* expressing women's dissatisfaction with limitations of domestic life and wish for careers and more active public life.
August 28, 1963		March on Washington where **Martin Luther King, Jr.** gives his "I have a dream" speech.
September 15, 1963		Bombing of Birmingham, Alabama, church killing four children.
November 22, 1963		Assassination of **President Kennedy.**
1964		Congress approves Tonkin Gulf Resolution authorizing increased military force in South Vietnam.
		Movie, *Dr. Strangelove: Or How I Stopped Worrying and Learned to Love the Bomb* presents a critical parody of cold war fears and American policy of Mutual Assured Destruction (MAD).
		Passage of the **Civil Rights** Act. Prohibits racial discrimination in public facilities and discrimination against women.
1965		President **Lyndon Johnson** announces his "**Great Society**" program—Medicare, Medicaid, and a "war on poverty."
		Voting Rights Act removes barriers used to restrict Blacks from voting.
		President Johnson orders operation "Rolling Thunder," the limited bombing of North Vietnam. 50,000 more troops sent to South Vietnam.
1965–1970s		Counterculture. Associated with "hippies," "yippies," the **anti-war movement.** Woodstock Festival in New York.
February 21, 1965		Malcolm X murdered by enemies within his own movement.
1967		Anti-war march on the Pentagon.
1968		**Civil Rights** Act ending racial discrimination in housing.
		Tet Offensive in Vietnam. A majority of Americans turn against the Vietnam war.
April 4, 1968		Assassination of **Martin Luther King, Jr.**
June 6, 1968		Assassination of Robert F. Kennedy.
August 1968		Riots at the Chicago convention of the Democratic Party.

Date	President	Event
1969	Richard Nixon, 1969–1974	President **Richard Nixon** begins negotiations with the Soviet Union to reduce nuclear missiles. Strategic Arms Limitations Treaty (SALT) formalized two years later.
		American withdrawal from Vietnam begins.
July 20, 1969		**Americans land on the moon.**
1970		American incursion in Cambodia sets off campus riots and protests. Students killed at Kent State University in Ohio.
June 1971		Daniel Ellsberg leaks the so-called "**Pentagon Papers.**"
1972		**President Nixon** opens relations with Communist China.
1973		Paris Peace Agreement. American troops withdrawn from Vietnam. **POWs** returned.
1973		*Roe v. Wade.*
August 8, 1974	Gerald Ford, 1974–1977	**President Nixon** resigns from office as a result of the Watergate scandal.
1975		South Vietnam falls to the **communists.**
1977	Jimmy Carter, 1977–1981	**Feminist movement** becomes international. First meeting in Houston, Texas.
1980		Microsoft licenses its computer software, MS-DOS (Microsoft Disk Operating System).
1980s		Legal **immigration** of Asians and Hispanics increases social diversity.
		America becoming a "knowledge and service" economy.
		AIDs epidemic begins.
1980–1988		The so-called "Reagan Revolution." A massive build-up of the American military, a more aggressive policy to combat Soviet influence, efforts to restore more political power to the states, and federal tax cuts.
1981	Ronald Reagan, 1981–1989	
1985		Mikhail Gorbachev becomes head of the Soviet Union. Begins programs of reform *glasnost* (openness), and *perestroika* (restructuring) to revitalize the Soviet economy.
April 25–26, 1986		Nuclear power plant at Chernobyl explodes. World's worst nuclear accident.
June 3–4, 1989	George H. W. Bush, 1989–1993	Chinese students demonstrate in Tiananmen Square for more freedoms. Suppressed by military force.
November 19, 1989		Destruction of the **Berlin Wall.**
1990s		Internet moves from college and military use to public use. Contributes to the worldwide computer and digital information revolution.

Date	President	Event
1991		**First Gulf War.** Iraqi forces defeated. Sovereignty restored in Kuwait.
		Ethnic wars and ethnic cleansing begins in the former Yugoslavia.
December 21, 1991		The Soviet Union officially ceases to exist. **Cold War** ends.
February 26, 1993	**William J. Clinton, 1993–2001**	**Al-Qaida** detonates a truck bomb under the World Trade Center.
1995		The Dayton Accords. NATO forces enforce the peace in the Balkans.
2001	**George W. Bush, 2001—**	American-led forces defeat the **Taliban** in Afghanistan and destroy **al-Qaida** training bases.
September 11, 2001		**Al-Qaida Terrorists** destroy the two World Trade Center towers and damage the Pentagon. Nearly 3,000 people killed. President George W. Bush declares War on **Terror.**
October 26, 2001		USA PATRIOT Act passed.
2002		The Euro becomes the currency for many countries in the European Union.
March 19, 2003		United States-led forces invade Iraq.
2004		The European Union expands from fifteen to twenty-five members.
		An interim regime established in Iraq.
		American policy in Iraq and conduct of the War on **Terror** become key issues in the election campaign for president of the United States.

ADDAMS, JANE

(b. September 6, 1860; d. May 21, 1935) Reformer, advocate for peace and social justice, lecturer, and writer.

Jane Addams began her public career in 1889 as the co-founder and leader of the Chicago social settlement Hull-House. Between 1890 and 1914, Addams and Hull-House led the settlement movement then at the forefront of progressive social reforms sweeping America, including the abolition of child labor and sweat shops, immigrant protection and education, and woman suffrage. During World War I, Jane Addams became an organizer and the principal advocate of the modern American woman's peace movement. From that position, both during and after World War I, she helped build and direct an international coalition of women peace advocates representing countries from most of the continents. For her efforts, she became the first American woman to receive the Nobel Peace Prize (1931).

Addams was educated in her small Cedarville, Illinois community, and at Rockford Female Seminary. Having grown to maturity in the aftermath of the American Civil War, Jane Addams was aware of the destructive power of war. During the Spanish-American War (1898), she made her first public speech as an antiwar advocate at a Chicago gathering. When World War I began in Europe, Addams worked to keep America neutral. She feared that U.S. entry into the war would stifle the momentum for reforms and social justice that she and her like-minded friends had achieved since the founding of Hull-House. Addams saw the settlement neighborhood as a microcosm for the world. There, people from Europe, whose national history had made them enemies, had learned to live together peacefully with mutual respect. Addams favored developing a focus on internationalism to replace what she called "war virtues" so often associated with nationalism. Addams believed that war was not an appropriate solution for disputes.

During late 1914, Addams served as chair of the Chicago Emergency Peace Federation and as a member of the Round Table Conference on War, which met in New York to propose mediation to end the conflict raging in Europe. Addams wanted to bring the nurturing powers she believed women possessed to stop that war. On January 10, 1915, Addams and women's suffrage leader Carrie Chapman Catt convened a group in Washington, D.C., which organized itself into the Woman's Peace Party with Addams as chair. It called for the

Jane Addams. © BETTMANN/CORBIS

Advocating American neutrality, she met with Woodrow Wilson and Edward House, Wilson's representative to European nations, testified against proposals for conscription and rearmament, fought calls for preparedness, and worked to rouse public opinion against entering the war.

When America did enter the war, many of Addams's friends abandoned her pacifist position to support American war efforts. Isolated and shunned, Addams remained steadfast to her pacifist ideals. During the war, she worked with Roger Baldwin and the National Civil Liberties Bureau to protest passage of the Espionage Act and state syndicalist laws, supported the position of conscientious objectors, and lectured tirelessly throughout the United States for food conservation on behalf of the U.S. Food Administration.

In July 1919, eight months after World War I ended, Addams presided over the second International Congress of Women in Zurich. There the Women's International League for Peace and Freedom (WILPF) was formed with Addams as its international president. Following the meeting, she presented the new organization's resolutions to the American delegation in Paris. These included condemnation of the terms of the Treaty of Versailles and a proposal for a League of Nations. Concerned about starving families in Europe, Addams and Alice Hamilton traveled throughout Europe for the American Friends Service Committee to investigate and draw attention to the deplorable conditions. From 1919 to 1929, Addams served as international president of the WILPF and then became honorary president until her death in 1935, in Chicago, following surgery for cancer.

immediate end to the fighting and argued for a new international order that included nationalization of the manufacture of armaments, democratic control of foreign policy, and women's suffrage.

To develop the vital international element of the peace movement, in April 1915 Addams led an American delegation of women to the Hague for the International Congress of Women, composed of representatives from neutral and belligerent powers. With Addams as international president, the International Committee of Women for Permanent Peace was formed at the Congress and charged with convening another congress at the cessation of hostilities. The women also appointed two delegations to meet with government leaders throughout Europe and promote the cause of continuous mediation as a means to end World War I.

Addams saw the destructiveness of war as she led the delegation to meet with statesmen from the belligerent governments. From the time she returned from Europe until America entered the war, she worked tirelessly to preserve America's neutrality and to seek a negotiated end to the conflict. Although she supported Henry Ford's peace ship idea, because of ill health she was unable to join the venture when the ship left in December 1915.

BIBLIOGRAPHY

Addams, Jane. *Newer Ideals of Peace*. New York: Macmillan, 1907.

Addams, Jane. *Twenty Years at Hull-House*. New York: Macmillan, 1910.

Addams, Jane. *Peace and Bread in Time of War*. New York: Macmillan, 1922.

Addams, Jane. *Second Twenty Years at Hull-House*. New York: Macmillan, 1930.

Addams, Jane. *The Jane Addams Papers*. Edited by Mary Lynn McCree Bryan et al. Ann Arbor: University Microfilms International, 1985–1986. Microfilm, 82 reels.

Davis, Allen F. *American Heroine: The Life and Legend of Jane Addams*. New York: Oxford University Press, 1973.

Linn, James Weber. *Jane Addams: A Biography*. New York: D. Appleton-Century Co., 1935.

Mary Lynn McCree Bryan

See also: **Americanization; Disarmament and Arms Control; Feminism; Peace Movements; Women, World War I; Women's Suffrage Movement.**

AFRICAN AMERICANS, WORLD WAR I

Shortly after U.S. involvement in World War I ended, American serviceman Daniel Mack died in his uniform. He wasn't killed on the battlefields of Europe, but like many other black Americans Daniel Mack was a casualty of World War I. Having fought in France to make the world safe for democracy, Mack returned to Sylvester, Georgia, determined to enjoy the benefits of freedom. Vowing to never yield to Jim Crow again, Mack ignored "white only" signs, earning himself thirty days in jail—thirty days he never served because a white mob dragged him from jail to the outskirts of town and beat him to death. Mack's story is more than a personal tragedy; it signifies the changes, hopes, and disillusionment that World War I brought to African Americans.

MILITARY SERVICE

For many African Americans in 1917, participation in World War I seemed to promise a better future. Living in a world characterized by racial discrimination and segregation, they believed that African Americans might earn full citizenship by closing ranks with whites during the war. Thousands volunteered for military service and two million registered for the draft. In the end, almost 400,000 African Americans mustered into the U.S. military, which was still a segregated institution. Most of them served in either army service units or as navy stewards, but two army divisions, the 92nd and the 93rd Provisional, enrolled 42,000 blacks as combat soldiers in segregated units. Some of these units performed poorly overseas, perhaps because of inferior training or leadership or simply because of the nature of a segregated army, but a number of African Americans served with such distinction that they received individual honors. France awarded hundreds of its coveted medal, the *croix de guerre*, to African-American soldiers who had shown exceptional courage and fortitude. In 1917, the United States opened an officer training school for African Americans in Fort Des Moines, Iowa. With a history of military honors, 750 battle deaths, and 5,000 wounded to their credit, returning African-American soldiers hoped that legal, if not social and economic, equality might now be a real possibility back home. Some, like Daniel Mack, resolved to turn these hopes into realities.

THE HOMEFRONT AND AFRICAN-AMERICAN MIGRATION

On the homefront, equality remained elusive, but the war did open some new opportunities to African Americans. The immigration restrictions enforced throughout the war and the absorption of white laborers into the military had left Northern industries desperate for a new supply of workers. Once locked out of Northern labor markets, African Americans now found themselves courted by Northern factory managers. Recruiters offered Southern blacks free transportation and high wages to relocate to Northern industrial areas such as Chicago, Cleveland, Saint Louis, and Detroit. Lured by these promises, tens of thousands of African Americans pulled up stakes and poured into the North. Despite Southern efforts to protect their labor pool by means of both conciliation and intimidation, more than 300,000 African Americans had left the South by 1920 and thousands more followed later.

Black migrants did not find everything to their liking in the North, but they did benefit from the move. Economically, the exodus proved a move upward; African Americans made more money in factories than they had ever made on Southern farms, and this foothold in American industry created a path to future financial success. Simple relocation also moved many African Americans from the ranks of the disenfranchised to the voting booth. At a time when Jim Crow legislation in the South prevented African Americans from voting, most Northern cities allowed citizens of any color to vote, and migrating African Americans suddenly found themselves part of the country's political scene. Wartime migration, however, had negative consequences as well as benefits.

POSTWAR LEGACY

As African Americans moved North, and as black soldiers returned from the war, racial tensions and violence escalated. African Americans increasingly found themselves the targets of white mobs who felt blacks were competing for their neighborhoods, jobs, and recreational areas. In what came to be called the Red Summer of 1919 for the bloodshed and violence that took place between whites and blacks all over the country, more than thirty-eight northern cities erupted in riots. Frustrated whites in Chicago drowned an African-American youth by pelting him with rocks from the shore. This ignited a week of lawlessness during which 38 people died and another 520 suffered injuries. In Omaha, Saint Louis, and elsewhere the same scene played out, with the same tragic results.

As increasing numbers of African Americans moved North, so did segregation. Northern cities, including Washington, D.C., passed laws to separate the races. President Woodrow Wilson even replaced African-American office holders with whites and initiated a systematic segregation of civil service jobs.

In the South, too, race relations deteriorated. The newly revived Ku Klux Klan became more visible and more violent in response to the perceived postwar threat of African Americans infected with foreign notions of liberty, equality, and fraternity. After 1915, the lynching

African-American soldiers returning home from Europe after World War I wearing the *Croix de Guerre,* a medal given by the French government for bravery in battle, 1918. GETTY IMAGES

of African Americans became commonplace in the South. From 1916 to 1919, almost 300 people, mostly Southern blacks, lost their lives to lynch mobs who either hanged them or burned them alive. A number of these, like Daniel Mack, were returning soldiers still in uniform. Southern cities such as Knoxville, Tennessee, and Tulsa, Oklahoma, experienced riots, although these were less common in the South than in the North. In Tulsa, angry whites laid waste to an entire black section of the city, burning thirty-five square blocks and murdering hundreds of men, women, and children because of their race. All over the South, conditions worsened for African Americans as the homefront effects of World War I sharpened racial tensions.

For African Americans who had expected better returns for their wartime service at home and abroad, peace brought great disillusionment. Northward migration conferred some political rights and some increased eco-

nomic power but did nothing to change African Americans' status as second class citizens and in fact spurred more incidents of mistreatment. Each new lynching deepened resentment, and accounts of African-American soldiers hanged without cause by military police in Europe further embittered African Americans. But the population shifts and renewed commitment to the ideals of equality and democracy that war brought on also gave birth to a new generation of educated African Americans committed to achieving more, both socially and culturally, than had been even dreamed of by their forebears. The Harlem Renaissance drew its strength from the sons and daughters of African Americans who had migrated North during the war. And common experiences pulled the African-American community together, building solidarity in the demand for racial equality. Men like W. E. B. DuBois took up where the Daniel Macks left off, calling upon African Americans of all classes to fight for freedom at home. Decades later, African Americans would march to World War II determined to secure a double victory—one for their country abroad against the Axis Powers and one for their race at home against inequality and segregation. When they returned to America, they were more resolved than ever to secure the liberties African Americans had dreamed of in World War I, and their determination jumpstarted the American Civil Rights movement.

BIBLIOGRAPHY

Barbeau, Arthur E., and Florette Henri. *The Unknown Soldiers: Black American Troops in World War I.* Philadelphia: Temple University Press, 1974.

MacGregor, Morris J. *Integration of the Armed Forces, 1940-1965.* Washington, DC: Center of Military History, U.S. Army: 1981.

Nalty, Bernard C. *Strength for the Fight: A History of Black Americans in the Military.* New York: Free Press, 1986.

Woodward, C. Vann. *The Strange Career of Jim Crow,* 3d revised edition. New York: Oxford University Press, 1974.

Melinda Lee Pash

See also: **Civil Liberties, World War I; Du Bois, W. E. B.; Women and World War I.**

AFRICAN AMERICANS, WORLD WAR II

As the Nazis began to dominate the European continent, African Americans continued to grapple with the realities of life in a racist society. Jim Crow segregation and its quiet cousin, de facto segregation, ruled the land. Violence undergirded this social structure and prevented blacks from gaining some measure of parity with whites. World War II gave blacks an opportunity to reinvigorate the struggle against discrimination and, coupled with other social and political developments, to change a nation.

THE QUEST FOR EQUALITY

The Great Migration of blacks, during the World War I era, from the South to the North and Midwest began a national demographic transformation. The process resumed with vigor in the 1940s as black Southerners flocked to the industrial centers of the North, Midwest, and far West. The build-up for war created new opportunities for blacks in expanding industries, where blacks earned higher wages than in farming or domestic service.

As America prepared for war, longtime labor organizer A. Phillip Randolph joined with the National Association for the Advancement of Colored People (NAACP) and the National Urban League to pressure the White House to desegregate the military and defense

industries. After an unsuccessful meeting with the president, Randolph and other grassroots activists planned a protest against racial discrimination for June 1941 to be held at the Lincoln Memorial. To avoid the embarrassment of having 10,000 or more blacks demonstrating in the nation's capital for a chance to work and fight for their country, Roosevelt relented and signed Executive Order 8802. Executive Order 8802 outlawed racially discriminatory hiring practices in the defense industries and created the Fair Employment Practices Commission (FEPC) to enforce the edict. Bolstered by this victory, most blacks threw their unqualified support to the president, thereby prompting the shift of black voters from the Republican to the Democratic Party. Despite this triumph, the stark realities of racial hostility did not fade. Thus, black leaders sounded the clarion call of the "Double V" campaign: war abroad against fascism and war at home against racism. The connection between the two battles is best exemplified by the fate of the black soldier.

MILITARY SERVICE

In spite of their heroic performances in World War I, which had been widely recognized in Europe, black soldiers were pariahs in the United States. Whites remained wedded to the presumption of black inferiority, disloyalty, and cowardice. Because of rampant discrimination, black leaders sought proportional representation of blacks in the Army's combat units. President Roosevelt and others urged the Army to adopt a quota system so that the numbers of black soldiers would be representative of their proportion in the general population. Following the 1940 Selective Service Act, the enlisted strength of the Army usually was 10 percent black. By September 1944, the 701,678 black troops in the Army comprised 8.7 percent of the total. These gains aside, black troops found themselves shunted to the bottom of the military's hierarchy, and the armed services continued their practice of segregating whites and blacks.

Military officials forced black soldiers into segregated service units. Military policy did not allow blacks into combat units until 1944, thus accounting for the fact that little more than 50,000 black troops engaged the enemy in combat. Blacks served courageously in every theater of action, yet routinely the military failed to honor their bravery.

For example, Dorie Miller, one of the heroes of Pearl Harbor, shot down at least two Japanese fighter planes despite the Navy's prohibition against combat training for black sailors. The Navy ignored Miller's courage until the black-owned media trumpeted the community's outrage. On May 27, 1942, Miller received the Navy Cross but perished just eighteen months later when a Japanese submarine sank his ship, the USS *Liscome Bay.* Sadly, Miller ended his career as it began: as a messman.

Several members of the Tuskegee Airmen, an all-African-American combat squadron that became one of the most highly respected fighter groups of World War II.

The military's unwillingness to recognize the valor of, or simply to protect, black soldiers exacerbated these inequities.

By the end of World War II, 294 Medals of Honor had been bestowed on America's soldiers, yet none had been awarded to a black soldier. Beginning in 1993, research by a team organized at Shaw University—a historically black university in Raleigh, North Carolina—found a pattern of discrimination in the distribution of the Medal of Honor and recommended that the disparity be rectified. One such recipient of the award was Sergeant Edward Carter. Carter, who was demoted in order to serve in a combat unit, single-handedly wiped out a German unit and captured two prisoners while suffering multiple bullet and shrapnel wounds across his body.

HOMEFRONT
Despite the heroics of Carter, Miller, and others, black soldiers faced violence and hostility at home. Expanding black neighborhoods and business centers increased the competition for physical, cultural, and political space in America's cities. The ensuing tensions erupted in racial clashes and riots throughout the war years, the worst coming in Detroit in 1943. The military's disdain for African Americans echoed in the events surrounding a 1944 work stoppage by 258 black soldiers following an explosion at Port Chicago, California. Of that number, 50 were tried and convicted of mutiny, despite representation from the NAACP's Thurgood Marshall and support from First Lady Eleanor Roosevelt. In addition, many black soldiers were beaten, maimed, shot, or lynched—often while in uniform—by mobs and local authorities. By 1945, many blacks believed that war had ended only on one front.

Ultimately, the successes of black activists encouraged a stronger push for racial justice. President Roosevelt's actions served as a prelude to the Truman administration's executive order integrating the military and its espousal of civil rights. The treatment and triumphs of black workers, voters, and soldiers radicalized a community that already was eager to end the last vestiges of racism. In this manner, World War II—and the black responses to it—paved the way for racial integration, the civil rights movement, and a wider debate on the nature of American citizenship.

BIBLIOGRAPHY

Allen, Robert. *The Port Chicago Mutiny.* New York: Amistad, 1993.

Brandt, Nat. *Harlem at War: The Black Experience in World War II.* Syracuse, New York: Syracuse University Press, 1996.

Carter, Allene. *Honoring Sergeant Carter: Redeeming a Black World War II Hero's Legacy.* New York: Amistad, 2003.

Converse, III, Elliott, et al. *The Exclusion of Black Soldiers From the Medal of Honor in World War II: A Study Commissioned By the United States Army to Investigate Racial Bias in the Awarding of the Nation's Highest Military Decoration.* Jefferson, NC: McFarland & Co., 1997.

James, C. L. R., et al, eds. *Fighting Racism in World War II.* New York: Monad Press, 1980.

George White, Jr.

See also: **Civil Liberties, World War II; Du Bois, W. E. B.; Labor, World War I; Labor, World War II; Roosevelt, Eleanor; Roosevelt, Franklin Delano.**

ALLIES, IMAGES OF

When Americans entered World War I, they held a less than flattering image of their British, French, and Russians, allies. Since gaining their independence, Americans had frequently defined their identity against what they perceived as a tired and corrupt Old World. A recurring image in the discourse surrounding American entry into the war was that of the United States as a vigorous, dynamic force juxtaposed with the torpid, decaying European powers. Whereas the United States stood for individual liberty and unfettered initiative, Europe still represented the kind of privileged, effete society Americans had rejected in 1776.

For some Americans this image made them fearful that devious European diplomats were duping them into an imperialistic war. But for others, the image of a stagnent Europe infused their entry into the war with a crusading zeal. Henry Cabot Lodge said of the war, "We are resisting an effort to thrust mankind back to forms of government . . . which we had hoped had disappeared forever from the world." The *New York Times* conjured up the image of "millions of free Americans flocking to the rescue of beleaguered and exhausted Europe." More significantly, President Woodrow Wilson saw America's effort as a crusade to finally bring an end to Europe's re-

actionary regimes and "make the world safe for democracy." Wilson hoped that the New World idealism of the Fourteen Points, the peace program he laid out at the close of World War I, and the League of Nations might eradicate the ills of the Old World.

In the brief time they were there, American soldiers and military hierarchy developed a similar image of their European allies as stuck in the past. General John J. Pershing, leader of the American Expeditionary Force, derided the European tactics of attrition and entrenchment, favoring instead a strategy based more on mobility and initiative. Many soldiers' first-hand accounts of Europe perpetuated the image of allies as archaic by ruminating on the quaint and archaic nature of European society and customs.

After the war, the failure of Europe to embrace Wilson's international vision led to a sense of disillusionment among Americans. The bickering among former allies in the peace negotiations seemed to confirm earlier suspicions of Europe's moral decay. As a result, when the United States entered alliances with Great Britain, Russia, and later France in World War II, a negative image of European allies remained.

WORLD WAR II

At the outset of World War II, the prospect for a strong alliance between the United States, Great Britain, France, and the Soviet Union seemed remote. Despite President Franklin D. Roosevelt's sympathies for the plight of the British, many of Roosevelt's advisors viewed Great Britain negatively. As Mark Stoler notes in *Allies and Adversaries* (2000), many of the Joint Chiefs of Staff still believed that Great Britain had drawn the United States into a war to protect its imperial interests in 1917 and feared that the same thing was about to happen again. Moreover, Roosevelt feared that the British lacked the resolve necessary to fight Nazism. The election of Winston Churchill as prime minister in May 1940 quickly dispelled Roosevelt's fears and altered the image of Great Britain for most Americans. Soon after the fall of France in 1940, Churchill declared, "there will be no negotiations between London and Berlin." Churchill represented the kind of uncompromising leader in both word and deed that convinced Roosevelt that Great Britain would prove a steadfast ally. By war's end, the United States and Great Britain had developed a "special relationship" that continued through the Cold War (1946–1991) and beyond.

Just as the British and U.S. political alliance contained initial tensions, the image that allied soldiers held of each other were not entirely positive at first. U.S. troops carried their own preconceived images of the British when they first arrived there in January 1942. Despite their common language, U.S. troops found many

American sailor and Red Cross nurse standing with British Tommies during a celebration for the signing of the Armistice, November 11, 1918. © BETTMANN/CORBIS

cultural differences between themselves and their allies. In particular, many found British civilians and troops to be more socially reserved. For example, the British did not avidly shake hands, and they were far less likely to speak freely with recent acquaintances. Some American soldiers considered this behavior a sign of aloofness. Many found the more class-based British army and the use of imperial troops to be a sign of outdated mores and a reactionary mindset. Similarly, many American soldiers left the war believing that the French were a tired and decaying power. The once-proud French military failed to instill fear in the American troops that fought against them in North Africa, nor did they inspire much confidence when they fought alongside them during the latter stages of the war. To the average G.I., the relative disarray of French forces in terms of organization and material seemed to confirm France's decline as a major world power. These images permeated the highest levels of American decision making. Both Roosevelt and General Dwight D. Eisenhower marginalized Charles de Gaulle, head of the French Committee on National Lib-

eration, in the planning for D-Day and the last stages of the war. Only de Gaulle's opportunistic seizure of Paris (much to the chagrin of many American soldiers) and the Allies' need for a viable civilian authority to administer the newly liberated France allowed de Gaulle to exert such authority over postwar France.

Although over time, the shared experience of battle and the desire to vanquish a common foe allowed the British, French, and American soldiers to set aside differences, many Americans returned home with a strong image of European decay. For many, the erosion of the once-mighty British and French empires before their very eyes confirmed the waning power of the Old World and the ascendancy of the New. Contact with the British and French served to inflate America's self-proclaimed identity as a virtuous and vigorous nation and helped propel America into the active global leadership role it was to adopt immediately after World War II.

The mutual suspicion between the United States, the United Kingdom, and France proved minor compared with the tensions inherent with the Societ Union. Here too, each side's initial image of the other made an alliance seem unlikely. Since the Bolshevik Revolution of 1917, the United States had viewed the Soviet Union with suspicion and contempt. For ideological and financial reasons, U.S. officials resented Soviet Communism's closed society and calls for world revolution. The Stalinist purges of the 1930s further outraged the American public. For their part, the Soviets resented America's decision to send troops against the Bolshevik revolution in 1918 and its refusal to recognize the Soviet Union until 1933. The necessities of war, however, dictated that each side put aside their differences and embrace a more positive image of the other.

In the United States, the Roosevelt administration cultivated an image of Joseph Stalin as a heroic wartime leader. Although the idea of Stalin as a kindly "Uncle Joe" struck some as absurd, the military advantages of an alliance with Russia made such an image necessary. Churchill shared Roosevelt's reservations about the nature of the Soviet state but revealed the pragmatism behind the Grand Alliance when he commented, "Any man or state who fights Nazism will have our aid." The Soviets also set aside their ideological problems with the United States and publicly lauded Roosevelt for his resolute stand against the Nazis. Although such positive images managed to hold the alliance together just long enough to defeat Germany and Japan, the end of the war quickly shattered the illusion of harmony. Almost immediately, the old suspicions reemerged, ushering in the Cold War.

As the experience of World War I and World War II reveals, America's image of its allies not only changes to suit the purposes of policy, it also influences the shaping of those policies. Moreover, the images that they hold of their allies often force Americans to further define their own identity, the values for which they fight, and their role in the global community. In such subtle ways war can affect American identity, culture, and society.

BIBLIOGRAPHY

Kennedy, David M. *Over Here: The First World War and American Society* New York: Oxford University Press, 1980.

Mead, Gary. *The Doughboys: America and the First World War.* Woodstock, NY: Overlook Press, 2000.

Schrijvers, Peter. *The Crash of Ruin: American Combat Soldiers in Europe During World War II.* Houndmills, Basingstoke, Hampshire, UK: Macmillan, 1998.

Stoler, Mark A. *Allies and Adversaries: The Joint Chiefs of Staff, the Grand Alliance, and U.S. Strategy in World War II.* Chapel Hill: University of North Carolina Press, 2000.

Strout, Cushing. *The American Image of the Old World.* New York: Harper and Row, 1963.

Mark Boulton

See also: **Enemy, Images of; Wilson, Woodrow.**

AMERICAN INDIANS, WORLD WAR I AND WORLD WAR II

On the eve of World War I, white Americans doubted many things about Indians living in their midst—their loyalty to the United States, their viability as citizens, even their right to landholdings and reservations. But few Americans of any color doubted the adeptness of Indians as warriors. From colonial times, Indians proved capable in warfare; Indian troops served in both armies of the Civil War, and during the Spanish-American War, the Philippine Insurrection, and the 1916 U.S. incursion into Mexico. Thus when the United States entered World War I in 1917, Indians naturally became one source of manpower for the American war machine. Having served well in one world war, Indians found themselves called to serve again when the United States entered World War II in 1941. Indian participation in these two wars helped to reshape tribal life and American society.

When Congress approved the Selective Service Act in May 1917, requiring all American males to register for the draft, a large percentage of American Indians did not even possess U.S. citizenship. Still, the law required all Native American males of military age to register, though only citizens could be drafted. In the end, 17,000 American Indians registered, and 6,500 draftees and 6,000 enlistees mustered into the U.S. military. Most of these troops served in integrated units and were part of every major battle on the Western Front. There, Indians often held dangerous positions like snipers and scouts, suffering battle death rates of 5 percent as compared to 1 percent for U.S. troops overall. The heroism displayed by these troops earned them citizenship in 1919, opening the door for 1924 legislation granting citizenship to all Indians.

After World War I, many non-Indian Americans, impressed with Indian soldiers and home front efforts, hoped that Indians would soon give up tribal identities and assimilate into the larger society. However, the war actually reinforced tribal identities for many of its participants. Many tribes sent their soldiers off with war dances and welcomed them home with time-honored cleansing rituals and victory dances. And, as veterans returned home, they struggled with the same economic inequalities that had existed before their departure. Although congressional granting of citizenship did not turn Indians into Americans, their new legal status did have implications for Indians in the next war.

The beginning of World War II in Europe in September 1940 prompted Congress that same month to pass the first peacetime draft in American history. As citizens, Indians were expected to register. Some argued exemption because they rejected U.S. citizenship, but after the legal ruling *Ex Parte Green* stated that neither tribal

Two Navajo Indian "code talkers" operating the radio during World War II. Beginning in 1942, "code talkers" used the Navajo language as an unbreakable military code. GETTY IMAGES

membership nor rejection of citizenship excluded Indians from military service, opposition to the draft waned. By March 1941 over 7,500 American Indians had registered. By the end of World War II, tribal societies had provided 25,000 servicemen, 800 nurses to the WACS and WAVES, and thousands of dollars in bond purchases and donations. Over 1,250 Indians became casualties of war. Additionally, scores of Indians left reservations to become urban workers in the home front effort to win the war.

The Navajo and Comanche "code talkers" are the best known Indian soldiers. Starting in 1942, they used the Navajo language as an unbreakable military code. Reminiscent of Choctaw soldiers recruited in 1918 to work the Army's telephone service and confuse German intelligence during World War I, these code talkers gained distinction during World War II for their invaluable service. Eventually, the 382nd Platoon formed just for Navajo code talkers.

Returning home after years of war, Native American veterans of World War II found themselves confronted with a society that had reshaped itself in their absence. Before war, American Indian society had been isolated, but the money soldiers sent home transformed the reservations by making refrigerators, radios, heaters, and even phonographs fixtures in Indian life. Also, not all Indians who left in the war job exodus returned at war's end. Many instead chose to make cities their permanent homes, as did some veterans. The soldiers, too, had changed. Exposed to white culture and opportunities in the military, many wanted an education and better pay, and many more had adopted Christianity. Though political activism would be the hallmark of another generation, some veterans lobbied for increased voting rights or sought to change drinking laws that made alcohol unavailable to Indians. Although not drastic, World War II changes did draw more Indians into mainstream culture and bring parts of that culture into reservation life. Similarly, non-Indian Americans found Indian faces a more familiar part of their world, and later a more familiar part of their political life.

Neither of the world wars revolutionized the relationship between Indian and mainstream American cultures. But by ensuring Indian citizenship and exposing Indians to a larger world, both wars paved the way for increased pluralism on the reservation and in American communities. This legacy of contact would provide future generations of warriors with a foundation for more complex, and sometimes less peaceful, interactions.

BIBLIOGRAPHY

Bernstein, Alison. *American Indians and World War II: Toward a New Era in Indian Affairs.* Norman: University of Oklahoma Press, 1991.

Britten, Thomas A. *American Indians in World War I: At Home and at War.* Albuquerque: University of New Mexico Press, 1999.

Franco, Jere' Bishop. *Crossing the Pond: The Native American Effort in World War II.* Denton: University of North Texas Press, 1999.

Holm, Tom. *Strong Hearts, Wounded Souls: Native American Veterans of the Vietnam War.* Austin: University of Texas Press, 1996.

Meadows, William C. *The Comanche Code Talkers of World War II.* Austin: University of Texas Press, 2002.

Townsend, Kenneth. *World War II and the American Indian.* Albuquerque: University of New Mexico Press, 2000.

Melinda Lee Pash

See also: **Conscription, World War I; Conscription, World War II; War, Impact on Ethnic Groups.**

AMERICAN LEGION

The American Legion was founded in Paris in 1919 by a group of volunteer army officers interested in forming a veterans' organization devoted to preserving wartime camaraderie, law and order, and democracy. The Legion devised both a broad-based political agenda and specific measures to secure greater veterans' benefits. The organization soon became the principal spokesman for World War I veterans and conferred directly with the White House and Congress on a range of social and political issues.

Adopting the motto "For God and Country," the Legion advocated what was called 100 percent Americanism. Many individual posts took an active role in combating radicalism during the first Red Scare in 1919–1920 by attacking suspected Bolsheviks and breaking strikes. The Legion maintained strong ties with law enforcement agencies throughout the interwar period, and in 1941 the Federal Bureau of Investigation recruited 33,000 legionnaires as official informants. Between 1920 and 1941, the Legion consistently championed a strong defense budget, immigration restrictions, and a universal draft to take the profit out of war (by paying soldiers, workers, and industrialists similar wages).

The Legion also devoted enormous energy to securing aid for disabled veterans, hospital care for needy veterans, and bonus service pay for all World War I veterans. The government, the Legion argued, had failed to distribute the financial burdens of the war fairly between soldiers and civilians. Whereas workers and industrialists earned record wages and profits, soldiers only received a dollar a day. The Legion wanted each veteran to receive additional retroactive pay for their wartime service. In 1924 the government granted this request by giving veterans an adjusted compensation bond that matured in 1945. In 1932 bonus marchers descended on Washington, D.C., to demand immediate payment of this money, but the Legion refused to endorse their movement. After the army forcibly evicted the bonus marchers, the Legion switched its position and successfully lobbied for an early bond payment in 1936.

Throughout the interwar years, the Legion also took an active interest in keeping the memory of World War I alive. The Legion built monuments and memorial buildings to commemorate the war, convinced the government to post an armed guard at the tomb of the unknown soldier in Arlington cemetery, and successfully pushed for Armistice Day to become a national holiday in 1938.

The chartering of individual posts was left to each state's Legion headquarters, a policy that gave southern states the power to reject applications from black posts.

Few African-American veterans, therefore, joined the Legion. In 1925 the Legion recognized 100 black posts, with an overall membership of 1,862 out of 380,000 potential members. Race was only one issue that divided Legion posts. The Legion's 11,000 posts ranged from conservative posts that readily cooperated with the Ku Klux Klan to urban chapters linked to unions.

Dues-paying legionnaires never comprised the majority of World War I veterans. Out of four million potential members, Legion rolls ranged from 843,000 in 1920 to 609,000 in 1925, only to soar to over one million in 1931. The Legion's opposition to immediate payment of the bonus resulted in a severe dip to 770,000 in 1933, but the organization rebounded to 1.1 million by 1941.

Legion posts often provided a launching pad for a career in local politics. In addition, Legion posts sponsored boy scout troops, built parks and playgrounds, organized baseball leagues, held patriotic ceremonies, promoted proper flag etiquette, ran child-welfare programs, and offered disaster-relief.

Through the Legion, World War I veterans made their greatest contribution to American society by authoring and lobbying for the Servicemen's Readjustment Act in 1944, also known as the G.I. Bill. This legislation helped the country avoid the mistakes made after World War I when veterans faced a difficult readjustment. The G.I. Bill gave World War II veterans access to unemployment compensation, low-interest housing and small business loans, college tuition, and health care. Thanks to the G.I. Bill, military service for the first time in the nation's history became a way to enter the middle class.

After much debate, the Legion decided to open its doors to World War II veterans in 1942. Proponents of this measure wanted to offer help to wounded ex-servicemen and worried that the Legion would lose influence over veterans' affairs if World War II veterans formed their own organization. In 1946, with 16 million prospective members returning home, Legion membership grew to 3.5 million.

Overall, the Legion exerted tremendous influence in veterans' affairs, national politics, antiradical activities, and community affairs in the interwar period and helped the nation interpret the significance of World War I.

BIBLIOGRAPHY

Keene, Jennifer D. *Doughboys, The Great War and the Remaking of America*. Baltimore, MD: Johns Hopkins University Press, 2001.

Pencak, William. *For God and Country: The American Legion, 1919–1941*. Boston: Northeastern University Press, 1989.

Rumer, Thomas A. *The American Legion: An Official History, 1919–1989*. New York: M. Evans, 1990.

Jennifer D. Keene

See also: **Armistice Day; Bonus March; G.I. Bill of Rights; Hoover, Herbert; Monuments, Cemeteries, World War I; Veterans' Benefits; Veterans of Foreign Wars.**

AMERICANIZATION

In 1916, while a deadly war raged in Europe, President Woodrow Wilson successfully ran for reelection on the slogan, "He Kept Us out of War." But by April 1917, however, events had pulled the United States into what was then called the Great War, a conflict that Wilson subsequently declared a crusade to "make the world safe for democracy." Reacting to the unpopular nature of the war, the growing peace movement, the fear of radicalism, and the ethnic diversity of the nation, the U.S. government created a high-pitched propaganda effort designed to instill patriotism, promote the war, and reaffirm the cultural hegemony of traditional white Protestant values. The campaign fueled a jingoistic fervor that escalated into mass hysteria and vigilantism. The result was a harsh Americanization movement that demanded nothing less than total conformity. Especially targeted were ethnic groups from Southern and Eastern Europe.

Once the United States entered World War I in April 1917, the government's new propaganda agency, the Committee on Public Information (CPI), hired an impressive group of writers, historians, photographers, and entertainers to sell the war to the American public using innovative advertising and marketing methods and the new film medium to promote loyalty and conformity by bombarding the nation with millions of official bulletins, pamphlets, and news releases, as well as articles and ads in mass magazines. Over 150,000 people served on CPI committees. The Liberty Loan campaign capitalized on the patriotic fervor with posters that draped the nation's cities and towns, presenting the purchase of war bonds as a demonstration of loyalty. A team of 75,000 Four Minute Men gave short, passionate patriotic speeches, and volunteer groups such as the American Protective League joined the small army of volunteers promoting the war. Some went to extremes in their attempt to unify the nation, keeping a watchful eye on their fellow Americans, reading private mail, bugging telephones, breaking into homes, and physically assaulting those suspected of disloyalty.

Throughout the country, nativists called upon the foreign-born to prove their allegiance to America. Consequently, the immigrant experience of World War I was one of oppression, forced assimilation, ruthless xenophobia, and harsh one-hundred-percent Americanism. The CPI directed much of its propaganda efforts at immigrants through foreign language materials designed to

Immigrant women from Hungary, Galicia, Russia, Germany, and Romania sew an American flag, ca. 1918. © CORBIS

strip them of their native cultures and loyalties. Public schools instructed the children of immigrants in "proper" Anglo-Saxon values and traditions and strongly encouraged them to take their lessons home. Ethnic presses fell under the sharp inspection of the U.S. government and faced financial burdens placed on them by the U.S. Postal Service, which demanded the right to scrutinize translations prior to publication. Many foreign presses shut down under the strain. Eventually, the U.S. government also forced all immigrants born in countries under the Central Powers to register with the government, labeling them enemy aliens. In this emotionally charged atmosphere of superpatriotism, the voices of the foreign-born, like those of radicals and pacifists, were effectively stifled.

Although many ethnic groups became victims of harassment, German Americans were particularly targeted. Many school boards instructed students to cut all references to Germany out of their textbooks and canceled classes in the German language, which was now considered treasonous. Libraries removed books on Germany,

officials in many cities forbade public orchestras to play Bach and Beethoven, and German art was removed from some city museums. Hamburgers, sauerkraut, and German measles became liberty sandwiches, liberty cabbage, and liberty measles. For many German Americans, war hysteria resulted in harassment, loss of employment, violence, and even death.

During the war, many ethnic communities demonstrated loyalty to their adopted nation with parades, speeches, fundraisers, and resolutions. Although many immigrants must have felt coerced into expressing loyalty to the United States, the situation was complex. Many immigrants, especially those from territories under the rule of the Austro-Hungarian Empire, genuinely supported the war effort. Many of them had fled the tyranny of the empire and sought freedom in America. They hoped that a war against the Central Powers would finally free their homelands from oppressive rule.

The foreign-born also expressed their loyalty through military service, and eventually almost one in every five soldiers in the U.S. army was foreign-born; the U.S. army included soldiers from forty-six different nations. With America's declaration of war, leaders from the Czech-, Slovak-, Polish-, and Jewish-American communities encouraged members of their ethnic groups who were not eligible to join the American military to join the Czechoslovak, Polish, or Jewish legions attached to the French and British armies.

At the end of the war, the hysteria that made so many immigrants suspect did not simply end. The war's end marked a period of upheaval. The excitement and permissiveness of the Roaring Twenties challenged traditional Victorian morality. Modernity did battle with traditionalism. The social stress and the zeal of war gave way to new fervors and culminated in the Red Scare, a resurgent Ku Klux Klan, fundamentalism, labor strikes, and prohibition. Anti-immigration hysteria fueled by postwar uncertainty and the turbulence of the 1920s pushed Congress into enacting the 1924 National Origins Act. This unequal quota system dramatically reduced the number of immigrants allowed into the United States from Southern and Eastern Europe, all but closing the door to future immigration. World War I and its aftermath helped usher in dramatic changes in American identity, culture, and society.

BIBLIOGRAPHY

Ford, Nancy Gentile. *Americans All: Foreign-Born Soldiers in World War I.* College Station: Texas A&M University Press, 2001

Higham, John. *Strangers in the Land: Patterns of American Nativism 1860–1925* (1955). New Brunswick, NJ: Rutgers University Press, 2002.

Kennedy, David M. *Over Here: The First World War and American Society.* New York: Oxford University Press, 1980.

Nancy Gentile Ford

See also: **Civil Liberties, World War I; Dissent in World War I and World War II; Ku Klux Klan; Red Scare.**

ARMISTICE DAY

At 11:00 A.M. on November 11, 1918, World War I, known as the "War to End all Wars," came to an end with the signing of the cease-fire agreement at Rethondes, France. One year later, November 11 was set aside as Armistice Day in the United States to remember the sacrifices made by men and women during that war. Veterans' parades and political speeches throughout the country emphasized the peaceful nature of the day, echoing the theme of national unity and the victory of democracy over tyranny.

Memorial Day, originally established after the Civil War to honor the war dead and to heal the sectional divisions remaining from that conflict, was, and remained, the traditional day on which the dead of all conflicts were honored through reverent ceremonies and the decoration of their graves with flags and flowers. Armistice Day, on the other hand, was designated as a national day commemorating America's participation in World War I and those who served: not only the dead, but the living.

Armistice Day observances in the United States were similar to those in France and Great Britain with processions, wreath-laying ceremonies, and a moment of silence to pay homage to those who died in the war. On the third Armistice Day after the war, November 11, 1921, America further followed the example of its allies by burying, with impressive ceremony, an Unknown Soldier in an elaborate tomb at Arlington Cemetery. The event not only bolstered efforts to make Armistice Day a national holiday, but established rituals intended to unify a homogenous nation still ambivalent about the nation's involvement in the war.

Although united in their desire to pay tribute to those who had fought and died, Americans could not agree on the precise nature and intent of Armistice Day commemorative rituals. The American Legion, the largest veterans' organization to emerge after the war, endeavored to ensure that the achievements of American veterans were remembered. Through hymns and prayers, ceremonies sponsored by the Legion emphasized the terrible cost of war and the need to work for a new, more harmonious world order. In accord with the belief that military strength ensures peace, Legion parades often included a military component from the various branches of the armed forces and rifle or artillery salutes to the dead.

Others preferred to strip Armistice Day of its militaristic character, emphasizing instead the tragedy of war and the hope of preserving peace through negotiation. In the 1920s a series of disarmament treaties and pacifist promises, such as those of the Kellogg-Briand pact of 1928, created a sense of optimism about the possibility that there might never be another war. Members of national peace movements believed war could be stopped only through disarmament and pacifism, whereas the American Legion maintained that military preparedness provided the best assurance against future wars. The lack of consensus within society reflected the ambivalence that still prevailed toward America's intervention in the First World War.

Despite years of political lobbying and campaigning by the Legion, Congress did not make Armistice Day a federal holiday until 1938. By this time, it was obvious that another war was imminent and that once again

Photo taken by *Life* magazine photographer Alfred Eisenstaedt in New York City, as the inhabitants celebrated the surrender of Japan during World War II. ALFRED EISENSTAEDT/LIFE (MAGAZINE).

Americans might be called to fight. Emotional memories of the previous conflict stirred isolationists and peace groups to urge the government away from another foreign entanglement toward stringent neutrality laws. Ultimately, patriotic fervor and the perceived need to defend the nation against such unprovoked attacks as the one on Pearl Harbor proved the decisive factors that united the

nation in fighting another world war. During the war observances of Armistice Day declined.

After World War II ended in 1945, Americans continued to observe Armistice Day on November 11 as the Legion opened its membership to a new generation of veterans. These Second World War veterans joined each year in the rituals and commemorative ceremonies established by previous veterans after the First World War. In 1954, the holiday was designated Veterans Day to honor veterans of all American wars and in 1971, President Nixon declared it a federal holiday on the fourth Monday in October in accordance with the Uniform Holidays Act. However, many Americans objected to this change in its traditional date, so in 1978 Congress restored the observance of Veterans Day to November 11.

BIBLIOGRAPHY

"Beginnings and Results of Memorial Day," *American Legion Weekly*, 26 May 1922, 16–17.

Piehler, G. Kurt. *Remembering War the American Way*. Washington, DC: Smithsonian Institution Press, 1995.

Worthington, R.C. "Homecoming." *American Legion Magazine*, November, 1938.

Internet Resources

"History of Veterans Day." U.S. Department of Veterans Affairs. Available from <http://www.va.gov/vetsday/>.

Lisa M. Budreau

See also: **American Legion; Monuments, Cemeteries, World War I; Veterans of Foreign Wars.**

BONUS MARCH

In the late spring and early summer of 1932, 40,000 middle-aged and impoverished World War I veterans descended on Washington, D.C., to demand immediate payment of their adjusted compensation certificates, or bonus. The government had given veterans these bonds to settle an earlier political dispute. World War I veterans returned home in the midst of the 1919 recession and soon grew angry with war profiteers. The draft, veterans argued, gave the government the power to determine who went into the army and who stayed at home. Those who went into the army received one dollar a day, while civilians earned high wages and profits in the booming wartime economy. The government, in veterans' eyes, had the responsibility of ensuring equality of sacrifice in time of total war by distributing the financial burdens of the war fairly between soldiers and civilians. In 1924 the government offered veterans a compromise. Instead of a cash settlement, veterans would receive a bond (worth approximately $1,000) that matured in 1945. With the economy improving, veterans accepted the government's offer without protest.

The Great Depression caused veterans to revive their call for immediate compensation. At first, they limited their requests to letters and telegrams. In May 1932 a group of veterans from Portland, Oregon, decided to cross the country to present their requests personally before Congress. The press picked up the story, and when the initial group of two hundred rode into the nation's capital atop trucks provided by the Maryland National Guard, they discovered that their trek had become a full-fledged mass movement. Thousands of veterans from throughout the country came to join the Oregon group, launching one of the greatest grassroots movements in the nation's history.

The veterans set up a makeshift camp on the Anacostia Flats, in sight of the Capitol. As the movement grew, over two dozen smaller groups occupied empty federal buildings downtown. A few Communists set up a camp at the fringes of the movement but had little influence over the majority of veterans. Despite intense media coverage and daily visits by veterans to individual congressmen, the Senate voted down a House-approved payment bill in June. The nation waited anxiously to see if the veterans would leave peacefully, be allowed to stay, or be forcibly evicted.

From the beginning, President Herbert Hoover and U.S. Army Chief of Staff Douglas MacArthur feared that the veterans had come to stage a Communist coup. On July 28 the police began evicting some bonus marchers from a downtown building slated for demolition and in the process shot two unarmed veterans. With tempers rising, District of Columbia officials asked Hoover for troops to help clear the area. Disregarding the advice of his aide, Major Dwight Eisenhower, MacArthur decided to personally command the eviction. MacArthur arrived at the scene in full dress uniform, leading one squadron of cavalry troops, two battalions of infantry, a mounted machine gun squad, and five tanks. The troops cleared the downtown camps, and then headed to the Anacostia Bridge to cross into the veterans' main camp. Hoover sent at least three messages to MacArthur telling him not to cross the bridge, but MacArthur ignored these orders. By midnight, the main veteran camp was in flames and the bonus marchers had fled.

In the political turmoil that followed the eviction, Hoover chose to stand by MacArthur and never publicly revealed the general's insubordination. The country saw Hoover's eviction of the bonus marchers as symbolic of his general unwillingness to grant direct relief to ease individual suffering during the Great Depression. By popularizing the image of Hoover as an uncaring president who was out of touch with the common man, the bonus march played a significant role in Hoover's defeat in the presidential election of 1932.

The new president, Franklin D. Roosevelt, was more successful in deflecting the bonus issue. During the two subsequent bonus marches, in 1933 and 1934, Roosevelt welcomed the few thousand veterans who came as conventioneers, housed them in an army camp out of the city, and then offered them places in the Civilian Conservation Corps to get them to disperse willingly. Roosevelt also went on the offensive, chiding veterans for making "special class" demands at a time of national crisis. Within a few years, however, the New Deal created so many special demographic categories eligible for federal aid that public support resurfaced for early payment. In 1936 Congress overrode a presidential veto and agreed to let veterans cash in their bonds immediately.

The bonus march was a legacy of World War I that helped shape the nation's response to the Great Depression and World War II. During the Depression, Americans were able to express their preference for a more activist state through their support of the bonus marchers. In 1944, hoping in part to avoid the political embarrassment of another veterans' march on Washington, D.C., the government passed the G.I. Bill, a comprehensive set of benefits for World War II veterans.

BIBLIOGRAPHY

Barber, Lucy G. *Marching on Washington: the Forging of an American Political Tradition.* Berkeley: University of California, 2002.

Daniels, Roger. *The Bonus March: An Episode of the Great Depression.* Westport, CT: Greenwood Press, 1971.

Keene, Jennifer D. *Doughboys, the Great War and the Remaking of America.* Baltimore, MD: Johns Hopkins University Press, 2001.

Lisio, Donald J. *The President and Protest: Hoover, Conspiracy, and the Bonus Riot.* Columbia: University of Missouri Press, 1974.

Jennifer D. Keene

See also: **American Legion; Hoover, Herbert; Roosevelt, Franklin Delano; Veterans' Benefits; Veterans of Foreign Wars.**

CATT, CARRIE CHAPMAN

(b. January 9,1859; d. March 9, 1947) President of the National American Woman Suffrage Association and founder of the League of Women Voters.

A leader of the woman suffrage movement, Carrie Chapman Catt was a peace advocate during most of World War I, then became an influential supporter of the American war effort. Born Carrie Clinton Lane, she demonstrated a strong independent streak early in life. She paid her own way through Iowa State College and after graduation worked as a high school principal. She married Leo Chapman in 1885, but he died of typhoid fever in 1886, leaving her nearly penniless. She scraped together a living as a lecturer and newspaper editorial assistant, and she joined the Iowa Suffrage Association, where she developed her organizational skills. In 1890, she married George Catt, a feminist and financially successful engineer. Elected president of the National American Woman Suffrage Association (NAWSA) in 1900, she served for four years, then headed the International Woman Suffrage Alliance.

When World War I began, Catt was sailing home from a conference in London where she and women from twenty-six nations had jointly written a manifesto pleading for a diplomatic solution to the mounting crisis. Although as women they lacked political power in their native lands, they hoped that together they could make a difference. The failure of the manifesto to influence events strengthened Catt's resolve to do all she could to obtain full political rights for women. She believed that women were inherently less inclined than men to favor war and that if nations were ruled by men and women equally war would become a rare occurrence. In her opinion, lasting world peace was unlikely to arrive anytime soon, but it was guaranteed never to arrive at all as long as the female half of the human race remained politically powerless.

From the first, Catt viewed the war in Europe as a catastrophe for humanity. In late 1914, she helped organize a peace parade in New York City, then enlisted the help of well-known pacifist and pioneer social worker Jane Addams to organize women's opposition to the war. Catt wanted Addams to spearhead women's antiwar activities so that her own name would not become prominent in the peace movement. Catt worried that she was so well known as an advocate of woman suffrage that if she became closely identified with pacifism she might harm the cause of woman suffrage among Americans who

Carrie Chapman Catt.

tism, and she hoped that after the war women's service to the nation would be rewarded by recognition of their right to vote. She kept the war-related contributions of women in general, and the NAWSA in particular, constantly in the news. Her strategy worked; after the armistice, many politicians who had formerly opposed woman suffrage now supported it on the grounds that women had proven themselves worthy of it during the war.

Through her wartime leadership of the NAWSA, and especially her success in encouraging women to take up war-related work, Catt helped change Americans' views of women's ability to participate fully in civic life. However, Catt never stopped hating war, and during the 1920s she devoted herself to the cause of world peace. Yet by the late 1930s she feared that the Nazis would destroy civilization and she denounced isolationism. She died in1947, happy to have seen the birth of the United Nations.

BIBLIOGRAPHY

Fowler, Robert Booth. *Carrie Catt: Feminist Politician.* Boston: Northeastern University Press, 1986.

Peck, Mary Gray. *Carrie Chapman Catt: A Biography.* New York: H. W. Wilson, 1944.

Van Voris, Jacqueline. *Carrie Chapman Catt: A Public Life.* New York: Feminist Press at the City University of New York, 1987.

Janis Appier

See also: **Addams, Jane; Civil Liberties, World War I; Feminism; Women and World War I; Women, Employment of.**

supported the war. Catt refused a leadership position in the peace movement, but she remained active behind the scenes, lending her formidable management skills and political connections. She occasionally met with President Woodrow Wilson to urge him to continue his policy of neutrality. Her participation in the peace movement, although low key, helped it stay alive.

In December 1915, Catt once again became president of the NAWSA, and over the next few years she led the woman suffrage movement to national victory. Her success lay in part in her adroit handling of the volatile issues of peace, patriotism, and woman suffrage. As America inched closer to war, most antisuffragists lumped suffragists and peace groups into a single category, calling them disloyal and pro-German. In February 1917, Catt called a meeting of the NAWSA and convinced the delegates that U.S. entry into the war was imminent and that to avoid being labeled subversive the organization must endorse war-readiness. After the United States entered the war, Catt served on the Woman's Committee of the Council of National Defense and worked to get women—especially suffragists—involved in war-related work. She wanted the public to associate the NAWSA with patrio-

CIVIL LIBERTIES, WORLD WAR I

During World War I, the Woodrow Wilson administration took unprecedented steps to mobilize public support for the war. In addition to a massive government propaganda campaign, Congress passed laws designed to silence dissent. Newspapers were censored, politicians were jailed, and mobs attacked those suspected of disloyalty. Some Americans organized to protest the erosion of democratic freedoms guaranteed by the Constitution, a group of rights that they called "civil liberties." Thus, while democratic freedoms were undermined during World War I, public concern over these policies inspired the beginnings of a twentieth-century movement to guard the right of Americans to criticize their government, even when their country is at war.

When President Woodrow Wilson called on Congress to declare war on Germany in April 1917, the government faced a formidable task. Millions of young men had to be drafted, equipped, trained, and shipped an ocean away. To accomplish this in time to break the military stalemate on Europe's western front, Wilson demanded unprecedented powers to mobilize American society.

In addition to drafting men and directing the economy, Wilson took steps to control public opinion, encouraging patriotic support for the war effort. The task was made more urgent because Americans remained deeply divided about the conflict. When Germany invaded France in 1914, most Americans shared Wilson's desire to remain neutral. His reelection in 1916 was widely considered a vote for the man who "kept us out of war." When he declared war five months later, many Americans still opposed involvement. Some German immigrants remained sympathetic to their ancestral home; socialists thought the war was inspired by capitalist greed; and various religious sects opposed all war on principle. Considering national unity essential to military success, Wilson took steps to silence these critics, guarding American society from what he called "the poison of disloyalty."

SILENCING DISSENT

In June 1917, Congress passed the Espionage Act, making it a crime for Americans to speak against their government's war effort, to incite disloyalty, or to encourage men to resist the draft. A year later, the more restrictive Sedition Act outlawed "disloyal, profane, scurrilous or abusive language" against the flag, the Constitution, and even the uniform of the armed forces. Those who continued to speak against the war risked heavy fines and jail sentences of up to twenty years.

The Espionage Act gave the U.S. postmaster general, Albert S. Burleson, the power to deny mailing privileges to any newspaper or magazine that seemed to give comfort to the enemy. The Trading-with-the-Enemy Act (1917) gave Burleson additional powers over America's foreign-language press. The postmaster wielded these censorship powers enthusiastically, and by war's end many of the nation's radical newspapers and magazines had been driven into bankruptcy. Those that survived agreed to toe the government's line on the war. Liberal and radical journalists complained to Wilson that his postmaster was violating the First Amendment guarantee of a free press, but the president generally supported Burleson's decisions. As one historian argues, during the war "only the administration's views of the larger issues found their way into print."

The government built an elaborate spy network to watch German immigrants and American radicals. Federal agents arrested hundreds for making anti-war speeches, and sometimes for informal and private remarks. Eugene Debs, four-time presidential candidate for the Socialist Party, was arrested in June 1918 for suggesting during a speech that young American men were "fit for something better than slavery and cannon fodder." Sentenced to ten years in prison, he defiantly ran for president in 1920 from his jail cell in Atlanta, and received almost a million votes. During the war, more than 2,000 men and women were arrested for "disloyal" speech, and over 1200 went to jail.

In addition to these attacks on free speech, the government violated basic legal protections in other ways. Some conscientious objectors were court-martialed and mistreated in military prisons. A 1918 law sanctioned the deportation of any non-citizen suspected of belonging to a revolutionary group; hundreds were deported without the benefit of a hearing. And on September 5, 1917, federal agents raided the offices of the Industrial Workers of the World (IWW), a radical labor union, and arrested hundreds, including most of the union's leadership. Although the IWW was neutral on the war, business leaders considered the union to be dangerously subversive. Following mass trials, hundreds of IWW members, including most of the leadership, were sent to federal penitentiaries, convicted not for their actions but for their ideas.

The government's disregard for the civil rights of dissenters encouraged private citizens to express their patriotism by attacking those they suspected of disloyalty. Citizen groups such as the National Security League and the American Protective League broke up anti-war meetings, assaulted speakers, and conducted illegal "slacker raids" to round up young men who had failed to register for the draft. Mobs attacked and in a few cases even lynched innocent German-Americans, their rage fueled by a steady diet of government propaganda against the "Huns." Even colleges and public schools joined in the attack on freedom of speech, firing teachers suspected of German sympathies. While Wilson and other federal officials denounced mob violence, they also encouraged citizens to spy on their neighbors, and gave official sanction to some vigilante groups.

SUPREME COURT AND CIVIL LIBERTIES

When the Espionage and Sedition Acts were tested in the Supreme Court in the months after the war, the justices unanimously upheld the conviction of wartime protestors. Congress has the right to regulate speech, Justice Oliver Wendell Holmes asserted in *Schenk vs. United States*, when the country faces "a clear and present danger." The court's claim that the government can limit basic American freedoms in times of war troubled some Americans, including many of Wilson's liberal supporters who feared that his war to "make the world safe for democracy" had undermined democratic principles at home. A new organization, the American Civil Liberties Union (ACLU; 1920), provided legal defense for those imprisoned for wartime speech. Raising public concern about government's new powers to regulate opinion, the ACLU and other groups pressured the government to grant an "amnesty" to many convicted under the wartime laws. As Americans tried in the early 1920s to "return to normalcy," most of those convicted under the Espionage and Sedition laws were released.

World War I serves as a stark warning that the stresses of modern warfare pose a threat to America's tradition of civil liberties. But this period also inspired what historian Eric Foner has called "the birth of civil liberties" in American society. First united in their opposition to government attacks on anti-war protesters in World War I, the ACLU and other rights groups have since won landmark cases that have helped to establish greater protections for dissenting voices in American society during times of war.

BIBLIOGRAPHY

Foner, Eric. *The Story of American Freedom.* New York: Norton, 1998.

Kennedy, David M. *Over Here: The First World War and American Society.* New York: Oxford University Press, 1982.

Murphy, Paul L. *World War I and the Origin of Civil Liberties in the United States.* New York: Norton, 1979.

Peterson, H. C., and Fite, Gilbert C. *Opponents of War, 1917–1918* (c. 1957). Westport, CT: Greenwood Press, 1986.

Preston, William, Jr. *Aliens and Dissenters: Federal Suppression of Radicals, 1903–1933.* Cambridge, MA: Harvard University Press, 1963.

Rabban, David. *Free Speech in its Forgotten Years.* Cambridge, UK: Cambridge University Press, 1997.

Rodney, Smolla. *Free Speech in an Open Society.* New York, Knopf, 1992; distributed by Random House.

Ernest Freeberg

See also: **Addams, Jane; Dissent in World War I and World War II; Du Bois, W. E. B.; Labor, World War I; Red Scare.**

CIVIL LIBERTIES, WORLD WAR II

The federal government, in response to periods of insecurity and conflict, sometimes restricts civil liberties in an effort to maintain national security. U.S. involvement in World War I brought about such restrictions, and World War II proved to be no different. In the wake of the attack on Pearl Harbor, the federal government took into custody almost 11,000 persons it considered enemy aliens. The arrest of the 8,000 Japanese Americans, 2,300 German Americans, and several hundred Italian Americans followed due process of law. However, on February 19, 1942, presidential action targeted one specific group for detainment. Executive Order 9066 provided the initial authority for the roundup and internment of approximately 120,000 Japanese Americans, including those who were American citizens. Congress later passed legislation to enforce the order. The Japanese Americans affected by the mandate, primarily those living on the West Coast, were divided and sent to ten detention centers located in California, Arizona, Idaho, Wyoming, Colorado, and Arkansas.

The War Relocation Authority served as the administration responsible for overseeing the detention centers. Life in the camps was humane for the occupants, but even efforts meant to help or entertain the detainees often proved to be culturally insensitive. In 1943 the federal government forced the internees to take a loyalty oath, forswearing "any form of allegiance or obedience to the Japanese emperor," and it asked if they were willing to serve in the United States military. Some Japanese-American men refused to serve and over 200 were sentenced to prison for their resistance. Others, however, served honorably. In fact, the 442nd Combat Regiment, composed of Japanese Americans, was the most decorated American unit in World War II and suffered the highest percentages of casualties and deaths.

The decision to intern Japanese Americans sparked opposition from the American Civil Liberties Union as well as from First Lady Eleanor Roosevelt. A series of court cases also challenged the wartime treatment of Japanese Americans. The first, *Hirabayashi v. United States* (1943) regarded in general the restrictions placed on all Japanese Americans on the West Coast. After violating a curfew imposed on Japanese Americans, Gordon Hirabayashi objected that the law infringed on his civil rights. He also challenged the federal order authorizing the detainment of Japanese Americans in camps. In its decision, the Supreme Court avoided the issue of internment and instead ruled on the curfew, arguing that wartime conditions sometimes made it necessary to "place citizens of one ancestry in a different category from others." The decision not only maintained the curfew but also sanctioned continued limitation of Japanese Americans' movement, regardless of their citizenship status.

Other court cases directly contested the internment of Japanese Americans. A key case resulted from the resistance of a Japanese-American man who attempted to avoid detention. Fred Korematsu ignored the orders for evacuation and remained in Oakland, California. After being arrested by the FBI, Korematsu argued in court

Japanese citizens waiting in line at the Japanese internment camp in Manzanar, California, March 24, 1942. AP/WIDE WORLD PHOTOS

that due process of law had been violated. Despite the expectations of many legal professionals, the Supreme Court did not strike down the legislation authorizing detainment. Instead, in *Korematsu v. United States* (1944) the Supreme Court upheld the detention of Japanese Americans.

Finally, the Supreme Court acknowledged that not all Japanese Americans posed a threat to national security. In April 1942 Mitsue Endo filed a petition of habeas corpus, protesting her detainment at the Topaz Camp in Utah. After two years, in *Endo v. United States* (1944), the Supreme Court ruled that the War Relocation Authority should make an effort to separate "disloyal" internees from "loyal" ones and release the latter from the detention centers. Following the decision, the government announced that all the camps would be closed and the detainees released. The last of the camps closed in 1946.

The detainment episode can be put into a larger context of discrimination toward Asians. Decades earlier, the federal government enacted such measures as the Chinese Exclusion Act of 1882 in order to curb Asian immigration. Although provoked partially by security fears, the wartime internment was ultimately another expression of the United States' racism toward Asians. In 1982 a presidential commission declared that racism, a deficiency of leadership, and war hysteria provided the impetus for the detention. A few years later, Congress passed the Civil Liberties Act of 1988, awarding $20,000 each, as well as an official apology, to more than 80,000 individuals who had been detained.

BIBLIOGRAPHY

Daniels, Roger. *The Decision to Relocate the Japanese Americans.* Philadelphia: Lippincott, 1985.

Daniels, Roger. *Prisoners without Trial: Japanese Americans in World War II.* New York: Hill and Wang, 1993.

Irons, Peter. *Justice at War: The Story of the Japanese Internment Cases.* New York: Oxford University Press, 1983.

Taylor, Sandra C. *Jewel of the Desert: Japanese American Internment at Topaz.* Berkeley: University of California Press, 1993.

Angela Frye Keaton

See also: Civil Liberties, Civil War; Civil Liberties, World War I.

CIVILIAN CONSERVATION CORPS (CCC)

Tagged "Roosevelt's Tree Army," or "the Soil Soldiers," the Civilian Conservation Corps (CCC) was not a military program, but it was modeled on military organization and incorporated the military spirit of public service. Established in 1933, the CCC was one of many programs in the New Deal's war against the economic depression. In his 1933 inaugural address, President Franklin D. Roosevelt asked Congress for "broad Executive power to wage a war" against the Depression and for power "that would be given to me if we were in fact invaded by a foreign foe." In many ways the New Deal's recovery programs were conceived as if the United States were at war, such as the National Recovery Administration that was modeled after the War Industries Board that President Woodrow Wilson had created to mobilize the nation's economy to win World War I.

Created during the first Hundred Days of Franklin D. Roosevelt's New Deal, the CCC employed primarily unmarried men between the ages of seventeen and twenty-eight to plant trees, fight forest fires, battle forest tree pests, stock fish, and conduct other conservation work in the national forests, national parks, and other public lands. The "Three Cs," as enrollees nicknamed it, was also a relief program that (at the start of the program) paid them thirty dollars a month, twenty-five of which was sent back to the employee's family.

MOBILIZATION AGAINST UNEMPLOYMENT

The CCC was part of Roosevelt's "war" to defeat the Great Depression, which had left 25 percent of the workforce idle. Officers from the U.S. Army, Naval, and Marine Reserves supervised the construction and maintenance of CCC camps where the enrollees lived. And CCC advocates suffused publicity with military language: Enlisting the unemployed to restore the nation's over-harvested forests and badly eroded streams was pronounced "the Moral Equivalent of War." It also employed World War I veterans; a total of 213,000 middle-aged former servicemen were part of the CCC.

Within two months of the 1933 legislation, 64,000 unemployed youth had been enrolled; by the end of the program in 1942, 3.19 million young men had served in the CCC. Only the War Department had experience with the mobilization of so many so quickly—a larger undertaking than the Spanish-American War, for example. Each agency involved relied upon military officers to oversee the construction of barracks, mess halls, recreation buildings, infirmaries, educational and library buildings, garages, tool sheds, and machine shops in the more than 4,500 camps. Some of these buildings were designed with such care that they are still used by government agencies; the commanding officer of each company also took charge of day-to-day administration of the camp. Park superintendents and district rangers, who supervised the men in the field, at times became impatient with the amount of time military men required the enrollees to spend in the camps, but they relied upon the discipline instilled there.

Less than half the enrollees were from urban areas; in fact, the majority of the young men were from communities not unlike the ones in which they were camped. The young men rose at 6 A.M., worked from 8 A.M. until 5 P.M., then had a choice of athletics, attending classes, or various entertainments in the evenings. Over 90 percent of the men attended at least one class during their six-month tour. They could earn both eighth grade and high school certificates as well as learn marketable skills such as typing. In the Great Smoky Mountains National Park of North Carolina and Tennessee, which boasted seventeen CCC camps, the men formed baseball teams and companies challenged each other to tournaments. Many of the camps published newsletters announcing the residents' achievements and sharing songs and stories.

BLACKS AND THE CCC

Although official policy prohibited discrimination, the 330,000 African Americans who served were segregated into colored units. The National Association for the Advancement of Colored People (NAACP) objected to this practice, and by the end of the program some northern camps were integrated. Most public agencies, such as the National Park Service, bowed to local customs in the matter of segregation. The War Department also selected whites as commanding officers, stating that using black officers "was still in the experimental stages." Because local and state communities complained about having black camps in their area, some African-American enrollees ended up serving on military reservations; others at the more remotely located national parks.

LEGACY

The CCC was the nation's first major and long-term effort to apply lessons learned from war-time mobilization to put the unemployed to work. In the early years, the CCC faced considerable opposition from local communities, who expressed fears that "bums" and "delinquents" would pollute the water, disturb the wildlife, drink, and ravage women. To counter these fears, the CCC established an aggressive publicity campaign, which not only sent camp officials to speak at the Rotary or other local civic organizations but also urged enrollees to write essays for local newspapers to explain the benefits of the program.

Nevertheless, like all New Deal programs, the CCC faced severe criticism from conservative congressmen, who labeled it socialism. It also faced a steady 8 percent desertion rate, as the primitive living experience and military order were not for everyone; this jumped to 20 percent toward the end of the program, when other jobs became plentiful. Despite criticism, the CCC work record was impressive. According to official records, they planted 2.36 billion trees, constructed 126,000 trails, built 6.6 million erosion-control dams, and spent 6.5 million man-days fighting forest fires. They restored streams, built fish hatcheries, and "planted" a billion fish in streams. Memoirs and oral histories also show that participants found considerable pride in their achievements. Unemployed and without job experience in the middle of the Great Depression, they were grateful for regular meals, new clothes, something to do, and of course, the great good fun of being in the woods with other young men their own age.

The CCC combined military discipline, employment, and public service. It put young men to work, rather than on welfare. It left a legacy of national service that not only contributed to the public good, but also helped individuals rebuild lives shattered by the Great Depression.

BIBLIOGRAPHY

Merrill, Perry H. *Roosevelt's Forest Army: A History of the Civilian Conservation Corps, 1933–1942.* Montpelier, VT: Perry H. Merrill, 1981.

Otis, Alison T., et al. *The Forest Service and the Civilian Conservation Corps: 1933–1942.* Washington, DC: U.S. Department of Agriculture, Forest Service, 1986.

Paige, John C. *The Civilian Conservation Corps and the National Park Service, 1933–1942: An Administrative History.* Denver, CO: National Park Service, U.S. Department of the Interior, 1985.

Salmond, John A. *The Civilian Conservation Corps, 1933–1942: A New Deal Case Study.* Durham, NC: Duke University Press, 1967.

Margaret Lynn Brown

See also: **New Deal; Roosevelt, Eleanor; Roosevelt, Franklin Delano.**

CLOTHING, WORLD WAR I AND WORLD WAR II

World War I and World War II required mobilizing the entire nation not only ideologically, but also in every aspect of life, including the clothing people wore. The wartime economy, the change in population demographics, the expanding domestic economy (with more people working), and the shift to women in the workforce all had a tremendous impact on fashion. Styles are always influenced by the function clothes must serve, economic factors, the availability of goods, social expression and social aspiration, Hollywood, and by what is worn by the armed forces. These influences affect fashion and fashion affects, and reflects, culture and society.

FASHION PRIOR TO WORLD WAR I

Before World War I, France was fashion's center. American women looked to French designers for direction and guidance. By following high fashions and staying current with the designers' most recent collections, people were able to distinguish between the social classes and set themselves apart, displaying their wealth and position.

Fashion for women in the late nineteenth and early twentieth centuries featured bustles and cinched waists. Women wore corsets that emphasized small waists and rounded behinds. In 1911, the stylish silhouette changed to a high-waisted, more tailored one that followed more closely the natural curves of a women's body. This style was very popular despite the fact that it was soon nicknamed the hobble skirt—skirts were so tight at the ankle that women who wore them could not take full steps.

While women's fashion were slowly becoming less confining and artificial, men's fashions were already comfortable and eminently wearable. For men, suits were the uniform of the day. A well-dressed man's wardrobe consisted of a morning suit with a cutaway jacket worn with a top hat, walking stick and a flower in the lapel; a frock coat (also worn with a top hat, walking stick and flower); and a lounge suit. The lounge suit of that era is recognizable today as a man's single-breasted, three-piece suit worn with a tie.

EFFECT OF WORLD WAR I AND WORLD WAR II ON FASHION

American fashion saw few influences directly related to World War I. France was only temporarily usurped as the world's fashion capital during the shipping blockade; after the war's end, it once again became the center of fashion. Within a few years, because of social changes due in part to the war and its aftermath, shorter skirts for women came into style for the first time.

Secretary of the Treasury William G. McAdoo, Miss Nona McAdoo, and *Colliers* editor Norman Hapgood on board the S.S. *Rochambeau* on June 15, 1915. Their clothing is typical of the styles of the era. © BETTMANN/CORBIS

World War II, however, strongly influenced American fashion. For example, with thanks to government issued (GI) underwear and with a little help from Marlon Brando and James Dean in the post war years, the ubiquitous T-shirt became fashionable. As in World War I, fashion imports from France were banned. And to limit fashion's appeal even more, in 1942 the U.S. Production Board issued Limitation Order 85 (L-85). This order's goal was to save 15 percent of domestic fabric production, as well as more than forty million pounds of wool cloth. Another goal was to freeze fashion, making older clothes more appealing.

L-85 dictated many of fashions' designs. No longer were details such as patch pockets, cuffs, and double pleats allowed. Rationing was the new key word. Women's clothes were less full and used less fabric. The shirtwaist, reflecting the new austere aesthetic, became popular. Hats were less showy. Shoes also had to comply with the new rules and no shoe could have a heel over 1½ inches. Because of these restrictions, styles did not change much during the war years. L-85 restrictions were lifted on V-E Day, May 8, 1945.

The L-85 restrictions were also applied to women's bathing suits; manufacturers could use a limited amount of fabric. This led to the introduction of the two piece swimsuit. Initially, these were styled with skirts and modest designs. As the restrictions were tightened, swimsuits became less modest. In 1946, the first bikini, named after the atomic bomb tests off of the Bikini Islands in the Pacific, was introduced.

Not only were women restricted to the amount of fabric available for clothes during the war, leaving many of them to make do with older clothing, but their new work roles changed their clothing needs. The newest item worn by women was not a froufrou French-influenced style, but men's coveralls and overalls.

It is impossible to discuss practical clothes without discussing hats and hairstyles for women. When working in factories, women were discouraged from wearing long hair loose like a favorite of the silver screen, Veronica Lake. They put away their fancy, feathered hats and donned a popular alternative—the turban wrap. Many women managed their dangerously loose, flowing hair by wearing snoods and tied-on kerchiefs. At the end of the Second World War, there was a return of extravagance with "Liberation" hats coming out of France, although hats were worn on fewer occasions, and by fewer women, than in the prewar era. The popularity of hats truly declined during the presidency of John F. Kennedy.

Military styles also had an impact on civilian clothing. The popular domestic silhouette, a strong padded shoulder, natural waist, and straight skirt, strongly resembled that of military uniforms. Clothes for both men and women were more severe, practical, and simple during World War II than in the past. Men's clothes were more masculine, and civilian men borrowed from the uniform both the Chesterfield and the officer's coat.

While civilian men's attire became more severe and serious, soldiers' uniforms became more casual. Dress uniforms were less common and bomber jackets were introduced. These jackets had more pockets than traditional coats, which enabled soldiers to carry more equipment. Another influential style was the reefer coat, also known as the Eisenhower. These short wool overcoats, worn by General Eisenhower, were made popular by the stories of the Atlantic escort ships called corvettes. They were seen as heroic and were bought by civilians in great numbers at Army surplus stores after the war's end.

Wartime restrictions on clothing also spawned rebellious styles. Popular with young men in the Hispanic communities of California, as well as among musicians,

CBS singing star Eleanor Steber modelling clothing made out of wrinkle-free fabric, in 1944. © BETTMANN/CORBIS

was the extravagant zoot suit. With its exaggerated shoulders, knee length jackets, baggy, cuffed pants, the zoot suit flouted the L-85 restrictions. Such styles gave these marginalized communities an outlet for social rage. Unfortunately, in Los Angeles men wearing zoot suits became targets of aggression from military personnel. Zoot-suiters were stopped, humiliated, beaten up and stripped. Los Angeles police did nothing to enforce the laws protecting the zoot-suiters. Instead, they arrested the beaten, naked men for disturbing the peace. In June of 1943 the situation escalated and Los Angeles experienced serious riots, stopped only when the War Department made Los Angeles out-of-bounds for all military personnel.

World War II brought lasting changes to fashion. Women's skirts became shorter, the bikini was introduced, and it became more common and acceptable for women to wear slacks. For men, formality and variety also changed. Prewar men had a larger wardrobe and were expected to dress differently for work, worship and for social occasions. With the long shortage of supplies during and after the war, men no longer dressed up routinely and the casual suit became acceptable for most occasions. Though France regained its dominance in fashion design with its introduction of the "New Look" in 1947, American and British designers became more influential in fashion. Utility has by now become de rigueur in both civilian and military clothing. The fashions adopted by Americans at war helped to shape the fashions of Americans at peace.

BIBLIOGRAPHY

Baker, Patricia. *Fashion of a Decade: The 1940's*. New York: Facts On File, 1992.

Escobar, Edward J. "Zoot-Suiters and Cops: Chicanos Youth and the Los Angeles Police Department during World War II." In *The War in American Culture, Society and Consciousness During World War II*, edited by Lewis A. Erenberg and Susan E. Hirsch. Chicago: University of Chicago Press, 1996.

Kellog, Ann T.; Peterson, Amy T.; Bay, Stefani; et al. *In an Influential Fashion*. Westport, CT: Greenwod Press, 2002.

Makrell, Alice. *An Illustrated History of Fashion: 00 Years of Fashion Illustration*. New York: Custom and Fashion Press, 1997.

Stimson, Ermina; Lessing, Alice; and Bower, Rhea. *Sixty Years of Fashion*. New York: Fairchild Publications, 1963.

Windrow, Martin, and Embleton, Gerry. *Military Dress of North America, 166–1970*. New York: Scribner, 1973.

Susan G. Contente

See also: **Labor, World War I; Labor, World War II; Economy, World War I; Economy, World War II.**

COCHRAN, JACKIE

(b. ca. 1910; d. August 9, 1980) Director of Women Airforce Service Pilots (WASP) during WWII; first woman to break the sound barrier.

The first woman to break the sound barrier, and the director of the Women Airforce Service Pilots (WASP) in World War II, Jacqueline (Jackie) Cochran held more speed, distance, and altitude records during her career than any other pilot, male or female. Although not as well known to the public as Amelia Earhart, she is called by many the greatest woman pilot in aviation history. Her flying career covered four decades, and some of her records still stand.

Orphaned as a child, Cochran was raised by poor foster parents in Pensacola, Florida, where she was born, although the year is uncertain. Her family name and that of her foster parents are unknown, but according to her autobiography, she chose the name "Cochran" out of a phone book. She had very little formal education and began full-time work in a cotton mill as a young girl. From there, she became a beauty operator and by the 1930s had started her own cosmetics firm in New York City. In 1932 Cochran began taking flying lessons at Roosevelt Field on Long Island at the suggestion of an aviator friend. The idea was partly to promote her company. After her third lesson she flew solo, and two weeks later she had her license. She bought her own plane, a Travelair, and immediately began advanced instruction.

Cochran married her aviator friend, Floyd Odlum, who was also an industrialist and banker, in 1936. A year earlier, she had been the first woman to enter the Bendix Transcontinental Air Race, and in 1938 she won it. In her silver P-35, she flew from Los Angeles to Cleveland, Ohio, in 8 hours, 10 minutes, 31 seconds. Using a new fuel system, she was also the first to finish the course nonstop. Also in that year she set a speed record for women, crossing North America in 10 hours, 12 minutes, 55 seconds in a converted P-35 racer. Several months later, she climbed to 33,000 feet, breaking the women's altitude record. She also won the Harmon trophy, the top prize for women aviators.

In 1939, when war was looming in Europe, Cochran wrote to First Lady Eleanor Roosevelt, suggesting that female pilots could release men for active duty by flying support missions. Nothing came of the idea at the time. But it was very much alive in Great Britain, where Cochran went in 1941 to study the operation. After President Franklin Roosevelt suggested she investigate ways in which women pilots could be used in the Army Air Corps, she returned to Great Britain with twenty-five American women pilots to help ferry planes. She became a captain in the British Air Force Auxiliary. After the

Pilot Jackie Cochran arriving in Cleveland in September 1946. TIME LIFE PICTURES/GETTY IMAGES

United States entered the war, Cochran was asked by General Hap Arnold to come home and teach American women to fly. In 1943 she became director of the Women Airforce Service Pilots.

In 1944, after records showed that the WASP did not have as many fatal and nonfatal accidents as the male pilots, Cochran campaigned to get her unit taken into the Army Air Force. But the war was coming to an end, fewer male pilots were needed for combat missions, and the men staged an effective campaign against admitting

the WASP program. It was disbanded in December, and Cochran was given the Distinguished Service Medal the following year.

A disappointed Cochran went back to civilian life and breaking records. In 1950 she set a new speed record for propeller aircraft. She was just getting started. In 1953 she broke the world speed record for both men and women, flying 652.552 mph in a Sabre jet. On March 1 of that year, she became the first woman to break the sound barrier. In 1960 she was the first woman to take off from an aircraft carrier and was the first woman to fly at Mach 2 (twice the speed of sound) in 1961. In 1964 she flew faster than any woman in previous history, reaching 1,429 mph.

In the early 1970s Cochran was devastated when told that her flying career must end because of a heart condition. She retired from the Air Force Reserve as a colonel and served as a consultant to the National Aeronautics and Space Administration (NASA). She died in Indio, California, on August 9, 1980.

Jackie Cochran was a pioneer for women flyers. She opened the door to women flying in the military. Although women make up just 4 percent of U.S. military pilots, since the 1990s their numbers have increased greatly, as have their roles from support to combat. Cochran's experience parallels in many ways that of other groups, especially minorities: society opening up and cultural barriers dropping as a result of Americans being at war.

BIBLIOGRAPHY

Cochran, Jackie, and Bucknum Brinley, Maryann. *Jackie Cochran*. New York: Bantam, 1987.

Internet Resources

"Jackie Cochran: Magnificent Woman in Her Flying Machine Climbed into the Cockpit and 'Broke the Bonds of Gender and Space.'" Dryden Flight Research Center, *The X-Press*. Available from <http://www.dfrc.nasa.gov>.

Rose Blue and Corinne J. Naden

See also: **Feminism; Roosevelt, Eleanor; Women, Employment of; Women and World War I; Women and World War II.**

CONSCRIPTION, WORLD WAR I

In the world wars of the twentieth century, fighting could not be confined to a handful of volunteer and professional soldiers. Nations had to be mobilized to provide millions of men. Military service had to be made mandatory through the draft, or conscription. Conscription expanded the powers of government, and whereas it was generally accepted by the populace as a patriotic duty, it also produced conflict on the homefront between the majority and those opposed to war, as well as those who believed the draft was unfair or incompatible with liberty.

CREATION OF THE DRAFT

In the spring of 1917, the peacetime U.S. Army totaled 135,000 men. After war was declared on Germany on

April 6, 1917, patriotism in the country ran high. Many men were immediately moved to volunteer to join the U.S. forces and fight the war. Still, this added manpower was not nearly enough. General John Pershing, who had command of the American forces in Europe, asked for millions of men for his army. A draft was necessary, insisted Chief of Staff Hugh Scott. Secretary of War Newton D. Baker agreed and convinced President Woodrow Wilson. Meanwhile, former president Theodore Roosevelt was pushing the idea of including a provision to organize a division of volunteers. Baker rejected this idea, and was supported by Wilson, who for political reasons did not want to get Roosevelt involved in the raising of an army.

Wilson's draft bill next had to clear Congress, and some lawmakers were promising a fight. In rural regions, especially the South, people cared little about the distant European war. All over America, people wrote to their representatives by the hundreds of thousands, expressing opinions both for and against conscription. One alternate to the president's bill proposed a trial volunteer army for a few months. Another proposal suggested the raising of a volunteer army while simultaneously preparing to implement the draft. The latter, known as the Dent bill after its sponsor in Congress, was a compromise popular in the parts of the country that favored isolationism.

On April 28, the Dent bill was put up for a vote in the House and failed to pass. This signaled rejection of the idea of a volunteer army and cleared the way for a draft bill's victory. Still, there was wrangling over the details of the bill. The president was able to compromise on some of the finer points and ultimately managed to get the final version through Congress. The Selective Service Act was signed into law on May 18, 1917. It authorized President Wilson to increase the regular army, to bring into federal service the National Guard and National Guard Reserve, and to raise military force by a selective draft.

ORGANIZATION AND LOGISTICS

The organization of the draft was relatively simple. Local draft boards would register men for the draft and decide on exemptions. The whole operation fell under the jurisdiction of the office of the Provost Marshal General in Washington. There were 4,648 local draft boards in the United States and the territories of Alaska, Hawaii, and Puerto Rico: at least one per county in every state, and more if the population density of the county was high. In New York City alone, for example, there were 189 draft boards. District boards were supervisory boards that oversaw about thirty local draft boards each. Draft board service was compulsory for those chosen; it was an unpaid post.

Initially men between the ages of twenty-one and thirty-one were required to register; later, registration included those aged eighteen through forty-five. The two-sided registration cards asked for a variety of information such as date of birth, place of birth, father's place of birth, address of next of kin, eye and hair color, and race. On June 5, 1917, 9.5 million men were registered.

There were 10,500 different draft lottery numbers. On July 20, 1917, a blindfolded Secretary Baker drew the first number from a bowl, followed by other dignitaries over the course of sixteen and one-half hours. A total of 1,374,000 men were called up that day. Anyone with a number that was picked by the lottery had to immediately report to his local draft board. Three more draft registrations were held in 1918 which increased the number of potential draftees by 13 million men. While there were no protests on the scale of the New York City draft riot during the Civil War, there were incidents of violent opposition in the rural South and resistance to the draft in the form of refusal to register.

Eventually, a total of 24 million American men registered for the draft, and 2.8 million were inducted into service. The men selected formed the National Army of the American Expeditionary Force. Physical examinations were conducted for those men who were drafted. If they passed the examination, they were shipped to a training center. Those who were too thin or otherwise failed the physical were rejected. About half of the 1.3 million men called up on the first day of draft were rejected, mostly due to health reasons.

It was a slow process. Most draftees were assigned to National Army divisions, and the first group took many months to get overseas. Construction of camps and cantonments, mostly on the East Coast, was authorized in May 1917. All in all, thirty-two camps were hastily established, about half for the National Army and the others for the National Guard.

PUBLIC REACTION TO THE DRAFT

During the Civil War, the draft had been a failure because a conscript could send a substitute to serve in his place or could buy an exemption. The Civil War draft had been seen largely as a poor man's draft. This time around there was more acceptance by the public because of the perceived fairness of the draft bill. Still, the legitimacy of the draft was challenged in the Supreme Court by a man who refused to register; it was upheld in an early 1918 decision.

The Committee on Public Information put out pamphlets to help the American public understand why the United States had entered the war. These free pamphlets included *The Great War: From Spectator to Participant; A War of Self Defense; Why America Fights Germany;* and

Uncle Sam in the 1917 recruitment poster by James Montgomery Flagg. © BETTMANN/CORBIS

Ways to Serve the Nation. An advertisement for toothpaste in a 1918 boys' magazine was titled "The Twice a Day Draft" and featured an "Enlistment Blank for Good Teeth—Good Health." Another advertisement for bicycle tires told readers to "Keep in Fighting Trim . . . if you're called to the colors, you'll be ready."

The biggest proponent of the conscription movement was a military preparedness group called the National Security League, with 100,000 members and 250 branches nationwide. This group was financed by big-city millionaires and corporations and had considerable political clout. Organized resistance to the draft came mainly from religious groups and political organizations including the No Conscription League, the People's Council for Peace and Democracy, and the Socialist Party of America.

People in different regions of the country reacted differently to conscription. For example, some southerners felt disenfranchised by what they perceived as a violation of their rights as citizens. Many southerners had isolationist views and did not wish to participate in the draft. During congressional debate, the Speaker of the House, a Missourian named James Beauchamp Clark, gave a passionate speech in which he equated being a conscript to being a convict. Five hundred farmers in Oklahoma planned to march in Washington, D.C., but were arrested before they could take action.

Men who objected to military service on the basis of religious beliefs or political ideals were known as conscientious objectors. About 65,000 men claimed objector status. Some were opposed to killing, others to the idea of the draft, which they believed was contrary to principles of liberty and freedom. However, only those who belonged to the historic "peace churches" were exempted from combat. President Wilson defined certain areas of service that were classified as "non-combatant," to which these men must accept assignment or suffer punishment. About 65,000 men claimed objector status, but the number of objectors was whittled down as thousands of men changed their minds while in training camp, and thousands more did not pass the physical exam.

The remaining four thousand legally-recognized objectors considered non-combatant service unacceptable. To them, true opposition to the war meant avoiding any service that furthered the war effort in any way. By the end of the war, however, many of these men had capitulated and were placed into the Medical Corps or on civilian duty. Nearly five hundred of the most stubborn objectors (known as absolutists) were court-martialed and imprisoned.

LEGACY OF THE DRAFT

After the armistice of November 1918, the Selective Service system was dismantled. Draft boards officially closed in March 1919, and the position of Provost Marshal General was discontinued in July 1919. The system was a success; during the Civil War, fifty years earlier, only 8 percent of the Army had been represented by draftees, compared with over 70 percent during World War I.

The end of the volunteer system as an effective means to raise a wartime army marked a change in the way America fought wars. This precedent was the forerunner of several drafts over the course of the twentieth century. Conscription was utilized again during World War II and during the Vietnam Conflict. With each rebirth of conscription, debate was reopened on the worthiness of the cause and the fairness of the system.

BIBLIOGRAPHY

Adams, James Truslow. *The March of Democracy.* New York: Scribner, 1933.

Chambers, John Whiteclay. *To Raise an Army: The Draft Comes to Modern America.* New York: The Free Press, 1987.

Eisenhower, John S. D., with Eisenhower, Joanne T. *Yanks: The Epic Story of the American Army in World War I.* New York: Free Press, 2001.

French, Paul Comly. *We Won't Murder, Being the Story of Men Who Followed Their Conscientious Scruples and Helped Give Life to Democracy.* New York: Hastings House, 1940.

Lawson, Don. *The United States in World War I: The Story of General John J. Pershing and the American Expeditionary Forces.* New York: Abelard-Schuman, 1963.

Richard Panchyk and Caren Prommersberger

CONSCRIPTION, WORLD WAR II

The draft, or more accurately, selective military conscription, was the primary means by which men were inducted into the American armed forces during World War II. The Selective Service Act of 1940 established the first peacetime military conscription in the nation's history and provided the blueprint by which men were drafted for the next thirty years.

DEBATES SURROUNDING PEACETIME DRAFT, 1940

When first proposed in 1940, pre-war conscription was extremely controversial. The push for draft legislation came from a small group of leaders that had been in the pre-World War I "Preparedness" movement. Led by attorney Grenville Clark, the Military Training Camps Association (MTCA) started a lobbying campaign for compulsory military service in May. On June 20, 1940, Senator Ed Burke (D., NE) introduced a modified version of the MCTA bill in the Senate with Congressman James Wadsworth (R., NY) introducing similar legislation in the House. The fall of France on June 22, combined with President Roosevelt's appointment of Henry L. Stimson as the Secretary of War, tilted the political balance towards passage.

Opponents included organized labor, major religious groups, the peace movement, most of the educational establishment, and Republican isolationist legislators. Some argued that the draft was unconstitutional, because in 1918 the Supreme Court had upheld conscription only in wartime. Labor leaders argued that the elitist interests pushing a draft were concerned with profit, not democratic principles. Many legislators wanted to see a volunteer effort tried before resorting to conscription. The bill passed in both houses of Congress by decisive majorities and was signed into law on September 16, 1940. It is generally accepted that Hitler's advance across Europe was the primary reason the law was enacted.

ADMINISTRATION

The Selective Service Act of 1940 limited service to one year, and forbad duty outside the Western Hemisphere.

U.S. Secretary of War Henry Stimson is blindfolded as he draws the first number for the nation's first peacetime military draft lottery on October 29, 1940. AP/WIDE WORLD PHOTOS

These restrictions on service reflected the nation's suspicions of militarism, its isolationism, and its reluctance to engage in military buildup except for defensive purposes. The act required every male from age 21 to 36 years old to register, and prohibited racial discrimination. Registered men could volunteer before called and pick their branch of service. The president could authorize deferments as he deemed necessary for the maintenance of public health, safety, or interest. An appeal system was established to dispute local board classification. Ministers and divinity students were exempted from service but not registration. Conscientious objectors (CO) were recognized "based on religious training and belief" and not required to be members of historic peace churches. Some 50,000 men were granted CO status and offered a choice between noncombatant military duty or alternate service.

The president was authorized to create a Selective Service System, eventually under the direction of General Lewis B. Hershey. Local civilian boards, composed of unpaid volunteers, were responsible for the actual classification and calls. National headquarters established the order of call via lottery, the priority of classification, and state quotas.

The draft revealed several problems. By the summer of 1941 half of the men drafted (mainly older men) had been rejected for medical exams or illiteracy. Based on this experience, the army affirmed its position that 18-to-21-year-olds made the best soldiers. Rapid expansion also created a backlog of inductees because training facilities were inadequate. The army asked Congress to extend term and service to train these men. Often misconstrued, the major congressional contest over the Service Extension Act of 1941 (passed by only one vote in the House) focused on the length of service for the first 600,000 draftees, not the existence of the draft itself.

After Pearl Harbor, Congress extended registration to ages 18 to 38, removed the overseas prohibition, and increased service to the duration of the war plus six

CONSCIENTIOUS OBJECTORS

Persons who have objected to war on religious or personal grounds have resided in the United States since the earliest colonization of America. Many have been part of particular religious groups, such as the Church of the Brethren, Quakers, Amish, and Mennonites. During the Revolutionary War conscription did not yet exist, yet non-participants might have been viewed as Tory sympathizers. Certain people were given exemptions from military service resister status at other points throughout history: in the Massachusetts colony in 1661 and in 1673 in Rhode Island. Yet some of the objectors were fined for their nonparticipation.

During the Civil War the Confederate government enacted conscription, though many well-to-do men paid to have other men take their places in the military forces, and objectors on religious grounds might have paid a $500 fine. In 1863 the Union passed the Conscription Act, which allowed an exemption if a person paid $300 to the War Department or supplied a substitute, and the following year it amended the act to allow individuals who objected on religious grounds to serve as noncombatants. However, as in the Revolutionary War, objectors—from both North and South—were often viewed as supporters of the enemy's cause.

The World Wars saw many changes in conscription. When the Selective Service Act was passed in 1917, only those objectors who were part of religious organizations known for opposing military activity were excused from military service. Some 4,000 objectors were drafted for noncombatant service, and some 450 objectors who refused to serve as noncombatants were tried in military courts and sentenced to serve prison time, though President Woodrow Wilson pardoned these objectors at the war's end. During World War II, the definition of a conscientious objector was changed to include those persons who chose not to fight for personal reasons, not only those who were part of established pacifist religious groups. The federal government also expanded opportunities for noncombatant service with the creation of Civilian Public Service Camps. Nevertheless, some 6,000 noncombatants—many members of the Jehovah's Witness religious group—were tried and imprisoned for declining to participate in alternative service.

During the 1960s and the Vietnam War, objectors on religious grounds received exemptions from combat, yet many others voiced their objections based on moral grounds and were still subject to the draft. Many of those who refused to serve in the military fled to Canada or Europe and became known as draft evaders. In 1974 President Gerald Ford offered evaders of the Vietnam War the opportunity to do two years of public service work in return for amnesty and repatriation.

---

months. In 1942 registration was expanded to ages 18 to 45, the Navy began using draftees, and volunteering was terminated. Yet by 1944 the draft was experiencing major shortages. Racism hampered mobilization. The army's policy of segregating facilities and military units limited the number of black men who could be trained for service and restricted their roles in the military. Ironically, southern draft boards complained that military segregation forced them to induct mainly white men and to exclude eligible Blacks from service. While shortfalls were due to increased manpower requirements for the planned invasion of Europe and a continued 50 percent rejection rate, a primary factor was the deferment policy.

CONTROVERSIES OVER EXEMPTIONS

Despite the theme of universal sacrifice, at the height of the war in 1944, critics claimed that the deferment process had become captive to politics, special interests, and to local biases. Selective Service was used as an indirect agent to keep labor in line by threatening induction. It was also used to balance the needs for industrial and military manpower. Occupation was a direct factor in determining deferment eligibility. Throughout the war various groups demanded and received deferments, including the medical community, college students, educators, scientists, agriculture, and the war industry.

Certain classes experienced significantly lower induction rates, notably farmers, fathers, and physicians. Of these, dependency deferments for fatherhood enjoyed especially strong public support. Because of a manpower shortage in early 1943, Hershey instructed local boards to disregard dependency deferments to meet calls. In response, Congress passed a bill that deferred all fathers until all other eligible men were taken. To fill the shortfall, induction was expanded to eighteen-year-olds. Nonetheless, by 1945 nearly one million fathers were drafted.

CONCLUSION

Conscription affected virtually every aspect of American life, from professional athletes such as Joe Lewis and Ted Williams to women's participation in the workforce. Once volunteering was prohibited in late 1942, the draft became the only way to enter the armed forces. Although it is difficult to separate the effects of military service itself from the entry method, the fact that the majority of men donned the uniform via the draft resulted in this becoming a common and normative experience for an entire generation. Public approval of the draft signaled a dramatic shift from pre-war attitudes. Perhaps the most fundamental postwar change was the American people's acceptance of keeping a large standing army in peacetime that included conscription.

The draft made an important contribution to victory in World War II. Selective Service registered 49 million men, selected 19 million, and inducted 10.1 million into an armed force of approximately 15 million. Public opinion polls consistently indicated the draft was perceived as fair. The deferment system managed manpower without destroying the nation's social structure. Because local boards controlled classification, Congress ensured national leadership was responsive to citizens' values over who fought and who did not. However, after VJ Day, congressional and public support for the draft waned as traditional opposition to peacetime conscription returned. Following several extensions, the World War II draft was allowed to expire March 31, 1947.

BIBLIOGRAPHY

Blum, Albert A. *Drafted or Deferred: Practices Past and Present.* Ann Arbor: University of Michigan, 1967.

Flynn, George. Q. *The Draft, 1940–1973.* Lawrence: University Press of Kansas, 1993.

Clifford, Gary, and Samuel R. Spencer, Jr. *The First Peacetime Draft.* Lawrence: University Press of Kansas, 1956.

O'Sullivan, John, and Alan M. Meckler, eds. *The Draft and Its Enemies.* Urbana: University of Illinois Press, 1974.

Rosemary Bryant Mariner

See also: **Civil Liberties, World War II; Labor, World War II.**

DEMOBILIZATION

Demobilizing the mass army and defense industry at the end of America's two world wars in 1918 and 1945 was an extremely complicated task. In 1918, American officials expected World War I to last another year and were taken by surprise when the Armistice was announced on November 11, 1918. With only preliminary planning for demobilization underway, the government did a hasty and poor job directing the shift from a wartime to a peacetime economy. During World War II, the government made significant strides preparing for demobilization well before victory was attained on the battlefield. In 1945, most Americans feared a return of the Great Depression once the war-fueled boom evaporated. Instead, the government found itself combating inflation.

WORLD WAR I

At the end of World War I, the government immediately dissolved the wartime agencies that had directed the nation's economic mobilization. Concocting a viable demobilization plan, therefore, fell to the War Department. Returning four million soldiers to the workforce at the very moment that government cancellation of thousands of wartime manufacturing contracts made jobs scarce threatened to wreak havoc on the national economy. The military considered plans to keep soldiers in the service until a job became available for them or letting soldiers who had served the longest leave first. But these plans were rejected as too cumbersome and politically unfeasible. Instead, the War Department embraced a strategy that was easy both to manage and explain to the American people: simply demobilize units when their military rationale for existing ceased. The War Department began by releasing the 1.5 million men training in domestic camps, and then brought overseas units home in the following order: casuals, surplus and special service troops, troops in England, U.S. Air Service personnel, troops in Italy, combat divisions, and Service of Supply troops.

The army, however, encountered huge problems even implementing this basic demobilization scheme. Over-crowded debarkation camps in France, the ongoing Spanish Influenza epidemic, and horrendous winter weather turned the demobilization experience into a nightmare for many troops. Americans became furious when soldiers who had survived the war died while waiting for a ship home. Soldiers staged protests overseas, sent petitions, and enrolled their families in the campaign to return them home quickly and safely. Congress launched several investigations into the government's mismanagement of the demobilization process.

The government offered unemployed ex-servicemen little help finding jobs, and as a result veterans soon demanded additional retroactive pay to ease their postwar suffering. In 1924, veterans received an adjusted compensation bond that matured in 1945. During the Depression, calls for immediate payment of this bond led to the Bonus March in 1932.

Veterans were not the only ones who suffered in the postwar recession. Millions were out of work and a wave of strikes that involved nearly 22 percent of the total workforce rocked the country. Gradually, the economy improved when some industries, such as automobiles and housing construction, began to revive and consumer spending increased. Agriculture, however, remained a sick industry throughout the so-called "roaring twenties." Farmers had taken out loans to expand production to meet the wartime demand for agricultural products and were particularly hard-hit by the cancellation of Allied food orders when the war ended.

WORLD WAR II

Intent on avoiding a repeat of these past mistakes, the government expected to play a larger role in guiding the demobilization effort once victory was declared against Germany and Japan in World War II. The military developed a complex point system that awarded each soldier points based on length of service, days in combat, time overseas, and number of children, to determine who went home first. When Germany surrendered on May 8, 1945, the military began a partial demobilization of high point troops. Once again, however, the end of the war came sooner than expected. Japan's capitulation on August 14, 1945 caught the military in the midst of transferring men from Europe to the Far East for the planned invasion. The military now fully confronted the logistical difficulties of dismantling an armed forces dispersed widely around the globe. Soldiers and the public clamored for troops' speedy return home, including wives who organized "Bring Back Daddy" clubs that sent baby shoes to congressmen. At the end of 1945, President Harry Truman worried that the quick pace of the demobilization was threatening the military's ability to assemble the needed occupation forces, and ordered a demobilization slowdown. This announcement led to a near-mutiny among overseas troops.

On the home front, several factors helped mitigate the expected rise in postwar unemployment. The GI Bill of Rights offered 16 million veterans unemployment compensation, housing loans, vocational education, and college tuition. These benefits strengthened veterans'

purchasing power and staggered their re-entry into the workforce. Large numbers of women, youth, and aged voluntarily left their wartime jobs. Industry returned to the pre-war standard of forty hours a week, and generous government payments for terminating $65.7 billion in wartime contracts also protected jobs. With the administration selling off government-owned defense plants and equipment at bargain prices, many businesses received an important capital infusion during the demobilization period that helped them accelerate production of consumer goods.

After the war, Americans finally had goods to buy with the considerable savings that high wartime wages had helped them amass during the war. During this surge of consumer spending, the government decided to lift wartime price controls, and soon inflation, rather than unemployment, posed a more serious economic threat. At the same time, unions mounted a series of strikes for higher wages. To cool the overheated economy, the government curtailed federal spending, jettisoned planned tax cuts, and forced settlement of major strikes in the railroad and coal industry.

Overall, demobilization was the last phase of total war for the United States after the two world wars. During World War II, policy makers had planned more carefully than their predecessors for the peacetime conversion, and successfully avoided a postwar depression. After both wars, however, the public had little patience for government missteps. Anxious to return to normal life as quickly as possible, Americans expressed their dissatisfaction with the government's demobilization policies through political protests, strikes, and demands for veterans' benefits.

BIBLIOGRAPHY

Ballard, Jack Stokes. *The Shock of Peace: Military and Economic Demobilization after World War II.* Washington, D.C.: University Press of America, 1983.

Keene, Jennifer D. *Doughboys, the Great War and the Remaking of America.* Baltimore, MD: Johns Hopkins University Press, 2001.

Severo, Richard and Milford, Lewis. *The Wages of War: When American Soldiers Come Home—From Valley Forge to Vietnam.* New York: Simon & Schuster, 1989.

Wecter, Dixon. *When Johnny Comes Marching Home.* Westport, CT: Greenwood Press, 1970.

Jennifer D. Keene

See also: **American Legion; Economy, World War I; Economy, World War II; GI Bill of Rights; Labor, World War I; Labor, World War II; Red Scare; Veterans of Foreign Wars.**

DISARMAMENT AND ARMS CONTROL (1898–1945)

During the forty-seven years between victories in the Spanish-American War (1898) and World War II (1945), the United States completed a remarkable transformation from regional to global military power, a transformation made painful at times by vigorous debate over whether to limit or expand America's armed forces. Social reformers, pacifists, and fiscal conservatives championed the cause of disarmament; others resisted calls for arms control from home and abroad, insisting that American military "preparedness" was vital. During the 1920s, in the backlash against American involvement in World War I, disarmament advocates enjoyed the diplomatic success of the Washington Naval Treaty system, but the naval arms control regime proved temporary. Ultimately the Great Depression, along with waning international cooperation and growing threats to global security, enervated the American arms control movement.

THE HAGUE CONFERENCE, WORLD WAR I
In 1899, U.S. armament policy was a source of political conflict. Future president Theodore Roosevelt and prominent naval strategist Captain Alfred Thayer Mahan advocated an expansion of American naval power to consolidate America's new empire in the Pacific and to compete with European colonialism. On the other hand, those who wished to restrict America's international role to the Western Hemisphere, along with anti-imperialists, condemned the expansion of American military power and instead supported diplomatic efforts to reduce armaments.

Although in 1899 the United States participated in the first of two international peace conferences at the Hague, the American delegate, Mahan, opposed limitation on naval armaments. Mahan's opposition was consistent with his revolutionary vision of the U.S. Navy's future as a force capable of global sea control. American naval planners had adopted Mahan's vision and already had begun transforming the U.S. Navy from a coastal defense force into an ocean-going navy. Many industrialists and members of Congress supported the construction of such a "blue-water" navy, believing that it would create jobs and increase profits for American companies. However, other Americans opposed expanding the U.S. Navy's mission and force structure. Isolationists in Congress and members of various domestic reform groups believed that increased armament was destructive because it would invite foreign entanglement, arms races, and increased instability, rather than increased security. The outbreak in 1914 of World War I in Europe seemed to confirm this belief. Social and political reformers, including women's rights activists, labor reformers, paci-

fists, and socialists, found common ground as arms control advocates. Jane Addams of the Women's Peace Party (and later of the Women's International League for Peace and Freedom) and Eugene V. Debs of the Socialist Party of America were among the "progressive internationalists" (Knock, p. 50) who urged President Woodrow Wilson to pursue peace and disarmament.

Wilson listened to disarmament advocates with a sympathetic ear. Even though the United States fought in World War I, Wilson echoed the concerns of progressive internationalists, notably in his "Peace without Victory" address to the U.S. Senate on January 22, 1917. Deeply critical of militarism and imperialism, Wilson called for a "community of nations" founded on several ideals, including general disarmament. Putting ideals into practice proved difficult, however, and the United States's refusal to join rendered the League of Nations ineffective, despite Wilson's hopes that the League would facilitate international dispute arbitration and arms control.

While publicly advocating arms control, Wilson simultaneously sought to strengthen the U.S. Navy as the backbone for a new world order; the Naval Act of 1916 was intended to create a navy "second-to-none" by the mid-1920s. After the war ended, however, the American people protested high levels of military spending, and Congress was reluctant to appropriate funds for naval construction. Postwar advocacy of peace and arms control was so strong that very few politicians, Democrat or Republican, were willing to accept the political risk of being branded anti-arms control. The public outcry against military spending (along with a deepening rift with Japan in the Pacific) prompted President Warren G. Harding to invite the world's sea powers to a conference to discuss trade in East Asia and naval arms limitation.

WASHINGTON NAVAL TREATY SYSTEM (1922–1936)
Naval and military officers were nearly universally excluded from the national delegations to the Washington Conference in 1921, a sure sign of the anti-militarist mood in the United States and Europe. Still, the prospects for an arms control agreement appeared slim, and foreign delegates were visibly surprised when U.S. Secretary of State Charles Evan Hughes immediately proposed a naval arms limitation regime that would require the United States to scrap a shocking number of capital ships, many of which had just been built or were still under construction. Hughes's proposal, combined with the public's demands for reduced military spending, helped propel and sustain the negotiations. Most notable of the resulting seven treaties signed in 1922 was the Five Power Treaty, which required the United States, Great Britain, Japan, France, and Italy to limit their navies' capital ships in

President Herbert Hoover (seated) with (standing, left to right) Arkansas Senator Joseph Robinson, Secretary of State Henry Stimson, Vice President Charles Curtis, Idaho Senator William Borah, Virginia Senator Charles Swaine, Secretary of the Navy Charles Adams, Indiana Senator James Watson, and Pennsylvania Senator David Reed, all assembled for the signing of the ratification of the Three-Power Treaty, 1930. © BETTMAN/CORBIS

terms of both size (tonnage) and armament (gun size), and to observe a ten-year "holiday" during which no new construction of capital ships would begin.

The Washington Treaty system satisfied the public's demands for arms limitation at the expense of "preparedness" advocates. Acceptance of international limitations on U.S. naval expansion devastated American navalists. Some took comfort in the treaty's recognition of American parity with Great Britain, the world's leading naval power, but this proved cold comfort indeed, as a strengthening peace movement and Republican legislators' meager naval appropriations combined to prevent the United States from building to its treaty limits. The U.S. Navy deteriorated during the 1920s as a result of continued anti-militarist sentiment and Republican budget-cutting, even though a subsequent naval arms control conference in Geneva in 1927 failed to impose

more stringent limitations. Only at decade's end did Congress approve new naval construction (fifteen cruisers and an aircraft carrier) and even then, President Herbert Hoover's administration (along with the governments of Great Britain and Japan) accepted new limitations on cruisers at the London Conference of 1930.

Effective for over ten years, the Washington Naval Treaty system ultimately disintegrated during the 1930s. American citizens were increasingly preoccupied by the economic troubles of the Great Depression; the United States became increasingly isolationist, and social activism regarding foreign policy issues, including disarmament, plummeted. A second conference in London (1935 to 1936) ended abruptly when Japan withdrew its delegation, and the collapse of the conference signaled the end of the Washington system. The United States had participated in other interwar disarmament initiatives (including the World Disarmament Conference in Geneva in 1932, a dismal failure, and a conference in 1925 that produced the Geneva Protocol on Poisonous Gases, which the U.S. Senate failed to ratify, owing in part to the chemical industry's lobbying campaign), but none had the impact of the Washington naval arms control regime.

COMING OF WAR AND REARMAMENT

The American initiative for the Washington Naval Treaty system grew largely out of domestic politics. Public attitudes in the United States after World War I were generally anti-war and anti-militarist, and the government was reluctant to increase military spending. Combined with an active peace movement, these pressures led American leaders to postpone the Navy's plans for expansion for nearly two decades. Only in 1938 did the United States Congress approve a substantial expansion of American naval forces through the Vinson bills, a series of legislative actions transforming the "treaty navy" into the two-ocean navy that cemented the United States's global power status during and after World War II. Many scholars describe the Washington system as the interwar period's primary arms control success story, as it helped for over a decade to prevent arms races among Great Britain, Japan, and the United States. Critics argue that the regime hampered the development of American naval force structure and doctrine, and weakened the United States's ability to deter Japanese expansionism in the Pacific region during the 1930s.

BIBLIOGRAPHY

Baer, George W. *One Hundred Years of Sea Power: The U.S. Navy, 1890–1990.* Stanford, CA: Stanford University Press, 1994.

Braisted, William Reynolds. *The United States Navy in the Pacific, 1909–1922.* Austin: University of Texas Press, 1971.

Buckley, Thomas H. *The United States and the Washington Conference, 1921–1922.* Knoxville: The University of Tennessee Press, 1970.

Chambers, John Whiteclay, II, ed. *The Eagle and the Dove: The American Peace Movement and United States Foreign Policy, 1900–1922,* 2d edition. Syracuse, NY: Syracuse University Press, 1991.

Fanning, Richard W. *Peace and Disarmament: Naval Rivalry and Arms Control, 1922–1933.* Lexington: The University Press of Kentucky, 1995.

Knock, Thomas J. *To End All Wars: Woodrow Wilson and the Quest for a New World Order.* New York: Oxford University Press, 1992.

Mahan, Alfred Thayer. *The Influence of Sea Power upon History, 1660–1783* (1890). New York: Dover Publications, 1987.

Jonathan M. DiCicco

See also: **Laws of War; Peace Movements, 1898–1945.**

DISSENT IN WORLD WAR I AND WORLD WAR II

There was significant American opposition to World Wars I and II. While American antiwar dissent was broader and sharper during World War I, dissent also existed during World War II. Even though antiwar dissent did not alter the conduct or duration of the conflicts, both world wars had a major impact on the American peace movement—and through the peace movement, on American society.

WORLD WAR I

World War I spawned the modern American peace movement. Led by male business and professional elites and supported by middle-class professionals, the prewar peace movement (respectable, practical, and reformist) sought to resolve conflict through international law, arbitration, and conciliation. By contrast, the modern, post-1914 peace movement, characterized by citizen-peace activists, women's peace organizations, and a progressive reformist impulse, was a more militant grassroots movement that sought both peace and social justice.

Opponents of World War I included radicals, pacifists, social gospel clergymen, social workers, feminist women, labor lawyers, liberal publishers, university professors, public school teachers, isolationists, and some German Americans. Opponents of U.S. intervention organized against President Wilson's preparedness campaign (1915–1917); after the United States entered the war in April 1917, many opponents continued to express antiwar dissent. Radicals, including socialists, anarchists, and syndicalists, argued that capitalism, imperialism, and the competition for markets caused the war. The Socialist Party of America (SP) and the Industrial Workers of the World (IWW) were the most important radical groups to oppose the war and the draft. In April 1917, the SP condemned the war, opposed American intervention, and vowed support for "all mass movements" against conscription. The IWW, a revolutionary industrial union opposed to capitalism and militarism whose members were known as Wobblies, led wartime strikes that disrupted wartime production. Individual radicals also opposed the war, including anarchists Emma Goldman and Alexander Berkman, who formed the No-Conscription League, which prompted their arrest.

Pacifists formed a number of organizations to oppose the conflict and the preparedness campaign. Jessie Wallace Hughan, a New York socialist pacifist feminist, founded the Anti-Enlistment League (1915), which collected pledges of war resistance to persuade the government to stay out of the conflict. The liberal American Union Against Militarism (AUAM, 1915), which was

Industrial Workers of the World poster declaring their stance against World War I, ca. 1917. UNIVERSITY OF ARIZONA LIBRARY SPECIAL COLLECTIONS

created to oppose the preparedness movement, claimed 6,000 members and 50,000 sympathizers nationwide. The Fellowship of Reconciliation (FOR, 1915) became the major religious pacifist organization in America. Founded by Jane Addams, the Women's Peace Party (WPP, 1915) provided a link between the peace and suf-

frage movements; in 1919, the WPP became the Women's International League for Peace and Freedom (WILPF). Proclaiming that women were more concerned than men with preserving human life, the WPP argued that females had a special role in the peace movement, and that the enfranchisement of women would promote peace in the political sphere. In 1915, a WPP delegation visited belligerent nations in an unsuccessful attempt to win neutral mediation of the conflict. The People's Council of America for Peace and Democracy (1917), dominated by left wing progressives and socialists, urged a quick negotiated peace. Finally, Quakers formed the American Friends Service Committee (AFSC, 1917) to organize conscientious objector-led reconstruction, humanitarian, and medical projects in wartime Europe.

Conscientious Objectors (COs) offered a particularly concrete expression of antiwar dissent. The Selective Service Act of 1917 effectively limited conscientious objection to members of the historic peace churches (Quakers, Mennonites, Brethren). Nearly 4,000 inductees obtained a CO exemption from active combat service. Of the 65,000 men who claimed CO status, 20,000 were inducted, of whom 16,000 dropped their objection during training. Another 450 absolutist COs were court-martialed and sentenced to military prisons, where some waged individual and collective rebellions to protest their mistreatment and to resist regulations that violated their conscience. Some religious leaders, particularly Protestant social gospel clergyman, opposed the war. For instance, John Haynes Holmes, a prominent religious pacifist, condemned World War I (and later, World War II). In addition to individual clergymen, denominations opposed to the war included, most notably, the historic peace churches and the Jehovah's Witnesses.

WORLD WAR I: GOVERNMENT SUPPRESSION

Antiwar dissidents were battered by legal and extralegal measures. The government, private agencies, and "patriots" conducted repressive campaigns against radicals, pacifists, and liberals who challenged the war. Federal legislation, most notably the Espionage Act and the Sedition Act, restricted dissent and promoted conformity. The government used the Espionage Act to convict many antiwar dissidents, including Eugene V. Debs, the SP leader who received a ten-year prison term for delivering an antiwar speech. Similarly, the federal government used the Espionage Act and the courts to suppress the IWW in a wartime campaign; the campaign culminated in a nationwide September 1917 raid and subsequent 1918 trial that convicted 101 IWW leaders and decimated the group. The Postmaster General suppressed radical periodicals shipped in the mail. The New York state legislature prohibited teachers from speaking against the war. New York City required teachers to sign loyalty oaths, though eighty-seven teachers refused. Nationwide, dissident public school teachers (and several university professors) were fired, suspended, and harassed for their antiwar and radical convictions. Private groups, including the American Protective League, the National Security League, and the American Defense Society, enforced the Espionage and Sedition Acts and attacked civil liberties and free speech. Also, citizen mobs attacked and in several cases murdered Wobblies.

Even though they did not prevent or shorten the war, antiwar activists had a significant impact on American society. First, the modern peace movement that emerged during World War I advanced peace and justice during the interwar period. Besides building a powerful interwar antiwar movement, the peace movement promoted social reform to abolish the social causes of war and injustice. Second, women, who played a prominent role in the wartime and postwar peace movement, challenged traditional gender roles by assuming a public voice on matters of war and peace, an issue previously dominated by men. Third, imprisoned COs, whose protests in jail created headaches for officials, led the government to liberalize provisions for COs in World War II. Fourth, peace activists made important contributions to the wartime and postwar civil liberties movement. In 1917, feminist pacifists, radicals, and socialists formed the New York Bureau of Legal Advice (BLA), while the AUAM created the Civil Liberties Bureau (CLB, later the independent National Civil Liberties Board, NCLB). Both groups provided free wartime counseling and legal assistance to COs and their families and to individuals persecuted for dissent. After the war, they provided legal services to legal aliens victimized by the Red Scare who awaited deportation. In 1920 the American Civil Liberties Union (ACLU), the successor to the NCLB, absorbed the work of the BLA. Thus, pacifists and the antiwar movement made a direct contribution to the founding of the ACLU and the promotion of civil liberties in the United States.

WORLD WAR II
Disillusioned by World War I, a powerful isolationist, or anti-interventionist, movement emerged during the 1930s. Anti-interventionists sought to prevent U.S. involvement in future wars by limiting American political and military commitments (but not trade) overseas. Ideologically and politically diverse, this anti-interventionist movement included the conservative America First Committee, liberal/left peace and pacifist groups, and the Socialist and Communist parties. To prevent a repetition of World War I, between 1935 and 1937 Congress enacted three neutrality acts that banned Americans from giving

loans to belligerents, from shipping munitions to belligerents, from traveling on belligerent vessels, and from arming American merchant ships.

Unlike World War I, antiwar dissent during World War II was largely confined to pacifists. After Pearl Harbor, public opinion, previously divided, overwhelmingly supported U.S. intervention. For instance, the America First Committee (an influential isolationist organization), Norman Thomas (the respected Socialist Party leader and peace advocate), and mainstream churches all reversed course and endorsed U.S. intervention. In December 1941, the House of Representatives approved a declaration of war with only one dissenting vote; in April 1917, fifty House members had voted against a similar declaration. Partly because antiwar dissent was marginal and posed no serious challenge to the war effort, the civil liberties of dissenters were generally tolerated and respected during World War II.

While the American peace and isolationist movements collapsed after Pearl Harbor, the established pacifist organizations and historic peace churches continued to oppose World War II. Pacifist organizations that opposed the war included the FOR, the WILPF, the AFSC, the War Resisters League (WRL, a secular radical pacifist group founded in 1923), and the Catholic Worker Movement (1933). The Peace Now Movement (1943) sought to unite pacifists and non-pacifists against the war. Between 1939 and 1945, pacifists opposed conscription, lobbied to liberalize the immigration laws to help refugees, assisted COs, advocated a negotiated peace, condemned the internment of Japanese Americans, and criticized the saturation bombing of German cities.

Even more than World War I, COs were a major element of the antiwar dissent during World War II. For COs, the Selective Service and Training Act of 1940 was a marked improvement over the World War I draft law. Unlike the World War I law which effectively restricted CO status to members of the historic peace churches, the World War II law broadened the religious test and granted CO status to any "person who by reason of religious training and belief, is conscientiously opposed to participation in war in any form." It also permitted COs to choose either "non-combatant service" under military control or "work of national importance under civilian direction." During World War II, 12,000 COs enrolled in Civilian Public Service (CPS), an alternative program to military service which promised them "work of national importance" under civilian control in 151 camps and units. In addition, 6,000 COs went to prison, and 25,000 other COs performed noncombatant work in the armed forces. Although religious COs comprised the vast majority of objectors, political objectors included African

Americans who refused to serve in a Jim Crow military, Puerto Rican nationalists who refused induction to protest Puerto Rico's colonial status, interned Japanese Americans who refused induction to protest their incarceration, socialists who refused to participate in a capitalist war, and pacifists who opposed war on political, humanitarian, and ethical (rather than religious) grounds.

In CPS and prison, radical COs staged nonviolent protests against racism, censorship, conscription, and the policies that dehumanized prison and marred the original vision of CPS. Disillusioned by CPS, COs resorted to work strikes, work slowdowns, hunger strikes, nonviolent sabotage, and walkouts to protest the absence of paid work, insignificant work assignments, and arbitrary camp management. Similarly, prison COs led nonviolent protests. For instance, at Danbury Correctional Institution, COs staged a 135-day work strike that abolished Jim Crow in the prison dining room. At Lewisburg Federal Penitentiary, COs waged a 65-day hunger strike that led officials to liberalize censorship policies.

POSTWAR LEGACY

Like World War I, World War II transformed the peace movement, which, in turn had a major impact on American society. Radicalized by World War II, COs such as David Dellinger, Bayard Rustin, George Houser, and James Peck, championed the nonviolent direct action and civil disobedience that marked postwar social activism. After World War II, COs and other pacifists, such as A.J. Muste, applied Gandhian techniques to advance peace and justice—most notably in the peace, civil rights, antinuclear, environmental, civil liberties, and women's movements. For instance, pacifists founded the Congress of Racial Equality (CORE, 1942), which spearheaded nonviolent direct action to win civil rights for African Americans; advised Martin Luther King, Jr. during the Montgomery Bus Boycott (1955–1956), and, afterwards, in the Southern Christian Leadership Conference and elsewhere; led the Committee for Nonviolent Action, a small radical pacifist group that organized dramatic direct action and civil disobedience protests at nuclear testing bases and missile sites; and provided leadership to the anti-Vietnam War movement. During the Cold War, pacifists also condemned both superpower blocs, opposed militarism, resisted conscription, and championed the right of dissent and conscientious objection. In these and other ways, the postwar peace movement, led by World War II COs, popularized nonviolent direct action and civil disobedience to promote peace and justice in America and abroad.

In conclusion, even though it did not prevent or shorten the conflicts, significant antiwar dissent existed during both world wars. Ever since World War I, part of the peace movement has advocated social reform to abolish the social causes of war. During and after both conflicts, the peace movement has advanced peace and justice in America.

BIBLIOGRAPHY

Alonso, Harriet H. *Peace as a Women's Issue: A History of the U.S. Movement for World Peace and Women's Rights.* Syracuse, NY: Syracuse University Press, 1993.

Bennett, Scott H. *Radical Pacifism: The War Resisters League and Gandhian Nonviolence in America, 1915–1963.* Syracuse, NY: Syracuse University Press, 2003.

Chambers, John W. *To Raise an Army: The Draft Comes to Modern America.* New York: Free Press, 1987.

Chatfield, Charles. *For Peace and Justice: Pacifism in America, 1914–1941.* Knoxville: University of Tennessee Press, 1971.

DeBenedetti, Charles. *The Peace Reform in American History.* Bloomington: Indiana University Press, 1980.

Doenecke, Justus D. *Storm on the Horizon: The Challenge to American Intervention, 1939–1941.* Lanham, MD: Rowman & Littlefield, 2000.

Early, Frances H. *A World Without War: How U.S. Feminists and Pacifists Resisted World War I.* Syracuse University Press, 1997.

Frazer, Heather T., and O'Sullivan, John, eds. *"We Have Just Begun To Not Fight": An Oral History of Conscientious Objectors in Civilian Public Service During World War II.* New York: Twayne, 1996.

Goossen, Rachel W. *Women against the Good War: Conscientious Objection and Gender on the American Home Front, 1941–1947.* Chapel Hill: University of North Carolina Press, 1997.

Jaffe, Julian F. *Crusade against Radicalism: New York during the Red Scare, 1914–1924.* Port Washington, NY: Kennikat Press, 1972.

Kennedy, Kathleen. *Disloyal Mothers and Scurrilous Citizens: Women and Subversion During World War I.* Bloomington: Indiana University Press, 1999.

Kohn, Stephen M. *Jailed for Peace: The History of American Draft Violators, 1658–1985.* Westmont, CT: Greenwood Press, 1986.

Peterson, H.C., and Fite, Gilbert C. *Opponents of War: 1917–1918.* Madison: University of Wisconsin Press, 1957.

Sibley, Mulford Q., and Jacob, Philip E. *Conscription of Conscience: The American State and the Conscientious Objector, 1940–1947.* Ithaca, NY: Cornell University Press, 1952.

Tracy, James. *Direct Action: Radical Pacifism from the Union Eight to the Chicago Seven.* Chicago: University of Chicago Press, 1996.

Wittner, Lawrence S. *Rebels Against War: The American Peace Movement, 1933–1983.* Philadelphia: Temple University Press, 1984.

Scott H. Bennett

See also: **Civil Liberties, World War I; Civil Liberties, World War II; Peace Movements, 1898–1945.**

DU BOIS, W. E. B.

⭐ (b. February 23, 1868; d. August 27, 1963) American
writer, sociologist, and civil rights leader.

William Edward Burghardt Du Bois was born in Great
Barrington, Massachusetts. His mother worked as a maid
for local white families, despite being partially paralyzed
in her hands and legs by a stroke. When Du Bois was
just a year old, his father left home, ostensibly to look for
work, and never returned. Though life was difficult and
money hard to come by, Du Bois was bright and articulate and he excelled in school. Most of his friends were
sons of the middle class white families in town. Du Bois's
upbringing was relatively free of racial discrimination.

In 1885, Du Bois moved to Nashville, Tennessee, to
attend historically black Fisk University, where, despite
his self-described "blithely European and imperialist"
outlook, he began to articulate his ideas about race relations and the importance of economics to American
notions of equality. After Fisk, Du Bois fulfilled his long-
held desire to attend Harvard. He received his Ph.D. in
1895 after falling under the spell of the burgeoning science of sociology.

Next came a series of teaching and research positions, first at tiny Wilberforce College in Ohio, then at
the University of Philadelphia after he moved there with
his new wife, Nina. In 1903, Du Bois published *The Souls
of Black Folk,* a collection of essays that became, and is
still considered, one of the most important books ever
written about the problems of African-American people
in the United States. In it, Du Bois separated his philosophy from those of the towering black thinkers of
American history, many of which he considered too focused on appeasement and delicately constructed acces-
sion. Not long after, Du Bois helped found the National
Association for the Advancement of Colored People
(NAACP) and went on to serve as the organizations' director of publication and as the editor of its magazine,
Crisis, for nearly a quarter of a century.

With the coming of World War I, Du Bois saw an
opportunity for black Americans to advance and to win
many of the freedoms and protections they had long
struggled for. He urged blacks to insist on their right to
serve their country by joining the armed forces, an idea
the military at first resisted. Later, he used his position
in the NAACP and as editor of *Crisis* to urge Congress
to allow blacks to become officers and to establish economic and occupational assistance for returning black
veterans. His writing about the moral conundrum of
black soldiers voluntarily defending a country that refused
to protect them from lynch mobs was widely read and
discussed, and immediately became part of America's political and social vocabulary.

W. E. B. Du Bois.

When the war ended, Du Bois used his increased influence and popularity to bring yet more attention to the
plight of black people around the world. The pan-African
Conferences that he organized, though lauded in certain
circles, were unsuccessful largely because of changing
ideas among black Americans about how to proceed in
the struggle for equality. As Du Bois had anticipated,
World War I had been a catalyst for blacks to gain equal
rights. For many black Americans who had served their
country, a return to the days of political and social repression seemed unthinkable. A new idealism and purpose were afoot. What was missing was a unified voice.
For many, like the orator and critic Marcus Garvey, the
only solution was separation and a return to Africa. Du
Bois' conflict with Garvey, who raised money to purchase
a line of sailing ships, was widely reported in the press
and served to forestall any attempts to create a viable pan-
African political movement.

In 1934, Du Bois resigned his position in the
NAACP when his own increasingly militant opinions
brought him into conflict with other leading figures within
the organization. He returned to Atlanta University,

where he had taught from 1897 until 1910, and during the next decade he published many books. Then, having been forced to resign due in part to his increasingly radical views, Du Bois continued to organize international summits to examine the plight of black people in America and abroad. He rejoined the NAACP, but was again ousted when his criticism of U.S. foreign policy became too vocal.

That criticism increased following World War II, with America's ascension to the position of world military superpower. It was in the post war period that Du Bois began to speak out most vocally about the dangers of American imperialism, which he saw as creating a new class of conquered, desperate, and ignored humanity. In 1945, he warned against these dangers at the birth of the United Nations and later convened another pan-African Congress to consider the question and a possible response.

Not all of these gestures met with universal approval among African Americans. Indeed, a visit to the USSR, which cemented the favorable view of socialism Du Bois had developed during the Great Depression, as well as his decision to join the Communist Party in 1961 further alienated him from the mainstream Civil Rights movement. That same year, Du Bois renounced his American citizenship and emigrated to Ghana, Africa, where he undertook the editorship of the massive and audacious *Encyclopedia Africana,* a work suggested by the country's president and Du Bois's friend Kwame Nkrumah, but never brought to completion.

Du Bois died some six months later, at the age of ninety-four, very far from the land of his birth. The board of the NAACP, with whom he had so often tangled, honored him as "the prime inspirer, philosopher and father of the Negro protest movement."

BIBLIOGRAPHY

Lewis, David Levering. *W. E. B. Du Bois: Biography of a Race: 1868–1919.* New York: Henry Holt, 1993.

Lewis, David Levering. *W. E. B. Du Bois: The Fight for Equality and the American Century 1919–1963.* New York: Henry Holt, 2000.

Marable, Manning. *W. E. B. DuBois, Black Radical Democrat.* Boston: Twayne, 1986.

Internet Resource

Hynes, Gerald. "A Biographical Sketch of W.E.B. DuBois." W.E.B. DuBois Learning Center. Available from <http://www.duboislc.org/man.html>.

Laura M. Miller

See also: **African Americans, World War I; African Americans, World War II; Civil Liberties, World War I; Civil Liberties, World War II.**

ECONOMY, WORLD WAR I

In April 1917, almost fifty-two years to the day after Lee's surrender at Appomattox, the United States entered the First World War. The federal government moved forward tentatively as it sought to mobilize the nation for its first great conflict since the Civil War. By November 1918, however, the federal government overcame its early handicaps and successfully marshaled the nation's human and economic assets to fight. In the process, Washington accumulated vast new powers, vindicated the ideas of a generation of reformers, and set the stage for New Deal and World War II reforms.

The first issue the Wilson administration faced as it prepared America for war in April 1917 concerned financing the mammoth cost of war. On this issue Progressives and their traditionalist opponents waged the first great battle. World War I cost an estimated $33.5 billion, and of this amount the government borrowed some $23 billion and raised some $10.5 billion through taxes. Progressive reformers had hoped to finance the bulk of the war through taxation but, faced with spiraling costs and congressional opposition to draconian taxes, Secretary of the Treasury William McAdoo sought greater reliance on generating revenue through the sale of government bonds. In the end, McAdoo's Liberty Bond Campaign contributed some $22 billion to the nation's war coffers. McAdoo's use of the Federal Reserve System to enlarge the nation's money supply eased the fiscal strain on the credit supply and facilitated the rise of the national debt from $1 billion to $20 billion. But it also brought about a doubling of the consumer price index between 1916 and 1920. Despite the Treasury Department's emphasis on borrowing and currency manipulation, Progressive reformers led by Wisconsin's Robert La Follette were not without success. Presaging Franklin Roosevelt's progressive tax policy of World War II, the 1917 and 1918 Revenue Acts proved significant in shifting the tax burden from the shoulders of the working class to the affluent. During the war federal receipts from consumption and excise taxes (taxes on certain goods and licenses) declined from 75 percent of total tax revenue to 25 percent, while revenue from income, corporate, luxury, and estate taxes grew from 25 percent to 75 percent of total tax revenue. Despite inflation, many working-class and farm incomes increased during the war. For the wealthy, after-tax income reached a plateau.

AGRICULTURE

The Wilson administration faced the enormous task of marshalling the nation's human and material resources. By Armistice Day the United States had raised a military of nearly 4.8 million soldiers and shipped over 20 million tons of food to Europe. None of this would have been possible without a mammoth increase in the power and authority of the federal government to organize the economy so as to support the war effort. In 1916, as part of its overall preparedness campaign, Congress created the Council of National Defense, made up of cabinet officers and leaders from business and labor. The council's major achievement involved the creation of various specialty coordinating agencies, including the Food Administration and the War Industries Board. In May 1917 President Wilson appointed Herbert Hoover as Food Administrator and charged him with raising U.S. agricultural production in order to furnish both domestic and European needs. Congress provided Hoover considerable power under the Lever Act, which gave him authority to control the production and distribution of key commodities such as meat and grain. The future president augmented his official powers with new voluntary measures, including conservation of key commodities through the observance of "meatless days" and "wheatless days." Hoover's policies paid off handsomely for all concerned. Food exports increased from some 7 million tons in 1916 to 18 million tons in 1918, and farm income soared as the Lever Act pegged commodity prices at often twice their prewar level.

INDUSTRY

In July 1917 the council created its second great coordinating agency, the War Industries Board (WIB), and charged it with coordinating war production and supervising labor-management relations. After ten inauspicious months, WIB leadership passed to Bernard Baruch. With sweeping authority, which included allocation of resources, production and price controls, the suspension of antitrust laws, and the use of the cost-plus contract, Baruch and the WIB brought coordination to the wartime economy.

Complementing the WIB's control over wartime industry, several federal agencies brought similar order to America's far-flung and diverse labor force. The United States Employment Service, for example, placed some 3.7 million workers in wartime industry. The War Labor Board (WLB), led by Frank Walsh and former president William Howard Taft, worked to ensure labor harmony and avert strikes. The WLB heard over twelve hundred labor management disputes and settled the vast majority in labor's favor. Under WLB auspices, workers won the right to collective bargaining and the eight-hour day while the nation's largest union, the American Federa-

tion of Labor, saw its membership rise from approximately two million in 1916 to just over four million in 1920. Private employers also sought to create harmony at the workplace through the use of welfare capitalism, a system in which employers sought to gain worker loyalty through benefits such as profit sharing and pensions.

Much less successful experiments in coordination, including the Emergency Fleet Corporation and the Aircraft Production Board, utterly failed to meet their respective obligations. The Shipping Board, for example, created by Wilson in April 1917, provided less than 500,000 tons of new merchant shipping—less than 3 percent of its goal of 15 million tons—by late summer 1918. Wartime agencies were far more successful when they simply took needed resources. The United States Shipping Board, for example, helped alleviate the merchant marine shortage by seizing a merchant fleet of some 3.5 million tons. When volunteer efforts failed to coordinate the nation's mammoth rail system by Christmas 1917, President Wilson placed the railroads under the control of the newly created United States Railroad Commission.

World War I ended on November 11, 1918, but its effect on the United States would continue for a generation. The war helped invalidate earlier ideas about the superiority of limited government in an industrial age and in the process vindicated the ideas of a generation of reformers about using government to regulate the economy and promote social justice. World War I set the stage for the reforms of the 1930s and contributed to the rise of the modern, powerful government, which would lead the nation through the challenges of World War II.

BIBLIOGRAPHY

Chambers, John W. *The Tyranny of Change: America in the Progressive Era, 1890–1920*. New York: St. Martin's, 1992.

Kennedy, David M. *Over There: The First World War and American Society*. New York: Oxford University Press, 1980.

Leuchtenburg, William. *The Perils of Prosperity, 1914–1932*, 2nd edition. Chicago: University of Chicago Press, 1993.

Link, William A., and Link, William S. *American Epoch: A History of the United States Since 1900*. New York: McGraw Hill, 1993.

Sidney L. Pash

See also: **Financing, World War I; Financing, World War II; Labor, World War I; Rationing; Women, Employment of.**

ECONOMY, WORLD WAR II

On December 8, 1941, a day after the devastating Japanese attack on Pearl Harbor, the United States declared war on Japan. On December 12, one day after Japan's Axis partners declared war on the United States, Congress reciprocated. Having embarked on its second world war in a generation, the federal government stumbled forward in an attempt to mobilize the nation for its greatest challenge since the Civil War. Despite the experience it had gained from World War I and even though it had begun mobilization prior to December 1941, the government, for myriad reasons, was unprepared for war and never managed to fully organize the nation for the twentieth century's final global conflict.

FINANCE

World War II cost the United States over $130 billion, and wartime finance soon proved to be an issue where the federal government excelled. For the most part, Washington financed this war, as it had World War I, through massive borrowing. In all, seven war bond campaigns raised some $135 billion. It also financed the war by transforming the tax code with the Revenue Act of 1942. Reflecting the progressive tax laws of World War I, this act raised the corporate, estate, excess profits, and gift taxes. It simultaneously revolutionized the tax code by tripling the number of wage earners paying federal income tax. By extending the income tax to millions of low to moderate wage earners, the 1942 legislation added 37 million Americans to the federal tax roles. War bonds and taxation also worked—in conjunction with the Anti-Inflation Act of 1942, which allowed the president to freeze wages and prices—to hold down the rate of inflation. From 1940 to 1945 the consumer price index rose a modest 28 percent.

FEDERAL OVERSIGHT

Whereas the federal government quickly met the challenge of financing the war, the same cannot be said for its mobilization of the nation's economy, which before December 1941 proved haphazard at best. Much of the blame for this rests with President Franklin Delano Roosevelt and his isolationist opponents. The president, on the one hand, was reluctant to vest the authority needed to control the wartime economy with any single person or agency. Isolationists, on the other hand, harangued the administration when it attempted to better prepare the nation for conflict. Not until May 1940, as France faced certain defeat, could President Roosevelt create the Office of Emergency Management (OEM), an agency with the power to effectively direct the transition from a peacetime to a wartime economy. The OEM successfully oversaw the transition from civilian to wartime production during the first six months of 1941, when shortages of energy and raw materials and a growing chorus of complaints led the president to transfer its mandate to the newly created Supplies Priorities and Allocations Board

World War II production poster from 1942. © SWIM INK/CORBIS

on August 28, 1941. This new board, however, proved to be neither more capable than the OEM nor more resistant to criticism, and in January 1942 the president abolished it in favor of the new War Production Board (WPB).

Largely the brainchild of Bernard Baruch, the leader of the World War I War Industries Board, the WPB soon proved a disappointment. Lacking control over war production and the allocation of resources, it failed to bring coordination and control to industry. Far more important, though often overlooked, was the Office of Economic Stabilization (OES), created in October 1942 to combat rising inflation. Its director, South Carolina Senator James Byrnes, used this mandate to gain control over the allocation of scarce raw materials and in the process gained control over wartime industrial production. Success at OES brought Byrnes even greater authority when in May 1943 the president named him head of the newly created Office of War Mobilization (OWM), a kind of super agency with complete power to direct wartime mobilization through control of raw materials, civilian and military production, and transportation.

LEGACY

Despite early problems in coordinating the wartime economy, the United States soon proved capable of supplying both American and Allied needs. Industrial production jumped from $8 billion in 1941 to over $30 billion the next year, and by 1944 American factories produced twice as much war material as the entire Axis. From December 1941 to August 1945, the United States produced over 274,000 aircraft, almost 5,600 merchant ships, 90,000 combat vessels, and 100,000 tanks. American industry supported a military of some 15 million and allowed the United States to provide $50 billion in Lend Lease aid to Axis opponents.

United States war production altered the course of the global conflict and in the process reshaped the lives of countless Americans. War mobilization ended the Great Depression even before the first bombs fell on Pearl Harbor as the gross national product rose from $91 billion in 1939 to $126 billion in 1941 to over $166 billion in 1945. Unemployment fell from 8 percent in 1940 to 5 percent in 1942 to 1 percent by 1944. Building on the experience of World War I, the federal government weighed in on the side of labor in order to avert strikes. The War Labor Board (WLB), created in January 1942, settled some 20,000 disputes involving 20,000,000 workers. With WLB help, union membership increased from 10 million to 15 million. Steady work and shortages of certain consumer goods contributed to a phenomenal rise in personal savings, from $3 billion in 1939 to $37 billion in 1944. For industrial workers, income rose some 70 percent during the war and farm income rose a staggering 300 percent. The war, in short, gave birth to the modern American middle class.

Just as war production reshaped the course of millions of individual lives, it also reshaped the contours of American business and industry. Prior to the 1939, 87 percent of Americans worked for firms with fewer than 10,000 employees. During the war years, however, large employers received the lion's share of defense orders and, therefore, the bulk of wartime profits. By 1944, 30 percent of Americans worked for these large employers. A similar process occurred in agriculture, where the number of family farms continued to decline while large farms, which relied on greater mechanization and freed labor for war work, increased in both number and acreage.

Although World War II officially ended with Japan's formal surrender on September 2, 1945, the war's effect on the American economy continues into the twenty-first century. The war ended the Great Depression, strengthened the union movement, made the income tax a shared burden, narrowed the gap between rich and poor, and increasingly made the typical employer a large, often anonymous, entity. At the same time, the war years showed both the limitations of government's power to organize the economy and the immense productive capacity that a union of capital and labor could achieve in time of national emergency.

BIBLIOGRAPHY

Goodwin, Doris Kearns. *No Ordinary Time: Franklin and Eleanor Roosevelt: The Home Front in World War II.* New York: Simon & Schuster, 1994.

Jeffries, John W. *Wartime America: The World War II Home Front.* Chicago: Ivan Dee, 1996.

Leuchtenburg, William E. *Franklin D. Roosevelt and the New Deal, 1932–1940.* New York: Harper & Row, 1963.

Link, William A., and Link, William S. *American Epoch: A History of the United States since 1900.* New York: McGraw Hill, 1993.

O'Neill, William. *A Democracy at War: America's Fight at Home and Abroad in World War II.* Cambridge, MA: Harvard University Press, 1993.

Sparrow, Bartholomew H. *From the Outside In: World War II and the American State.* Princeton NJ: Princeton University Press, 1996.

Sidney L. Pash

See also: **Financing, World War II; Labor, World War II; Profiteering; Rationing.**

ENEMY, IMAGES OF

The way that people visualize the enemy during wartime often has little to do with the actual reasons for the war or the actual character of the enemy. The images of the enemy that dominate the public mind reflect the limited information available to the public, the public's collective predispositions, and elite strategies to shape opinion, including government propaganda and political debate. The specific images of the enemy that are presented in official propaganda reflect the government's judgment as to the best way to build and maintain support for the war effort. Enemies are routinely portrayed and viewed as cruel, treacherous, barbaric, or inhuman, and enemy motivations are almost always oversimplified and delegitimized. Scholars have long debated the reasons for these negative images, whether rooted in human psychology, the survival instincts of both individuals and societies, ethnic and racial prejudice, or manipulation by authority figures. In general, scholars agree that images of the enemy are rooted in nonrational sources and may have dysfunctional effects.

There is significant variation among the types of enemy images that emerge in different places and times. In

World War II poster encouraging Americans to work hard, with caricatures of Hitler, General Tojo, and Mussolini, ca. 1942. © CORBIS

the American context, images of the enemy seem to be formed both by American political values and by national stereotypes. American leaders have generally framed wars as fights for American political and social ideals, such as democracy and freedom. But these abstract goals have often been filtered through stereotypes that portray specific adversaries as "naturally" undemocratic or totalitarian. For example, during World War II, the Japanese were portrayed as militaristic and fanatically devoted to a totalitarian regime, an image that built on both American political values and national/racial stereotypes. However, it is probably more accurate to characterize the foreign policy motivations of both mass publics and élites in the United States as a complex blend of idealism and pragmatism. American images of the enemy are probably correspondingly complex in both source and effect.

THE SPANISH-AMERICAN WAR AND THE PHILIPPINE INSURRECTION

The early history of the Spanish-American War (1898–1899) was marked by American sympathy for the Cuban insurrectionists, whom many Americans viewed as freedom fighters opposing a colonial power just as had the early American revolutionaries. As the American press reported and often exaggerated the brutal anti-guerrilla tactics of the Spanish, Americans soon came to hold a view of Spain as a decadent, cruel, and tyrannical Old World empire that was heir to the worst European traditions, including monarchy and popery (a term used negatively to identify Roman Catholicism). When the American battleship *Maine* sank in Havana's harbor after a mysterious explosion, American newspapers built up a powerful patriotic frenzy, creating pressure on the U.S. government to go to war against Spain. President William McKinley and other American leaders justified the ensuing war as a war for freedom and human rights.

Victory in the war brought the United States new territories, including the Philippine Islands. The U.S. government now faced a dilemma as to what to do with the inhabitants of these territories. At first, American views of the Filipinos were benign but condescending. The notion that they were childlike and unfit for self-government was used to justify plans to colonize the Philippine Islands in order to civilize and democratize Filipino society. As a rebel insurgency against the United States gained momentum, however, American leaders branded the Philippine insurgents as thugs, brigands, and bandits, and refused to recognize their political aspirations and motivations as legitimate. As the guerrilla war continued (from 1899 to 1902), the United States found itself in an ironic position: although it was dedicated to a liberating and civilizing mission, it was forced to fight a brutal guerrilla war using some of the same tactics that it had criticized Spain for using in Cuba just a few years before.

WORLD WAR I

During World War I, public attention and a powerful government propaganda effort focused on Germany. President Woodrow Wilson framed World War I ideologically as a battle for peace, democracy, and national self-determination. Kaiser Wilhelm and other German leaders were portrayed as undemocratic, militaristic aggressors. A variety of official and unofficial organizations made the case for war by means of propaganda posters and speeches. The Four Minute Men, a quasi-official speaker's bureau, gave speeches portraying Germany and the Germans themselves as cruel (referring to German atrocities against American shipping and against Belgian civilians), treacherous, and even as un-Christian because of Germany's alliance with Ottoman Turkey, a Muslim country. Anti-German propaganda led to broad suspicion of German immigrants and German-Americans at home and to a movement for "100 percent Americanism." It also contributed to the passage of the Alien and Sedition Acts in 1918, which restricted immigration and freedom of speech.

WORLD WAR II AND AFTER

Like World War I, World War II was mostly framed as an ideological battle between freedom and totalitarianism. However, important differences separated official and popular views of Nazi Germany and Imperial Japan. For the most part, official propaganda about Germany focused on the ideology and leadership of the Nazi party, and tended to portray the German people as the victims of their government. By contrast, the portrayal of the Japanese enemy as cruel, treacherous, and subhuman extended to the Japanese population itself. Accordingly, American troops in the Pacific felt free to fight a war of annihilation, while at home American authorities felt justified in placing Japanese-Americans on the West Coast in internment camps.

After 1945, appeals to traditional American political values and national and racial stereotypes would continue to characterize images of the enemy in the Cold War era. Whether future images of American enemies will be less vulnerable to racial biases, however, remains an open question.

BIBLIOGRAPHY

Aho, James Alfred. *This Thing of Darkness: a Sociology of the Enemy.* Seattle: University of Washington Press, 1994.

Herle, Vilho. *Enemy with a Thousand Faces.* Westport, CT: Praeger, 2000.

Keen, Sam. *Faces of the Enemy: Reflections of the Hostile Imagination.* San Francisco: Harper and Row, 1986.

Lehmkuhl, Ursula, and Fiebig-von Hase, Ragnhild, eds. *Enemy Images in American History.* Providence, RI: Berghahn Books, 1997.

Lippman, Walter. *Public Opinion.* New York: Harcourt. 1922.

McDougall, Walter. *Promised Land, Crusader State: The American Encounter with the World since 1776.* Boston: Houghton Mifflin, 1997.

Seabury, Paul, and Codevilla, Angelo. *War: Ends and Means.* New York: Basic Books, 1990.

Zaller, John. *The Nature and Origins of Mass Opinion.* Cambridge, U.K.: Cambridge University Press, 1992.

Alfred Saucedo

See also: **Allies, Images of; Propaganda, War.**

FEMINISM

Carrie Chapman Catt, America's leading suffragist, helped organize the international suffrage movement in 1902. Feminists from developed nations met regularly to exchange strategies for winning the vote in their countries.

VOTES AND PACIFISM

Beyond winning the vote the feminists wanted to mobilize womanpower, worldwide, to prevent or stop wars. In 1915, a year after the First World War began, Catt, Jane Addams and other leading feminists formed the Women's Peace Party. Women, it argued, were "the mother half of humanity." Maternal pacifists said motherhood gave women a unique biological, social, and political viewpoint through their relationship not just to men and children, but also to the nation and the world. They believed that motherhood legitimized and motivated the solidarity of all women in condemning war, and that whereas men had conflicting interests and ambitions, women all over the world shared concern for the creation and preservation of human life. Motherhood thus became a potent symbol for pacifists, as reflected in a popular song of 1915, "I Didn't Raise My Boy to Be a Soldier."

In 1915 Addams and other pacifists joined Henry Ford's venture to plead directly with the belligerents for peace. President Woodrow Wilson, recognizing the influence of the peace movement, presented American entry into the war as a final desperate step to end all wars—then proposed a League of Nations to prevent future wars from starting. America's participation in the war silenced most of the pacifists, except for the socialists who saw further evidence of a capitalist conspiracy to profit from human misery. Addams actively supported the Food Administration's successful efforts to bring housewives' skills to bear on the world food crisis.

ACTIVISM IN THE 1920s

The feminist movement in America has largely focused on the domestic legal rights of women. Winning the vote in 1920 was the American feminists' great triumph, but they were not united on what to do next. Male politicians in the early 1920s scrambled to adjust to the new electorate; many supported policies they thought women wanted, such as pacifism, prohibition of alcholic liquors, welfare programs, and expansion of health services and schools. By the decade's end it was clear that women did not comprise a separate voting block, and the politicians turned to other issues.

The most energetic feminist campaigns after suffrage was won promoted world peace. After the war the pacifists reemerged. They had been reinvigorated by getting the vote in most major countries, and by the terrible knowledge that the Great War had failed to solve the world's problems. In the United States they failed to convince the nation to join the League of Nations or the World Court, but both went into operation anyway and attracted support from most feminists.

By 1921, the Women's International League for Peace and Freedom (WILPF) founded in 1915 had grown to twenty-two national affiliates. They united for the same goals they sought at home: to emphasize women's unique role as mothers and nurturers; to promote moral reform and fight against prostitution ("white slavery"); and to demand political rights and the pursuit of peace. Some were socialists who wanted to protect poor working class women from exploitation by capitalist employers. The rhetoric of the WILPF referred to women as "mother-hearts," "guardians, nurses & preservers," "Mothers of the Human Race," "carriers of life," "Mothers of the Nations," and "guardians of the new generations." Its members believed nature had made women morally superior to men. They believed in their hearts that their common gender could and would unite women across the world in the cause of peace in a way that transcended narrow national interests.

Feminists in America and Europe redoubled their efforts for peace in the 1920s. They promoted the 1925 Geneva Protocol, which successfully prohibited the use of poison gas and bacteriological weapons. Even more stunning success came in 1928, with the Kellogg-Briand pact that outlawed war as an instrument of national policy. It was ratified by most countries, incorporated into the United Nations Charter in 1945, and is still in effect; it has made formal declared wars between independent countries quite rare.

ISOLATIONISM

Pacifist feminism played a major role in the isolationist mood that formed U.S. national policy in the mid and late 1930s. But not all feminism was pacifist. The "realist" feminists controlled important organizations. Alarmed at the rise of ruthless militaristic dictatorships, realists argued that true peace required such threats to be ended. They were especially active against Japan, which launched large-scale invasions of China in the 1930s. Led by novelist Pearl Buck, who romanticized the work of American women missionaries in China, religious public opinion strongly supported military aid to China and deeply distrusted Japan. The WILPF kept to its pacifism, but lost most of its members.

WORLD WAR II

After Pearl Harbor, pacifist sentiments were rarely expressed by feminist leaders. Congresswoman Jeanette Rankin cast the only vote against war with Japan and did not run for reelection. Few women entered politics during the war. Perhaps the most notable new figure was Clare Boothe Luce, a leader in New York City society and culture, who was elected as a conservative Republican to Congress.

What little organized feminism existed was split on the debate over special laws protecting women in the workplace. The laws were on the books, strongly supported by labor unions and liberals (led by Eleanor Roosevelt) on the grounds that women were unable to bargain collectively to protect themselves, and needed the government's help. However, the growing numbers of educated, middle class women helped keep alive the feminist dream of an equal rights amendment to the Constitution that would end the protections, and thus validate the claim that women could be fully independent citizens and workers with exactly the same status as men.

The wartime labor shortage led to the repeal of traditional restrictions against married women holding white collar jobs in offices, stores, banks, and public schools. Millions of factory jobs opened for women, but most were in the munitions industry that everyone realized would shut down when peace arrived. Most of the new women factory workers were required to join unions, but except for some left-wing CIO unions, they were not welcomed by the male leadership. Liberal feminists supported the expansion of social services to the new workers, such as day care centers, but there was no organized effort to guarantee postwar access to blue collar jobs that had traditionally been monopolized by men.

WACS, WAVES, SPARS, Wasps and Women Marines marked a dramatic breakthrough in the role of women as militarized defenders of the nation. Most feminists seemed uncertain of the wisdom of this new development, and few tried to mobilize opinion on their behalf, although by contrast, military nursing won widespread praise. Instead of renewed feminism during the war, there was an intense interest in the nuclear family, as expressed in the Baby Boom. It began in 1941 as both middle class and working class women, black and white, reversed decades-long trends to later marriages and smaller families.

Feminism peaked in the immediate aftermath of World War I, as the grateful nation rewarded women with the vote and turned its attention to women's issues such as pacifism and prohibition. World War II had the opposite effect. Feminism seemed to reach a nadir in 1945 as America prepared to welcome back its male veterans with a celebration of home, family, fertility, and suburbia, with scant regard for women's independent role or independent voice at home or abroad.

BIBLIOGRAPHY

Alonso, Harriet Hyman. *The Women's Peace Union and the Outlawry of War, 1921–1942*. Knoxville: University of Tennessee Press, 1989.

Foster, Carrie A. *The Women and the Warriors: The U.S. Section of the Women's International League for Peace and Freedom, 1915–1946*. Syracuse, NY: Syracuse University Press, 1995.

Hartmann, Susan M. *The Home Front and Beyond: American Women in the 1940s*. Boston: Twayne Publishers, 1982.

Jeffreys-Jones, Rhodri. *Changing Differences: Women and the Shaping of American Foreign Policy, 1917–1994*. New Brunswick, NJ: Rutgers University Press, 1995.

Rupp, Leila J. *Worlds of Women: The Making of an International Women's Movement*. Princeton, NJ: Princeton University Press, 1997.

D'Ann Campbell

See also: **Rosie the Riveter; Women and World War I; Women and World War II; Women's Suffrage Movement**

Fundraising for the "Second Liberty Loan," in 1917.
ICM ARCHIVES/LANDOV

FINANCING, WORLD WAR I

The outbreak of World War I found the United States unprepared for the enormous strains the war would place on its fiscal system. When the guns finally fell silent in 1918, the United States had embraced a significantly different tax system, seen its government assume a dramatically enlarged place in the financial affairs of its citizens, and changed from an international debtor to an international creditor nation.

PREWAR TAXES

Before 1914, the American government had customarily received much of its income from the tariff. After wartime conditions shrank foreign imports, the duties collected on "vices" such as alcohol and tobacco products, cosmetics, and playing cards eclipsed the tariff as the largest source of revenue. The adoption of the Sixteenth Amendment in 1913 had legalized the income tax, but Congress embraced this change without much eagerness. The initial rates were so low and the exemption so high that 98 percent of American families paid no income tax whatsoever.

Such a system could never pay for a major war. The total cost of the war, $33 billion, was forty-two times as large as receipts from all sources in 1916, the last prewar year. The financial decision facing the nation as it con-

fronted the prospect of mobilization was whether to expand the income tax dramatically or to attempt a substantial broadening of the sin taxes. If duties were imposed on a much wider range of consumer commodities, the effect would be to establish a national sales tax. The issue was highly controversial.

THE INCOME TAX

Progressives in Congress had long hoped to use Congress's taxing power to reduce economic inequity by taxing the wealthy. In 1916, when President Woodrow Wilson asked for funds to support military preparedness, they saw their chance. Since many Progressives were opponents or only half-hearted supporters of war preparedness, they demanded an expansion of the income tax in return for their support. They contended that since Eastern businessmen were the principal advocates and beneficiaries of preparedness, they should pay for it. As the powerful North Carolina congressman Claude Kitchin put it, if the "New York people" were compelled to pay for preparedness, they would be less disposed to support it (Kennedy, p. 16).

WAR BONDS

Bonds are a form of interest-incurring loans and are sold through commercial banks. In 1863 the U.S. Congress created a national banking system in order to raise money to finance the American Civil War, and since then bonds have been used to finance other wars as well. After the United States entered World War I in April of 1917, the U.S. Treasury Department borrowed money using a series of bond issues. Although the first four bond issues were called "liberty loans" or "liberty bonds," the fifth and last was known as the "victory loan." These long-term bonds totaled some $21 billion, of which the liberty bonds accrued interest from 3.5 to 4.5 percent and the victory bonds accrued interest at 3.5 to 4.7 percent. Citizens were strongly encouraged to demonstrate their patriotism by buying these bonds. Posters the with slogan "Beat Back the Huns with Liberty Bonds" were plastered to walls, and speakers canvassed the nation, appearing at churches, rallies, factories, theaters, and other venues.

The Revenue Act of 1916 and its companion measures, the War Revenue Acts of 1917 and 1918, differed in detail but not in philosophy. They imposed more steeply graduated income taxes, thus pursuing a redistributive, soak-the-rich policy. Personal exemptions to individual income taxes were reduced to $1,000 for a single person and $2,000 for a married couple, above which a standard tax was imposed—2 percent in 1917 and 12 percent in 1918. To these were added surtaxes ranging from 1 percent for incomes above $5,000 to 65 percent for incomes above $1,000,000.

In addition, businesses were required to pay excess profits taxes on net income exceeding 7 to 9 percent of invested capital as measured during a three-year prewar period. These rates were graduated from 20 to 60 percent in 1917, reaching a theoretical cap of 80 percent in 1918. Taxes on excess corporate profits accounted for more than half of all monies collected in 1918. Between individual and corporate taxes, the Wilson administration was successful in obtaining financial support for the war from America's most affluent families. The richest 22 percent of U.S. taxpayers contributed 96 percent of all individual tax receipts in 1918. Also to tap the assets of the wealthy, Congress introduced a new and steeply

graduated estate tax and imposed excise duties on automobiles, jewelry, cameras, motor boats, and yachts.

WAR BONDS

Wilson's policies were less effective in reaching the great resources of the middle classes. Treasury Secretary William G. McAdoo orchestrated an elaborate and innovative campaign intended to prod Americans of average means to furnish financial support to the war effort by emphasizing the voluntary purchase of war bonds. Appealing to what he termed America's "profound impulse called patriotism," McAdoo drummed up support for a series of four Liberty Loans, arranging for celebrities, including the movie stars Douglas Fairbanks and Mary Pickford, to appear at bond rallies (Kennedy, p. 105). The nation's best-known illustrators drew posters entreating the public to contribute, and an army of Four-Minute Men gave patriotic speeches in movie theaters and elsewhere extolling the importance of buying bonds. Even the Boy Scouts turned out as bond salesmen under the slogan "Every Scout to Save a Soldier." In the third Liberty Loan campaign of 1918, at least half of all American families subscribed.

Nevertheless, the bond campaign was flawed. The social pressure compelling citizens to purchase was often heavy handed, echoing Wilson's infringement of freedom of speech and his mistreatment of conscientious objectors. Most significantly, the Federal Reserve System encouraged its member banks to lend money freely for the purchase of war bonds. This was the equivalent of the government printing money, and because of it the Wilson administration failed to meet its goal of financing half the cost of the war through taxes. The increased money supply was also rampantly inflationary and prices doubled by 1918 despite an ill-fated attempt at price control.

HELPING THE ALLIES

As the financier of its European allies, Uncle Sam fared much better. Prior to the war, Britain had dominated international trade, but German submarines among other things ensured that this was no longer possible. The United States moved to replace Britain as purveyors to Latin America and as the dominant world shipping power. Whereas in 1914 the United States was a net international debtor in the amount of $3.2 billion, massive British and French purchases soon reversed this situation. American banks and exporters extended long-term loans to their customers, and in 1917 and 1918 the U.S. Treasury extended huge loans to Europe. Britain had originally bankrolled the Allied governments, but its war-weakened reserves led to the primacy of the U.S. Treasury as the world's preeminent banker. By the end of the war, the United States had lent more than $10 billion to foreign governments, almost half of it to Britain, and it flexed its financial muscles by requiring that its loan money be spent on U.S. products. This ensured that the United States would be the arsenal and breadbasket of Europe.

By war's end, the United States had become the world's most important trading nation as well as its largest banker. Its tax-collecting arm, the Bureau of Internal Revenue, had quadrupled in size, and the income tax, which now produced thirty-one times as much revenue as it had in 1916, had solidified its position as the most powerful fiscal device of the modern U.S. state. Nearly 23 million Americans, or about 22 percent of the U.S. population, had voluntarily subscribed $7 billion to the Fourth Liberty Loan. By 1918, the United States was spending more on defense each day than any other belligerent, and it had succeeded in raising a greater proportion of its wartime expenditures from its citizens' taxes and loans than had any other nation. These achievements denoted the strength, patriotism, and willingness to sacrifice of an aroused and determined democracy.

BIBLIOGRAPHY

Brownlee, W. Elliot. *Federal Taxation in America: A Short History.* New York: Woodrow Wilson Center Press, 1996.

Gilbert, Charles. *American Financing of World War I.* Westport, CT: Greenwood, 1970.

Kennedy, David M. *Over Here: The First World War and American Society.* New York: Oxford University Press, 1980.

Schaffer, Ronald. *America in the Great War: The Rise of the War Welfare State.* New York: Oxford University Press, 1991.

Stuart D. Brandes

See also: **Civil Liberties, World War I; Economy, World War I.**

FINANCING, WORLD WAR II

World War II was the most expensive war in American history, exceeding all other conflicts in economic impact. Nearly forty million Americans paid income taxes for the first time, and an elaborate price control system touched the life of every consumer. To sell war bonds, the U.S. government made direct and frequent contact with more than 90 percent of the American population. The U.S. government financed a massive expansion of the nation's defense industry, so that by 1945 the government owned billions of dollars worth of factories and machinery.

PLANNING

During the two years before the United States entered the war, the enormity of America's financial burden became apparent. At the war's peak, federal expenditures

were twelve times greater than in the last peacetime year. President Franklin D. Roosevelt hoped to pay for half the cost of the war, or more, out of current income, but collecting such a colossal sum was a daunting task. Roosevelt was determined not to rely too heavily on loans, but borrowing was inevitable.

The Japanese attack on Pearl Harbor angered, frightened, and unified the nation, but although the public was eager to contribute to the war effort, Roosevelt's economic policies still faced difficulties. Some members of Congress disliked Roosevelt's political agenda in any form, and others were reluctant to face reelection after raising taxes. Roosevelt's greatest problem, however, was how to tap into the middle and lower income levels. Rampant consumer spending had led to large price increases during World War I.

BROADENING THE INCOME TAX

Tax experts generally agreed that the income tax was the fairest, most effective way to draw upon the spending power of the middle class. Some leaders preferred a national sales tax, but against the opposition of the president the idea went nowhere. The treasury proposed a tax on individual spending, but the plan's complexity doomed it as well. The income tax, formerly the domain of the wealthy alone, would have to be broadened to apply to Americans of average income.

In 1941 and again in 1942, Congress lowered income tax exemptions and adopted steeply graduated rates. These ranged from 13 percent on the first $2,000 of individual income up to 82 percent on income above $200,000. Gift and estate taxes were also broadened, and a graduated tax on excess corporate incomes added to the progressive nature of the tax structure, which became the highest in American history. Excise taxes on alcoholic beverages, tobacco, and gasoline rose dramatically as well.

Because the taxpaying public perceived the income tax as a levy that should apply only to the wealthy, the government feared noncompliance. "Suppose we have to go out and try to arrest five million people?" Treasury Secretary Henry Morgenthau said. To keep this from happening, and because most Americans were ignorant of the procedure for filling out an income tax form, the treasury devised a clever and effective public relations campaign, such as *The New Spirit.* Responding to this and other appeals, most Americans made a good-faith effort to pay their taxes.

COLLECTION AT THE SOURCE

The income tax was a bountiful source of income, but it had one great disadvantage: Before 1943, it was paid only quarterly. Since defense spending was producing huge daily deficits, tax collection had to be accelerated. The

THE NEW SPIRIT

More than two-thirds of the American population attended at least one movie each week during World War II, offering an ideal opportunity for a patriotic appeal. Early in 1942, the treasury department asked the Disney studio to produce *The New Spirit,* a short animated film featuring Donald Duck paying his income taxes. Arming himself with an aspirin bottle and aided by an animated ink bottle and pen, Donald finds that filling out his tax form is surprisingly painless. With three deductions for his dependents Huey, Dewey, and Louie, Donald's tax is only $13 on his actor's income of $2,501. More than thirty-two million people saw the film, which was shown on twelve thousand screens, and 37 percent of the moviegoers reported that it had a positive effect on their willingness to pay their taxes.

answer was to put the income tax on a pay-as-you-go basis-in other words, to withhold a sum for tax purposes from every paycheck, with a small reconciliation payment (or refund) due at year's end. The problem with this scheme was that, in the year the change was made, taxpayers would have to pay their taxes twice, once for the previous year and again for the current year. Although this was Roosevelt's preference, many argued that it would be an unfair burden. They demanded that in return for accepting the pay-as-you-go system taxpayers be excused from making the prior year's annual payment. Against Roosevelt's wishes, Congress agreed to forgive three-fourths of a year's tax payments, a compromise that transferred the payment to the shoulders of postwar taxpayers.

WAR BONDS

The World War I system of marketing war bonds through propaganda posters, pamphlets, and patriotic rallies was resurrected and expanded in World War II. Between the wars, most American families had acquired radios, which simplified the government's work in appealing for funds. Patriotic pleas, presented by performers such as the cowboy star Roy Rogers, flooded the airwaves. The treasury even presented its own variety show, *The Treasury Star Parade,* to coax the public to purchase war bonds regularly.

To reach people with the lowest incomes, the treasury made the purchase of bonds much easier. Bonds sold

for $50 in World War I, but in WWII the treasury sold stamps—which could be used to buy bonds—in denominations ranging from $0.10 to $5. The Series E bond, which sold for $18.75 but could be redeemed for $25 in ten years, was the most popular. (Sixty years later, a modified version, the Series EE, was still available.)

WAGE AND PRICE CONTROLS

Taxes and war bonds diverted consumer spending, but if wages rose significantly consumers might bid against the government for scarce resources. To prevent this, and to preserve equity in the economy, in April 1942 the government instituted a system of wage and price controls. Wages and retail prices were restricted according to a fixed schedule, and Roosevelt limited the compensation of business executives to $25,000 after taxes.

Initially, the price control system worked well. But as rising production demands placed pressure on scarce resources, flaws began to appear. The first was in the price of steel, which was vital to warships and tanks. Controlling the price of gasoline was an even thornier problem, and a shortage of rubber arose due to the Japanese capture of Southeast Asia. Driving was restricted: the government rationed gasoline, imposed a nationwide speed limit, and attempted to prohibit all motoring for pleasure. No wartime measure was more unpopular or difficult to enforce. A lively market for illegal, or black market gasoline developed, but in spite of the black market inflation during World War II was comparatively modest. Whereas the cost of living doubled during World War I, inflation was held to about 28 percent during World War II.

FOREIGN LOANS

The Roosevelt administration was skittish about making loans to foreign governments. Many Americans believed that during the 1930s America's World War I allies had improperly suspended payments on their debts, and they were leery of lending money again. To address this difficulty, Roosevelt proposed to lend only military equipment, all of which was to be returned after the war. The lend-lease program adroitly avoided the issue of whether debts would be repaid after the war.

DEFENSE PLANTS

In wartime, the United States had traditionally relied on converting existing factories to defense production. In World War II, to encourage plant conversion and expansion, the government again offered liberal tax incentives and paid attractive, high-incentive prices. In return, contractors agreed to a system of price renegotiation that was intended to prevent swollen profits. But the existing manufacturing facilities could not produce the immense

Actress Carole Lombard at the podium during a World War II bond rally in January 1942. She was killed in a plane crash while flying home to California from this Indianapolis, Indiana, rally. TIME LIFE PICTURES/GETTY IMAGES

quantities of planes and tanks that World War II required. New plants had to be built, and only the government could supply the capital necessary to finance them.

In 1940, Congress created the Defense Plant Corporation, which could build an entire factory and then lease it to a contractor. This firm financed about 30 percent of the new facilities that were built during the war, and the government came to own major portions of the synthetic rubber, aircraft, magnesium, and aluminum businesses. By the war's end, the government had invested billions of dollars in factories and machinery and owned about one-sixth of the nation's industrial capacity. Since there was little postwar need for many of these facilities, the government sold them to the highest bidder in an auction popularly known as Uncle Sam's garage sale. Some contractors realized excellent bargains, purchasing equipment or even whole factories at a fraction of their cost.

When the war ended, America's financial strength was unrivaled. The United States possessed the most powerful revenue source ever devised, the mass-collected personal income tax. It had claim to billions of dollars in military equipment that was in the possession of its wartime allies, and it owned a significant portion of the nation's manufacturing capacity. It had successfully limited the wages and salaries of the nation's workers and managers, and it had restricted the prices of nearly all consumer products. About 40 percent of the cost of World War II was financed out of current revenue, an improvement on the Civil War (28 percent) and World War I (36 percent). The nation could be rightfully proud of a job well done.

BIBLIOGRAPHY

Blum, John Morton. *V Was for Victory: Politics and American Culture during World War II.* New York: Harcourt Brace Jovanovich, 1976.

Brandes, Stuart D. *Warhogs: A History of War Profits in America.* Lexington: University Press of Kentucky, 1997.

Brownlee, W. Elliot. *Federal Taxation in America: A Short History.* Washington, DC: Woodrow Wilson Center Press; New York: Cambridge University Press, 1996.

Jones, Carolyn C. "Mass-Based Income Taxation: Creating a Taxpaying Culture, 1940–1952." In *Funding the Modern American State, 1941–1995: The Rise and Fall of Easy Finance,* edited by W. Elliot Brownlee. Washington, DC: Woodrow Wilson Center Press; New York: Cambridge University Press, 1996.

Perrett, Geoffrey. *Days of Sadness, Years of Triumph: The American People, 1939–1945.* New York: Coward, McCann & Geoghegan, 1973.

Winkler, Allan M. *Home Front U.S.A.: America during World War II.* Wheeling, IL: Harlan Davidson, 2000.

Internet Resources

Thorndike, Joseph J. "Historical Perspective: Wartime Tax Legislation and the Politics of Policymaking." Tax History Project. Available from <http://www.taxhistory.org>.

Stuart D. Brandes

See also: **Financing, World War I.**

FORD, HENRY

(b. July 30, 1863; d. April 7, 1947) American industrialist, creator of the first mass-produced automobile.

Technological genius and headline maker, Henry Ford was the creative force behind an industry that changed the culture of the United States. His Model T automobile put Americans on the road. People were no longer isolated on remote farms or in small villages. It was Ford's belief that the car was intended for ordinary people, not exclusively for the wealthy. This most rapid change ever in the lives of average citizens was completed in less than two decades.

Ford was born on a farm himself, near Dearborn, Michigan, on July 30, 1863, one of eight children. By 1893, he had completed his first gasoline engine model. Six years later, with backers, he formed the Detroit Automobile Company, which became the Ford Motor Company. That became the Cadillac Motor Car Company after he left in 1902 to start another Ford Motor Company. Incorporated in 1903, the company produced only a few cars until it introduced the famous Model T in 1909.

Almost as revolutionary as his famous car was the advanced production technology that Ford had in operation by 1913. Automobiles were put together on a moving assembly line, with different parts installed as they moved down the line. The result was a completed chassis every ninety-three minutes. Ford changed the way America manufactured its products.

A man of genius and prejudice, Ford was immovable when convinced he was right. A pacifist, he was totally against U.S. involvement in World War I. He cast himself as the country's leading peace advocate, and because of his widespread influence with the average citizen, many Americans opposed U.S. entry into the war.

In what is known as the Peace Ship episode, Ford even chartered an ocean liner to sail to Europe on a stop-the-fight mission. The effort was loudly ridiculed by government officials. When the British liner *Lusitania* was sunk by a German submarine in 1915, killing 1,198 passengers, Ford remarked that they were fools to get on the boat in the first place. Known as an anti-Semite, he blamed

Assembly line at the Ford plant in Willow Run, Michigan, where B-24 bombers were constructed during World War II. THE LIBRARY OF CONGRESS

the Jews for starting the war, although he never explained just how that could have been managed. During the 1920s, he was behind many anti-Semitic publications.

During the 1930s, Ford favored the U.S. neutrality legislation that tried to keep the United States out of World War II. He went a step further and opposed the Roosevelt administration's lend-lease policy of aid to Great Britain. Ford testified before the Senate Foreign Relations Committee and opposed cooperating with Britain and the Soviet Union to fight Hitler. In 1940, influenced by famed aviator Charles Lindbergh, he joined the America First committee, dedicated to keeping the country out of war. Ford, Lindbergh, and other top U.S. industrialists were accused of pro-Nazi attitudes. These isolationist sentiments, shared by many in America at the time, were complicated by the fact that Ford had investments in Germany, including a large plant near Cologne. However, when the Nazi government took control of all foreign business in the country, Ford decided not to in-

vest any more money in the Cologne plant. It was taken over by the Nazis just before they invaded Poland in 1939.

Despite his isolationist-pacifist leanings, Ford played a major role in World War II. After the Japanese bombed Pearl Harbor in 1941, he immediately threw the might of his production lines into the war effort. His plant at River Rouge, Michigan, was already the country's most important factory, a monument to maximum operations without wasted time. He changed military transportation as well with the production of the Jeep, the all-everything vehicle, produced along with aircraft engines at River Rouge. Ford's Willow Run plant in Michigan began to build B-24 bombers immediately after the attack on Pearl Harbor and the first aircraft came off the assembly line on May 1, 1942. The factory eventually produced one bomber per hour for a total of more than 86,000 by the end of the war.

Henry Ford died on April 7, 1947, at the age of eighty-four. He had many detractors because of his authoritative, racist attitudes, but no one could deny his contribution to U.S. military might during World War II.

BIBLIOGRAPHY

Bennett, Harry, as told to Paul Marcus. *We Never Called Him Henry.* New York: Fawcett, 1951.

Brinkley, Douglas. *Wheels for the World: Henry Ford, His Company, and a Century of Progress, 1903–2003.* New York: Viking, 2003.

Bryan, Ford R. *Beyond the Model T: the Other Ventures of Henry Ford.* Detroit, MI: Wayne State University Press, 1990.

Jardim, Anne. *The First Henry Ford: A Study in Personality and Business Leadership.* Cambridge, MA: MIT Press, 1970.

Wallace, Max. *The American Axis: Henry Ford, Charles Lindbergh, and the Rise of the Third Reich.* New York: St. Martin's, 2003.

Corinne J. Naden and Rose Blue

See also: **Economy, World War I; Economy, World War II; Labor, World War I; Labor, World War II; Peace Movements.**

GI BILL OF RIGHTS

In 1944, social and economic concerns, higher education, veterans' issues, and federal legislation merged in a way never before experienced in the history of the United States with the passage of the Servicemen's Readjustment Act, more commonly known as the GI Bill of Rights. This single piece of legislation simultaneously changed the lives of millions of veterans who served in World War II and affected social, economic, and educational development in the United States for decades to follow. Both veterans and historians frequently argue that the GI Bill was one of the most influential and beneficial pieces of legislation passed by the federal government in the twentieth century.

In light of events following World War I, particularly the Bonus Army's Washington protests, President Franklin D. Roosevelt's administration strove to develop legislation that would provide compensation for veterans, help them adjust to postwar society, and keep them from overloading the workforce as soon as the war ended. The economic and employment issues raised following World War I contributed to the comprehensive nature of the GI Bill, which was the first legislation to include all veterans and provide them with more than just basic living allowances. These efforts to develop a program of benefits for the veterans of World War II began well before the war ended.

The National Resources Planning Board Conference on Postwar Readjustment of Civilian and Military Personnel, a group organized by Roosevelt, first met on July 17, 1942. In June 1943, the Conference presented a report that advocated providing veterans with twelve months of schooling at any level and three years of education for a select number of veterans who showed particular aptitude. They also suggested that there would be a need for limited vocational training. Another group, the Osborn Committee of the Armed Forces Committee on Postwar Educational Opportunities for Service Personnel, also focused on the issue of educational opportunities for veterans. By the fall of 1943, the American Legion joined in the movement and began to work on a comprehensive bill that would include medical care, unemployment compensation, education and vocational training, home and farm loans, and a system of furlough pay. Jack Cejnar, the American Legion's acting director of public relations, eventually labeled their proposed program the GI Bill of Rights.

On June 22, 1944, President Roosevelt signed the GI Bill of Rights into law. Title Two of the measure dealt with the education and training of veterans. All veterans who had served at least ninety days in the military and were not more than twenty-five years old when they enlisted had the chance to receive one year of schooling. They could also receive additional education equal to the amount of time they served, a monthly subsistence allowance while in school, and money for fees, tuition, books, and supplies.

In addition to financial assistance, the bill offered the veterans a fair amount of freedom in their educational decisions. The veterans attended their schools of choice. The government also refrained from imposing itself on the schools' administrators and their curriculum decisions. Evidence of the bill's influence on higher education is evident in the fact that at some colleges veterans made up over half of the student body in the late 1940s. During the bill's peak year, 1947, nearly 49 percent of all college students in the United States were veterans. From the GI Bill's enactment in June 1944 to its end on July 25, 1956, close to 7.8 million veterans, of an eligible 15 million, received education and training with the assistance of the bill. Of these, approximately 2.2 million attended colleges and universities and 3.5 million attended other schools. An additional 2.1 million received on-the-job training and farm training. Over the twelve years the bill was in place for World War II veterans, the education program cost $14.5 billion.

In addition to addressing issues of education for the veterans, the GI Bill provided veterans with home, farm, and business loans that helped them to establish themselves financially after the war. These loans contributed to their ability to buy homes, purchase farmland and farming equipment, or start their own businesses. Also, under the GI Bill's 52–20 clause, all veterans were eligible to receive $20 a week for 52 weeks while they looked for work, which in that era was a significant contribution to living expenses. Only about one-fifth of the money set aside for the 52–20 Club, as this program was known, was distributed because most returning veterans promptly found work or used the bill's education benefits.

The broad nature of the coverage provided by the GI Bill indicated the societal goals of the legislation's authors. Thus, the GI Bill received significant political and public support, as veterans returning from the "good war" were viewed as heroes and the public believed they deserved extra acknowledgment. Its wide scope had extensive impact on society and education. Higher education in America dramatically changed and grew as a result of the bill; some schools tripled in size in less than a decade. Instead of flooding the job market on their return, as had happened after World War I, these veterans opted to receive education and training that ultimately made them strong contributors to society. Additionally, home ownership became increasingly accessible as a result of the loans made available by the bill. In essence, the GI Bill democratized many of the dreams held by Americans.

BIBLIOGRAPHY

Gubin, E. K. *Veteran's Handbook for Veterans of World War II and Their Dependents, Including an Explanation of the GI Bill of Rights.* Washington, DC: Army Times, 1945.

Kandel, Isaac Leon. *The Impact of the War upon Higher Education.* Chapel Hill: University of North Carolina Press, 1948.

Mohr, Clarence L. "World War II and the Transformation of Southern Higher Education." In *Remaking Dixie: The Impact of World War II on the American South*, edited by Neil R. McMillen. Jackson: University Press of Mississippi, 1997.

Olson, Keith W. *The G.I. Bill, the Veterans, and the Colleges.* Lexington: University Press of Kentucky, 1974.

Ross, Davis R. B. *Preparing for Ulysses: Politics and Veterans during World War II.* New York: Columbia University Press, 1969.

Kathryn St.Clair Ellis

See also: **American Legion; Demobilization; Veterans' Benefits; Veterans of Foreign Wars.**

GOLD STAR MOTHERS PILGRIMAGE

Gold Star Mothers derived their name from the gold star they displayed on service flags in their homes and armbands during America's participation in World War I (1917 to 1918). Each gold star publicly represented a son or daughter killed in war service and brought recognition to women for sacrificing a child for the nation.

Initially, there was no specifically named organization, but rather a collection of unofficial women's groups formed for mutual companionship and comfort. Commemorative organizations such as the American Legion offered affiliation for the Gold Star women. The American Gold Star Mothers, Inc. (AGSM) received official Federal Charter in 1928.

Controversy over the Gold Star pilgrimages—government-subsidized visits to the European grave sites of those killed overseas during the war—reflected lingering doubts in America over what World War I had accomplished. Debates over where the dead should be buried after the war further fractured the nation and added to questions regarding war aims. Many argued that the war dead should remain together, interred overseas in ground over which they had fought and died. Others believed the government should bring fallen soldiers

The president of the American Gold Star Mothers with a French Gold Star Mother at Dony Cemetery, France, in October 1925. © BETTMANN/CORBIS

home. In 1919, the issue was resolved when family members were asked to make the final decision concerning the disposition of the dead. Once the debate concerning overseas versus domestic burial was resolved, the issue of the Gold Star Pilgrimages could proceed.

One issue dominated the efforts of the Gold Star Mothers almost as soon as the Armistice ending World War I was signed: appeals to Congress for organized, subsidized travel to Europe to visit the graves of their loved ones buried in American cemeteries overseas. Difficult logistical and economic questions were raised during congressional debates regarding the pilgrimage legislation. Dominating the hearings were budgetary objections, questions of logistics, and more sensitive issues such as eligibility under the proposed legislation, since many believed fathers should not be excluded from the visits. The congressional debate over the Gold Star Mothers pilgrimage was also a forum for questioning American involvement in World War I by drawing American attention to the loss of life, and a forum for

reinforcing American isolationism and anti-militarism expressed in the Kellog-Briand Pact of 1928.

PILGRIMAGE

In March 1929, President Calvin Coolidge signed legislation authorizing Gold Star Mothers and widows with next of kin buried overseas to travel to Europe as guests of the United States government. Five million dollars was allocated to cover all expenses for pilgrimages that began in May 1930 and concluded in August 1933.

The army's Quartermaster Corps was designated with logistical responsibility for the Gold Star pilgrimages of mothers and widows. Relatives of more than 30,000 soldiers were contacted and approximately 14,000 women were found eligible to make the two-week trip abroad. Eventually, 6,693 women accepted the government's invitation, including widows if they had not remarried. The average pilgrim was between sixty-one and sixty-five years of age, but many were over seventy and frail or in poor health.

From the moment pilgrims left their homes, all reasonable expenses were paid. The lavish care extended by the government to the mothers and widows during their journey served to highlight the exceptional nature of their contribution. They were greeted by civic officials in New York at city hall receptions, boarded luxury liners, travelled cabin class, stayed at first-class hotels, and had an army officer, physician and nurse accompany them abroad. Pilgrims were escorted to the graves of their loved ones, then each group spent a week in either Paris or London where they were honored by the French or British government.

Though the government claimed to treat all women alike, African-American women invited to participate in the pilgrimage did so on the same segregated basis as their sons and husbands who had fought and died. They travelled as a separate group on commercial steamers, were accommodated in separate hotels, rode separate trains upon arrival in France, and were even provided separate entertainment. Neither the protest of African-American organizations nor the refusal of some women to participate in the pilgrimage succeeded in persuading the War Department to alter its policy on segregation.

As a public act of commemoration, the pilgrimages united women's groups in remembrance and possibly assisted the participants in the process of consigning the dead to memory. The experience also offers a remarkable "insight into the way many mothers and society at large attempted to portray and define the relationship that existed between mother and son and the nation's war dead" (Piehler, p. 102). The unprecedented pilgrimage legacy represents an unconventional attempt by the government to justify war losses while demonstrating that personal sacrifices had not been made in vain.

BIBLIOGRAPHY

Gillis, John R., ed. *Commemorations: The Politics of National Identity.* Princeton, NJ: Princeton University Press, 1994.

Piehler, G. Kurt. *Remembering War the American Way.* Washington, DC: Smithsonian Institution Press, 1995.

Risch, Erna. *Quartermaster Support of the Army: A History of the Corps 1775–1939.* Washington, DC: U.S. Army Center of Military History, 1989.

Lisa M. Budreau

See also: **Monuments, Cemeteries, World War I; Feminism; Women, World War I; Women, World War II.**

HEMINGWAY, ERNEST
(b. July 21, 1899; d. July 2, 1961) Author.

Ernest Hemingway was one of America's foremost novelists. He began his career as a newspaper reporter and Red Cross volunteer in World War I. Hemingway became part of the "Lost Generation" of writers, artists, and poets after World War I who were disillusioned with American society and its creed of progress following the brutality of that war. Like many of that generation, the experience of war shaped their view of life. War also left an indelible mark on Hemingway's personality that would haunt him until his suicide.

Growing up in Oak Park, Illinois, Hemingway was torn between two paths. His mother taught him to appreciate art and music. His father, a country doctor, taught him the delights of the outdoors, including hunting. When his father forbad Ernest from joining the Army after America declared war on Germany in 1917, the young Hemingway became a reporter with the *Kansas City Star*. It was there, among newspaper men, that he began to learn the style that would make him one of the twentieth century's most famous and widely-read authors: short, declarative sentences and an aversion to the prettified descriptions and mannered prose of the last century.

Still, even covering the excitement of local police precincts and hospitals wasn't enough for Hemingway. He craved the action and glory like in the stories he'd invented as a child, imagining himself as the dashing hero. After six months with the Kansas City Star, he decided he had had enough of newspaper work.

Hemingway enlisted in the American Red Cross as an ambulance driver and within a few weeks was in Italy, where he got his first taste of modern mechanized warfare: bloody, brutal, and unremitting. In his letters home, he described his shock at the dismembered bodies and the corpses of innocent civilians. The sight of dead women at an exploded munitions factory in Milan, Italy, seems to have troubled him particularly. A few weeks later, on July 8, 1918, he got his second taste of war when an artillery shell exploded nearby, sending more than 200 fragments into his leg.

It was while he was recovering from this wound that Hemingway met and fell deeply in love with a young nurse named Agnes von Kurowsky. Though she rejected him and broke his heart, Agnes would appear as the doomed nurse so loved by Frederic Henry, an American

Ernest Hemingway (seated center, with glasses) and a group of war correspondents covering the Spanish Civil War, ca. 1937. © HULTON-DEUTSCH COLLECTION/CORBIS

in the Italian ambulance service, in Hemingway's novel of World War I, *A Farewell To Arms* (1929).

No longer fit for the ambulance service, Hemingway returned to newspaper work, taking a position with the *Toronto Star* in 1920. After a year, he married Hadley Richardson and relocated to Paris to cover the Greco-Turkish War. A short time later, in 1923, *Three Stories and Ten Poems* made its appearance, as did Hemingway's first son, John.

It was during this time, too, that Hemingway became attached to a collection of disaffected expatriate Americans in Paris, a group of people who became the basis for his first noteworthy novel, *The Sun Also Rises* (1926). Among them was the typical Hemingway surrogate, the damaged, cynical and still hopeful Jake Barnes. Later yet, Hemingway would employ his recollections as a reporter covering the civil war in Spain, and supporting the Loyalist cause against the fascists, to weave his most daring and structurally complex novel, *For Whom the Bell Tolls* (1940). These were innovative works of fiction: lean, cold, and immediate. His people were often soldiers, or hunters, or fighters, and their lives were etched in Hemingway's simple, muscular prose, without

embellishment. With *A Farewell To Arms* and his many short stories, these novels became the foundation of Hemingway's literary reputation.

By the time he was thirty, Ernest Hemingway was a world-renowned writer of novels, short stories, and nonfiction. But all was not well. The adult Hemingway was capable of decidedly childish behavior. The bullying tendencies he had displayed as a young man too often re-asserted themselves, to disastrous effect. He fell out with old friends and influences. Gertrude Stein he alienated; Sherwood Anderson, sometimes described as the grand-father of Hemingway's prose style, he ridiculed merci-lessly in his novel *The Torrents of Spring* (1926). His four marriages were rocky.

In the late 1930s Hemingway again sought adventure and a cause. He volunteered with other American idealists to fight against the fascists in Spain. He observed this bloody civil war—one that became a prelude to World War II—and made it the context for one of his most successful novels, *For Whom the Bell Tolls*, which was adapted for film in 1943. In 1944 he became a war reporter covering the American campaign in Germany. His love of conflict took him beyond observation into combat under the guise of being a reporter. A man seeking the exhilaration of war, Hemingway seemed lost as a man and writer in peace.

As Hemingway aged, more problems appeared. The prose style, once celebrated, seemed often to descend into self-parody. Critical opinion turned against him. His novel *Across the River and Into the Trees* (1950) was widely panned. Another effort, *Islands in the Stream* (published posthumously in 1970) he forsook as too poor. Not until the publication of his short novel *The Old Man and the Sea* (1952) did he regain the reputation of his early career. The book won Hemingway the 1953 Pulitzer Prize. A year later, he received the Nobel Prize in Literature.

It was, perhaps, too little, too late. Hemingway's drinking, always heroic, grew worse. He underwent bouts of paranoia and depression. Legendarily accident prone, he suffered a number of debilitating injuries. During a visit to Africa in 1954, he was involved in not one, but two nearly-fatal airplane crashes; his premature obituary was widely published. Hemingway sneered, but he suffered grievous wounds. Physical pain exacerbated his drinking and robbed him of his ability to work.

On 2 July 1961, Ernest Hemingway took his own life, having attempted suicide once already that year. A number of noteworthy works, among them *A Moveable Feast* (1964), *The Nick Adams Stories* (1972), and *The Dangerous Summer* (1985) were published after his death.

BIBLIOGRAPHY

Brenner, Gerry and Rovit, Earl. *Ernest Hemingway.* New York: Twayne Publishers, 1995.

Dolan, Marc. *Modern Lives : A Cultural Re-reading of the "Lost Generation."* West Lafayette, IN: Purdue University Press, 1996.

Oliver, Charles M. *Ernest Hemingway A to Z: The Essential Reference to the Life and Work.* New York: Facts on File, 1999.

Reynolds, Michael. *Hemingway: The Final Years.* New York: Norton, 1999.

Laura M. Miller

See also: **Journalism, World War I; Literature, World War I; Literature, World War II; Motion Pictures, World War I and World War II.**

HOLOCAUST, AMERICAN RESPONSE TO

The American response to the Holocaust is characterized by a series of fluctuating policies. One must first examine the attitude of Americans towards the persecution of Germany's Jewish population under the Nazi regime and then examine how these attitudes changed once the war began in 1939.

PERSECUTION AND IMMIGRATION, 1931–1939

As Jews in Germany faced increasing acts of violence and discrimination sponsored by Hitler's government, some American Jewish leaders and American Christian liberals urged the U.S. State Department to alter their standards with regards to German Jewish immigration. By 1936 U.S. immigration officials did change their considerations to include the level of a German Jew's education, job skills, and affidavits of support from American relatives. In just one year this new policy led to a near doubling in the amount of visas granted to German Jews.

The immigration situation became further complicated in 1938 with the Nazi annexation of Austria and the subsequent increase in persecuted Jews living in the former Austrian lands. President Franklin Delano Roosevelt suggested that the immigration laws be further liberalized and added that the application wording of "Jewish refugees" should be changed to "political refugees." It has been argued that he was motivated to change this wording because he was well aware that public opinion polls demonstrated an American perception that Jews already held too much power. It should also be mentioned that due to the effects of the Great Depression, President Roosevelt understood that many Americans were unwilling or unable to extend humanitarian aid to foreigners. Even among some Jewish groups in America, there were divided opinions regarding the crisis in Germany and Austria.

The year 1938 turned out to be a pivotal year for it saw an increase in immigration quotas, the unsuccessful introduction of a congressional bill to aid 20,000 German Jewish children, and an international conference to discuss the Jewish refugee question. In July 1938, Evian, France, became the host site for a conference of thirty-two nations. Most of the nations in attendance were there to explain why their countries could not alter immigration restrictions to accept additional Jewish refugees. In this respect the American delegation was no different from the other countries present. Perhaps the only positive result of the Evian meeting was the creation of the Intergovernmental Committee on Refugees (IGCR), commissioned by the attendees to negotiate with the Nazis about Jewish immigration. Unfortunately, with war looming on the horizon, nothing substantial came of this new committee.

WAR AND JEWISH REFUGEES, 1939–1941

As Nazi Germany invaded Poland on September 1, 1939, the American public was consumed with worries of possible internal subversion. This overwhelming fear of potential enemy spies on American soil led to a major shift

Prisoners in the Auschwitz concentration camp in Poland greeting their liberators on January 27, 1945. UNITED STATES HOLOCAUST MEMORIAL MUSEUM

in American policy towards refugees. In an ironic twist, as Jews in Europe faced increased danger, immigration legislation was now altered to make it increasingly more difficult for them to gain entry to America. By 1941 Congress had made immigration so restricted that only a very small percentage of European immigration quotas were met.

From 1933 to 1941 most of the officials who had been working on the Jewish refugee question had aimed at the resettlement of Jews outside of Nazi-occupied Europe; now their focus shifted to rescue and aid efforts. By 1941 the Nazis had initiated a policy of planned extermination of Europe's Jewish population. By late 1941 the western press began to carry reports of Nazi atrocities. But to many Americans, the idea of mass annihilation of an entire group of people was unimaginable. Linked to this sense of disbelief was the memory that Americans had been tricked by British propaganda into believing that Germans had committed atrocities in Belgium in World War I. There was a tendency to discount much of the reported suffering as just Allied propaganda. In addition, officials in the U.S. government had decided by

1941 that military objectives were to be given top priority; any civilians suffering persecution by the Nazis would best be served by an Allied victory. In short, the argument was to win the war, thereby saving lives in general.

PROTEST AGAINST EXTERMINATION, 1942–1945

Some prominent individuals, such as Gerhart Riegner of the World Jewish Congress in Switzerland, attempted to provide hard evidence of the systematic murders being carried out against Europe's Jewish population. Many government officials ignored Riegner's attempts to prove murders were indeed taking place, but by 1942 the State Department could no longer reasonably deny the accuracy of Riegner's information. President Roosevelt met with five Jewish leaders, one of whom was Rabbi Stephen Wise (president of the American Jewish Congress) on December 8, 1942. A few days after this meeting the U.S. and eleven Allied governments issued a denunciation of Hitler's extermination policy in a joint declaration. Although the statement publicly verified that there was in fact a Nazi atrocity campaign underway, it included no plan of rescue.

As public awareness increased regarding the reality of the "Final Solution," various groups attempted to hold demonstrations and marches. Yet public opinion polls documented an actual increase in anti-semitism rather than a decline. The official American view began to alter only after the summer of 1943 as the tide of war began to change in favor of the Allies. Another contributing factor in the changing view was the role of Henry Morgenthau, secretary of the treasury, and a group of young, non-Jewish Treasury Department staff who shared the belief that the State Department had purposely dragged its feet in the aid and rescue of Jews. Josiah DuBois drafted a document to prove the group's beliefs. Morgenthau toned down the report and then submitted it to the president.

After reading the report, President Roosevelt created the War Refugee Board (WRB), with John Pehle heading the newly-created organization. At first, Pehle and the WRB met with resistance. However, in time, the WRB successfully obtained assistance from a variety of sources, including Pope Pius XII, the Red Cross, and Swedish businessman, Raoul Wallenberg. The WRB also considered a proposal that the Allies bomb Auschwitz-Birkenau, but ultimately the board concluded that such action would only bring about a temporary disruption of the concentration camp's activities.

LEGACY

Nazi atrocities committed against Jews did not play a decisive role in the minds of most American people. American politicians, for their part, were not willing to risk military personnel's lives in order to save foreign civilians. American Jewish leaders were not able to convince the American people that saving the lives of Jews in Europe should not be a minor issue. In the words of scholar Yehuda Bauer, "the record of the great democracies . . . does not generate a sense of pride, to put it mildly." (Bauer, p. 302).

In April and May 1945 various concentration camps were liberated by the Americans, the British, and the Soviets. Camps such as Buchenwald, Dachau, Mauthausen, Theresienstadt, and Bergen-Belsen revealed their horrors to the rest of the world. Perhaps the most stunning release of information was the British liberation of inmates at Bergen-Belsen. When films taken at the camp showed how the prisoners had suffered from a lack of food and water and the ravages of disease (37,000 inmates died prior to liberation), most Americans reacted with disgust and feelings of guilt. President Harry S. Truman, responding to American reactions, commissioned Earl G. Harrison, a Princeton law professor, to examine what could be done to aid Jews now living in the displaced person (DP) camps. In the end, the Harrison report was quite critical of the U.S. Army's treatment of Jewish DPs

and it recommended that 100,000 Jews be allowed to emigrate to Palestine. Harrison's report was released publicly in September 1945 but the British, in control of Palestine, refused to support the movement of so many Jews into the region. Most polls of the time reveal American support for Jews moving out of the DP camps and into Palestine, yet most American politicians refused to interfere in what was regarded as a "British" problem. Throughout 1946–1948 there was an internal battle between Arabs and Jews in Palestine over a Zionist state, ending on May 14, 1948, with the establishment of the state of Israel. While many Americans believed the Holocaust was the catalyst to Israel's creation, evidence suggests that Israel might have developed more rapidly had it not been for events in Europe.

Nevertheless, the Holocaust left an indelible impression on American values and identity. It contributed to the post-war American and international efforts to define "Crimes Against Humanity" and "Human Rights," and to create a permanent international court of justice to deter holocausts. In the twenty-first century Americans continue to debate whether the nation is obligated to use its military power to stop new forms of extermination, such as ethnic cleansing.

BIBLIOGRAPHY

Bauer, Yehuda. *A History of the Holocaust.* New York: Franklin Watts, 1982.

Breitman, Richard, and Allen Kraut. *American Refugee Policy and European Jewry: 1933–45.* Bloomington: Indiana University Press, 1987.

Feingold, Henry L. *The Politics of Rescue.* New Brunswick, NJ: Rutgers University Press, 1970.

Feingold, Henry L. *Bearing Witness: How America and Its Jews Responded to the Holocaust.* New York: Syracuse University Press, 1995.

Friedman, Saul. *No Haven for the Oppressed: United States Policy Toward Jewish Refugees, 1938–1945.* Detroit, MI: Wayne State University Press, 1971.

Laqueur, Walter. *The Terrible Secret: Suppression of the Truth about Hitler's "Final Solution."* New York: Penquin, 1982.

Marrus, Michael. *The Unwanted: European Refugees in the Twentieth Century.* New York: Oxford University Press, 1985.

Morse, Arthur D. *While Six Million Died: A Chronicle of American Apathy.* New York: Random House, 1967.

Newton, Verne W., ed. *FDR and the Holocaust.* New York: St. Martin's Press, 1996.

Wyman, David. *The Abandonment of the Jews, 1941–45.* New York: Pantheon Books, 1984.

Beth Griech-Polelle

See also: **Propaganda, 1895–1945; Radio and the Power of Broadcasting; Roosevelt, Franklin Delano.**

HOOVER, HERBERT

⭐ (August 10, 1874; October 20, 1964) Thirty-first president of the United States (1929–1933).

Herbert Hoover dedicated nearly fifty years to public service in roles ranging from international relief administrator to president of the United States. Few Americans played as significant a part in American wars or international relations as did Hoover during, and between, the great wars of the twentieth century. Hoover's activities on behalf of the U.S. government and nongovernmental international relief agencies during World War I first garnered him international renown. Deeply influenced both by the Quaker faith and the positivism of the Progressive era, Hoover applied the tenets of cooperative voluntarism and efficiency to the spheres of international relations and trade throughout his long public service.

While living in London in 1914, Hoover witnessed firsthand the commencement of European hostilities and the effects of World War I on noncombatants. As chairman of the American Committee, Hoover volunteered to assist Americans stranded in Europe, helping to repatriate thousands and giving material assistance to those in dire financial conditions. From 1914 to 1917, Hoover acted as the chairman of the Commission for Relief in Belgium (CRB), the nongovernmental international relief agency that raised millions of dollars to relieve the hardships of Belgians struggling to survive between two warring armies. The CRB distributed the aid with the grudging recognition of the belligerent nations.

After the United States entered the war, President Woodrow Wilson appointed Hoover the United States Food Administrator. In this capacity, Hoover managed the conservation and distribution of food material during the U.S. mobilization. Through a publicity campaign stating "Food Will Win the War," Hoover challenged Americans to voluntarily conserve their consumption of vital foodstuffs to help feed the American and Allied armies and Allied nonmilitary populations. By "Hooverizing" on "meatless Tuesdays" and "wheatless Wednesdays," Americans reduced food consumption by 15 percent without mandated rationing.

In 1919 Hoover played a notable role in the Versailles peace process as an economic advisor. More important, he became the director of the American Relief Administration (ARA) in war-ravaged Europe. The ARA ultimately fed 350 million people in twenty-one countries. Hoover acquired the label of the "Great Humanitarian" for his Herculean efforts to stave off starvation and material privation in postwar Europe.

Under Presidents Warren G. Harding and Calvin Coolidge, Hoover served as secretary of commerce. In

Herbert Hoover inspecting a food shipment bound for Europe. GETTY IMAGES

this position, Hoover emphasized the interdependence of the American and European economies in his attempts to redress the war debt and reparations issues. Hoover also called upon his wartime experiences with relief. In 1927, when the Mississippi river flooded in seven states, Hoover helped raise $15 million for the American Red Cross relief effort by appealing directly to the American people in a radio address.

Based on his successful career in public service, Hoover easily won the 1928 presidential election. During his term, he encountered a number of issues relating to American experiences during World War I. In the interests of peace and economic stability, Hoover attempted to lead the world toward disarmament and implemented the Kellogg-Briand Pact outlawing war. The U.S. government under Hoover sanctioned and paid for Gold Star Mothers to travel to Europe to attend the graves of their slain sons. In 1932, during the height of the Great Depression, Hoover faced the unwelcome presence in Washington, D.C., of 20,000 World War I veterans demanding immediate payment of their bonus. Fatefully, the Bonus March, and its dispersal at the hands of the U.S. Army, emerged as a symbol of Hoover's supposed disregard for American suffering during the Depression. Hoover lost the 1932 election to Franklin D. Roosevelt.

STARVATION IN EUROPE AND AMERICAN RELIEF

During World War I the Allies used naval blockades to prevent the enemy from getting supplies from other sources, thus turning hunger into a weapon. As a result, the elderly and children suffered the most because soldiers and military support people received priority in the rationing of food and other necessities.

As the driving force behind the CRB (Commission for Relief in Belgium), which provided foodstuffs to occupied Belgium and France with the assurances of the German government that none of these supplies would be used by the German military, Herbert Hoover was in a position to assess the need for humanitarian relief in other war-torn countries as well. Hoover foresaw the likelihood that at war's end most of the population of Europe, winners and losers alike, would face famine and illness, in part a result of the blockade, in part because of the inability to farm and raise livestock. Hoover did not support the blockade. "I do not believe in starving women and children," he later wrote, recalling, "I did not believe that stunted bodies and deformed minds in the next generation were the foundation upon which to rebuild civilization."

In advance of America's likely entrance into the war, Hoover ordered the stockpiling of food and medical supplies. He left the CRB in capable hands in order to manage the American Relief Administration (ARA), which was responsible for mobilizing food and medical supplies. To Allied thinking, bread ranked with bullets in the inventory of war priorities. Thus the goal of the ARA was to procure enough exports from the United States, Canada, and the West Indies to make up the large deficits of the Allies and certain neutral countries (and after the armistice all of Europe) and to do so without ruining the U.S. economy.

Hoover solicited the voluntary cooperation of individuals, food producers, and restaurant owners to reduce the amount of food consumed by Americans at home. Farmers also voluntarily stepped up production of crops and livestock, so that no Allied servicemen or American civilians were issued short rations during America's involvement in the conflict. After the United States entered the war in 1917, a complex shipping and distribution system was put into place. Like the CRB, the ARA operated as separate departments: one for provisioning of rations, for which people paid a meager sum; and another for benevolence, for which necessities were given at no cost. Hoover ordered that ten to twelve million children in the liberated countries get first priority for provisions for many of them were dangerously malnourished. In the year following the Armistice, the ARA brought in and distributed 27 million tons of food, seeds, clothing, medical and other supplies together valued at $5.5 billion. Among its numerous activities, the ARA directed coal mines and railroad operations and ran a delousing program to obliterate the typhus epidemic that cost over 10,000 lives in eastern Europe. In addition to supervising general relief activities, Hoover created the privately funded Children's Relief Fund, which cared for some 8 million children in central and eastern Europe.

Hoover's post-presidential career showed no signs of weakening his commitment to public affairs. Hoover emerged as a staunch critic of the Roosevelt administration's foreign policy and cautioned that a slide into another world war would have catastrophic effects on American liberties. Although Hoover opposed U.S. involvement in the European conflict between 1939 and 1941, he continued to coordinate humanitarian assistance to noncombatants by aiding Finland and establishing the Polish Relief Commission. After Pearl Harbor, Hoover supported the war and stressed the need for international organizations to construct a lasting peace. Summoned by President Harry Truman, Hoover reexamined food shortages in the United States and conducted worldwide surveys as a member of the Famine Emergency Commission. Until his death in 1964, Hoover cautioned Americans about the spread of Communism but also the expansion in size and scope of the federal government. From World War I to the Cold War, Herbert Hoover was a prominent administrator and public servant, and an influential voice in American society during war.

BIBLIOGRAPHY

Best, Gary Dean. *Herbert Hoover: The Postpresidential Years, 1933–1964.* Stanford, CA: Hoover Institution Press, 1983.

Gelfand, Lawrence E., ed. *Herbert Hoover: The Great War and Its Aftermath, 1914–1923.* Iowa City: University of Iowa Press, 1979.

Nash, George H. *The Life of Herbert Hoover,* 3 vols. New York: Norton, 1983–1996.

Wilson, Joan Hoff. *Herbert Hoover: Forgotten Progressive.* Boston: Little, Brown, 1975.

Internet Resources

The Herbert Hoover Presidential Library-Museum. Available at <http://www.hoover.archives.gov>.

The Hoover Institution on War, Revolution, and Peace. Stanford University. Available at <http://www-hoover.stanford.edu>.

Stephen R. Ortiz

See also: **Bonus March; Gold Star Mothers Pilgrimage; Red Cross, American.**

IMPERIALISM

The close of the nineteenth century witnessed the end of the United States' wars with Native Americans in the western regions of the continent. Along with this military triumph came the close of the American frontier. For many, these two developments signaled the dawning of a new age in the American experience. For others, it foretold a continuation of the tragic flaws in American politics and culture. The repercussions of the Spanish-American War helped to crystallize the issues regarding American imperialism in a new century.

CAUSES AND DEBATES OVER IMPERIALISM

For many turn-of-the-century politicians and business leaders such as Albert Beveridge and William McKinley, William Rockefeller and Russell Sage, the United States needed to expand its production of export goods because domestic consumers no longer could absorb the output of American industries. The saturation of the domestic economy resulted in disastrous, cyclical depressions and financial panics. The response of workers was to unionize, strike, picket, and otherwise clamor for economic reforms that would protect them from the rapacious actions of corporations, banks, and railroads. Although most labor unions opposed the build up to war during the mid-1890s, some workers supported the notion of imperialism because of the promise of greater job security and higher wages by expanding foreign markets. By the time the Spanish-American War took place in 1898, most workers supported it. Consequently, many argued for American imperialism based on the notion that expansion would result in greater business profits, enhanced job creation, and fewer social cleavages. Another point of contention was the perception of America's place in history.

Some writers in this period harkened to America's own experience of breaking away from Britain and believed that the United States should not impose the colonial yoke on anyone else. The philosopher William James was a noted anti-imperialist who castigated the saber-rattling of the period as unprincipled. Others countered by asserting that the "Founding Fathers" had envisioned America as a "city on the hill," which would serve as a beacon of freedom and civilization to the rest of a benighted world. In this interpretation, often invoked by Theodore Roosevelt and political scientist John Burgess, American imperialism simply was another means by which Americans could teach the meaning of liberty and democracy to others. This view gained currency as European imperialists justified their brutal regimes as civilizing missions of one form or another. Indeed, European imperialism served as an incentive in a different way. Roosevelt and his Navy mentor, Alfred T. Mahan, argued that for the United States to remain a great nation, it had to control certain islands, waterways, and build an isthmian canal to connect the Atlantic and Pacific Oceans. Pursuant to this line of reasoning, America could only ensure its strength and security through empire-building. Rudyard Kipling's poem, "The White Man's Burden," encouraged these sentiments. Although many Americans embraced the idea of the United States as a reluctant savior of the world's downtrodden, a vocal number were troubled by the manner in which the rhetoric of salvation differed from the reality of pacification, particularly of people of color. The American Anti-Imperialist League, led by men like Mark Twain, grew from the latter opinion and found powerful evidence to support its position in the aftermath of the Spanish-American War.

UNITED STATES INTERVENTION

The American military's refusal to allow the Cuban rebels to confer on Spain's surrender, the imposition of the Platt Amendment onto the burgeoning government of Cuba, and the destruction of the Filipino insurrection in the early 1900s all seemed to confirm the fears of many that U.S. imperialism meant an extension of the cloak of White Supremacy across the globe. The Platt Amendment (1901), which gave the U.S. the right to intervene in Cuban affairs, stifled self-determination in Cuba. With specific regard to the insurrection in the Philippines following American occupation, Filipino noncombatants made up roughly 90 percent of the more than 200,000 casualties in a war which included the relocation or eradication of entire villages, the implementation of concentration camps and the indiscriminate killing of women and children. Torture, a sad fact of the conflict, was best represented by the "water cure." When using the water cure, U.S. soldiers and physicians forced large volumes of water—sometimes with salt added—into the mouths or noses of Filipinos until they cooperated with their interrogators.

RACISM AND IMPERIALISM

While some were disturbed by the potential for brutality in American imperialism, others opposed it because of its implications for the national identity. These critics feared that American annexation of Cuba, Guam, Puerto Rico, and the Philippines eventually would mean that people in each territory would claim citizenship rights in America. In a nation already violently subjugating its Black, Red, and Yellow populations, the idea of bringing more people of color into the fold was disturbing. Within this debate, African Americans publicly asserted that U.S. im-

perialism meant the extension of American racism across the seas. Indeed, this sentiment was reflected in the oft quoted, though truncated, prophesy by W. E. B. Du Bois: "[t]he problem of the twentieth century is the problem of the color line—the relation of the darker to the lighter races of men in Asia and Africa, in America and the islands of the sea" (*The Souls of Black Folk*, p. 54.).

Indeed, Du Bois' legendary meditation, *The Souls of Black Folk*, captured, in many ways, the numerous factors that fueled the debate over the validity of the extension of American power beyond its borders: economic concerns regarding industrial expansion, jobs, and access to raw materials and foreign markets; ideological concerns pertaining to the notion of American exceptionalism; cultural concerns about race, the people who were certain to fall under the shadow of American might, and whether that shadow concealed a sword or a shield. Adding to this volatile mix was the cementing of European colonialism across Africa and Asia. By the outbreak of World War I, the United States' dealings with Mexico and other parts of Latin America convinced many that America had created an informal empire. Because of vocal opposition in many quarters, the first halting strides of American imperialism in the twentieth century were hotly contested and the competing discourses represented conflicting visions of what America should be.

BIBLIOGRAPHY

Lewis, David Levering. *W.E.B. Du Bois: Biography of a Race, 1868–1919.* New York: Henry Holt & Co., 1993.

Ninkovich, Frank. *The United States and Imperialism.* Malden, MA: Blackwell Publishers, 2001.

Williams, William A. *The Tragedy of American Diplomacy.* New York: Dell Publishing Co., 1972.

Zinn, Howard. *A People's History of the United States: 1492–Present* New York: Harper Perennial, 1995.

Zwick, Jim, ed. *Mark Twain's Weapons of Satire: Anti-Imperialism Writings on the Philippine-American War.* Syracuse, NY: Syracuse University Press, 1992.

George White, Jr.

See also: **Du Bois, W. E. B.; McKinley, William; Peace Movements, 1898–1945; Roosevelt, Theodore.**

ISOLATIONISM

Isolationism is the belief that the United States must limit its involvement in world affairs. Although deeply ingrained in the national character, isolationism grew into a dominant issue only after American participation in World War I. Prior to that war, isolationism took the form of an ideology that opposed imperialism and the existence of a standing army. It did not prevent significant American involvement in both Latin America and the Far East. By the late 1890s, as the nation moved toward war with Spain over the fate of Cuba, isolationism remained a relatively insignificant issue. The hesitancy of Presidents Grover Cleveland and William McKinley to wage war was attributable not to isolationist sentiment but rather to anti-imperialism, doubt over the prospects for successful Cuban self-government, and reluctance to fight a European power.

LEGACY OF WORLD WAR I

As America inched toward war with the Central Powers after the outbreak of World War I in the summer of 1914, isolationism once again failed to prove itself a deciding factor. From the outset of the conflict, the United States grew deeply involved as both creditor and munitions supplier to the nations fighting Germany while clinging to the traditional policy of neutrality in European affairs. Although the powerful Socialist Party of America and progressives from both major parties opposed American entrance in the war out of fear that domestic reform would suffer, their opposition did not prove decisive. Rather, divided ethnic loyalties, vain hopes for a U.S.-brokered diplomatic settlement, and the lack of a land force capable of large-scale intervention explain President Woodrow Wilson's decision to avoid entering the war until 1917.

Similarly, isolationism had far less to do with the Senate's rejection of the Versailles Treaty of 1919, which brought the war to a close and created the League of Nations, than did other issues. Many Senate opponents feared that membership in the League would limit American sovereignty by requiring the United States to join fellow League members in waging war against future aggressors. Others balked at membership in an organization that included both Asian and African nations, and some objected to the League's oversight of domestic affairs such as immigration and labor policy. Although Midwestern and Western progressives, known as the Irreconcilables, unequivocally opposed membership, fifty-three senators, reflecting prevailing public opinion, approved membership with few, if any, reservations. The ultimate failure of the Senate to approve membership had far more to do with political differences and President Wilson's refusal to compromise with the Senate's League opponents than with isolationism.

During the interwar period isolationism grew into a potent force. Americans were mourning their losses in World War I, and suspicion was growing that France, Britain, or even American finance and munitions interests had maneuvered Wilson into declaring war. Isolationism began to warp American diplomacy and slowed

the nation's reaction to German, Italian, and Japanese aggression. It prompted the Senate to approve the 1935 Neutrality Act, requiring the United States to embargo all war material to belligerent powers; the 1936 Neutrality Act, forbidding U.S. loans to nations at war; and the 1937 Pittman Resolution, prohibiting Americans to travel on the ships of belligerent powers.

However, although these acts were an important gauge of public sentiment, they do not convey the complete picture. The force of isolationist sentiment should not, in fact, be overstated, as the United States remained an active participant in interwar world affairs. The United States supported naval disarmament at the 1921–1922 Washington Conference and the 1930 London Conference, and it pioneered the abolition of war in the 1928 Kellogg-Briand Pact. Isolationist sentiment did not prevent the gradual expansion of the United States Navy during the 1930s nor its phenomenal growth after the fall of France in June 1940. Moreover, the army's meager growth is attributable in large part to America's traditional disdain for a large peacetime army coupled with the effects of the Great Depression rather than to isolationism.

AMERICAN RESPONSE TO WORLD WAR II

Following France's surrender, concern for England's survival mounted, and interventionism gradually eclipsed isolationism. In September 1940 President Roosevelt announced his agreement with England in which England would receive fifty American destroyers in exchange for eight British bases. That same month Congress approved the first peacetime draft in American history. Following Roosevelt's reelection to an unprecedented third term in November 1940, the president moved swiftly to extend ever-greater aid to the Axis foes. In March 1941 Congress approved the Lend-Lease Act, with an initial appropriation of $7 billion. Over the next four months, Roosevelt extended U.S. naval patrols deep into the Atlantic, dispatched U.S. ground forces to Greenland and then Iceland, and froze Japanese assets in the United States.

In the final months before Pearl Harbor, isolationism proved troublesome but ever more negligible. Historians have pointed to polls indicating that more than 80 percent of the American public firmly opposed American entry into the war as late as October 1941. But public sentiment did not hamstring the president. In August Roosevelt met with British Prime Minister Winston Churchill for four days in Placentia Bay off the Newfoundland coast. The following month he ordered the Atlantic Fleet to shoot on sight any Axis warships in America's Atlantic neutrality zone. In November Congress dealt isolationists a body blow when it repealed the

The crowd at the 1941 America First Committee rally in the Chicago Arena listen to the organization's chairmen General Robert Wood and Colonel Charles Lindbergh give speeches promulgating isolationism and cutting off aid to Britain. TIME LIFE PICTURES/GETTY IMAGES

1939 Neutrality Act, paving the way for U.S. vessels to convoy war material to Britain. Isolationism, in short, does not explain Roosevelt's decision to avoid war with the Axis in the autumn of 1941. Rather, with Lend-Lease aid flowing to the main Axis opponents and with industry and the armed forces still mobilizing for conflict, strategic interest dictated that the United States remain out of the global war.

With the Japanese attack on Pearl Harbor, isolationist sentiment all but vanished. In July 1945 Congress approved the Bretton Woods agreement, which established both the International Monetary Fund and the World Bank. That same month the Senate approved the United Nations Charter with only two dissenting votes, committing America to an internationalist future.

Although a significant issue between the world wars, isolationism faded rapidly after 1941. With the onset of the Cold War in summer 1945 and the extraordinary de-mands that the global conflict forced on the United Sates, isolationism moved to the fringes of American society, where it has remained ever since.

BIBLIOGRAPHY

Dallek, Robert. *Franklin D. Roosevelt and American Foreign Policy, 1932–1945.* New York: Oxford University Press, 1979.

Dallek, Robert. *The American Style of Foreign Policy.* New York: Oxford University Press, 1983.

Leuchtenburg, William E. *Franklin D. Roosevelt and the New Deal, 1932–1940.* New York: Harper and Row, 1963.

Patterson Thomas, G.; Clifford, Garry J.; and Hagan, Kenneth J. *American Foreign Relations*, Vol. 4. Boston: Houghton Mifflin, 2000.

Sidney L. Pash

See also: **Disarmament and Arms Control, 1898–1945; Peace Movements, 1898–1945; United Nations.**

JAPANESE AMERICANS, WORLD WAR II

Less than three months after the Japanese attack on Pearl Harbor on December 7, 1941, President Franklin D. Roosevelt signed Executive Order 9066, which resulted in the mass removal and incarceration of all Japanese Americans living on the West Coast. The government's decision, made in the context of long and often intense anti-Japanese sentiment on the West Coast, ultimately resulted in the imprisonment of 119,803 Japanese Americans. American citizens constituted almost two-thirds of these prisoners held without trial. Although many inmates eventually obtained wartime releases from the camps, forced exile from their homes and incarceration produced lasting consequences.

The government's decision to incarcerate Japanese Americans was in part attributable to Americans' racist attitudes. General John L. DeWitt of the Western Defense Command, for example, explained the need to imprison all Japanese Americans by asserting that "a Jap is a Jap. . . . It makes no difference whether he is an American citizen, he is still Japanese" (Grodzins, p. 362). DeWitt expressed the widespread racial belief that Japanese Americans were disloyal and devious. Wartime hysteria also contributed to the government's policies. Allegations of subversive Japanese-American activities at Pearl Harbor, which remain unsubstantiated today, reinforced fears held by many Americans of sabotage, espionage, and fifth column activities. DeWitt and West Coast politicians such as California Attorney General Earl Warren supported these rumors by warning that the absence of sabotage immediately after December 7 suggested a well-concealed plan to attack later.

As the military, newspapers, and the public demanded a response to the supposed threat of Japanese Americans, the government moved toward removal and incarceration. Within seventy-two hours of Pearl Harbor, in fact, DeWitt forwarded the first proposal for the mass exile of Japanese Americans, which was supported by Major General Allen W. Gullion, the Provost Marshal General, and Karl R. Bendetsen, chief of the Aliens Division in Gullion's office. Although Attorney General Francis Biddle expressed misgivings, the Justice Department deferred to the War Department's claims of "military necessity."

Executive Order 9066, issued on February 19, 1942, allowed the military to exclude "any or all persons" from "military areas." Despite the nonspecific language, the

Ed Ichiyama on April 3, 2003, at a Medal of Honor exhibit following ceremonies marking the sixtieth anniversary of the forming of the Army's World War II 442nd Regimental Combat Team, made up almost entirely of Japanese Americans. The team was one of the most decorated units in U.S. military history. AP/WIDE WORLD PHOTOS

decree affected only Japanese Americans. The military's initial control over the inmates was eventually transferred to the civilian War Relocation Authority (WRA). By mid-1942 the WRA began a program to release many of its prisoners. Fearing that camp life bred frustration, fear, bitterness, and the possibility of the permanent institutionalization of Japanese Americans, the WRA initially allowed temporary releases for seasonal agricultural labor and later permitted indefinite releases for higher education and employment.

Military service provided another avenue of escape from the camps. Although the War Department had decided to reject Japanese Americans for military service after Pearl Harbor, the military soon reversed its position and allowed WRA inmates to volunteer and serve. The army officially announced its new policy in January 1943; the special combat team formed as a result, the 442nd, subsequently earned fame with its slogan "Go for Broke" and its reputation as the most decorated unit of its size. In early 1944 the War Department reinstituted the draft for all eligible Japanese Americans, both inside and outside the camps. Although the War Department also changed its regulations so Japanese Americans could be assigned as

individual replacements in both theaters, most draftees continued to serve with the segregated 442nd. The Military Intelligence Service Language School received top priority, and any Japanese American who met its linguistic qualifications was sent there. By the end of the war, about 23,000 Japanese Americans—about one-half from the continental United States—had served in the military.

The mass exile and incarceration of Japanese Americans during World War II had important consequences for American society and culture. The government's actions suggest that substantial prejudice existed at home during a war fought against fascism. Both the Supreme Court, in its *Hirabayashi, Korematsu* and *Endo* decisions, and Congress strongly supported the wartime camps. This support led to Title II of the Internal Security Act of 1950. Title II established what Congressmen defined as "fairer" camps for Communists in the event of an internal security emergency declared by the president. Title II was not repealed until 1971. In 1983 the Commission on the Wartime Relocation and Internment of Civilians (CWRIC) released *Personal Justice Denied*, which noted that exile and incarceration had resulted from "race prejudice, war hysteria, and a failure of polit-

GERMAN AMERICANS DURING WORLD WARS I AND II

Japanese-Americans were not the only group to feel the sting of discrimination because of war with their country of origin. In World War I, when the United States declared war on Germany, German-American citizens were also discriminated against and made objects of suspicion. Many citizens questioned the loyalty and patriotism of recent German immigrants because they spoke a different language and practiced different customs. In some communities Americans insisted that the German language not be taught in school or spoken in public. Some people changed the name sauerkraut to victory cabbage to remove any reference to Germany and to show their loyalty to the United States. Some Germans changed their names so they sounded more English. During World War II, German-Americans and Italian-Americans experienced less suspicion and hostility, which was likely the result of over a generation of integration in American society. American resentment focused on Japanese-Americans because of Japan's attack on the United States and also because that attack released strong racial hostility that had been partly kept in check by peace.

John P. Resch

ical leadership." As a result of the CWRIC's report, which led to passage of the Civil Liberties Act of 1988, redress payments of $20,000 to surviving prisoners of the camps began in the late 1980s.

BIBLIOGRAPHY

Daniels, Roger. *Concentration Camps, North America: Japanese in the United States and Canada During World War II*. Malabar, FL: Robert E. Krieger Publishing Company, 1981.

Daniels, Roger. *Asian America: Chinese and Japanese in the United States Since 1850*. Seattle: University of Washington Press, 1988.

Grodzins, Morton. *Americans Betrayed: Politics and the Japanese Evacuation*. Chicago: University of Chicago Press, 1949.

Harth, Erica, ed. *Last Witnesses: Reflections on the Wartime Internment of Japanese Americans*. New York: Palgrave, 2001.

Robinson, Greg. *By Order of the President: FDR and the Internment of Japanese Americans*. Cambridge, MA: Harvard University Press, 2001.

Allan W. Austin

See also: Civil Liberties, World War II; War, Impact on Ethnic Groups.

JOURNALISM, SPANISH-AMERICAN WAR

Many historians consider the Spanish-American War to be a conflict that American journalists not only reported but helped create. The United States had complex motives for going to war against Spain in 1898; sympathy for its Cuban neighbors mixed with the nation's own global ambitions. But Americans were also driven to war by their emotions, stirred by a series of newspaper stories.

For decades, Cuban patriots had waged guerrilla warfare against Spanish rule. Outnumbered and poor, the revolutionaries tried to disrupt the Cuban economy by burning sugarcane plantations. The Spanish retaliated harshly, executing suspected rebels and herding peasants into camps where thousands succumbed to disease and starvation. These brutal measures provided stirring copy for American journalists, who invariably sympathized with the Cuban underdogs.

Still, the public might have paid little attention to the conflict had it not coincided with a newspaper circulation war in New York. At the end of the nineteenth century, more than half a dozen newspapers competed in the influential New York market. The leader was Joseph Pulitzer's *World*, which pioneered a "new journalism" that appealed to a broad audience through reforming crusades, catchy headlines, and sensational human interest stories. In 1895, Pulitzer was challenged by William Randolph Hearst, an impulsive millionaire who bought the New York *Journal* and took Pulitzer's techniques to an extreme that critics called yellow journalism.

Although he probably felt genuine concern for the Cubans, Hearst also recognized the ingredients of a great story. One *Journal* reporter recounted that Hearst sent the artist Frederic Remington to provide sketches of the conflict. Finding no fighting, Remington cabled to Hearst, asking to come home. Hearst allegedly replied, "You furnish the pictures and I'll furnish the war." Some doubt that such an exchange ever took place, but the tale captures Hearst's arrogant determination not simply to report events but to provoke them.

When the Spanish searched some Cuban women on an American ship, Hearst's headline screamed, "Does Our Flag Protect Women?" He used Remington's lurid and misleading drawing, suggesting that male soldiers had strip-searched the women, to underscore the point. Hearst also championed the cause of Evangelina Cisneros, a young woman imprisoned for attempting to

New Yorkers gathering around a bulletin board with news from the New York *Journal* during the Spanish-American War, ca. 1898. The *Journal,* along with another New York newspaper, the *World,* were the pioneers of "new journalism." It was the sensationist stories by these two newspapers that became known as "yellow journalism." © CORBIS

kidnap a Spanish officer. Cisneros claimed she was only trying to repel his advances. Hearst depicted the beautiful Cisneros as a symbol of national liberation, a "Cuban Joan of Arc," and recruited leading American women to campaign for her release. When Spain refused, Hearst sent a reporter to break Cisneros out of jail, bringing her to New York in October 1897 for a triumphant reception. These were examples of what Hearst proudly called "journalism that acts."

Many of Heart's excesses were denounced by rival papers, but his escapades drew readers, encouraging other

yellow papers to offer sensational accounts of the Cuban conflict. The battle of words was further fueled by Cuban exiles. Eager to draw Americans into the war, these Cuban propagandists fed stories to eager editors, including false reports of Cuban victories and exaggerated tales of Spanish atrocities. The Cubans scored a direct hit against their foe when they intercepted a cable sent by Enrique Dupuy de Lôme, Spain's ambassador in Washington, in which he ridiculed President William McKinley. Hearst printed the telegram with a headline denouncing it as "the worst insult" ever.

The wreck of the USS *Maine* in the Havana, Cuba, harbor in 1898. Although there was no direct evidence that linked Spain to the explosion of the *Maine,* the destruction of the ship influenced the United States to declare war on Spain. © BETTMANN/CORBIS

Hope for a peaceful resolution was destroyed on February 15, 1898, when the USS *Maine,* an American battleship moored in Havana harbor, exploded, killing 266 sailors. No evidence linked Spain to the tragedy, and a 1976 Navy investigation concluded that the explosion was probably an accident. Most American papers withheld judgment, but Hearst insisted that the *Maine* was destroyed by an "enemy's secret infernal machine," a claim

the *Journal* supported with a fanciful illustration of an imaginary Spanish mine. Hearst assembled his own committee of U.S. congressmen to visit Havana harbor; they traveled on his yacht and filed stories for the *Journal.*

Historians have often blamed Hearst and Pulitzer for whipping up war fever, but McKinley declared war, on April 11, 1898, for more complex reasons. Although newspapers did contribute to public resentment against

Spain, U.S. leaders were also responding to real, ongoing turmoil in Cuba and understood the war as a chance to advance America's global interests. Although Hearst boasted that this was "the *Journal*'s war," that claim exaggerates his actual influence on public opinion.

In spite of the excesses of yellow journalism, the record of journalists in what one historian has called "the correspondents' war" is not all negative. Many newspapers avoided and even criticized the sensationalism of the yellow press. Before the war, some journalists risked imprisonment to expose human rights abuses against the Cubans. During the conflict, several journalists reported on American military incompetence, while others risked their lives to provide first-hand accounts of battle, including stirring tales about the Rough Riders that made Teddy Roosevelt a national hero. Some fine reporting was done by Richard Harding Davis, Sylvester Scovel, and the novelist Stephen Crane. African-American reporters sometimes challenged the nation's imperialist expansion, especially as the war devolved into a bloody three-year effort to subdue the Philippines.

Although the Spanish-American War was not caused solely by a circulation battle among New York newspapers, the story of yellow journalism's distortions and interventions in Cuba remains a cautionary tale about the power of the mass media to shape public opinion and create war fever that government can use to carry out its military and economic policies.

BIBLIOGRAPHY

Browne, Charles H. *The Correspondents' War: Journalists in the Spanish-American War.* New York: Scribner, 1967.

Campbell, W. Joseph. *Yellow Journalism: Puncturing the Myths, Defining the Legacies.* Westport, CT: Praeger, 2001.

Marks, George P., ed. *The Black Press Views American Imperialism (1898–1900).* New York: Arno, 1971.

Pérez, Louis A., Jr. *War of 1898: The United States and Cuba in History and Historiography.* Chapel Hill: University of North Carolina Press, 1998.

Swanberg, W. A. *Citizen Hearst: A Biography of William Randolph Hearst.* New York: Scribner, 1961.

Ernest Freeberg

See also: Imperialism; Journalism, World War I; McKinley, William.

JOURNALISM, WORLD WAR I

World War I had a great impact on journalism. The attempt of the Woodrow Wilson administration to censor not only newspaper accounts of the war but books, magazines, and other attempts to present the truth caused a strong reaction by the press in the effort to gain journalistic freedom. Moreover, the public relations manipulation of the Wilson administration, what we would today call "spin doctoring," led to a significant increase in objectivity of press accounts during and after the war.

Walter Lippmann, a highly respected journalist and commentator, warned at the time that manipulation of the press through government's "public relations" was highly dangerous, and could send nations spinning into war. That legacy of distrust has continued to the present day, with perhaps a pause for World War II when there was less public display of pessimism regarding the war's aims.

The military began its own newspaper during World War I, the *Stars and Stripes*. Although it tried to censor articles that it deemed inappropriate, it often failed and stories of the ingenuity of its reporters are legendary. Additionally, it was a source of change in overall American life. The increase in American advertising connected with the war, for example, was a clear example of tying patriotism to American commercial enterprise. The new cigarette Lucky Strike, launched in 1917, got a great boost from the war through its connection with the American doughboy. The Bull Durham Company's slogan tied rolling your own to "The 'Makings' of a Nation." Thirty-six million sacks, two million pounds, of Bull Durham were sent to American troops in Europe monthly, and ads stated that every single one was "chock-full of real American sentiment and love for you." For those people who weren't smokers, there was chewing gum, heavily advertised in *Stars and Stripes*.

The press influenced the way many people viewed the average doughboy. It presented a picture of the wholesome soldier, plugging along with optimism in the face of trying circumstances. Soldiers were depicted as human, people readers could recognize, a tradition that has carried on to the present day.

After the war the press remained suspicious of government attempts to manipulate reporting. Journalists developed a strong creed, holding that with very few exceptions the government should trust the professionalism of the press over claims of "national security." There was a strong sense that too often public officials simply wished to hide their errors, rather than protect public interests, when they claimed national security as a means for their imposition of censorship.

Therefore, the press since World War I has embraced a doctrine of objectivity to protect itself, and the public, from government wartime propaganda. Walter Lippmann advocated the application of the scientific method to the press and its sources. It would, he hoped, serve as a check on subjective interpretation of facts. This was also a means of protest against the famous "Red

Scare" in which the government went on a witch hunt to jail anyone who appeared to be against the war or who expressed radical ideas during its aftermath.

World War I witnessed major attacks on the press and its members who dared oppose the official Wilson Propaganda line. This led to the embrace of objectivity at a time when it was difficult to be objective. During the war *The Stars and Stripes* showed an interesting mix of independence and literary elegance while walking a fine line to keep from being censored beyond credibility. Skepticism of government sources has affected press relations ever since, and has placed journalists in an adversarial role with respect to official representatives of the government.

BIBLIOGRAPHY

Applegate, Edd. *Print and Broadcast Journalism: A Critical Examination.* Westport, CT: Praeger Publishers, 1996.

Bovée, Warren G. *Discovering Journalism.* Westport, CT: Greenwood Press, 1999.

Connery, Thomas B., ed. *A Sourcebook of American Literary Journalism: Representative Writers in an Emerging Genre.* New York: Greenwood Press, 1992.

Cornebise, Alfred E. *The Stars and Stripes: Doughboy Journalism in World War I.* Westport, CT: Greenwood Press, 1984.

Durham, Meenakshi Gigi. "On the Relevance of Standpoint Epistemology to the Practice of Journalism: The Case for 'Strong Objectivity.'" *Communication Theory* 8, no. 2 (1998): 117–140.

Iggers, Jeremy. *Good News, Bad News: Journalism Ethics and the Public Interest.* Boulder, CO: Westview Press, 1998.

Stoker, Kevin. "Existential Objectivity: Freeing Journalists to Be Ethical." *Journal of Mass Media Ethics* 1, no.1 (1995): 5–22.

Willis, Jim. *Journalism: State of the Art.* New York: Praeger, 1990.

Frank A. Salamone

JOURNALISM, WORLD WAR II

By all measures, war reporting came of age between 1939 and 1945. The global conflagration of World War II elicited a massive response from the free press around the world. In countries under repressive regimes, print journalism and radio continued as well, but their effectiveness was compromised by rigid central control and the dictates of party propaganda.

In the United States, newspapers and radio broadcasting were already covering the war in Europe beginning with the German invasion of Poland on September 1, 1939, and the declaration of war two days later by France and Great Britain. Likewise, in the Far East correspondents were fanning out to chronicle the territorial aggressions of Imperial Japan. Even though America did not go to war officially until after the Japanese attack on Pearl Harbor on December 7, 1941, the press was by that time deeply involved in reporting the impending conflict for the United States.

Wartime print journalists fell into roughly three categories: 1) wire service reporters for the two major organizations, the Associated Press and United Press; 2) stringers and correspondents for the large metropolitan daily newspapers like the *New York Times*, *Chicago Tribune*, and *Los Angeles Times*; and 3) correspondents or freelance writers for weekly magazines like *Life*, *Time*, *Newsweek*, and the *New Yorker*. The majority of these journalists were sent overseas to cover the battles from the frontlines after receiving press accreditation by the War Department. They wore uniforms, yet they were considered noncombatants and not allowed to carry sidearms or to fire any kind of weapon at the enemy. Because of their proximity to the actual fighting, a number of American journalists were killed, wounded, or captured. Some who were captured were later executed by the enemy.

Journalists during the war in Europe were allowed to cover virtually all phases of the military operations, including actual combat. Usually, this consisted of "hitching a ride" in a jeep with officers and enlisted men and going up to the front where the fighting was taking place. Typically, they would interview the soldiers and jot down what they saw in terms of the casualties and battlefield successes, then return at the end of the day to press headquarters to type up the story, clear it through censors, and send it back by radio via London for cable transmission to New York and other cities. Each reporter signed a pledge to clear all stories through military censorship. Journalists who failed to do so were subject to military tribunals, but were more likely to be sent home. Most correspondents honored the pledge and scrupulously submitted all stories to censors who would use blue pencils and razor blades to eliminate words that might "give aid and comfort to the enemy." Thus, important stories were often delayed several days to a week before they appeared in American newspapers and magazines.

In 1942 President Franklin D. Roosevelt established the Office of War Information (OWI), and under the leadership of Elmer Davis it served to promote public support for the American war effort at home and abroad. Davis and the OWI played an instrumental role in prodding the American military to divulge greater information to journalists and to release more graphic imagery related to the cost of war. At the same time, the OWI, along with the military, actively encouraged journalists to report favorable stories supportive of the war effort and

War correspondent Ernie Pyle (second from right) on Okinawa in 1945. Ernie Pyle was one of the best-known journalists during World War II. © CORBIS

guidelines on what reporters should avoid covering. Although Second World War journalism would be marked by greater objectivity and depth of reporting than the bombastic coverage of the First World War, many journalists responded to the calls of military officials and the OWI to produce coverage that remained supportive of the war.

BILL MAULDIN AND ERNIE PYLE

Two of the most famous World War II journalists were Bill Mauldin and Ernie Pyle. Mauldin, an army enlisted man, was actually a gifted cartoonist for *Stars and Stripes*, the army's free daily newspaper. Mauldin's "Willie and Joe" drawings, later collected in *Up Front*, made him the favorite of GIs and their families back home. The Willie and Joe cartoons depict grizzled, dog-faced soldiers who retain the will to fight but who have grown weary of the numbing routine of cold, hunger, and the bureaucratic mindlessness of the army. As Mauldin wrote, they were men "who are able to fight a ruthless war against ruthless enemies, and still grin at themselves."

Ernie Pyle was probably the best-known journalist of World War II. His weekly columns for Scripps-Howard newspapers were entitled "The Roving Reporter." Pyle won a Pulitzer prize for his eloquent reporting during the Italian campaign. His famous "Captain Waskow" story, describing the anger and sadness of the men when their beloved captain's body is brought down from an Italian mountain, was the centerpiece for this recognition. Pyle's close friend and fellow journalist Don Whitehead, who covered the war for the Associated Press, remembers how the story was created: "He [Pyle] was absolutely whipped physically and mentally. I was with him in the room where he wrote the story. He asked me to read it, because he was afraid he had lost his touch. He said, 'I don't think it's worth a damn. I've just lost my feeling.' I read it and then told him, 'My God, Ernie, if you've lost your touch writing that story, I hope I can lose mine!'" Pyle was shot dead by a Japanese sniper on the island of Ie Shima, near Okinawa, on April 17, 1945, fulfilling his premonition that he would not live through the war.

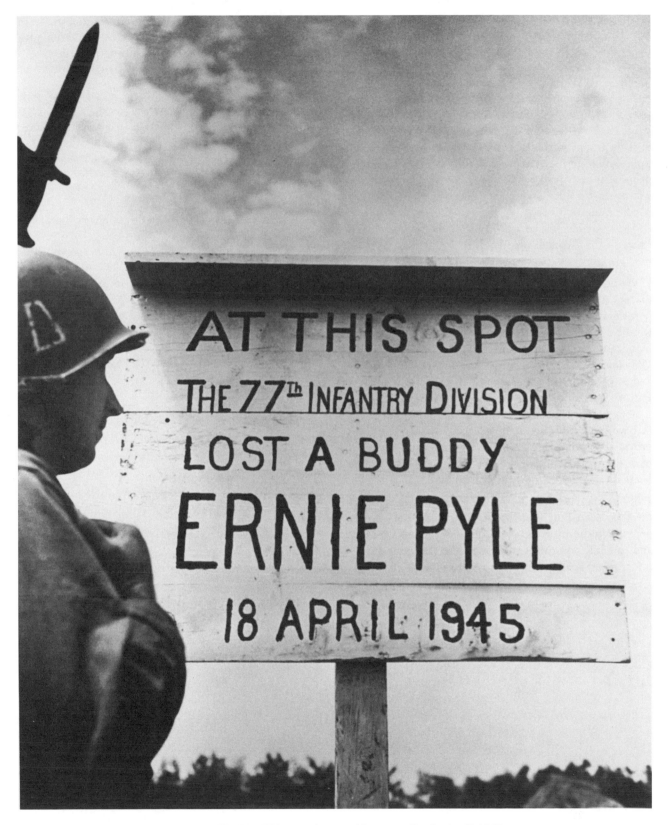

Memorial to Ernie Pyle, who was killed in Okinawa by machine gun fire in April 1945. © CORBIS

STARS AND STRIPES AND RADIO

The U.S. military provided its own unique coverage of the war in the Pacific and in Europe through *Stars and Stripes*. This soldier's newspaper originated in 1861 during the Civil War and resurfaced in World War I in 1918, but its publication was short-lived and did not continue after 1919. *Stars and Stripes* reemerged as a tabloid on April 18, 1942, with its primary aim as a morale booster for U.S. troops, and has been published ever since. Multiple editions of the newspaper during the European campaign reflected the far-flung operational theaters of the war against Hitler and Mussolini—North Africa, the Mediterranean, Europe. A Pacific version of *Stars and Stripes* was inaugurated in May 1945 as the war moved closer to the Japanese mainland.

Another essential perspective in the media coverage of World War II was afforded by radio. The major broadcasters, ABC, CBS, and NBC, all sent journalists to report the war. Some of the most famous of these reporters were Edward R. Murrow, best known for his poignant broadcasts from London during the Nazi air raids; William L. Shirer, whose riveting reports from Berlin and Paris described the Battle of Britain and the fall of Paris in 1940; and others such as Eric Sevareid, Charles Collingwood, and Howard K. Smith, who would go on to have successful careers in television news. Live radio provided an immediacy in the living rooms of Americans back home that anticipated the "television war" of the Vietnam conflict in the 1960s and 1970s.

Although wartime journalists covered campaigns and the men who fought in them, they could not entirely practice freedom of the press. Journalism was censored and carefully controlled to support the war effort by reinforcing an image of Americans at war that would maintain morale on the homefront. Thus in journalism, as in other facets of American life, war redefines, and often restricts, liberties taken for granted during peacetime.

BIBLIOGRAPHY

Bernstein, Mark; Lubertozzi, Alex; and Rather, Dan (CD Narrator). *World War II on the Air: Edward R. Murrow and the Broadcasts that Riveted a Nation*. Naperville, IL: Sourcebooks, 2003.

Knightley, Phillip. *The First Casualty, From the Crimea to Vietnam: The War Correspondent as Hero, Propagandist, and Myth Maker*. New York: Harcourt Brace Jovanovich, 1975.

Mauldin, Bill. *Up Front*. New York: Norton, 2000.

Meyer, Robert E., ed. *The* Stars and Stripes *Story of World War II*. New York: D. McKay, 1960.

Murrow, Edward R. *In Search of Light: The Broadcasts of Edward R. Murrow, 1938–1961*. New York: Knopf, 1967.

Pyle, Ernie. *Brave Men*. Lincoln: University of Nebraska Press, 2001.

Reporting World War II, Part 1: American Journalism 1938–1944, Part 2: American Journalism 1944–1946. New York: Library of America, 1995.

Romeiser, John B. *Beachhead Don: Reporting the War from the European Theater: 1942–1945*. New York: Fordham University Press, 2004.

Shirer, William L. *Berlin Diary: The Journal of a Foreign Correspondent, 1934-1941*. New York: Knopf, 1941.

Tobin, James. *Ernie Pyle's War: America's Eyewitness to World War II*. New York: Free Press, 1997.

Internet Resource

European and Pacific *Stars and Stripes*. Available from <www.estripes.com>.

John B. Romeiser

See also: **Literature, World War II; Propaganda, War.**

LABOR, WORLD WAR I

World War I had a profound impact on American society, expanding the size, role, and power of the federal government and dramatically changing its relationship with both business and labor. Wartime expansion brought together government and corporate America as never before, planting the seeds for the massive bureaucratic state that would become the American political economy. Prior to the war, many Progressive reformers fought for a more active government and regulation of businesses to combat abuses in the workplace and problems associated with the rapidly growing cities. In the absence of the right to bargain collectively, workers struggled with low wages, long hours, unsafe working conditions, child labor, and other prolonged forms of exploitation. It would take a world war to bring about improvement for many working Americans. But although World War I brought gains for the national trade unions, and especially for the American Federation of Labor (AFL), the Industrial Workers of the World (IWW) became a victim of wartime hysteria and antiradicalism.

WAR INDUSTRIES BOARD

When the United States entered World War I, it became clear that it needed an organization to oversee the manufacturing and distribution of war products that were so desperately needed by both the American and Allied troops. By the summer of 1917, President Woodrow Wilson's administration had established the War Industries Board (WIB)—under the leadership of the Wall Street stock speculator Bernard M. Baruch—to serve as the center of industrial mobilization. WIB war contracts ensured a rapid increase in production by negotiating fair prices that guaranteed company profits. Government wartime agencies had unparalleled control over shipping and trade and virtually took over the operation of the nation's railroad, telephone, and telegraph systems. The Lever Act and the Fuel Control Act of 1917 gave President Wilson unmatched power over food production, commodity prices, raw materials, and the nation's fuel resources. These changes did not occur without the assistance of big business, and many corporate leaders became dollar-a-day men, heading up the some five thousand newly created federal agencies for the token payment of one dollar per day.

Government war contracts translated into business expansion, and over a million new laborers were needed for industry and agriculture. But massive military mobilization

U.S. Employment Service Department of Labor poster from ca. 1919. © SWIM INK/CORBIS

coincided with the sudden waning of immigration, creating a critical labor shortage. The war also reignited long-standing domestic labor problems. With inflation rising and prices escalating, in 1917 workers demanded immediate changes through thousands of strikes, involving more than one million workers.

AMERICAN FEDERATION OF LABOR

Faced with labor unrest that drained the nation and disrupted production, President Wilson set up the National War Labor Board (NWLB) to address laborers' issues, stabilize the workforce, and arbitrate between labor and management. Labor attorney Frank Walsh steered the NWLB and proved to be sympathetic to the problems facing the American worker. Former president Howard H. Taft joined Walsh at the helm. Samuel Gompers, president of the AFL, quickly allied trade unionism with support of the war and became a member of the NWLB. The AFL was a union of skilled workers with a membership of over two million in 1914. Unlike the IWW, which denounced the nation's capitalist economic system

as oppressive and exploitative, AFL leaders believed that business unionism would bring about increased democracy and a redistribution of capital in the workplace.

Government regulation of the American labor force brought changes for most workers. Men deemed indispensable to the war economy received exemptions from the draft, and those who were ineligible for military service due to age or health continued in their positions; however, African Americans and women made inroads into jobs from which they had previously been excluded, and Mexican contract laborers were allowed to fill some positions. Improvements for workers included increased wages, reduced hours, and perhaps most significantly the NWLB supported workers' right to organize and bargain collectively with management. With war contracts in hand, the government also pressed for the eight-hour day, overtime pay, and enforcement of the federal ban on child labor. These changes brought about an expansion of union membership from 2.7 million in 1916 to over 5 million by 1920, over 3 million of whom were in the AFL.

INDUSTRIAL WORKERS OF THE WORLD

However, in the supercharged patriotic atmosphere of World War I, labor radicals came to be considered enemies of the state, and Justice Department officials pursued IWW leaders and dismantled the union. The Industrial Workers of the World (also known as the Wobblies) were a socialist union that developed in opposition to the AFL's restrictive focus on skilled workers to the exclusion of the unskilled. It was organized as an inclusive industrial union, accepting all workers regardless of skill level or trade. Unlike the AFL, the IWW denounced the ongoing conflict as a capitalist's war and continued its struggle to reform the nation's economy. Rising concerns over the IWW's wartime expansion, especially in jobs necessary to the war industry, led the U.S. government to take action—harassing, arresting, jailing, and at times deporting IWW leaders under a broad interpretation of the wartime Espionage Act. It was in this atmosphere that the U.S. government arrested and jailed IWW leaders and tried IWW President William Haywood under the Federal Espionage and Sedition Acts, after he called a strike in a war-sensitive industry. Haywood was convicted and sentenced to thirty years in prison but fled the county when he was released on bail. The antiradical frenzy continued into the postwar period, and the government's harassment and prosecution of IWW leaders seriously crippled membership in the Industrial Workers of the World.

POSTWAR PERIOD

With the Armistice of November 11, 1918, the United States looked forward to a new and brighter future. The war had dramatically increased the federal government's regulatory role and gave it unprecedented power to oversee the economy. It also resulted in renewed corporate consolidation and a new collaboration between the government, business, and labor.

But the economic boom that had improved the lives of many American workers came to a sudden end with postwar inflation and rising unemployment, which coincided with the return of some four million soldiers, sailors, and marines. Within months of the end of World War I, canceled government contracts and renewed economic hardship led to relentless strikes as workers struggled to keep the gains they had made during the war. In 1919 alone, over 3,300 strikes involving more than four million workers shook the nation. The U.S. Labor Department reported strikes in twenty-four states. In 1919, an anti-Communist red scare and a national recession magnified the intensity of the postwar crisis. By the early 1920s, economic improvements and the celebratory mood of the Roaring Twenties gave the nation hope that the worst was behind it, but in 1929 the Great Depression began, putting an end to that hope.

BIBLIOGRAPHY

Hawley, Ellis. *The Great War and the Search for a Modern Order: A History of the American People and Their Institutions, 1917–1933,* 2d edition. New York: St. Martin's Press, 1992

Kennedy, David M. *Over Here: The First World War and American Society.* New York: Oxford University Press, 1980.

McCartin, Joseph A. *Labor's Great War: The Struggle for Industrial Democracy and the Origins of Modern American Labor Relations, 1912–1921.* Chapel Hill: University of North Carolina Press, 1997.

Nancy Gentile Ford

See also: **Economy, World War I; Financing, World War I; Ford, Henry; Women, Employment of.**

LABOR, WORLD WAR II

In the eight years prior to the attack on Pearl Harbor, the American labor movement had experienced the greatest growth and most dramatic changes in its history. The number of workers in trade unions had increased from under three million at the beginning of 1933 to over ten million by the end of 1941. The Congress of Industrial Organizations (CIO) had come into existence, initially as a split from the American Federation of Labor (AFL) in 1935, to organize unskilled and semi-skilled workers in mass production industries on an industrywide basis—mobilizing hundreds of thousands in steel, autos, electrical appliances, meat-packing, and other basic industries.

In the mainstream American labor movement, the CIO had also represented a new kind of unionism previously associated with radicalism in the form of socialism and communism. In this "social unionism," labor unions actively involved themselves in politics—supporting public housing and health care, social welfare programs for those unable to work, and anti-Fascist foreign policy initiatives, along with more traditional labor legislation.

LABOR'S CONTRIBUTION

From 1939 to 1941, labor was marked by conflicts. Communists joined with CIO president John L. Lewis and non-Communist anti-interventionists in the CIO to oppose U.S. involvement in the war, whereas socialists like Walter Reuther of the UAW supported the Roosevelt administration's "arsenal for democracy" policy of providing aid for England. On the homefront, the African-American socialist A. Philip Randolph pushed the Roosevelt administration into banning discrimination in the rapidly expanding defense plants by threatening a march on Washington in 1941. In the aftermath of the Japanese attack on Pearl Harbor on December 7, 1941, the labor movement united in its support for the war.

Following Pearl Harbor, the Roosevelt administration established a War Labor Board (WLB) with broad powers. AFL and CIO unions agreed to a "no-strike pledge" for the duration of the war, compulsory arbitration to settle differences between labor and management, a wage-freeze policy connected to the administration's price-freeze policy, and a "maintenance of membership" policy, which in effect compelled employers and workers to accept union representation in exchange for war production contracts and jobs. By the war's end, union membership had grown to 14.7 million, five times what it had been at the beginning of the Roosevelt administration.

During the war, workers engaged in "wildcat strikes" (strikes without union approval). A major coal strike by the United Mine Workers in 1943 led Congress to pass the War Labor Disputes Act, known as the Smith-Connally Act. This act was the first federal anti-strike legislation in United States history and a precursor of the postwar Taft-Hartley Act. Despite these upsets, the labor movement's contribution to the war effort was enormous.

First, as President Roosevelt stated often, the most important battle for Americans was the "battle of production," and the United States was, by 1944, outproducing all of its Axis enemies and providing vital military supplies and foodstuffs to Great Britain and its Soviet and Chinese allies, who were tying down the great bulk of German and Japanese ground troops in Europe and Asia. The labor movement, particularly the industrial unions of the CIO, also made possible the mobilization of over eight million new female workers, and the shift of existing female workers from service jobs to basic industry. Overall, the percentage of women in the labor force grew from 25 percent to 36 percent during the war and only the Soviet Union surpassed the United States in its effective mobilization of female labor for the war effort. The role of the CIO unions, particularly the United Electrical Workers, led by leftists, in raising the issue of equal pay for equal work for women and in pressing for policies to reduce the income gap between men and women were precursors of later campaigns for women's rights, including the availability of daycare facilities.

Beginning with President Roosevelt's Executive Order banning discrimination in the war production industries and establishing a Fair Employment Practices Committee (1941), black workers became a more important part of the industrial labor force than ever before. Although the military remained segregated, the integration of work in the factories—a difficult process that sometimes inspired wildcat "hate strikes" by white workers and led directly to a major race riot in Detroit in 1943—was also essential to winning the "battle of production" and the war itself.

LABOR AND POLITICS

Politically, labor contributed to the egalitarian and democratic ideology with which the war was fought. This ideology was symbolized by the poster for Franklin Roosevelt's 1944 reelection campaign by the artist Ben Shahn. The poster showed black and white war production workers united in solidarity and friendship, and its caption, "After the war, full employment," summed up the ideal that the labor movement strove for as a postwar program. President Roosevelt paid lip service to this program when he campaigned in 1944 for a "second bill of rights"—economic and social rights like the right to a job, housing, education, and health care—to supplement the original Bill of Rights. The press dubbed this program the Economic Bill of Rights, and both supporters and opponents saw it as the center of the New Deal's postwar agenda.

Politically, though, the labor movement experienced both gains and losses. The CIO had created a Political Action Committee which scored impressive gains in the 1944 primary and general elections, forcing Martin Dies, the leader of the House Un-American Activities Committee, into political retirement and helping to elect Roosevelt and many pro-labor New Deal candidates

LEGACY

Without the gains in organization and confidence that American workers experienced in the 1930s, organized labor's huge contribution to the nation's World War II victory would have been more difficult to imagine. The war to a great extent muted the conflict between capital and labor over the nation's future, of which the New Deal was at the center. During the war both liberal labor and conservative pro-business forces had made large gains—the former from the increase in membership, the latter through the vast increase in corporate profits that the industrial expansion had produced. Although the domestic political effects of the development of the Cold War (1946–1991) limited labor's growth and reversed some of its gains from the 1930s and 1940s, the union movement held onto many of those gains in urban industrial states until the 1980s. In the process, the labor movement—even though it was challenged by the anti-union provisions of the Taft-Hartley Law (1947) and drained of much of its militancy by purges against Communists and other radicals—still contributed to the huge increase in the American people's standard of living in the postwar era.

BIBLIOGRAPHY

Fraser, Steve. *Labor Will Rule: Sidney Hillman and the Rise of American Labor.* New York: Free Press, 1991.

Harris, William H. *The Harder We Run: Black Workers Since the Civil War.* New York: Oxford University Press, 1982.

Lichtenstein, Nelson. *Labor's War at Home: The CIO in WWII.* Philadelphia: Temple University Press, 2003.

Milkman, Ruth. *Gender at Work: The Dynamics of Job Segregation During WWII.* Urbana: University of Illinois Press, 1987.

Norman Markowitz

See also: **Economy, World War II; Financing, World War II; Propaganda, War; Rosie the Riveter; Women, Employment of.**

LATINOS, WORLD WAR I AND WORLD WAR II

As far back as the Revolution, Latinos in the United States have made important contributions to the American military and war efforts. However, it was not until the twentieth century that the Latino community played significant roles in the military. World War I marked the beginning of assimilation for many Latinos, and World War II saw an increasing number of Latinos in the military. The two world wars also influenced the Latino homefront, as Latinos moved into new occupations and dealt with wartime discrimination.

LATINOS IN WORLD WAR I

Although a lack of records makes it difficult to precisely measure the role of Latinos in the U.S. military during

World War I, documentation demonstrates their important, though largely unrecognized, contribution to the war effort. Many Latinos from states such as Texas and New Mexico served during World War I.

Because the United States was largely unprepared for war, the military had to induct and train soldiers quickly. Many of the new recruits spoke little or no English, including some Latinos. At first, these men were sent to development battalions at military training camps, where they were given little attention. Sometimes ridiculed by English-speaking soldiers, many Latinos and other ethnic minorities wanted to leave the military. In response, the military developed the Camp Gordon Plan, in which soldiers were separated into language groups with officers who spoke the language of the soldiers. Once this communications gap was bridged, their military training then continued in their native language. Most of the Latinos who received such training were at the Camp Cody, New Mexico, training camp.

Some Latinos saw combat duty, and a few received honors. Nicolas Lucero, a nineteen-year-old soldier from Albuquerque, won the French Croix de Guerre. Marcelino Serna, an enlisted man in the army, fought on the front-line trenches of France, where he earned numerous medals. However, despite capturing twenty-four German soldiers, he never received the Medal of Honor. An officer told Serna that he would not receive such an award because he was merely a private and that he could never advance to a higher level because of his limited English-language skills.

At the same time, for many Latinos in Texas and other states, World War I represented their first experience with assimilation into mainstream U.S. society. For the first time, the government and society in general sought active involvement of Latinos in national life. Although some Latinos refused to register for the draft to protest being treated as second-class citizens, others hoped that active participation in the war effort would increase opportunities for them. Much discrimination remained, and Hispanic participation in World War I can be seen as the start of a struggle for equal rights in the twentieth century.

LATINOS IN WORLD WAR II

Exact figures for the number of Latinos who fought in World War II are not known. Estimates range from 250,000 to 500,000, or about 2.5 to 5 percent of the number of soldiers who fought in the war. The only precise information available is for Puerto Ricans, who numbered about 53,000. In addition, some 200 Puerto Rican women formed part of the Women's Army Corps. One reason why it is difficult to know the number of Latinos is that, with few exceptions, they were not segregated into their own units. Rather, soldiers of Hispanic descent could be found throughout the military, particularly those units that originated in the Southwest.

Latinos were among the first U.S. soldiers who saw combat in the war. Before the bombing of Pearl Harbor, the United States sought to bolster the defense of the Philippines. Two of the units sent came from the New Mexico National Guard, which contained a heavy representation of both Hispanic officers and enlisted men. In part, these men were selected for their Spanish-speaking abilities because many in the Philippines still spoke Spanish.

A number of Hispanic soldiers received honors for their participation in the war. One of the most famous is Private José P. Martínez. Martínez was born in 1920 in Taos, New Mexico, to a family with a long line of Spanish-speaking ancestors in New Mexico. In 1927 his family moved to Colorado seeking a better life. Both Martínez and his brother were drafted during the war. Martínez was killed in action in the Aleutian Islands in an attack on Japanese positions in May 1943. He was the first Hispanic Medal of Honor recipient during World War II. Today, Martínez's name can be found on scholarships, a chapter of the Disabled American Veterans, and an American Legion post.

The heroics of soldiers such as Martínez helped to temper anti-Hispanic sentiments in the military that resulted from the Zoot Suit riots in Los Angeles in June 1943. Confrontations between servicemen and Mexican-American youths, known as *pachucos*, erupted into a race riot in that city. The police did little to stop attacks by soldiers on the Hispanic community, and the media played up the anti-Hispanic sentiments. U.S. enemies in the war used the riots as propaganda against the United States.

Many other Latinos served in noncombatant roles during the war, including numerous Hispanic members of the 713th Railway Operation Battalion of the Military Railway Service. Also known as the Santa Fe Battalion, the 713th was formed at Camp Clovis, New Mexico, in 1942 of experienced railway personnel. The unit went to North Africa in 1943, where it operated trains, built new track, and repaired old track along the coast of North Africa to supply U.S. and British units. The 713th later served in Italy, France, and Germany.

Latinos also played an important role on the home-front during World War II. During the Great Depression, many Hispanic Americans, especially Mexicans, had been repatriated because of a lack of jobs. However, once the United States entered the war, there was great demand for additional workers to replace those who left their jobs for the military. The governments of Mexico and the United States forged an agreement known as the Bracero Program, which brought Mexican contract laborers to work in agricultural jobs in the United States starting in 1942. By 1947 some 200,000 Mexican workers came to the United States under this program. The Bracero Program allowed these workers both to earn an income and to show their patriotism.

Many other Latinos worked in the defense industry during World War II. Traditionally, they had been excluded from such jobs. However, with the onset of the war and the demand for new workers, Latinos could be found in shipyards, armament factories, and aircraft facilities. In 1941 there were no Mexican Americans in the shipyards of Los Angeles, but by 1944 there were more than 17,000. Most of these Mexican-American workers toiled in the lowest-paying jobs in the defense industry. Thousands of Mexican-American women joined the ranks of defense workers, often working as riveters in factories. Formerly limited to jobs as maids, garment workers, or farm laborers, Mexican women in defense jobs found higher wages and an opportunity to intermingle with female workers of other racial groups.

The history of Latinos in the first half of the twentieth century illustrates one of the ironies of America's wars. World Wars I and II provided expanded and new opportunities for Latinos, as it did for African Americans, to advance economically and to integrate further into the society. Latinos demonstrated their patriotism by either carrying arms or supporting the war effort with their labor. Latinos built on their achievements to challenge discrimination. In this way, multiculturalism and the extension of civil liberties in America were as much outcomes of two world wars as were victories over imperialism and totalitarianism abroad.

BIBLIOGRAPHY

Christian, Carole E. "Joining the American Mainstream: Texas's Mexican Americans During World War I." *Southwestern Historical Quarterly* 92, no. 4 (1989): 559–595.

Morin, Raul. *Among the Valiant: Mexican-Americans in WWII and Korea.* Alhambra, CA: Borden Publishing, 1966.

Rosenfeld, Paul, and Culbertson, Amy. "Hispanics in the Military." In *Hispanics in the Workplace*, edited by Stephen Knouse et al. Newbury Park, CA: Sage Publications, 1992.

Takaki, Ronald. *Double Victory: A Multicultural History of America in World War II.* Boston: Little, Brown, 2000.

U.S. Department of Defense. *Hispanics in America's Defense.* Washington, D.C.: Office of the Deputy Assistant Secretary of Defense for Military Manpower and Personnel Policy, 1990.

Ronald Young

LITERATURE, WORLD WAR I

The literature of war of the 1920s and 1930s revealed unprecedented disillusionment and pessimism in America's best young writers. The wartime experiences of this "Lost Generation" shattered their faith in society, in the value of idealism, and in the significance of the individual life. The powerful antiwar books of the 1920s and 1930s helped encourage pacifism and isolationism in the years before Pearl Harbor.

With the striking exceptions of Ezra Pound's "Hugh Selwyn Mauberly" (1920) and T. S. Eliot's "The Wasteland" (1922), most American poetry about the war employs stale diction to uphold platitudes about heroism, patriotism, and sacrifice. (Alan Seeger's popular "A Rendezvous with Death" [1915] rises somewhat above the general level.) Marxist periodicals printed strident antiwar verse during the period of American neutrality.

Mainstream war writing published in 1917–1918 was strongly conventional and propagandistic. Writers romanticized the war as an opportunity to cultivate patriotism and character, to oppose Prussian militarism, and to offer one's life for democracy and civilization. A rare example of the pacifist spirit is Ellen N. La Motte's fictionalized memoir *The Backwash of War* (1916). La Motte's narrator, a nurse volunteer with the French army, sees appalling suffering and is also disturbed by European attitudes toward sex; the book's circulation was curtailed by the publisher after America entered the war, apparently to avoid a confrontation with pro-war organizations or newly enacted federal censorship restrictions. Typically the war was called the "Great Adventure." Arthur Guy Empey's best-selling *Over the Top* (1917) enthusiastically recounted his front-line service as an American in the British army.

Popular novelists strongly supported U.S. involvement, both during and after hostilities. As Edith Wharton wrote in *The Marne* (1918), America "tore the gag of neutrality from her lips, and with all the strength of her liberated lungs, claimed her right to a place in the struggle. The pacifists crept into their holes." In *One of Ours* (1922), which won the Pulitzer Prize, Willa Cather depicts the war as a force that lends meaning to an officer's life; his battlefield death makes up for years of frustration on a Nebraska farm.

War-veteran writers, however, found little to redeem their actual military experiences. *Three Soldiers* (1921), by John Dos Passos, depicts a military machine that destroys the artist and the hard worker alike. In Elliott Paul's *Impromptu* (1922), the army turns a soldier into a dependent cur. Amid confusion, incompetence, and horror, the Marine in *Through the Wheat* (1923), by Thomas Boyd, ends as a soulless automaton. Boyd's angry combat novel contrasts with John Thomason's Marine sketches *Fix Bayonets!* (1925), which extols the virtues of humor, endurance, and courage under fire without the cloying sentiment of most civilian writers.

The Enormous Room (1922), a novel by the poet e. e. cummings, conveys the intellectually stifling climate of the war years by fictionalizing cummings's confinement in a French jail for suspected political dissent. This often hallucinatory novel concentrates on the power of authority and the powerlessness of the artist. Cummings wrote a number of bitter antiwar poems in the 1920s and 1930s.

An affair between Lieutenant Frederic Henry and nurse Catherine Barkley is the focus of Ernest Hemingway's best-selling *A Farewell to Arms* (1929). Pointless bloodshed and pompous rhetoric have turned Henry's frontier faith in physical courage into an exercise in vanity. Sex, plus disdain for the frauds of the world, keeps the two lovers sane. Barkley's unexpected death leaves Henry, now a deserter, seething against a life in which suffering and death are the only realities.

The war affects all society in Dos Passos's *1919* (1932) and Mary Lee's *"It's a Great War!"* (1929), the lone novel by a female civilian employed by the U.S. army. Lee's protagonist, college-educated New Englander Anne Wentworth, first sees war in an army hospital where most of the patients, black and white, suffer from spinal meningitis or venereal disease. Besides wartime nursing, Lee dramatizes changing sexual mores, rear-echelon inefficiency, demoralization, loss of religious faith, and the public's unalterable provincialism and greed. Back in the United States, Wentworth discovers that the war has isolated her from most of her own as well as from her parents' generation.

In *1919*, Dos Passos depicts America at home and overseas. His many characters express the undirected explosive energy of a nation suddenly thrust onto the world stage. More vigorously than any other novel, *1919* emphasizes the disparity between proclaimed democratic ideals and the forces of dog-eat-dog capitalism and an impersonal military. Dos Passos shows postwar America as a hypocritical, hedonistic powerhouse more divided than ever between haves and have-nots.

William March, author of *Company K* (1934), remains one of the few highly decorated American soldiers of any war to have interpreted his experience in fiction. This profoundly pessimistic novel uses 113 narrators to tell the story of a rifle company from boot camp through the Armistice and back into civilian life. Their experiences are presented as tragedy, black humor, error, vision, and pure horror. For March, industrialized warfare

is a whirling "circle of pain," with the soldiers of both sides imprisoned by forces that make future wars inevitable. Some of the men are forever haunted by what they have seen and done.

In 1924 Laurence Stallings co-scripted, with Maxwell Anderson, the play *What Price Glory?*, a combination of comedy and drama that censors later tried to close for supposed disrespect to the military. That same year Stallings published *Plumes*, an autobiographical novel about the difficult readjustment of a wounded officer. A dying veteran is a central presence in William Faulkner's debut novel *Soldier's Pay* (1926).

The upshot of war for the immobile doughboy in Dalton Trumbo's macabre *Johnny Got His Gun* (1939) is truly a living death. In Katherine Anne Porter's apocalyptic story "Pale Horse, Pale Rider" (1939), a more symbolic take on a similar theme, young Miranda watches America dissolve into a nightmare of propaganda, legally enforced political conformity, mounting casualties, and epidemic disease. Her only solace comes in fever dreams of the past and from her hope for something better after death.

Although William Faulkner tried to redeem the war's disasters with Christian symbolism in *A Fable* (1954), the antiwar pessimism and revulsion of novelists like Hemingway, March, Trumbo, and Porter remains definitive. For many writers, World War I was more than a mere personal trauma or a tragic historical episode. To some it had been fought, in the words of Ezra Pound, merely "for a botched civilization." To others, more bitter still, it revealed a world without meaning, without progress, without hope. Their work helped banish the glorification of war from American literature. It also helped to shape American culture, society, and identity in the years between World War I and World War II, reinforcing the notions of pacifism, isolationism, and materialism.

BIBLIOGRAPHY

Cooperman, Stanley. *World War I and the American Novel.* Baltimore, MD: Johns Hopkins University Press, 1967.

Matsen, William E. *The Great War and the American Novel.* New York: Peter Lang, 1993.

Van Wienan, Mark W. *Rendezvous with Death: American Poems of the Great War.* Urbana: University of Illinois Press, 2002.

Walsh, Jeffrey. *American War Literature 1914 to Vietnam.* New York: St. Martin's, 1982.

J. E. Lighter

See also: **Hemingway, Ernest; Journalism, World War I; Propaganda, War.**

LITERATURE, WORLD WAR II

Writers have long drawn on the experiences of war to examine themes such as race, power, democracy, and human behavior under conditions of stress. Partly through addressing these and similar issues with unprecedented candor and realism, U.S. war literature matured during and after World War II. Hundreds of war novels eventually appeared, some of outstanding craftsmanship. Many American poets did impressive work, and wartime journalism and postwar memoirs often exhibited a new subtlety and clarity. Only the most popular or original works and writers can be described here.

World War II novels comprise the most varied category in U.S. war literature. Harry Brown tells of small-unit combat in *A Walk in the Sun* (1944). John Hersey's *A Bell for Adano* (1944) suggests that the integrity of most Americans abroad will ultimately outweigh the arrogance and cruelty of a few. Hersey also wrote *Into the Valley* (1943) and *Hiroshima* (1946), both reportorial classics, as well as the novels *The Wall* (1950), about the Warsaw Ghetto, and *The War Lover* (1959), a Freudian tale of bomber pilots in England.

Saul Bellow's *Dangling Man* (1944) ends disturbingly before its draftee protagonist goes overseas. Life in North Africa and Italy beguiles the GIs in John Horne Burns's *The Gallery* (1947). Like many novels, *The Gallery* features self-seeking officers, decent enlisted men, and kind-hearted foreign women, but a chapter about gay Allied soldiers was controversial. John Hawkes's surrealistic *The Cannibal* (1949) portrays occupied Germany as a landscape of gothic horrors, and Jerzy Kozinski takes a macabre view of Nazi-occupied Poland in *The Painted Bird* (1965). William Gardner Smith's *Last of the Conquerors* (1948) shows black soldiers in occupied Germany as better treated by German civilians than by fellow Americans. John Oliver Killens's *And Then We Heard the Thunder* (1962) dramatically portrays a comparable social contradiction in wartime Australia.

Three ambitious, more or less pessimistic, novels appeared in 1948. Irwin Shaw's *The Young Lions* unites the fates of three infantrymen, two American and one German. Shaw emphasizes that the United States has its racists and tyrants as well as Germany; here, however, they have not yet gained the upper hand. German expatriate Stefan Heym's *The Crusaders* spotlights a psychological warfare unit; while endorsing the Allied cause as just, Heym criticizes American hypocrisy and naivete in Europe. In his deeply pessimistic *The Naked and the Dead*, Norman Mailer mixes realistic details of the Pacific war with profound fears about the future of democracy. In this novel, war has given frightening power to autocrats like General Cummings and sadists like Sergeant Croft.

Only chance and heroic endurance, embodied in Private Ridges and Private Goldstein, offer a glimmer of hope in a dark human and natural landscape.

The vivid and moving *Mask of Glory* (1949), by Dan Levin, offers a leftist perspective on Marine heroism in the Pacific. Though disdained by critics as cliched and superficial, Leon Uris's *Battle Cry!* (1953) was enormously popular. Richard Matheson's *The Beardless Warriors* (1960) shows teenagers coming to grips with battle. *Face of a Hero* (1950), by Louis Falstein, dramatizes the bombing of southern Europe, and Edward L. Beach's *Run Silent, Run Deep* (1959) does the same for the submarine war.

Questions of discipline and psychology distinguish Herman Wouk's Pulitzer Prize-winning *The Caine Mutiny* (1951). The tyrannical Captain Queeg's irrationality leads a handful of officers to seize command during a typhoon. Once a court-martial clears the alleged mutineers, their own attorney angrily upholds Queeg, whose service helped protect America even before Pearl Harbor; few then were willing to accept that responsibility. Many readers find this last-minute vindication of Queeg unconvincing.

James Jones published the best-selling *From Here to Eternity* in 1951, describing the life of the rebellious Private Prewitt in Hawaii before Pearl Harbor. Considered shocking in language and detail at the time it was published, its brutal depiction of army life angered some skeptical critics. But Jones's ability to write powerfully and insightfully about soldiers was confirmed in *The Thin Red Line* (1962), an outstanding combat-oriented novel. In the sex-charged *Whistle* (1978) Jones writes bleakly of returned veterans of Guadalcanal.

The U.S. Army Air Force in Joseph Heller's *Catch-22* (1961) is a world of caricatures and tortured logic. But beneath the slapstick, *Catch-22* satirizes greed, gullibility, ambition, corruption, and complacency. Captain Yossarian is at the mercy of corrupt and inept bosses and colleagues. He finally rejects a system that demands infinite loyalty despite its cruelty to the individual. Heller's theme is that of the individual in an irrational, impersonal society, but during the Vietnam War many readers eagerly endorsed military idiocy as the book's actual message.

In *Slaughterhouse Five* (1969), Kurt Vonnegut shuttles Private Billy Pilgrim between 1945 Dresden, a future America, and a zoo on the planet Tralfamidor. Hardly a straightforward "antiwar" novel, *Slaughterhouse Five* seems to counsel resignation in the face of the world's horrors. Also influenced by science fiction, Thomas Pynchon's avant-garde *Gravity's Rainbow* (1973) focuses on Nazi development of "vengeance weapons" near the end of the war.

Although critics do not generally regard them as being successful as literature, Herman Wouk's epic-scale *The Winds of War* (1971) and its sequel, *War and Remembrance* (1978) employ enormous historical research to substantiate the war's tragedy and the influence of history on the individual.

The best war poetry was personal and understated. War poets included Howard Nemerov, Louis Simpson, Karl Shapiro, Phyllis McGinley, John Ciardi, James Dickey, Lincoln Kirstein, and others. Anthologies of war poems often include Richard Eberhart's "The Fury of Aerial Bombardment," Randall Jarrell's "Eighth Air Force," and Winfield Townley Scott's "The American Sailor with the Japanese Skull."

Outstanding American overseas journalists included Ernie Pyle (whose newspaper columns frequently personalized the ordinary GI), Richard Tregaskis, John Hersey, Margaret Bourke-White, Quentin Reynolds, John Steinbeck, and Martha Gellhorn. CBS radio correspondent Edward R. Murrow became famous for the economy and impact of his written as well as his spoken words.

World War II is the subject of many distinguished memoirs and other nonfiction accounts. *The Longest Day* (1959), by Cornelius Ryan, is an early example of oral history. *The Warriors* (1958), by former intelligence officer J. Glenn Gray, ponders the psychology of men at war. Senior officers' memoirs, such as General Dwight Eisenhower's *Crusade in Europe* (1948), are complemented by the works of junior officers and enlisted men; some notable examples are James Fahey's *Pacific War Diary* (1956), Eugene Sledge's *With the Old Breed on Peleliu and Iwo Jima* (1981), Samuel Hynes's *Flights of Passage* (1988), Raymond Gantter's *Roll Me Over* (1997), and William A. Foley, Jr.,'s *Visions from a Foxhole* (2002).

American writers on the subject of World War II created a body of work unsurpassed in quality by the literature of any other American war. Novels, autobiographies, and poetry explored the effects of war on individuals. Unlike the disillusionment that characterized the literature of World War I, in general World War II literature was neither pessimistic nor antiwar. Instead, it presents war in its complexity as a tragic but perhaps inevitable part of the human condition. Reflecting the views of their own generation, authors writing about World War II generally accepted the justness of that war and the necessity of ridding the world of Nazi totalitarianism and Japanese militarism. World War II literature helped to make that war, later called the "good war," a defining moment in affirming America's democratic values and the nation's identity as a moral people. Later in the century the literature of the Vietnam War would take American war literature down a starkly different path.

BIBLIOGRAPHY

Beidler, Philip D. *The Good War's Greatest Hits*. Athens: University of Georgia Press, 1998.

Cowley, Malcolm. "War Novels: After Two Wars." In *The Literary Situation*. New York: Viking, 1954.

Homberger, Eric. "United States." In *The Second World War in Fiction*, edited by Holger Klein et al. London: Macmillan, 1984.

Reporting World War II, 2 vols. New York: Library of America, 1995.

Shapiro, Harvey, ed. *Poets of World War II*. New York: Library of America, 2003.

Walsh, Jeffrey. "Second World War Fiction"; "Second World War Poetry." In *American War Literature 1914 to Vietnam*. New York: St. Martin's Press, 1982.

J. E. Lighter

See also: **Hemingway, Ernest; Journalism, World War II; Propaganda, War.**

MANHATTAN PROJECT

The Manhattan Engineer District, a secret U.S. government project begun in 1942 to develop an atomic bomb, was managed by Brigadier General Leslie Groves and undertaken by the U.S. Army Corps of Engineers. Undertaken at the urging of physicists Leo Szilard, Eugene Wigner, Edward Teller, Enrico Fermi, and Albert Einstein, the project responded to the threat of atomic weapon development by Nazi Germany. Ultimately, the U.S. effort brought together intelligence operatives, leading physicists, chemists, and engineers, as well as thousands of managers and workers at four major sites.

The best known of these sites, Los Alamos, in New Mexico, was the scientific and design headquarters of the project. Directed by the physicist J. Robert Oppenheimer, the Los Alamos site developed the theoretical knowledge behind the bomb and pieced together the designs for the two types of devices used on the Japanese cities of Hiroshima—a uranium bomb (code-named Little Boy)—and Nagasaki—a plutonium device (code-named Fat Man)—in August 1945.

However, the lesser known sites, such as the Radiation Laboratory in Berkeley, California, the Metallurgical Laboratory at the University of Chicago, and the two atomic manufacturing centers, Oak Ridge, Tennessee, and Hanford, Washington, each made major contributions to the Manhattan Project as well. Berkeley's laboratory, the product of Ernest Lawrence's work on the physics of radiation, produced the theoretical and practical knowledge that drove the electromagnetic separation process in Oak Ridge. The Metallurgical Laboratory in Chicago, headed by Arthur Compton, created the first chain reaction, and established a pilot plant for the manufacture of plutonium, built in Oak Ridge.

Full-scale uranium separation took place in the massive industrial facilities of Oak Ridge, Tennessee. Built as a secret city, the facility drew workers from throughout Appalachia and the South with high wages and promises of housing and a better life. At the three major plants of Oak Ridge—chemical separations (K-25), electromagnetic separations (Y-12), and the plutonium pilot plant (X-10)—engineers, managers, and workers struggled to produce atomic material pure enough to power the bombs being designed and assembled at Los Alamos. The Hanford, Washington, site, built and managed by the Du Pont Corporation, comprised massive camps of workers building and manning a facility to

THE TECHNOLOGY OF WORLD WARS I AND II

War has always driven technological advances. United States involvement in the two great global conflicts of the twentieth century impelled the development of weapons of a hitherto unsurpassed efficacy and sophistication. Many of the weapons developed for World War I saw their genesis in the nineteenth century and remain in use in the twenty-first.

The Springfield 1903 Rifle

The Springfield was a bolt-action (single-shot) rifle was issued to United States troops during World War I, and was in wide use during the first half of the twentieth century. The Springfield 1903 was developed after observation of weapons used during the Spanish-American War (1898). Spanish troops were armed with German Mauser 98 rifles, which were superior in many ways to those available to U.S. troops. A prototype of the Springfield was developed in 1900 and went into production in 1903 at the federally-owned Springfield Armory in Geneseo, Illinois. The gun was adapted for German-style pointed ammunition—the Springfield rounds, designated "Cartridge, Ball, Caliber .30, Model of 1906," led to the term .30-'06 (or "thirty-ought six"); this ammunition is used in countless small arms in the twenty-first century. The Springfield was so obviously modeled on the German Mauser that the U.S. government had to pay royalties to the German manufacturer Mauserwerke.

The M1 Garand

The federally-owned Springfield Armory in Geneseo was also the site of the development of the only full-power, semiautomatic standard infantry rifle used during World War II. This rifle replaced the Springfield due to its superior speed of fire—it was a clip-loading rather than a bolt-action weapon, and therefore could be fired multiple times before needing to be reloaded. The M1 Garand remains the most popular high-powered target semiautomatic in the world into the twenty-first century.

The Norden Bombsight

The Norden Bombsight (NBS), an optical precision device used to target bombs from aircraft to ground locations much more accurately than had before been possible, was one of the most secret weapons developed and used by the U.S. before and during World War II. Before it was introduced, there was no precise way to guide bombs to specific targets. Bombardiers simply dropped bombs near their intended targets. "Carpet bombing" and the "Blitzkrieg" approach of bombing enemy territory guaranteed a high rate of destruction and massive civilian casualties. The Navy Bureau of Ordnance began development of the NBS in 1922. In 1932 the prototype Mark XV was introduced, and the configuration of the NBS was largely unchanged throughout its functional life. Its accuracy during Allied bombing runs made it one of the most important technical developments of World War II. It was used with the first guided bombs—the forerunners of the guided missile. The NBS was used in 1967 and 1968 in the Vietnam War before it was superceded by more accurate equipment.

The Army Signal Corps was the source of most developments in the nation's communications and electronics technology in World War II. In World War I, wire had proven its worth as a communications tool and was used in most tactical and administrative signal equipment. Radio did not lend itself to secrecy and had serious drawbacks in reliability and ease of use, and in the 1930s the Signal Corps focused on researching long-range radio capabilities. The laboratories developed compact switchboards for corps and division levels. Work on a military version of the teletype printer also began, as did development of the military field typewriter. The Army Signal Corps worked to decrease the size of vehicular radios that had to be removed and set up on the ground; infantry, cavalry, and armored divisions suffered the limitations of the equipment's stationary ground use and limited range. Equipment weight was a major concern, along with limited wave range. Navigational radio emerged from World War I: it could be used for intelligence gathering or as a means of taking bearings from fixed radio sites. This concept, first used in ships and planes, has been refined throughout the twentieth century and into the twenty-first to such a degree that it can be used by individuals and has been installed in commercially manufactured automobiles.

Marie Lazzari

Los Alamos National Laboratory, ca. 1940–1950. Los Alamos, in New Mexico, was the scientific and design head-quarters for the Manhattan Project: the development of the atomic bomb. © CORBIS

create plutonium, a man-made element, for use in the Fat Man device.

Secrecy was the watchword of the project, both among workers and scientists. General Groves' system of compartmentalization meant that almost all project employees, military or civilian, had knowledge of only their small piece of the atomic puzzle, with no overview of how the entire project fit together. However, some information did make its way to the Soviet Union before the close of the war, through the efforts of Soviet agents like Los Alamos physicist Klaus Fuchs.

After the successful atomic test at Alamogordo, New Mexico, on July 16, 1945, the atomic bomb became an important implement of U.S. military and diplomatic policy. At the summit of American, British, and Soviet leaders in Potsdam, Germany, in July-August 1945, President Harry Truman warned an unsurprised Joseph Stalin of the existence of a powerful new weapon. However, the August 6, 1945, dropping of the atomic bomb on Hiroshima took the world (and many Manhattan Project personnel) by surprise. The dropping of the second bomb two days later, on August 8, demonstrated that America

was willing and able to use atomic weapons again to bring about Japanese capitulation.

The decision to use the atomic bomb was made by President Truman, against the advice of scientists such as James Franck, who urged the U.S. government to warn Japan first about the atomic bomb, or to demonstrate the bomb for Japanese observers first.

The U.S. sought a target area for the bombs that would hamper the Japanese war effort and provide the Japanese with a full demonstration of the bomb's devastation. Secretary of War Henry Stimson vetoed the consideration of Kyoto as a target because of its cultural value to the Japanese people. Two cities not yet bombed, Hiroshima and Nagasaki, both major cities with military ports, were chosen instead as the first targets for the atomic bombs.

After the bombs' detonations, the wartime Japanese government, at the command of Emperor Hirohito, abandoned its plan for massive resistance to U.S. invasion and surrendered on August 14, 1945. The devastation of the bombing, which killed more than 60,000 in Hiroshima and more than 30,000 in Nagasaki, would become known only in the weeks to come. More than

100,000 people injured by the atomic bombs' blasts and radiation were forced to cope with its impact for the rest of their lives.

The significance of the Manhattan Project has been assessed from various perspectives. The historian David Kennedy has written, in *Freedom from Fear*, that the Project

> stands as the single best illustration of the American way of war—not so much for the technological novelty of the bombs, or the moral issues they inevitably raised, but because only the Americans had the margins of money, material, and manpower, as well as the undisturbed space and time, to bring an enterprise on the scale of the Manhattan Project to successful completion. (p. 668)

On the other hand, the Project forever changed warfare, international relations, and America's sense of security. Atomic weapons in the hands of governments or terrorists created the possibility of a nuclear holocaust. That specter of mass destruction would not only affect America's defense policy but also help to shape the nation's postwar society and culture.

BIBLIOGRAPHY

Kennedy, David M. *Freedom from Fear: The American People in Depression and War, 1929–1945*. New York: Oxford University Press, 1999.

Boyer, Paul. *By the Bomb's Early Light: American Thought and Culture at the Dawn of the Atomic Age*. NY: Pantheon Books, 1985.

Committee for the Compilation of Materials on Damage Caused by the Atomic Bombs at Hiroshima and Nagasaki. *The Physical, Medical, and Social Effects of the Atomic Bombings*. New York: Basic Books, 1981.

Groueff, Stephane. *Manhattan Project: The Untold Story of the Making of the Atomic Bomb*. Boston: Little, Brown and Co., 1967.

Groves, Leslie. *Now it Can Be Told*. New York: Harper and Row, 1962.

Jones, Vincent. Manhattan: *The Army and the Atomic Bomb*. Washington, D.C.: United States Army, 1985.

Sherwin, Martin. *A World Destroyed*. New York, Vintage, 1987.

Russell Olwell

MCKINLEY, WILLIAM

(b. January 29, 1843; d. September 14, 1901) Twenty-fifth president of the United States (1897–1901).

William McKinley served fourteen years in the House of Representatives and two terms as Governor of Ohio before being elected twenty-fifth president of the United States in 1896. In 1901 he was shot by an anarchist and died from his wounds eight days later.

During his term in office McKinley oversaw the transformation of the United States into both a world and an imperial power. He took office in March 1897 a firm believer in peaceful American overseas expansion. The two-year-old Cuban revolution against Spain, however, complicated his hope of achieving this. Since the outbreak of fighting in 1895, congressional and public opinion in support of the revolution had pressed his predecessor Grover Cleveland to take decisive action; and upon becoming president McKinley too felt this pressure. He initially asked the Spanish government to moderate its often brutal tactics for dealing with the Cuban situation, but by early 1898 Spanish reforms had failed to bear fruit.

During the winter of 1898 a series of shocks and a final miscalculation by the president brought about war. The publication of a stolen letter written by the chief Spanish envoy to the United States, Enrique Dupuy de Lome, which implied that Spain would never change its tactics in Cuba and described McKinley as a "bidder for the admiration of the crowd," enflamed public opinion. Within days the nation endured a second shock, and its collective mood turned white-hot with the destruction of the battleship USS *Maine* in Havana Harbor. The following month McKinley took a desperate gamble to avoid war, assuage public opinion, and end the insurrection in Cuba when he demanded that Spain agree to an immediate cease-fire followed by negotiations and eventual Cuban independence. Whereas Spain was amenable to a cease-fire it could not countenance all American demands, especially the call for Cuban independence, and so declared war on the United States on April 23, 1898.

American naval forces largely determined the outcome of the war in two key battles. On May 1 Commodore George Dewey's Pacific Fleet destroyed its Spanish counterpart in Manila Bay. Just over two months later, on July 3, elements of the U.S. Atlantic Fleet destroyed Spanish naval forces in Cuba as they attempted to break the blockade around Santiago Harbor. With victory in Asia and the Caribbean, President McKinley accepted an armistice, which included the cession of Cuba, Guam and Puerto Rico to the United States.

The Administration now faced the critical question of what to do with the territory it had acquired as a result of the armistice. McKinley and Congress had already exposed an expansionist hand when the president introduced a resolution to annex Hawaii, which Congress dutifully approved in July 1898. Guam and Puerto Rico quickly became part of America's burgeoning global empire, while Cuba gained its independence after granting the United States a lease, which it still possesses, on the naval base at Guantanamo Bay.

Possible American acquisition of the Philippines generated heated controversy between the so-called anti-imperialists, who formed the Anti-Imperialist League in November 1898, and a powerful pro-imperial coalition that included McKinley, leading members of the Senate, and future president Theodore Roosevelt. Although the Treaty of Paris, in which Spain ceded the Philippines to the United States for $20 million, still faced a bitter Senate fight, McKinley decided to annex the islands in October 1898. He concluded that the Philippines were not prepared for self-government and that if the United States allowed Philippine independence, the new nation would likely be gobbled up by one of the major imperial powers.

On February 4, 1899, two days before the Senate ratified the Treaty of Paris, American and Philippine forces exchanged fire in Manila, thus beginning the so-called Philippine Insurrection. This war for Philippine independence ended in 1902 with an American victory that cost the United States over 4,000 dead and the Philippines at least 200,000 dead. The Philippines remained an American possession until 1946.

While creating an American empire in the Pacific and Caribbean, McKinley supported traditional anti-imperial American diplomacy in China. Faced with the prospect of China's territorial disintegration in 1899, McKinley reluctantly backed the decision of Secretary of State John Hay to circulate the first Open Door Note to the great powers, which called for equal access to the China market. McKinley acted even more forcefully a year later when he dispatched American troops to join an international relief force headed to Peking to rescue foreigners from the anti-western Boxer rebels. McKinley then backed a second set of Open Door notes that urged the international community not to colonize China. The Open Door notes formed the bedrock of American Far Eastern diplomacy for the next forty years.

Taken as a whole, McKinley's expansionist foreign policy may be seen as a continuation of traditional American manifest destiny ideology. While the American empire had its domestic opponents, a consensus developed by the time of McKinley's election that held that overseas expansion would serve American economic development by securing foreign markets and investment outlets, and that it would enhance internal stability by ending the boom and bust cycle that had characterized the American economy in the last decades of the nineteenth century. This consensus also held that American expansion would benefit those brought under United States control. Although apparently polar opposites, both the conquest of the Philippines and the Open Door for China were manifestations of an ideology that sought markets to conquer, men to civilize, and souls to save.

William McKinley.

McKinley brought America onto the world stage. His successor, Theodore Roosevelt, built on McKinley's accomplishments and gave America a leading role to play, especially in the Caribbean and the Far East. A generation later, Theodore's cousin, Franklin Delano Roosevelt, led America in war against Japan in order to defend the American empire and the American principles that reached their apex under William McKinley.

BIBLIOGRAPHY.

LaFeber, Walter. *The New Empire: An Interpretation of American Expansion, 1860–1898.* Ithaca, NY: Cornell University Press, 1963.

May, Ernest R. *Imperial Democracy: The Emergence of America as a Great Power.* New York: Harcourt, 1961.

Paterson, Thomas G., Clifford, J. Garry and Hagan, Kenneth J. *American Foreign Relations: A History.* Vol. 4. Boston: Houghton Mifflin, 2000.

Sidney L. Pash

See also: **Imperialism; Monuments, Cemeteries, Spanish American War**

MEDICINE, WORLD WAR I

The Great War was a staging ground of carnage, diseases, and psychological disorders on scale that dwarfs suffering in peace time. Millions of people who otherwise would have escaped such ravages were killed, maimed, and scarred for life. While the extent and devastation of the war affected battlefield care and post-combat treatment, loss of relatives, crippling injuries, impaired health, and psychological disorders also had a profound effect on social attitudes and culture after the war ended.

The First World War was the first in which battlefield fatalities outnumbered deaths by battlefield disease. Heavily armored tanks, machine guns and gas warfare replaced the antiquated cavalry and cannons of past conflicts. Great advances in prostheses were made. Gunshot wounds were now irrigated with antiseptic fluid (Carrel-Dakin treatment), which helped prevent gangrene. Most importantly, hygiene became an ever-present issue.

Throughout the war, soldiers fought, ate, slept, washed, and relieved themselves in narrow trenches surrounded by dead, decomposing bodies and hungry diseased rats. To make matters worse, the body louse, also known as the "chat," was rampant. Since lighting fires on the front lines was prohibited because they would attract sniper fire, soldiers often had to huddle in close groups in cold weather, thus enabling infestation. Besides being a vector for diseases like typhus fever, which killed millions of German and Russian troops on the Eastern Front, the body louse can spread very quickly, producing up to twelve eggs per day. When conditions allowed, soldiers made social events of picking off these lice from clothing hair, and skin; these events were often called "chats" or "chatting up."

Although lice were bothersome, and on occasions deadly, they may have saved many lives. Louse feces caused "Trench Fever," also known as the "Five Day Fever," marked by high-grade fever, aches, and rashes. Soldiers suffering from Trench Fever had to be evacuated from the lines. However, rarely did anyone die from this condition.

Trench Foot, another ailment facilitated by bad hygienic conditions, was the result of prolonged periods in wet soggy boots in cold, water-filled trenches. Feet swelled, blistered, and caused intense pain. Though this was not usually deadly, if it was not treated gangrene could set in, necessitating amputation. To avoid Trench Foot, soldiers were required to change socks and wash feet whenever possible.

The outbreak of venereal diseases in wartime France increased because many women, whose husbands had

TRIAGE

From the French word *trier* "to sort out," triage means to sort casualties of war or other wounded persons according to the seriousness of their injuries, the need for immediate treatment, and the availability of a place for treatment. This medical prioritization system was developed during World War I, when there were usually not enough doctors or medical supplies at field hospitals. Physicians and support personnel had to balance time-consuming and high-intensity treatment against treating the lightly wounded in order to send them back to their military units. Later *The Geneva Convention for the Protection of War Victims: Armed Forces in the Field,* one of the four *Geneva Conventions of 1949,* would stipulate: "Only urgent medical reasons will authorize priority in the order of treatment to be administered." Triage procedures are also used today in hospital emergency rooms and in disaster relief situations.

been killed, became prostitutes for financial and other reasons. During the war the control of licensed prostitution, which had been enforced by the "police de moeurs," became less rigid. According to one U.S. Navy physician, 50 percent of prostitutes were infected with syphilis in its primary and secondary stages. All of these women were infected with gonorrhea. To protect soldiers the U.S. military used measures such as semi-monthly inspections of troops, warnings, prophylaxis, and in some cases, loss of pay for illness.

Shell shock, later called war neurosis and now known as post-traumatic stress disorder (PTSD), was a popular label for neuropsychiatric casualties of the war. Victims of this condition, who were initially believed to have suffered from concussions due to exploding shell blasts, often exhibited starry-eyed looks, violent tremors, expressions of terror and sometimes blindness and paralysis. Although the treatment of this multi-symptom condition varied, Americans such as U.S. Army psychiatrist Dr. Thomas Salmon developed a program consisting of rest, food, access to a warm shower, and assurance that victim was neither cowardly nor ill. Many victims suffered from the psychological damage caused by the war for the remainder of their lives.

One might say that the war ended with a cough, not a bang. In 1918, the year of the Armistice, more people

American Red Cross ambulances being loaded with stretchers in front of the 1st Line Hospital, at the foot of Monte Grappa on the Italian front, ca. 1914–1918. ©CORBIS

died from Spanish Influenza than from combat. Of course, "Spanish flu" was a misnomer for the pandemic that wreaked havoc across the world. It is believed that the disease began at a Kansas army training facility in 1917, spreading throughout North America, and was brought to the European front by American troops. Somewhere along the line, as a result of increasing human antibodies, it mutated. By the time it reappeared in the United States in the fall of 1918, influenza brought on the added complication of pneumonia. Health providers could treat only the symptoms. By 1919, after a reign of terror that killed between 22 and 40 million people worldwide and over 675,000 Americans, the virulent form of flu simply vanished. Today's virologists are still unlocking the mysteries of the virus.

During the war 4.7 million Americans were mobilized; of these, about 4 million were in the Army, 600,000 served in the Navy and 79,000 were Marines. In total, 116,708 American servicemen died during the war, including 53,513 killed in battle. These statistics do not reveal the stories of the many survivors who became physically and/or psychologically impaired from the toll of war. However, the medical community gained new understanding of military medicine, leading to preparation for the onslaught of the next major conflict of the century just twenty-one years later.

BIBLIOGRAPHY

Armstrong, James F. "Philadelphia, Nurses and the Spanish Influenza Pandemic of 1918." *Navy Medicine,* March–April 2001: 92.

Jones, Franklin D. "Psychiatric Lessons of War." In *War Psychiatry,* edited by Franklin D. Jones, et al. Falls Church, VA: Office of the Surgeon General, U.S. Army, 1995.

Keegan, John. *An Illustrated History of the First World War.* New York: Alfred A. Knopf, 2001.

Miller, M.G. "Of Lice and Men: trench fever and trench life in the AIF." Paper presented at the Second Anzac Medical Society meeting, France, October 1993.

Surgeon General, U.S. Navy. *Annual Report to the Secretary of the Navy.* Washington, DC: Government Printing Office, 1918.

André B. Sobocinski

See also: **Medicine, World War II; Red Cross, American.**

MEDICINE, WORLD WAR II

The purpose of military medicine during World War II was the same as in previous wars: to conserve the strength and efficiency of the fighting forces so as to keep as many men at as many guns for as many days as possible. What transpired between 1939 and 1945 was a cataclysmic event made worse by the nature of the weapons the combatants used. The use of machine guns, submarines, airplanes, and tanks was widespread in World War I; but in World War II these weapons reached unimagined perfection as killing machines. In every theater of war, small arms, land- and sea-based artillery, torpedoes, and armor-piercing and antipersonnel bombs took a terrible toll in human life. In America's first major encounter at Pearl Harbor, the survivors of the Japanese attack could describe what modern warfare really meant. Strafing aircraft, exploding ordnance, and burning ships caused penetrating injuries, simple and compound fractures, traumatic amputations, blast injuries, and horrific burns, to name just a few. Total U.S. battle deaths in World War II numbered 292,131 with 671,801 reported wounded or missing.

Conserving fighting strength and enabling armies and navies to defeat the enemy also meant recognizing that disease, more than enemy action, often threatened this goal. For example, during the early Pacific campaign to subdue the Solomon Islands, malaria caused more casualties than Japanese bullets. Following the initial landings on Guadalcanal, the number of patients hospitalized with malaria exceeded all other diseases. Some units suffered 100 percent casualty rates, with personnel sometimes being hospitalized more than once. Only when malaria and other tropical diseases were controlled could the Pacific war be won.

The military's top priority organized its medical services to care for battlefield casualties, make them well, and return them to duty. The systems developed by the army and navy worked similarly. In all theaters of war, but particularly in the Pacific, both army and navy medicine faced their greatest challenge dealing with the aftermath of intense, bloody warfare fought far from fixed hospitals. This put enormous pressure on medical personnel closest to the front and forced new approaches to primary care and evacuation.

ARMY MEDICS AND NAVY CORPSMEN

The most dramatic and demanding duty an army medic or navy hospital corpsman could have was with army infantry or Marine Corps units in the field. Because the Marine Corps had always relied on the navy for medical support, corpsmen accompanied the leathernecks and suffered the brunt of combat themselves. Many of them and their army counterparts went unarmed, reserving their strength for carrying medical supplies.

Army medics or navy corpsmen were the first critical link in the evacuation chain. From the time a soldier suffered a wound on a battlefield in France or a marine was hit on an invasion beach at Iwo Jima, the medic or corpsman braved enemy fire to render aid. He applied a battle dressing, administered morphine and perhaps plasma or serum albumin, and tagged the casualty. Indeed, one of the lingering images of the World War II battlefield is the corpsman or medic crouched beside a wounded patient, his upstretched hand gripping a glass bottle. From the bottle flowed a liquid that brought many a marine or soldier back from the threshold of death. In the early days of the conflict that fluid was plasma. Throughout the war, scientists sought and finally developed a better blood substitute, serum albumin. Finally, in 1945, whole blood, rich in oxygen-carrying red cells, became available in medical facilities close to the battlefield.

If he was lucky, the medic or corpsman might commandeer a litter team to move the casualty out of harm's way and on to a battalion aid station or a collecting and clearing company for further treatment. This care would mean stabilizing the patient with plasma, serum albumin, or whole blood. In some cases, the casualty was then evacuated. Other casualties were taken to a divisional hospital, where doctors performed further stabilization including surgery, if needed. In the Pacific, where sailors, soldiers, and marines were doing the fighting, both navy and army hospital ships, employed mainly as ambulances, provided first aid and some surgical care for the casualties' needs while ferrying them to base hospitals in the Pacific or back to the United States for definitive care. As the war continued, air evacuation helped carry the load. Trained army and navy nurses, medics, and corpsmen staffed the evacuation aircraft.

MEDICAL ADVANCES

World War II brought about many advances in medicine. The military moved quickly to reduce the impact of malaria and other tropical diseases. Personnel trained in preventive medicine attempted to control malaria-spreading mosquitoes by spreading oil on breeding areas and spraying DDT. Physicians, medics, and corpsmen dispensed quinine and atabrine as malaria suppressants.

Advances in combat surgery saved countless lives. Surgical removal of dead or dying tissue—debridement—reduced the danger of infection as did the delayed closure of wounds. Surgeons skilled in orthopedics preserved limbs that in previous wars would have been amputated.

Medics move a casualty from the battlefront via a trench in August 1944, near Brest, France. LANDOV

For the first time, miracle drugs—the sulfas and penicillin—were widely used to combat infection. By the last two years of the war, penicillin was also being mass-produced in the civilian community.

Not all wounds are physical. In a previous era, the psychologically wounded suffered from "nostalgia" during the Civil War, and "shell-shock" in World War I. In World War II this condition was termed combat exhaustion or combat fatigue. Although the World War I experience of treating men at the front had been successful, military psychiatrists and psychologists at the beginning of World War II had to relearn those lessons. Nevertheless, the care givers soon recognized that given a respite from combat, a safe place to rest, regular food, and a clean environment, 85 to 90 percent of patients could again become efficient warriors. The more psychologically damaged received therapy in military hospitals.

By 1945 the war had left a decided impact on the practice of medicine, with implications both for the military and civilian communities. The combat theaters were testing grounds for medical evacuation procedures, the use of blood substitutes, advanced surgical techniques, new miracle drugs, preventive medicine practice, and the treatment of psychiatric disorders.

BIBLIOGRAPHY

Beadle, Christine, and Hoffman, S. "History of Malaria in the United States Naval Forces at War: World War I through the Vietnam Conflict." *Clinical Infectious Disease* 16 (1993): 320–329.

Cowdrey, Albert E. *Fighting for Life: American Military Medicine in World War II.* New York: Free Press, 1994.

Herman, Jan K. *Battle Station Sick Bay: Navy Medicine in World War II.* Annapolis, MD: Naval Institute Press, 1997.

Levin, Dan. "Briefing for Iwo Beach." *Hospital Corps Quarterly* 18, no. 5 (May 1945): 35–36.

Maisel, Albert Q. *Miracles of Military Medicine.* New York: Duell, Sloan and Pearce, 1943.

McGuire, Frederick L. *Psychology Aweigh!: A History of Clinical Psychology in the United States Navy, 1900–1988.* Washington, DC: American Psychological Association, 1990.

Shephard, Ben. *A War of Nerves: Soldiers and Psychiatrists of the Twentieth Century.* Cambridge, MA: Harvard University Press, 2001.

U.S. Navy Medical Department Administrative History, 1941–1945: Narrative History. Vol. 2, chapters 9–18. Unpublished typescript in the BUMED Archives, Washington, DC.

Jan Kenneth Herman

See also: **Medicine, World War I; Red Cross, American.**

MEMOIRS, AUTOBIOGRAPHIES

The war memoir has always been a genre in American literature. The Revolutionary War had no sooner ended than some of its key figures wrote and published accounts of their experiences. Yet these, like most of the war memoirs published after the Civil War, were written by senior officers less concerned to document the war experience than to tell the stories of battles or campaigns and justify their own conduct in them. Although common soldiers, nurses, civilians, and others outside headquarters wrote letters and kept diaries—a tradition that dated back to the Revolutionary War and continued in the Civil War—few of their records were published until the twentieth century.

THE SPANISH-AMERICAN WAR

The most influential memoir of the Spanish-American War (1898–1899) is Theodore Roosevelt's *The Rough Riders* (1899). There are only a few others, among them George Kennan's *Campaigning in Cuba* (1899); John Bigelow's *Reminiscences of the Santiago Campaign* (1899); George A. Andrews's *A Soldier in Two Armies* (1901); Ralph Delahaye Paine's *Roads of Adventure* (1922); and Charles Johnson Post's *The Little War of Private Post* (1960). Even fewer books emerged from the Philippine Insurrection (1899–1902), although the historian A. B. Feuer has collected and published many valuable accounts in *America at War: The Philippines, 1898–1913*.

WORLD WAR I

Not until World War I did the war memoir written from the common soldier's or junior officer's perspective become a major literary genre in the United States. This is attributable to the nature of the war itself, which, unlike any previous conflict, involved entire populations; to the growing literacy of those populations; and to the exploitation of literature as a propaganda weapon by the belligerent governments. American memoirs published during the war, for example James Rogers McConnell's *Flying for France* (1917), were less concerned with accurately portraying the war experience than with encouraging recruiting and boosting civilian morale.

War memoirs became especially popular after the Treaty of Versailles, especially during two brief periods that dated roughly from 1919 to 1922 and from 1929 to 1933. The second period was inspired by the 1929 publication in English translation of *All Quiet on the Western Front*, a war novel by the German writer Erich Maria Remarque. In Europe, especially in Britain and France, many—but by no means all—of the memoirs published during these years expressed some form of disillusionment with war and the social and political traditions seen as having incited war. These memoirs were not necessarily representative of most veterans' experiences, but they found much greater favor with the pacifist-minded European public than did those that justified the war, which were largely ignored.

In America, by contrast, patriotism remained popular and memoirs of disillusionment were the exception to the rule. *No Hard Feelings!* (1930), by the Congressional Medal of Honor winner John Lewis Barkley, is perhaps the best representative of the type. Aviation memoirs such as Norman Archibald's *Heaven High, Hell Deep* (1935) also attracted particular public interest in the United States, perhaps because they allowed readers to envision war as a chivalrous affair and avoid the harrowing images of the trenches. Yet, although most American memoirists affirmed the cause for which they fought, almost all of them decried war itself and urged their country to remain uninvolved in future European conflicts. Some of the best American memoirs, most notably Hervey Allen's *Toward the Flame: A Memoir of World War I* (1926; 2003), Thomas Barber's *Along the Road* (1924), and Elton Mackin's *Suddenly We Didn't Want to Die: Memoirs of a World War I Marine* (1993), used an understated but powerfully effective realism to express their experiences and feelings about them.

WORLD WAR II

Unlike World War I, World War II did not inspire an explosion of memoir-writing. Nevertheless, after 1945 war memoirs maintained a significant share of the American popular market, while in Europe the war memoir practically disappeared as a literary form. The best-known American World War II memoir is Audie Murphy's *To Hell and Back* (1949), which inspired a movie and helped to make the author a popular hero. Yet most American World War II veterans presented a far less positive picture of war than had their fathers. This was true of works published before the 1960s—Lester Atwell's bitter 1958 memoir *Private*, for example—but became even more so during and after the Vietnam War. In the 1960s antiwar novels by veterans, such as Joseph Heller's *Catch-22* (1961) and Kurt Vonnegut's *Slaughterhouse-Five* (1969) reflected the public mood. By the time these novels appeared, memoirs that attempted to reaffirm the old patriotic ethos were no more acceptable to the American reading public than they had been to Europeans in the 1930s, and for the most part disappeared from print.

The public market for war memoirs shriveled in the 1970s and 1980s. Since the 1990s, however, scholarly interest in the war memoir as a historical source and art form in its own right has increased. This interest is driven partly by the emergence of an academic approach to history that emphasizes the experiences of individuals instead of the usual narratives of battles and campaigns, and partly by the desire to preserve the stories of generations that are rapidly dying off. Whatever the cause, the effect has been overwhelmingly positive: letters, diaries, and manuscript memoirs are being archived, studied, and published in unprecedented volume.

This trend has led to far greater depth and balance in our understanding of the experience of warfare, revealing, for example, the wartime lives of women, African Americans, and minorities in and near the firing line, and of workers, farmers, doctors, and other civilians on the home front. The study of memoirs and other firsthand accounts of wartime has both exposed the nature and extent of problems such as racism, and helped to explain the remarkable resilience in battle of the U.S. armed forces. It also has shown the sheer variety, not just of actual war experiences, but of reactions to those experiences by the participants themselves.

Edward Lengel

See also: **Hemingway, Ernest; Literature, World War I; Literature, World War II.**

MITCHELL, BILLY

(b. December 29, 1879; d. February 19, 1936) Commander of Air Service, First U.S. Army during World War I, and airpower theorist.

Billy Mitchell's leadership was instrumental in the early development of American air forces, and his ideas about airpower exert their influence to this day. He served as the top combat commander of the Air Service of the American Expeditionary Forces in World War I. Afterward he became an outspoken proponent of airpower, resulting in a court-martial that shortened his military career. As a civilian he continued to widely publicize his beliefs until his death.

William Mitchell was born on December 29, 1879 in Nice, France. He grew up in the Midwest and joined the army during the Spanish-American War. His father was a U.S. senator, and Billy used that connection to garner a second lieutenant's commission in a volunteer signal company. After a rather uneventful tour in Cuba, he served in the Philippines during the insurrection there. He did well in these early assignments, and soon accepted the army as his career. He eventually became involved with the development of the Aviation Section of the Signal Corps. He began his own flight training in the fall of 1916, and was sent to France as an aeronautical

Colonel Billy Mitchell (far right) at his court martial. Mitchell provoked the court martial in order to draw attention to his ideas for changing military air power strategies. COURTESY OF THE LIBRARY OF CONGRESS

observer in early 1917. He learned much from the British and the French that he would apply in helping to create an air service for the American Expeditionary Forces in World War I.

Mitchell witnessed firsthand the futility of French assaults on German trenches. He was impressed by French aircraft designs and French concepts of concentrated airpower as a modern tactical weapon. However, he much preferred the type of air operations conducted by the independent British Royal Flying Corps under the command of Major General Hugh Trenchard. The RFC emphasized that command of the air over the battlefield could be accomplished only by an incessant air offensive. Mitchell may have also picked up some ideas from Italian theorists Gianni Caproni and Giulio Douhet.

Colonel Mitchell got along well with General John J. Pershing, who appointed the aggressive airman Chief of Air Service, First United States Army. Mitchell clashed with the first Chief of the Air Service, AEF, Ben-

jamin Foulois, but had better relations with Mason Patrick, his replacement. During the Battle of St. Mihiel, Mitchell earned a promotion to Brigadier General. He loosely commanded the largest concentration of aircraft during the war, a total of over 1,480 British, French, Italian, and American planes, and quickly achieved air superiority. His aircraft continued to support friendly units and bomb enemy troop concentrations during the subsequent Meuse-Argonne campaign. Though he was fascinated by new ideas such as strategic bombing and dropping troops by parachute, the war ended before Allied airmen really had a chance to try them.

Though Mitchell exaggerated his prescience in his memoirs, he did develop a vision for future American airpower from his World War I experience that emphasized its revolutionary and offensive nature. He returned home to become assistant chief of the Air Service. After Mitchell sank the battleship *Ostfriesland* in a much ballyhooed, and somewhat rigged, demonstration in 1921, the Joint Army-Navy Board recognized the possible vulnerability of ships to aerial bombardment, but their report fell far short of condoning the revolutionary changes Mitchell desired.

Always willing to attract attention to further his cause, Mitchell deliberately provoked a court-martial in 1925 by accusing the War and Navy Departments of "incompetency, criminal negligence, and almost treasonable administration of the National Defense" because of their failure to build-up or maintain their air components. He had achieved some success in 1921 because the public was prepared to accept the concept of using inexpensive airplanes against seaborne invasions, but four years later Americans were even more devoted to a return to "normalcy," isolationism, and economical government. Mitchell had also profited from inept opposition from the Navy in 1921, while the War Department proved more adept in the way it handled his court-martial.

After his conviction for insubordination Mitchell resigned from active duty in 1926. His treatment enraged some supporters in the House of Representatives and attracted the media attention he desired, facilitating his efforts to get many of his ideas into print. He continued to refine his views about an independent air force attacking enemy vital centers until his death in 1936, publishing five books and many more articles in journals and newspapers. His unyielding radical views about airpower had little immediate impact on developments in military aviation, but they did help condition the public to accept the changes that were to come.

Mitchell's ideas eventually had great significance in shaping the emerging American air service. Two of his disciples, Henry "Hap" Arnold and Carl Spaatz, were especially important in achieving Mitchell's goal of an independent air service with a strong strategic bombing force. Arnold led the Army Air Forces during World War II, while Spaatz succeeded him and guided the new United States Air Force into existence in 1947. Mitchell's ideas contributed to American air doctrine, and he is still perceived within the Air Force as an example of principled leadership to emulate, willing to sacrifice his personal career to further airpower ideals.

BIBLIOGRAPHY

Hurley, Alfred F. *Billy Mitchell: Crusader for Airpower*. Bloomington: Indiana University Press, 1975.

Mets, David R. *The Air Campaign: John Warden and the Classical Airpower Theorists*. Maxwell Air Force Base, AL: Air University Press, 1999.

Mitchell, William. *Memoirs of World War I*. New York: Random House, 1960.

Conrad C. Crane

MONUMENTS, CEMETERIES, SPANISH-AMERICAN WAR

On February 15, 1898, a massive explosion shattered the American battleship *Maine* in Havana Harbor, killing 260 men. Although the exact cause is unknown, the sinking was widely attributed to deliberate sabotage by Spain. By April 1898, public pressure was such that despite all his efforts to hold back the tide of pro-war sentiment in the United States, President McKinley asked Congress for a declaration of war. Stirred by the slogan, "Remember the Maine," the Spanish fleet in the Philippines was sunk in retaliation for the American deaths. Although the Spanish-American War, known as the "splendid little war" for the United States, was short in duration it resulted in territorial gain, the occupation of the Philippines, and a bloody insurrection by the Filipinos that lasted more than three years and cost thousands of lives.

Americans had traditionally resisted becoming involved in the affairs of other nations, so it was necessary to justify the war as something other than an imperialist action by a bellicose military force. The war was portrayed as a necessary conflict that had strengthened the nation, but many Americans remained doubtful about what had been accomplished. The efforts of their army and navy were exalted, particularly the triumph of Admiral George Dewey, which was seen as appropriate revenge for the cowardly attack on the *Maine*. A grateful nation welcomed Dewey's victory with ceremony and a parade through a victory arch in New York. Colonel Theodore Roosevelt, consummate hero of the Rough Riders, used this moment of national exuberance to praise the war as a national and essential unifying force. The nation was quick to honor its dead with memorials erected in Arlington National Cemetery, including a special monument to the legendary Rough Riders; but Roosevelt's rhetoric sharply contrasted the tension and disunity that followed those short months of glory.

No national monuments were built by the federal government to honor the American troops that fought in the subsequent Philippine Insurrection, as it proved to be extremely controversial among the American public. Many opponents of intervention believed the bloody campaign against the Filipinos was immoral. When the McKinley administration decided to retain the Philippines and govern it as an American possession, further fierce debate ensued within the United States, for such imperialist actions were thought contrary to the true American ethos. The nation's involvement in the insurrection was soon forgotten. The Dewey Arch in New York was torn down as the admiral's fame and reputation quickly diminished in the aftermath of the unpopular conflict.

A funeral service at Arlington Cemetery for soldiers who died during the Spanish-American War, 1899. ©CORBIS

Despite public derision, memory of the *Maine* persisted as efforts were introduced to have the ship raised. Congress appropriated funds in 1910 and two years later Americans across the country paid tribute to those who died upon the sunken vessel. New York streets were crowded, bells tolled, flags were lowered, and coffins containing the sailors' remains were carried through the streets in solemn procession. Burial took place in Arlington Cemetery beneath the ship's recovered mainmast, which became part of the funerary memorial to those who had lost their lives aboard the ship. Other relics of the ship were incorporated in monuments across the country. Throughout the early 1900s, the annual anniversary of the sinking, on February 16, continued to invoke memorial services in New York and elsewhere.

"Time served to transform the *Maine* from a crass jingoistic symbol into a more ambiguous and tragic one" (Piehler, p. 91). To many Americans this symbol was an image of American military might as a tool for humanitarian causes, rather than one of aggression. Some used it to argue for preparedness and felt it supported the notion that war was a noble and heroic enterprise, while others believed the *Maine* and the conflict it represented should serve as a reminder that war must be avoided at all costs.

Ambiguity surrounding America's participation in the Spanish-American War continued to influence public opinion in the years preceding the First World War. The same tension that existed between America's rise to power and its traditional reluctance to become involved in imperialistic action was a key factor in the widespread move toward isolationism. Ultimately, this contributed to the nation's decision to avoid participation in the League of Nations following the Armistice.

BIBLIOGRAPHY

Piehler, G. Kurt. *Remembering War the American Way.* Washington, DC: Smithsonian Institution Press, 1995.

Renehan, Edward J., Jr. *The Lion's Pride: Theodore Roosevelt and His Family in Peace and War.* New York: Oxford University Press, 1998.

Samuels, Peggy and Harold. *Remembering the Maine.* Washington, DC: Smithsonian Institution Press, 1995.

Lisa M. Budreau

See also: **Monuments, Cemeteries, World War I; Monuments, Cemeteries, World War II.**

MONUMENTS, CEMETERIES, WORLD WAR I

By the First World War Armistice of 1919, America's war dead, substantially fewer than the loss suffered by other nations, numbered more than 75,000. Honoring a promise made in 1918, the War Department agreed to provide a home burial to all who died in its foreign service. Alternatively, Americans could choose to leave their loved ones buried in national cemeteries overseas. The American government turned to its people in search of a compromise on the issue. In place of consensus, widely divergent views prompted a democratic response that supported individual choice, with the result that over 30,000 U.S. bodies were left buried overseas.

The American Battle Monuments Commission (ABMC) assumed control of these cemeteries and promptly established full authority over the commemoration of America's military achievements on behalf of the nation. In this case, no public endorsement was sought from citizens at home as commissioners with powerful political agendas attempted to create an image of national solidarity abroad. In doing so, they concealed individual, cultural, and religious identities behind celebratory images of a united nation with power and dominion overseas.

For those families whose loved ones had never been found, there would be no personal headstones. The weapons of widespread destruction used during the First World War resulted in an inordinate number of men unaccounted for, graves that had been totally destroyed during battle, and vast numbers of dead who remained unidentifiable. For the four and a half thousand American "unknowns," national political and military leaders in the United States followed the example of England and France, each of which buried one unidentified soldier in 1920.

After resolving disagreements over where the body should be buried, how many unidentified bodies should be returned, and the best day for burial, America laid the body of an unidentified soldier to rest at Arlington Cemetery on November 11, 1921 and designated it the nation's "Unknown Soldier." Assurance of anonymity mattered more than rank, race or social status because the Unknown Soldier symbolised the ideal of national community. Even the marble tomb placed over the grave caused tension, for the public remained undecided as to whether it should symbolize war or peace. Five years passed before Congress finally authorized a white marble compromise. Three allegorical figures of Peace, Valor and a dominant central Victory were depicted on a simple sar-

---

TOMB OF THE UNKNOWN SOLDIER

On November 11, 1921, a horse-drawn procession went from the Capitol Rotunda to Arlington National Cemetery. In a casket on a caisson were borne the remains of an unknown soldier from World War I who had died in France. Veterans from the conflict attended this ceremony in honor of their fallen fellowmen, including General Pershing, who represented all of the soldiers who had died and been buried in American cemeteries in France. Though seriously ill, former President Woodrow Wilson, who had seen America through this war, was also in attendance. The grave was covered by a temporary granite tomb.

On November 11, 1932, a simple yet elegant sarcophagus of Colorado marble was set in place. One side bears the inscription: "Here rests in honored glory an American soldier known but to God." In later years the remains of soldiers from World War II, the Korean War, and the Vietnam War were also interred here, and the memorial was renamed the Tomb of the Unknown Soldier. In 1999, however, the Pentagon announced that no new remains would be added to the memorial because new technology made the likelihood of there being unidentified remains in the future remote.

Specially trained guards from the 3rd United States Infantry (The Old Guard) guard the tomb 24 hours per day, 365 days per year, and visitors to the monument may watch the changing of this guard. If someone approaches too closely to the memorial, the guards have been instructed to apprehend the trespasser using whatever force necessary.

IN FLANDERS FIELDS

Each May before Memorial Day, members of the Veterans of Foreign Wars (VFW) solicit donations for their Veterans Assistance Programs. Donors receive a small, artificial red poppy, a symbol that harks to this famous poem by Canadian physician John McCrae, who died in France in 1918. During World War I over 25,000 American servicemen were interred in American cemeteries in northwestern France.

> In Flanders fields the poppies blow
> Between the crosses, row on row,
> That mark our place; and in the sky

> The larks, still bravely singing, fly
> Scarce heard amid the guns below.

> We are the Dead. Short days ago
> We lived, felt dawn, saw sunset glow
> Loved and were loved, and now we lie
> In Flanders fields.

> Take up our quarrel with the foe:
> To you from failing hands we throw
> The torch; be yours to hold it high.
> If ye break faith with us who die
> We shall not sleep, though poppies grow
> In Flanders fields.

---

cophagus. America, an ambivalent nation struggling with the memory of war focused its remembrance on victory, not death, in order to justify the sacrifices made.

Despite the lack of consensus in American society, construction of memorials continued overseas throughout the 1930s, culminating in the completion of several minor monuments, three major monuments, and eight large cemeteries, each with chapels. In conjunction with the government's Fine Arts Commission, the ABMC shaped an American presence across the former Western Front. Though borrowing much from British war cemetery practice, the ABMC sought to make cemeteries distinctly American with features such as park-like settings and smaller headstones with greater space between graves. Temporary wooden crosses were replaced with uniform white marble crosses or Stars of David, minimizing individual characteristics in an effort to submerge individual identity to the nation's cause.

To form the American presence overseas Paul Cret, a foreign-born architect, was appointed to create the designs for America's civic architecture abroad. Cret's favored choice of classicism contributed to the international debate concerning modernism and classicism that engaged the profession during the 1920s and 1930s. His work provided a bridge between the end of Beaux-Arts historicism and the rise of modernism, closely paralleling the nation's struggle to build continuity between the past and the complex contemporary world its citizens had inherited.

Ambivalence and delay marked the post-war commemorative effort in which a heterogeneous population, late into the conflict and with smaller numbers of war dead than other nations, sought to commemorate the experience that led to America's new world role. Despite the massive death tolls experienced in the Civil War, the past left Americans at home unprepared for the challenge of memorializing the recent war's casualties.

Graves scattered across Europe and the United States complicated efforts to collectively mourn the dead, just as distant battlefields and ABMC restrictions prevented cooperative attempts to mark the war in a personal and meaningful way. Efforts to commemorate at home reflected the feelings within the nation at large as various factions within American society pursued their own constructions of war memory. Sharp differences emerged at home over the types of memorials that would best define the nation. Progressive reformers urged Americans to build living memorials with utilitarian purpose such as bridges, parks, libraries, playgrounds, and community centers. They were met with stern opposition from artists, monument makers, and professional art organizations insisting that statues, paintings, and other artistic expressions would be more appropriate. Ultimately, some of the finest sculptors in the nation were called upon to design suitable memorials numbering more than 950 statues and plaques dedicated to honoring the men and women war heroes.

While commemoration of the First World War in the United States followed patterns similar to those of other countries, the nation was forced to consider dimensions absent from memorialization as practiced abroad. These added dimensions required a unique and innovative commemorative response to the tenuous connection between national war aims and the high cost of war. Yet, despite the solemn pageantry and hero worship that marked more than a decade of governmental effort to memorialize the war, the resulting symbols failed to mask

Tomb of the Unknown Soldier at Arlington Cemetery, Virginia. AP/WIDE WORLD PHOTOS

the post-war tension, divisiveness, and political rancor of a disillusioned society.

BIBLIOGRAPHY

American Battle Monuments Commission. *American Armies and Battlefields in Europe, a History, Guide and Reference Book*. Washington, DC: United States Government Printing Office, 1938.

Meigs, Mark. *Optimism at Armageddon, Voices of American Particpants in the First World War*. London: Macmillan Press Ltd, 1997.

Piehler, G. Kurt. *Remembering War the American Way*. Washington, DC: Smithsonian Institution Press, 1995.

Lisa M. Budreau

See also: **Armistice Day; Gold Star Mothers Pilgrimage; Public Opinion; World War I, Visual Arts.**

MONUMENTS, CEMETERIES, WORLD WAR II

The scale of U.S. casualties in World War II was unlike anything seen before. In total, 400,000 Americans died during the war. The patriotism and emotions surrounding several key events led to the creation of numerous permanent remembrances. The key groups involved in creating these memorials have usually included a mix of veterans, artists and architects, and politicians.

CEMETERIES

Because American casualties occurred overseas, by 1945 hundreds of temporary foreign cemeteries had been created. At the time, Undersecretary of War Kenneth Royall was quoted as saying that he had spoken to many men going into battle who said if they were killed in action they wished to be buried in the countries they were fighting to liberate. Still, many families wanted their loved ones buried in the United States, so between 1947 and 1954 the army's American Graves Registration Service oversaw the repatriation of 172,000 American dead. In 1947, fourteen overseas sites were selected as permanent cemeteries by the Secretary of the Army and the American Battle Monuments Commission. The dead whose families had requested foreign burials were to be relocated from temporary cemeteries to the nearest permanent one. More than 93,000 World War II dead are buried in the permanent cemeteries in Europe, Africa, and Asia.

These cemeteries are located near sites where the Allies fought major battles against the Axis. The land was donated by the host countries for use by the United States in perpetuity. There was some delay in the Philippines because the government objected to making any of the temporary sites permanent. Finally, in 1948, the government allowed the establishment of a permanent cemetery on part of the former Fort William McKinley in Manila, a rough site that required considerable landscaping.

Prominent architects were selected to design each of the overseas cemeteries; each site was to have a chapel, a permanent way to record the names of the missing in the area, and explanatory maps of the local battles in which Americans fought and died. The designers were responsible for everything from the layout of the graves to the statuary and visitors building at each site. In 1949, the permanent burials were complete, and construction of the associated memorials was completed during the 1950s and early 1960s. The many rows of uniform white gravestones at each site make a bold visual impression.

MONUMENTS AND MEMORIALS

The Marine Corps War Memorial was based on a photograph shot by Joe Rosenthal after the taking of the South Pacific island of Iwo Jima on February 23, 1945. In the photograph, six marines plant the American flag atop Mount Suribachi, and this image captured the imagination and stirred the patriotism of Americans at home. Soon after, senators and citizens alike began to promote the idea of a monument based on the photo. Sculptor Felix de Weldon made a small clay model of the scene within days of seeing the picture and was later commissioned to recreate the scene in bronze. He worked from photographs and from poses by the three surviving flag-raisers, creating a work in which thirty-two-foot-high marines raise a sixty-foot-high flag. At a final cost of $850,000, the memorial was erected in 1954 and dedicated by President Eisenhower.

The USS *Arizona* Memorial was built to honor those who died during the attack on Pearl Harbor, Hawaii. On the morning of December 7, 1941, the *Arizona* exploded after being hit by a bomb, and she sank in less than nine minutes with 1,177 of her crew aboard. Numerous ships and aircraft were damaged or destroyed that day, and U.S. military and civilian losses totaled 2,388, with another 1,178 wounded. Because the *Arizona* is the final resting place of so many of the day's dead, a memorial was built over the midsection of the battleship.

Suggestions for the memorial began in 1943, but steps to establish it were not taken until 1949, when the Pacific War Memorial Commission was established. In 1950, a flagpole was erected over the sunken *Arizona* and a commemorative plaque placed under the flagpole. President Eisenhower approved the creation of the memorial in 1958. Using a combination of private donations and public funds, construction was completed in 1961. The 184-foot structure was designed by architect Alfred Preis and consists of three sections: the entry and assembly rooms, a central area for ceremonies and observation, and the shrine room, where the names of those killed on the *Arizona* are engraved on the marble wall.

HOLOCAUST MEMORIALS

Americans are not the only victims of World War II remembered in the United States. Interest in memorializing the Holocaust was strong during the decades following the war, in part because many Jews had immigrated to the United States during the early twentieth century and had relatives who perished in Europe. Further, Holocaust survivors immigrated to the United States in the years following the war.

Around the country, various memorial museums created exhibits and educational programs about the Holocaust. The largest of these is the United States Holocaust Memorial Museum in Washington, D.C. By displaying artifacts such as victims' shoes, the museum memorializes the lost. In forcing visitors to confront the scale of the Holocaust, the photos, shoes, and other effects serve the same purpose as gravestones. The hexagonal Hall of Remembrance within the museum is a national memorial to the Holocaust victims and contains an eternal flame and memorial candles.

THE WORLD WAR II MEMORIAL AND THE PROCESS OF MEMORIALIZATION

With the close of the twentieth century and the aging of the World War II generation, public interest in honoring veterans increased. The idea for a national World War II memorial was first proposed in 1987 by a veteran in Ohio. In 1993, President Bill Clinton signed a law au-

The snow-covered Iwo Jima Monument in Arlington, Virginia. AP/WIDE WORLD PHOTOS

thorizing the construction of a World War II memorial in Washington, D.C. The design was selected by a ten-member design jury and a twelve-member architect-engineer evaluation board. These panels consisted of prominent architects, critics, scholars, and veterans.

Among the considerations were originality, appropriateness, and construction feasibility.

Architect Friedrich St. Florian's winning design was selected from a pool of four hundred. Key features include a memorial plaza, fountains, forty-three-foot memorial arches, and a semicircle of seventeen-foot-high granite pillars. The $67 million price tag was paid mostly by private donations.

Critics were numerous. Some said the design was bland or too reminiscent of fascist architecture. Others were upset about the memorial's location at the eastern end of the reflecting pool on the National Mall, where they felt it invaded the sacred space linking the Washington Monument and the Lincoln Memorial. Despite protests, construction was begun in 2001.

The perception of World War II veterans as the "greatest generation" helped create public support for remembrances of all kinds. On Memorial Day 2004, the World War II Memorial was officially dedicated, the nation's first large-scale tribute to all 16 million Americans who served in the armed forces during the war.

The memorialization of those who lost their lives during World War II has occurred in numerous locations all across the nation. This reflects the fact that more Americans fought and died during World War II than in any other war. The perception of a just cause and the personification of the evil enemy (Adolf Hitler) helped polarize American society like never before. The American legacy of World War II has been met kindly with the passage of time, especially in recent years as the generation that lived through the war is thinning out and as the trials of 9/11 brought out American patriotism in full force once again.

BIBLIOGRAPHY

Bradley, James, with Powers, Ron. *Flags of Our Fathers.* New York: Bantam, 2000.

Nishiura, Elizabeth, ed. *American Battle Monuments: A Guide to Military Cemeteries and Monuments Maintained by the American Battle Monuments Commission.* Detroit, MI: Omnigraphics, 1989.

Rajtar, Steve, and Franks, Frances Elizabeth. *War Monuments, Museums, and Library Collections of 20th Century Conflicts: A Directory of United States Sites.* Jefferson, NC: McFarland, 2002.

Internet Resources

American Battle Monuments Commission. Available from <http://www.abmc.gov>.

"Graves Registration." Quartermaster Museum. Available from <http://www.qmfound.com/graves_registration.htm>.

United States Holocaust Memorial Museum. Available from <http://www.ushmm.org>.

National WWII Memorial. Available from <http://www.wwiimemorial.com>.

"U.S.M.C. War Memorial." National Park Service. Available from <http://www.nps.gov/gwmp/usmc.htm>.

Richard Panchyk and Caren Prommersberger

See also: **Monuments, Cemeteries, World War I.**

MOTION PICTURES DURING WORLD WARS I AND II

The American motion picture industry began making war movies soon after its first filmmakers stepped behind their cameras and yelled, "Action!" Over the many decades since, American audiences have come to experience war—its spectacle, excitement, sacrifice, and tragedy—via the larger-than-life visions projected on the nation's countless silver screens. Because the Hollywood film industry blossomed during the early decades of the twentieth century, it was inevitably shaped by America's involvement in the World Wars. And, conversely, the films produced and distributed by Hollywood's studios contributed directly to the nation's war efforts. When the call to war was sounded, filmmakers and audiences alike lined up for duty. Their films reflected as well as shaped American culture.

THE EARLY YEARS

The history of cooperation between Hollywood studios and the War Department/Department of Defense is almost as old as the history of American cinema itself. In 1914, barely twenty years after Thomas Edison's first moving pictures were exhibited in New York City, filmmaker D. W. Griffith employed engineers from West Point as technical advisors on his Civil War epic, *Birth of a Nation* (1915). The film startled audiences with its large-scale, realistic battle sequences, and set a standard for spectacle against which all contemporary war and historical films were judged.

The financial and critical success of *Birth of a Nation* helped to establish the film as a template for the many war movies that would follow. Audiences proved willing to overlook certain weaknesses in plot and characterization if the battle scenes were exciting and appeared authentic. To that end, Griffith borrowed Civil War artillery pieces from West Point and nearly bankrupted himself and the studio in his efforts to secure period costumes and to build convincing locations. *Birth of a Nation* set standards in other ways as well. As Lawrence Suid notes, American films made before the Vietnam era seldom focused on any but the most glamorous aspects of war: "Battle was not always shown as pleasant, but the films made it clear that pain was necessary for ultimate victory" (p. 3).

WORLD WAR I

By 1916, the nation was deeply divided on the question of war itself, with President Woodrow Wilson, joined by much of the Democratic Party and members of various progressive movements, struggling to maintain his non-interventionist policy toward Europe—this despite growing numbers of attacks on American civilians abroad and America's growing financial interests in the war. That ambivalence is reflected in the anti-war movies of the day, including Griffith's *Intolerance* (1916), Herbert Brenon's *War Brides* (1916), and Thomas Ince's *Civilization* (1916), all of which depict the toll of war without seriously addressing its root causes or complexities. Though lambasted by critics, *Civilization,* in particular, was a massive hit, and some have argued that its popularity and its pacifist sentiment contributed directly to Wilson's re-election.

Soon after April 6, 1917, when America declared war on Germany, Hollywood filmmakers, like much of the general population, mobilized to support the war effort. Popular pacifist films from the year before were now heavily censored, if not banned entirely, and movie stars began to pitch liberty bonds. Even Griffith, despite his muddied feelings toward the war, made *Hearts of the World* (1917), a contribution to the British propaganda effort. Studio films were equally polemical. *The Four Horsemen of the Apocalypse* (1921) was the most popular of the lot, but its success can be attributed in large part to its leading man, Rudolph Valentino, then Hollywood's brightest star.

Historian Andrew Kelly notes that Hollywood films of the war years are notable not for their quality or artistic innovations, both of which were stifled by the rampant paranoia and economic problems of the day, but for their impact on the motion picture business at large. "The American film industry had come of age by 1918," Kelly writes, while Europe's studios crumbled under the machinery of war (p. 27). By the end of World War I, American films had secured new audiences worldwide and the movie-going public back home had grown weary of battle scenes, no matter how great a spectacle they offered.

THE INTERWAR YEARS

A notable change in the cultural climate had occurred by 1924, however, when King Vidor set out to make a realistic war movie told from a soldier's perspective. Hollywood again turned to Washington, this time requesting from the Army trucks, thousands of men, and a hundred airplanes. *The Big Parade* (1925) found great success with audiences and critics alike, despite its complex representation of man in war. The film's protagonist, John Gilbert, is shipped to the western front, where he loses a leg and watches his two best friends die before returning to a very different life back home. Ultimately, *The Big Parade* questions accepted notions of heroism and imagines war as a deeply flawed and very human en-

Movie poster from World War I picture, *Under Four Flags.* © CORBIS

deavor. That the War Department so enthusiastically supported such a production distinguishes the isolationist 1920s and 1930s from the two decades that followed.

The other landmark film of the interwar years is *All Quiet on the Western Front* (1930), Lewis Milestone's adaptation of Erich Maria Remarque's blistering anti-war novel. Told from a German perspective, the film was a risk for Universal Pictures that proved wise: *All Quiet on the Western Front* won two Academy Awards, including Best Picture and Best Direction, and is now considered one of the greatest war films of all time. The Russian-born Milestone, who had edited Army film footage while in the Signal Corps, and his German cinematographer, Karl Freund, commanded a cast of thousands and a budget of nearly $1.5 million, but their film soars on its cutting between epic battle sequences and smaller, more quiet moments. The most memorable is a shot of the lead character being killed as he reaches for a butterfly, a single image that encapsulated widespread anti-war sentiment.

Ingrid Bergman (as Elsa Laszlo) and Humphrey Bogart (as Rick Blaine) in the World War II classic movie, *Casablanca*.
THE KOBAL COLLECTION

THE BUILDUP TO WAR

By the end of the 1930s, the American film industry was nearing its pinnacle, having weathered the storm of the Depression with comparative ease. Hollywood produced a string of recruiting pictures throughout the decade, including *Here Comes the Navy* (1934), *Devil Dogs of the Air* (1935), and *Submarine D-1* (1937), all directed by naval reservist Lloyd Bacon; but, mirroring the climate of the country and the White House, studio executives typically steered clear of storylines that addressed head-on German aggression in Europe. The most popular war film of the era, in fact, is the most popular film of all time: the Civil War romance, *Gone with the Wind* (1939).

Like every other facet of American life, the course of Hollywood film history was dramatically altered by the events of December 7, 1941. The three months preced-

ing Pearl Harbor had seen the opening of a Senate investigation into the production of "propaganda" films by the major Hollywood studios. Leading isolationists accused the studios of attempting to hasten America's involvement in World War II by producing "preparedness" films such as *Dive Bomber* (1941), *Sergeant York* (1941), *Confessions of a Nazi Spy* (1939), and Charlie Chaplin's *The Great Dictator* (1940), which was deemed "prematurely anti-fascist" by Senator D. W. Clark (D-Idaho). The investigation proved to be little more than political posturing, however, and was abruptly abandoned when America entered the fray.

WORLD WAR II

When President Roosevelt declared war, Hollywood studios proved more than willing to take advantage of the explosive level of public interest in modern combat (and the box office revenue it generated). Likewise, the War Department became keenly aware of how the cinema might be used for its own purposes. A symbiotic relationship quickly developed, and by the end of 1942 several films based on actual events and made with the assistance of the armed services were released to a public brimming with patriotism and clamoring for swift and decisive victory. *Wake Island* (1942), *Air Force* (1943), and *Bataan* (1943) depict the Marines, Air Force, and Army respectively in their heroic efforts following devastating "real life" setbacks in the South Pacific.

This first wave of World War II films helped to establish what would become the standard service film. A "crusty old sergeant" serves as father-figure to a heterogeneous pack of raw recruits. His brave young men fight nobly against insurmountable odds, all in hope of returning to their faithful women "back home." The collective message of such films, quite simply, was that America was in for a good, hard fight, but that through perseverance and bravery, democracy would inevitably triumph over fascism. Steven Spielberg, like so many filmmakers before him, would return to this template six decades later with *Saving Private Ryan* (1998).

The American film industry's contributions to the war effort extended far beyond the service film genre. Many actors enlisted in active service, most notably Jimmy Stewart, who was inducted into the Army Air Corps nine months *before* Pearl Harbor and eventually flew twenty missions with the 445th Bomb Group. The studios also produced a series of propaganda, training, health, and bond-buying films that often featured Hollywood's biggest stars. Those stars included Mickey Mouse, Donald Duck, and the stable of popular Walt Disney characters. The animation studio at Warner Brothers likewise enlisted the talents of its Looney Tunes crew—director Chuck Jones, writer Theodor "Dr. Seuss" Geisel, and voice artist Mel Blanc among them—to bring to life Private Snafu. Personifying "Situation Normal, All Fucked Up," a common expression among soldiers of the day, Private Snafu would regularly make outlandish mistakes and teach valuable lessons in the process.

In the final years of World War II, the studios continued to churn out timely combat films, including *Thirty Seconds Over Tokyo* (1944), *They Were Expendable* (1945), and *The Story of G. I. Joe* (1945). But the war also served as a backdrop to films from other genres. The most famous example is *Casablanca* (1942), Michael Curtiz's romance starring Humphrey Bogart. Rick's Place, the Moroccan night club in which most of the film is set, serves as a microcosm of its day, with a cast of characters that includes Nazis and "good Germans," freedom fighters and politically-neutral French, Americans and Soviets. World War II also found its way into the plots of comedies such as Preston Sturges's *The Miracle of Morgan's Creek* (1944) and *All Hail the Conquering Hero* (1944), and also Alfred Hitchcock's thrillers, *Lifeboat* (1944) and *Notorious* (1946).

CONCLUSION

America's war movies are snapshots of their day, capturing, for example, the isolationist mood of the 1930s and the patriotic zeal of the 1940s. They are like public landmarks for the fallen soldiers and for the nation's crises, landmarks around which the American public rallies, mourns, and protests. As America entered the Cold War, that trend continued. The battlefields of the Western Front, Normandy, and the South Pacific served metaphorically for Korea, Vietnam, and the potentially apocalyptic stand-off between the United States and the Soviet Union. Fighting war on the big screen is surely entertainment and big business, but it is also catharsis, a safe venue for Americans to confront the consequences of their nation's conflicts.

BIBLIOGRAPHY

Basinger, Jeanine. *The World War II Combat Film: Anatomy of a Genre.* Middletown, CT: Wesleyan University Press, 2003.

Chambers, John Whiteclay II, and Culbert, David, eds. *World War II: Film and History.* New York: Oxford University Press, 1996.

DeBauche, Leslie Midkiff. *Reel Patriotism: The Movies and World War I.* Madison: University of Wisconsin Press, 1997.

Dick, Bernard F. *The Star-Spangled Screen: The American World War II Film.* Lexington: University of Kentucky Press, 1985.

Kelly, Andrew. *Cinema and the Great War.* London: Routledge, 1997.

Koppes, Clayton R., and Black, Gregory D. *Hollywood Goes to War: How Politics, Profits, and Propaganda Shaped World War II Movies.* New York: Free Press, 1987.

Shindler, Colin. *Hollywood Goes to War: Films and American Society 1939–1952.* London: Routledge & Kegan Paul, 1979.

Spears, Jack. *The Civil War on the Screen and Other Essays.* South Brunswick, NJ: A. S. Barnes, 1977.

Suid, Lawrence H. *Guts and Glory: Great American War Movies.* Reading, MA: Addison-Wesley, 1978.

Darren Hughes

See also: **Stewart, Jimmy; Wayne, John.**

MUSIC, WORLD WAR I

World War I had a significant impact on U.S. music-making and its reception, different from other wars in the challenge posed to a U.S. symphonic and operatic musical culture that was so deeply rooted in Austro-Germanic music as to be considered a musical colony of the Central Powers. At the same time, as with all wars, music performed important functions such as the bolstering of morale, military recruiting, and the assertion of at least the illusion of a unified national identity. Ironically, a conflict that was promoted as one that would preserve freedom led to domestic censorship of German music and the internment and deportation of orchestral musicians. Fueled by the Committee on Public Information—the federal government's information ministry, led by George Creel—many citizens of the United States demonstrated their loyalty to the country in ways that both embraced the culture of the Allies and simultaneously denounced anything related to the culture of the Central Powers. Creel's volunteer corps, the Four-Minute Men, gave lectures explaining the motives and purposes of the war, and beginning in September 1918 they augmented their speeches with music, leading audiences at movie theaters to sing along with projected stills that had the song lyrics and related images.

POPULAR MUSIC

Between the European outbreak of World War I in 1914 and the point at which the United States joined the Allies in April 1917, musical sentiments reflected popular anxieties over U.S. involvement. The burgeoning sheet music industry that had prospered around the region called Tin Pan Alley in New York City since the 1890s offered up songs like "I Didn't Raise My Boy to Be a Soldier"; brisk sales of the sheet music were followed by a recording, released in March 1915, which was popular until it was withdrawn in April 1917. With the U.S. entry into the war, song titles quickly shifted to ones like "I Didn't Raise My Boy To Be a Coward" and "America Needs You," reflecting the need to persuade young men to enlist in the military and providing a musical equivalent to recruiting posters such as James Montgomery Flagg's famous "I Want You for U.S. Army."

Some popular songs from England that were originally associated with British soldiers entering into the war became hits in the United States, including "Pack Up Your Troubles in Your Old Kit Bag" and "Keep the Home Fires Burning." War themes were reflected in many other songs, including "You're In the Army Now" and "K-K-K-Katy," billed as "The Sensational Stammering Song Success Sung by the Soldiers and Sailors." Perhaps the single most famous U.S. song to originate from World War I, George M. Cohan's "Over There" was first performed publicly at a Red Cross benefit concert in New York City in the fall of 1917. Cohan said that the memorable three-note melodic hook ("O-ver there") was a dramatization of a bugle call; the disjunct, triadic melody suggests a militaristic optimism that di-

minished as the war progressed. Soldiers on the front entertained themselves with topical songs like "Hinky-Dinky, Parley-Voo?" and "Hail! Hail! The Gang's All Here," as well as songs like "My Old Kentucky Home" or "I Want to Go Back to Michigan," which simply reminded them of home.

CLASSICAL MUSIC AND CENSORSHIP

Censorship began to affect many things associated in the popular mind with the Central Powers. Sauerkraut became "liberty cabbage," dachshunds became "liberty pups," and the triple meter dance rhythm so popular at the turn of the century in Viennese operettas and Tin Pan Alley waltz songs was replaced with the strong duple patterns of the march and the foxtrot. Educators and politicians in many cases prevented the teaching of the German language in public schools. In California, the State Council for National Defense attempted to purge all public school music books of any songs derived from German sources; as a result, the music books of countless schoolchildren had pages torn out, rendering them largely unusable.

The reaction of professional music companies in larger urban areas varied. Although there were no official policies restricting the performance of German music, there were laws restricting the activities of "enemy aliens"—individuals not born or naturalized as U.S. citizens. A ban on alien employment in Washington, D.C., meant that many major orchestras could not perform in the nation's capital. In Pittsburgh, the symphony banned all German music from its programs, while orchestras in New York City restricted their bans to living German composers. The Metropolitan Opera Company, also in New York City, banned all German music from its repertoire following the U.S. entry into the war, a harsher measure than was taken in England, where operas by Mozart and Wagner were still performed, although in English translations. The famous Austrian violinist Fritz Kreisler took a hiatus from concertizing after being banned in Jersey City and Pittsburgh. Frederick Stock, the German-born conductor of the Chicago Symphony Orchestra, and several of his players also opted for a voluntary wartime retirement (before the war, rehearsals had typically been held in German). Geraldine Farrar, a famous opera singer born in Massachusetts, was alleged to have pro-German sentiments, and when she starred in Cecil B. DeMille's film *Joan the Woman* in 1917 she eliminated any doubts about her loyalty by wrapping a U.S. flag around her body and singing "The Star-Spangled Banner" in the lobby of a Boston theater.

"THE STAR SPANGLED BANNER"

Although the United States did not have an official national anthem until Congress and President Herbert

OVER THERE

American singer, dancer, and songwriter George M. Cohan penned the top "hit" of World War I in 1917, during a forty-five minute commuter train ride from New Rochelle, New York to New York City. In 1942 President Franklin Delano Roosevelt presented Cohan with the Congressional Medal of Honor to acknowledge this song, which inspired listeners during both world wars.

Johnnie get your gun, get your gun, get your gun
Take it on the run, on the run, on the run
Hear them calling you and me;
Every son of liberty.
Hurry right away, no delay, go today,
Make your daddy glad to have had such a lad.
Tell your sweetheart not to pine,
To be proud her boy's in line.

Chorus:
Over there, over there

Send the word, send the word, over there,
That the Yanks are coming, the Yanks are coming
The drums rum-tumming everywhere.
So prepare, say a pray'r,
Send the word, send the word to beware.
We'll be over, we're coming over,
And we won't come back till it's over over there.

Johnnie get your gun, get your gun, get your gun,
Johnnie show the Hun, you're a son-of-a-gun.
Hoist the flag and let her fly,
Like true heroes do or die.
Pack your little kit, show your grit, do your bit.
Soldiers from the ranks, from the towns and the tanks,
Make your mother proud of you,
And to liberty be true.

Chorus

Hoover declared one on March 3, 1931, "The Star-Spangled Banner" played a prominent role during World War I. Based on an English song connected to a drinking society, "The Star-Spangled Banner" was used, with different words, by both sides during the Civil War. The U.S. Service Bands needed a distinctive tune when performing with other Allied bands, and in 1916 President Woodrow Wilson signed an executive order making it the official anthem of the armed forces. The U.S. Marine Band, when conducted by the German-born William F. Santelmann, concluded all its concerts with "The Star-Spangled Banner," and a concert program from July 3, 1916, contained perhaps the first instruction that the entire audience was required to stand at attention as the anthem was played. Rising during the playing of "The Star-Spangled Banner" became a kind of loyalty test, and on May 6, 1919, a man was shot in the back three times for refusing to stand.

Orchestras were expected to open their programs with "The Star-Spangled Banner" as a sign of loyalty. The most infamous instance involved Karl Muck, a highly regarded conductor who led the Boston Symphony Orchestra after building a distinguished career in his native Germany. In October 1917, the Boston Symphony was to perform in Providence, Rhode Island; management had refused a request to open the concert with "The Star-Spangled Banner." Although not involved in that decision, Muck was quickly branded a traitor by powerful voices, including that of Theodore Roosevelt, who was quoted in the *New York Times* (November 3, 1917) as saying that "any man who refuses to play the 'The Star-Spangled Banner' in this time of national crisis, should be forced to pack up and return to the country he came from." A Boston Symphony concert planned for Baltimore, the birthplace of the national anthem, was cancelled after a former Maryland governor, Edwin Warfield, volunteered to lead a violent mob in protest. Despite Muck's eventual performances of "The Star-Spangled Banner" and his offer to resign his conducting post, the charges against him continued to build, and after being arrested in March 1918 he was sent to Fort Oglethorpe, Georgia, where he was imprisoned as an enemy alien with Ernst Kunwald, the (former) conductor of the Cincinnati Symphony. An investigation by the Justice Department found Muck guilty only of "alleged proGerman sympathies and utterances" (Tischler 81) and he was deported shortly after the end of the war, in August 1919. Boston's next two conductors were French.

MUSIC IN THE CONCERT HALL

One consequence of the anti-Germanism within professional orchestras was that more U.S.-born musicians were hired and promoted. In September 1918, an U.S.-born violinist assumed the position of concertmaster with a major U.S. orchestra for the first time when Frederick Fradken became the concertmaster with the Boston Symphony. Although the percentage of German works programmed by orchestra and opera companies declined during 1917 through 1919, the void was not generally filled by the works of U.S. composers. The maverick U.S. composer Charles Ives, whose music was not widely heard during his lifetime, responded to the sinking of the *Lusitania* in his piece "From Hanover Square North at the End of a Tragic Day the People Again Arose" and to the role of the U.S. soldier in the song "He Is There!" which he revised in 1942 under the title "They Are There!" By the 1920s, German repertoire had reasserted itself within U.S. musical culture.

BIBLIOGRAPHY

Arnold, Ben. *Music and War: A Research and Information Guide.* New York and London: Garland, 1993.

Badal, James J. "Prisoner: 1337; Occupation: Conductor, Boston Symphony Orchestra." *High Fidelity/Musical America* 20, no. 10 (October, 1970): 55–60.

Horowitz, Joseph. *Understanding Toscanini: A Social History of American Concert Life.* Berkeley: University of California Press, 1994.

Lowens, Irving. "L'affaire Muck: A Study in War Hysteria (1917–1918)."*Musicology* 1, no. 3 (1947): 265–274.

"Send Dr. Muck Back, Roosevelt Advises." *New York Times,* November 3, 1917.

Tischler, Barbara L. *An American Music: The Search for an American Musical Identity.* New York: Oxford University Press, 1986.

Watkins, Glenn. *Proof through the Night: Music and the Great War.* Berkeley: University of California Press, 2003.

Neil W. Lerner

See also: **Music, World War II; USO.**

MUSIC, WORLD WAR II

During World War II, the music industry made significant contributions to the U.S. war effort. It also endured wartime constraints and benefited from the extraordinary changes brought about by the war. By war's end, American music was ready to march to different tunes as a result of the social, cultural, and technological changes of the war years.

PATRIOTIC SONGS

Songwriters leaped into the fray early. By 1941 people were taking sides musically, even though many Americans still debated whether the United States should get involved in the war in Europe. "The Last Time I Saw Paris," by Jerome Kern and Oscar Hammerstein, won an Academy Award that year for Best Song. It evokes wist-

ful memories of one of the world's most beloved cities, which had been under German control since June 1940. A competitor for the award, the bouncy, reveille-inspired Andrews Sisters' hit, "Boogie Woogie Bugle Boy," describes one young man's draft experience. Many listeners could relate to the lyrics because of legislation passed in 1940 authorizing America's first peacetime military draft.

After Japan's attack on Pearl Harbor, the music industry faced new challenges. In addition to trying to attract listeners who were dealing with the war's difficulties and dislocations, the industry had to contend with government demands for songs that would inspire support for the war. The Office of War Information (OWI), created by Congress in 1942, pushed music producers to record patriotic or war-related songs. Producers did not welcome the government's interference. They believed they knew best what music would sell. One music executive, quoted by Kathleen E. R. Smith in *God Bless America*, protested that he did not want to lose money on fighting songs until "such time as the Government is ready to foot the bill" (p. 104). Smith notes that during the entire war only twenty-seven songs with war-related themes reached the top-ten charts, and most did not last there long. "Coming in on a Wing and a Prayer" and "Praise the Lord and Pass the Ammunition" were two popular songs with war themes, the latter based on a comment attributed to a navy chaplain at Pearl Harbor. Other war-related songs occasionally made the charts, including "Corns for My Country," "Der Fuehrer's Face," and "You're a Sap, Mr. Jap."

ESCAPIST AND SENTIMENTAL SONGS

Despite the existence of some songs with war themes, *Billboard* and *Variety* record charts show that the public preferred lighthearted, escapist songs, such as "Mairzy Dotes," a goofy novelty hit on what mares, lambs, and kids eat, or songs that described people's personal experiences. During the war years, female singers like Frances Langford and Dinah Shore became more prominent as they interpreted women's concerns. Lyrics reflecting both male and female perspectives often dealt with separation and loneliness, even though OWI discouraged these themes as depressing. Examples include "Don't Get Around Much Anymore," "I Don't Want to Walk Without You," "It's Been a Long, Long Time," and "Waitin' for the Train to Come In."

Three popular holiday songs from the early 1940s, "White Christmas," "I'll Be Home for Christmas," and "Have Yourself a Merry Little Christmas," exemplify this trend. Each is suffused with longing for a holiday "just like the ones I used to know." The first two employ dreams as a way to reach that ideal, the third anticipates the occasion "if the fates allow." All three sound uncer-

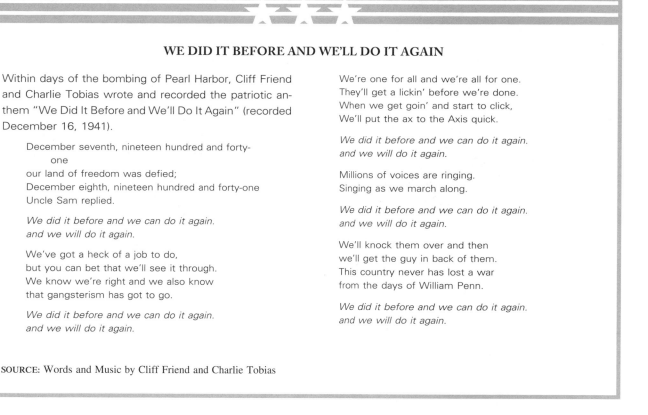

WE DID IT BEFORE AND WE'LL DO IT AGAIN

Within days of the bombing of Pearl Harbor, Cliff Friend and Charlie Tobias wrote and recorded the patriotic anthem "We Did It Before and We'll Do It Again" (recorded December 16, 1941).

December seventh, nineteen hundred and forty-
one
our land of freedom was defied;
December eighth, nineteen hundred and forty-one
Uncle Sam replied.

We did it before and we can do it again.
and we will do it again.

We've got a heck of a job to do,
but you can bet that we'll see it through.
We know we're right and we also know
that gangsterism has got to go.

We did it before and we can do it again.
and we will do it again.

We're one for all and we're all for one.
They'll get a lickin' before we're done.
When we get goin' and start to click,
We'll put the ax to the Axis quick.

We did it before and we can do it again.
and we will do it again.

Millions of voices are ringing.
Singing as we march along.

We did it before and we can do it again.
and we will do it again.

We'll knock them over and then
we'll get the guy in back of them.
This country never has lost a war
from the days of William Penn.

We did it before and we can do it again.
and we will do it again.

SOURCE: Words and Music by Cliff Friend and Charlie Tobias

---

tain that life could ever be the same again after the war, but they do offer hope. Striking an especially responsive chord, Irving Berlin's "White Christmas" became the best-selling single of all time.

TROOP AND HOMEFRONT MORALE

Musicians made other contributions to the war effort. Many performed in United Service Organization (USO) shows. Glenn Miller enlisted in the army and organized the Army Air Force Orchestra. It toured America and Europe and brought Miller's version of swing to the troops. The popular bandleader, who also performed at Bond Drives and made V-Disks (records produced specifically for servicemen), disappeared in 1944 when his plane was lost over the English Channel. The composer Irving Berlin created a musical, *This Is the Army*, to help raise money for the Army Emergency Relief Fund. He included his World War I tune, "Oh, How I Hate to Get Up in the Morning," and added new songs on enlisted men's concerns. The show raised millions and played on Broadway and for U.S. troops at home and overseas. In the movie version, Kate Smith sang Berlin's inspirational "God Bless America." For their efforts, Smith and Berlin received U.S. Medals of Freedom. Cincinnati Orchestra conductor Eugene Goossens challenged composers to create a special fanfare to honor people involved in the war effort. Aaron Copland responded with "Fanfare for the Common Man" in 1943.

MUSIC INDUSTRY

The music industry was greatly altered by the movement of people during the war years. As musicians joined the military, big bands either shrank or disbanded, creating a trend toward smaller, more intimate musical groups. As Philip Ennis notes in *The Seventh Stream*, in addition to military enlistments fifteen million people "crossed county lines" as a result of the war, and this "movement of people was unquestionably the most pervasive and important fact of the war years" (p. 121). This migration brought different groups into contact, which spread music styles such as "race" and "hillbilly" music. The emergence of black music styles led *Billboard* to add the Harlem Hit Parade chart in 1942. During the war years, country music surged in popularity as Southerners joined the military or left home for defense work.

War-related technologies also changed the music industry. For example, the capture of Germany's magnetic tape technology, a simple production method that produced high-quality sound, allowed small, independent producers to cut records outside of the control of the major record labels and later fostered the development of rhythm and blues and rock and roll.

Glenn Miller and his Chesterfield Orchestra in June 1942. Miller formed the Army Air Force Band, which played in war zones in England and on the continent of Europe, until his mysterious disappearance in a plane over the waters of the English Channel in 1944. GETTY IMAGES

Socially, culturally, and technologically, the war years set the stage for the sweeping changes of the 1950s and 1960s—changes popular music would both inspire and describe.

BIBLIOGRAPHY

Ennis, Philip H. *The Seventh Stream: The Emergence of Rock 'n' Roll in American Popular Music.* Hanover: Wesleyan University Press, published by University of New England Press, 1992.

Erenberg, Lewis A. "Swing Goes to War: Glenn Miller and the Popular Music of World War II." In *The War in American Culture,* edited by Lewis A. Erenberg and Susan E. Hirsch. Chicago: University of Chicago Press, 1996.

Lingeman, Richard. *Don't You Know There's a War On?* New York: Nation Books, 2003.

Livingston, Jeffrey C. "'Still Boy-Meets-Girl Stuff': Popular Music and War." In *America's Musical Pulse*, edited by Kenneth J. Bindas. Westport, CT: Greenwood Press, 1992.

Malone, Bill C. *Country Music USA*, rev. ed. Austin: University of Texas Press, 1985.

Smith, Kathleen E. R. *God Bless America: Tin Pan Alley Goes to War.* Lexington: University Press of Kentucky, 2003.

Whitburn, Joel. *Pop Memories 1890–1954.* Menomonee Falls, WI: Record Research Inc., 1986.

Internet Resources

Patriotic Melodies. "Fanfare for the Common Man." The Library of Congress. Available from <http://www.loc.gov>.

Marie L. Aquila

See also: **Music, World War I; USO.**

NATIONAL ANTHEM

Though a celebrated part of American culture today, "The Star Spangled Banner" has not always been America's national anthem. In fact, some people might argue that the song wasn't always American. How did Francis Scott Key's poetic tribute to the defense of Fort McHenry during the War of 1812 come to be one of the most revered and recognizable songs in America, gaining legal status as the official song of the United States?

When Key, a slaveholder, lawyer, and sometime poet, penned the "Star Spangled Banner," he wanted to give words to his emotions after witnessing the 1814 defense of Baltimore from British invasion. Just after dawn, Key looked to see whether the British or the Americans had taken the day. What he saw stirred him—a huge American flag, the "star-spangled banner," still flying at the fort. On the back of a letter Key immediately began composing his lyrics to the tune of an old English drinking song. Within days, the song became a handbill. Then, a Baltimore newspaper printed it, followed by newspapers around the country. By the 1890s, the Army and Navy had adopted the "Star Spangled Banner" as their official song, and in the midst of World War I President Woodrow Wilson ordered it played on all official occasions.

By the end of World War I, the Veterans of Foreign Wars and other patriotic and civic groups began lobbying Congress to make "The Star Spangled Banner" America's official song, but some Americans opposed it because the music was English in origin and the range of notes made it difficult to sing. Prohibitionists pointed out that the song was based on a drinking song, which they felt was inappropriate for a dry country's anthem. Still others rejected its archaic wording, and Peace Movement activists deplored the song's martial spirit. Teachers complained that it did not do enough to teach young Americans how to be good citizens in peacetime as well as in war. Several groups suggested Katharine Lee Bates's "America the Beautiful" as an alternative. But, on March 3, 1931, after twenty years of wrangling and the introduction of some forty bills and joint resolutions in Congress, President Herbert Hoover signed the bill making "The Star Spangled Banner" the official anthem of the United States.

When it was written, "The Star Spangled Banner" reflected the patriotic mood of the new republic and helped make the flag a venerated symbol of America. Today, it still holds special meaning for Americans. Its familiar choruses inspire American pride and optimism. Some opposition to the anthem still exists among those who favor other songs, but the attacks on the World Trade Center and Pentagon on September 11, 2001, rekindled the anthem's popularity.

BIBLIOGRAPHY

Kroll, Steven. *The Story of the Star Spangled Banner: By Dawn's Early Light.* New York: Scholastic, 1994.

Lord, Walter. *The Dawn's Early Light.* New York: Norton, 1972.

Molotsky, Irvin. *The Flag, the Poet, and the Song: The Story of the Star Spangled Banner.* New York: Plume, 2001.

Melinda L. Pash

See also: **Patriotism; Peace Movements.**

NATIONAL GUARD

The militia tradition, with its origins in the Minutemen of the Revolutionary War, is enshrined in the U.S. Constitution. By 1898 voluntary military units receiving state support were commonly called the National Guard. Guard units joined the Volunteer Army that had formed to fight the Spanish-American War, providing the majority of over 200,000 volunteers supporting an active army of 60,000. Although regular army units did most of the fighting in Cuba, guard volunteers played a major role in the Philippine Insurrection (1899–1902.) After the war, critics claimed that massive volunteering had overwhelmed the War Department's mobilization effort. As with the regular army, the National Guard became the subject of major postwar legislative reforms.

From 1898 to 1945 debates surrounding National Guard reform reflected a tension between the professional officer corps and citizen-soldier militia that dated to the Revolutionary War. Army officers, many of them West Point graduates, claimed the guard was militarily unprepared and physically unfit. They charged that Guard officers failed to meet federal standards and received commissions because of political influence. The guard, citing their historical record, asserted that such complaints were contrary to fact and that army officers were attempting to create a European-style army at odds with American tradition. The guard wanted to retain their state affiliations, including unit integrity and command, while serving as the nation's frontline reserve force. In opposition, army reformers advocated a national reserve force under War Department control using individual replacements that would either supplant the guard or restrict it to domestic defense duties.

The Militia Act of 1903 (commonly known as the Dick Act after Ohio congressman and National Guard Major General Charles Dick) established two classes of militia. The Organized Militia (National Guard) was under dual federal-state control and received federal funding and equipment. In return, these units had to meet federal training and organizational standards. The Unorganized Militia was a pool of males, between the ages of eighteen and forty-five, with emergency state and federal military obligations. Significantly, the Dick Act recognized the National Guard as the nation's ready reserve force and acknowledged presidential authority to call militia troops into national service for nine months.

The National Defense Act of 1916, passed as World War I raged in Europe, designated the National Guard as the army's primary reserve. The president's authority to mobilize the National Guard for the duration of emergencies was recognized, and federal training requirements and funding (including drill pay) were expanded. Additionally, National Guardsmen were required to meet the same enlistment standards as the regular army and take a dual oath to their state and the United States.

On April 6, 1917, when America declared war on Germany, 66,000 guardsmen were still serving on the Mexican border after being activated in response to Pancho Villa's incursions. By August 1917 almost 380,000 guardsmen in sixteen divisions were on active duty. The American Expeditionary Force (AEF) was still undergoing training when the German offensive started in March 1918, so the ready National Guard 26th "Yankee" and 42nd "Rainbow" Divisions were sent immediately into battle. By war's end over 433,000 guardsmen had served in the Great War. Eighteen of the forty-three divisions sent to France were National Guard, representing about 40 percent of the AEF.

During the Second World War, after France fell to Hitler's forces in 1940, President Franklin D. Roosevelt ordered the National Guard into federal service. Between September 1940 and October 1941 over 300,000 guardsmen were called up. Rapid mobilization led to numerous problems for both active and reserve forces, including major equipment shortages and high discharge rates. The army's training maneuvers in Louisiana, Tennessee, and the Carolinas during the fall of 1941 were a mobilization high point. As part of the largest army field exercises ever conducted, guard divisions participated fully and acquired valuable experience. However, some critics viewed the guard as especially lacking in combat readiness.

After the Japanese attack on Pearl Harbor on December 7, 1941, the National Guard provided the backbone of available divisions for the early war effort. At the time of the attack, eighteen of the army's thirty-four divisions were in the guard and provided critical offensive combat capability in the Pacific. The guard's 34th Division was the first army division deployed to the European Theater, and the division participated in the 1942 North African amphibious assault. The army's longest-serving division commander was Ohio National Guard Major General Robert Beightler of the 37th "Buckeye" Division. By 1945, the eighteen guard divisions had seen extensive combat in both the Pacific and European theaters. World War II again proved that the National Guard was a ready and reliable standing reserve force.

BIBLIOGRAPHY

Chambers, John W. *To Raise an Army: The Draft Comes to Modern America.* New York: Free Press, 1987.

Cooper, Jerry M. *The Rise of the National Guard: The Evolution of the American Militia, 1865–1920.* Lincoln: University of Nebraska Press, 1997.

Crossland, Richard B., and Currie, James T. *Twice the Citizen: A History of the United States Army Reserve, 1908–1983.* Washington, DC: Office of the Chief, Army Reserve, 1984.

Millett, Alan R. "The Constitution and the Citizen-Soldier." In *The United States Military under the Constitution of the United States, 1789–1989,* edited by Richard H. Kohn. New York: New York University Press, 1991.

Ohl, John K. *Minuteman: The Military Career of General Robert S. Beightler.* Boulder, CO: Lynne Rienner Publishers, 2001.

Internet Resource

Doubler, Michael. "Century of Change, Century of Contribution: A Militia Nation Comes of Age." National Guard Association of the United States. Available from <http://www.ngaus.org/ngmagazine>

Rosemary Bryant Mariner

See also: **Conscription, World War I; Conscription, World War II.**

NEW DEAL

The New Deal refers to the domestic reform program that President Franklin Delano Roosevelt pursued from 1933–1941. Given that the New Deal coincided with the rise of the Axis powers and the coming of the Second World War, military issues had a key bearing on the President's reforms.

REARMAMENT: THE NAVY

President Roosevelt took office in March 1933, less than two years after the Japanese conquest of the Chinese province of Manchuria. During the Manchurian crisis, the Hoover administration considered a naval demonstration, but soon learned that the United States Navy would not prove a credible deterrent to the Japanese. Accordingly, and with economic recovery definitely in mind, President Roosevelt allocated nearly $240 million in Public Works Administration (PWA) relief money for naval construction in 1933. The following year, the President's support proved critical in securing congressional approval for the 1934 Vinson-Trammel Act that appropriated money for a sustained naval expansion program through 1942.

Over the next two years, the Navy's General Board and the State Department worked to block the Japanese bid for naval parity at the 1936 London Conference. With its bid rejected, Japan refused to renew treaty limitations, thus freeing the Roosevelt Administration to pursue further fleet funding. In May 1938, with the economy still staggering from a sharp drop the previous year (the so-called Roosevelt Recession), Congress approved a second Vinson Act, which authorized the construction of some seventy additional warships. With the fall of France in June 1940, naval construction became a top priority and Congress approved the construction of additional combat ships totaling 1,325,000 tons.

REARMAMENT: THE ARMY

While the navy enjoyed sustained growth after 1933, the army did not. In part, isolationist sentiment, which reached its height in the mid-1930s, prevented increased funding for the army, as did the nation's long-standing anti-peacetime-army ideology. By 1939, however, with the Sino-Japanese war in its second year and Europe poised on the precipice of war, the President secured over $500 million in appropriations for the Army. Congress, meanwhile, approved money for the new Civilian Pilot Training Program in order to increase the number of skilled aviators. Following the invasion of Poland in September 1939, Roosevelt approved a modest increase in manpower for both the regular army and the National Guard. Between May and October 1940, as Germany struck west, brought France to its knees, and prepared for an invasion of England, the President secured some $17 billion for the armed forces. The army gained $8 billion, enough money to equip over 1.2 million men by October 1941. In May 1940 alone, Congress appropriated enough money to build a staggering 50,000 warplanes a year. In September 1940, Congress also passed the first peacetime draft in American history, thus paving the way for a vast expansion in military manpower. As the world crisis deepened during 1941, Congress appropriated an additional $26 billion for the army.

Working behind the scenes, New Deal internationalists also strove to bolster the nation for war. Prodded by internationalists such as the State Department's Herbert Feis, the Director of the Reconstruction Finance

Thousands of spectators and marchers show support for the National Recovery Administration (NRA) in a parade on Fifth Avenue, New York City, September 13, 1933. The NRA was established under the National Industrial Recovery Act, an emergency measure designed to encourage industrial recovery and help combat widespread unemployment. AP/WIDE WORLD PHOTOS

Corporation (RFC) Jesse Jones established a string of RFC funded agencies to coordinate the stockpiling of strategic raw materials. These companies, which included the Metals, Petroleum, and Rubber Reserve Company, stockpiled vast amounts of critical raw materials for the nation's war effort while, in effect, preclusively purchasing critical commodities in advance of the Axis. Another RFC subsidiary, the Defense Plant Corporation, oversaw the refurbishment or construction of some 2,300 defense plants.

While the RFC played a major role in preparing the nation for war, other New Deal agencies played parts as well. The PWA, for example, in addition to its role in naval expansion, played a critical role in aiding the Army Air Corps. The PWA funded the purchase of over 100 warplanes and the construction of some 50 military airfields. The Tennessee Valley Authority, meanwhile, sup-

ported the war effort through the creation of additional hydroelectric facilities to serve the needs of the aluminum industry and the nuclear facility at Oak Ridge, Tennessee.

By 1942 full-scale mobilization and war succeeded in doing what the New Deal could not, and the Great Depression at long last came to an end. With the economy flourishing, New Deal recovery programs gradually expired. In 1942 Congress terminated funding for the Civilian Conservation Corps and in 1943 Congress terminated the Works Progress Administration.

LEGACY

The New Deal is mainly known for its efforts to end the Depression and for its programs, such as Social Security. Besides economic recovery and social reform, Roosevelt also used the New Deal to lay the foundation of rearmament at a time when most Americans opposed spending money on weapons and becoming involved in foreign conflicts. Under the banner of putting people back to work, Roosevelt had strengthened the navy and expanded the army. The outbreak of World War II and the attack by Japan on Pearl Harbor found America ready to move from a peacetime to a wartime economy. Thus, the New Deal created legacies that, along with the lessons of World War II and the Cold War, have helped to shape American society—the necessity of military preparedness and the creation of what President Dwight Eisenhower would later call "The Military-Industrial Complex."

BIBLIOGRAPHY

Dallek, Robert. *Franklin D. Roosevelt and American Foreign Policy, 1932–1945.* New York: Oxford University Press, 1979.

Leuchtenburg, William E. *Franklin D. Roosevelt and the New Deal, 1932–1940.* New York: Harper and Row, 1963.

Paterson, Thomas G., Clifford, Gary J., and Hagan, Kenneth G. *American Foreign Relations, Vol. 2: A History Since 1895.* Boston: Houghton Mifflin, 2000.

Internet Resources

Center for Military History. "Mobilization: The US Army in World War II, Fiftieth Anniversary." Available from <http://www.army.mil/cmh-pg/documents/mobpam.htm>.

Public Broadcasting Service. "Brother Can You Spare a Billion?" Available from <http://www.pbs.org/jessejones/jesse_ww2_2.htm>.

"TVA Goes to War." Available from <http://www.tva.com/heritage/war/index.htm>.

Sidney L. Pash

See also: **Civilian Conservation Corps (CCC); Roosevelt, Eleanor; Roosevelt, Franklin Delano.**

PATRIOTISM

War and patriotism are often two sides of the same coin because warfare produces strong feelings of nationalism as well as challenges to the nation's culture and society. Patriotism not only has made Americans feel more strongly about their ideals, but also has led to excesses in which those ideals of tolerance and defense of basic rights are compromised in the name of patriotism. Although patriotism became a common way of expressing national identity, it also divided Americans and created disputes about the meaning of loyalty.

Some of America's most important patriotic holidays and rituals of patriotism either originated or gained familiar, contemporary characteristics between the Spanish-American War and the end of World War II.

NINETEENTH AND EARLY TWENTIETH CENTURIES

The Spanish-American War helped give patriotic celebration new national significance. A shift occurred in the meaning of Memorial Day, a holiday first called Decoration Day that originated in the 1860s with local ceremonies held to honor soldiers who died in the Civil War by decorating their graves with flowers. By the 1890s, northern states celebrated Memorial Day on May 30 to remember those who had given their lives for the Union, while southern states had separate holidays to commemorate the Confederate war dead.

The Spanish-American War contributed to sectional reconciliation, as soldiers from all parts of the country served together under the American flag. After the war was over, the commander of the Grand Army of the Republic (GAR), an organization of Union veterans, urged members of his organization to celebrate Memorial Day by placing flowers on the graves of fallen Confederates. Another GAR commander declared, "We had a new Union, no Northerners, no Southerners, but Americans all" (O'Leary, p. 146). Sectional differences, of course, persisted, but Memorial Day started to become a national holiday. In addition, a new national organization, the Veterans of Foreign Wars (VFW), emerged after the Spanish-American War.

Heavy immigration, especially from nations in southern and eastern Europe, created new concerns about loyalty and patriotism. As early as the 1890s, the GAR called on public schools to establish programs of citizenship education, which included pledging allegiance to the flag. Americanizing immigrants became a matter of national

A 1916 Independence Day parade in Boston. © CORBIS

importance after the beginning of war in Europe in August 1914. Even as President Woodrow Wilson sought to keep the United States out of war, he worried that the divided loyalties of recent immigrants threatened national cohesion. At the president's urging, citizens celebrated the Fourth of July in 1916 as "Americanization Day."

Wilson also proclaimed the first national observance of Flag Day in 1916 and marched in a parade draped in a flag. The Pledge of Allegiance became a daily ritual in many public schools, although some advocates of Americanization worried about an ambiguity in the original version that Francis Bellamy, a Baptist minister, had written in 1892. They insisted that in a diverse society with many people who had been born in other countries, citizens should pledge allegiance not to "my flag" but to the "flag of the United States of America," a change that Congress formally recognized in 1942.

WORLD WAR I

After U.S. entry into World War I in 1917, the federal government played an unprecedented role in arousing pa-

triotism. A Committee on Public Information rallied public support for the war by creating an army of 75,000 Four-Minute Men—speakers who gave brief, stirring, patriotic talks in local communities. Gold Star Mothers also became part of the war effort when Wilson decided to recognize those who had given their lives in battle by having their mothers wear a black arm band with a gold star. Wilson encouraged representatives of various ethnic groups to demonstrate their commitment to the war effort during Fourth of July celebrations in 1918, including a parade in the nation's capital called "Democracy Triumphant" that he personally reviewed.

Yet patriotism, at times, went to excess, as zealots sometimes measured loyalty by ethnicity or nationality. Some communities prohibited the teaching of German in the public schools. German-Americans occasionally became the targets of mob violence. Citizens who opposed U.S. involvement in the war or criticized the Wilson administration's policies faced not only challenges to their patriotism, but also the possibility of conviction and imprisonment under the Espionage and Sedition acts.

Even the end of the war on November 11, 1918, did not bring a return to peace on the home front. A wave of strikes, including some that turned violent, and several terrorist bombings produced a postwar Red Scare, as many patriotic Americans worried that "hyphenated Americans" with radical or revolutionary ideas threatened homeland security.

In 1919, veterans of the American Expeditionary Force that had fought in Europe founded the American Legion, which became an important organization in shaping patriotic observances after World War I. The American Legion helped secure recognition of Armistice Day—November 11—as a national holiday in 1938. In 1954, after World War II and the Korean War, the name changed to Veterans Day, to honor those who served in all U.S. wars. The American Legion also drew up a code of flag etiquette that Congress accepted, with few changes, in 1942.

WORLD WAR II

World War II produced an outpouring of patriotism, which the federal government directed toward boosting the war effort. Each year during the war millions of citizens celebrated "I Am an American Day" on the third Sunday in May. The holiday began in 1940 as a way of encouraging naturalized citizens to accept American values; it was intended to protect against the dangers of fascism and communism. After the Japanese attack on Pearl Harbor, "I Am an American Day" helped solidify public determination to do everything possible to win the war. More than a million people turned out for celebrations in New York City in 1945, and one thousand other communities held events to mark the occasion.

Because of its similarity to Nazi ritual, the traditional salute of the flag with arm extended and palm down while reciting the Pledge of Allegiance changed after America entered the war. That salute, as one West Virginia official put it, was "too much like Hitler's." During the war and thereafter, the usual practice was to hold the right hand over one's heart while pledging allegiance. Jehovah's Witnesses, who refused to accept any salute because of their religious beliefs, became targets of harassment and violence.

By 1945, there were more patriotic holidays than there had been a half century earlier and their observance conformed to national standards as well as local practices. The federal government and large organizations like the American Legion had helped make patriotism and its expression a significant part of national culture.

BIBLIOGRAPHY

Fried, Richard M. *The Russians Are Coming! The Russians Are Coming! Pageantry and Patriotism in Cold-War America.* New York: Oxford University Press, 1998.

Hansen, Jonathan M. *The Lost Promise of Patriotism: Debating American Identity, 1890–1920.* Chicago: University of Chicago Press, 2003.

Kennedy, David M. *Over Here: The First World War and American Society.* New York: Oxford University Press, 1980.

O'Leary, Cecilia Elizabeth. *To Die For: The Paradox of American Patriotism.* Princeton, NJ: Princeton University Press, 1999.

Chester J. Pach, Jr.

See also: **Armistice Day.**

PEACE MOVEMENTS, 1898–1945

For any society, participation in war invariably raises debates over the causes and consequences of involvement. Such debates often reveal preexisting divisions in society and tend to reflect larger social debates over national identity. When peace movements developed in the United States in response to a series of crises between 1898 and 1945, they raised important questions as to the nature of American society and values.

THE SPANISH-AMERICAN WAR (1898) AND THE PHILIPPINES WAR (1898–1902)

The United States' decision to help Cuban insurgents overthrow their repressive Spanish colonial rulers in 1898 led to its acquisition of overseas territories for the first time. Although the majority of Americans supported these events, a vocal minority did not. In particular, when American soldiers became embroiled in a bitter fight against nationalists in the former Spanish colony of the Philippines, a peace movement emerged in opposition to America's newly discovered imperialist impulse. The movement attracted some notable figures (including former presidents Harrison and Cleveland, social reformer Jane Addams, and industrialist Andrew Carnegie) decrying what they saw as Americans betraying their anticolonial, freedom-loving heritage. Less altruistic opponents of the war such as labor leader Samuel Gompers argued that the incorporation of foreign territory might lead to an influx of cheap foreign labor. Similarly, South Carolina senator Ben "Pitchfork" Tillman exemplified turn-of-the-century Anglo-Saxon racism when he warned of the dangers of a more racially diverse Union.

At the end of 1898, some peace proponents coalesced into the Anti-Imperialist League. But despite the notoriety of some league members, it lacked widespread public support and consequently had limited political power. America held on to Spain's former colonies and continued to repress the burgeoning nationalist movement in the Philippines.

WORLD WAR I (1914–1918)

When war broke out in Europe in 1914, the threat to American interests seemed remote. Consequently, a majority of Americans opposed direct involvement. Indeed, despite his clear sympathies for the allied cause, Woodrow Wilson won the 1916 presidential election largely on the promise that "He Kept Us out of the War." However, by April 1917 the pressures of cultural and economic ties to the allies and Germany's policy of unrestricted submarine warfare combined to make Americans more accepting of the need for involvement.

In the three years before the start of the conflict and Wilson's official declaration of war, several groups tried to prevent the sacrifice of American lives on European battlegrounds. Pacifists—many of them members of the Progressive movement—opposed the war on moral grounds. Some of the same opponents of the Philippines War resurrected their opposition to U.S. militarism. Andrew Carnegie gave funds to peace organizers even before war had broken out in Europe. Jane Addams joined with leading feminists such as Carrie Chapman Catt to form the Woman's Peace Party in 1915. Applying the same line of argument put forward in support of the temperance and suffrage movements of the time, Addams saw it as a woman's natural role to temper the aggressive nature of man. Similar peace movements, such as the American Union against Militarism and the League to Enforce Peace, argued for nonintervention up to 1917.

Militant workers swelled the ranks of peace movements during World War I. Many saw the war as a distraction from the bitter struggle for workers' rights and social reform at home. Socialist and Communist parties in America opposed the war for its decimating effects on the working classes. They charged that only industrialists and financiers profited from the conflict. The Industrial Workers of the World (IWW) even advocated industrial sabotage against arms manufacturers. However, not all labor groups opposed the war. Samuel Gompers, of the more conservative American Federation of Labor (AFL), welcomed the new bargaining power that the demands of wartime production gave workers.

The cumulative effect of such peace movements succeeded in keeping the United States out of World War I for three years. However, once Wilson declared war in 1917, most opposition forces retreated voluntarily. Patriotic campaigns backed by restrictive legislation such as the Espionage Act of 1917 muffled many remaining cries for peace. One notable exception was the People's Council of America (PCA), which lasted from 1917 to 1919. The PCA attracted mostly disaffected workers from the Socialist Party and other radical labor groups. The PCA too fell victim to government repression during the "Red Scare" of 1919.

THE INTERWAR YEARS AND WORLD WAR II (1918–1945)

Largely as a reaction to the bitter negotiations that followed World War I in Europe, the U.S. retreated into a position of relative isolation after 1918. For pragmatic and ideological reasons, the United States did nothing in response to growing militarism in Italy, Germany, and Japan. The country did trumpet the 1928 Kellogg-Briand Pact, which called for an end to war as a means of settling diplomatic disputes, but it was in no mood to back up its provisions by force. Ultimately, the pact did nothing to deter aggressors.

In response to events in Europe and the Far East, several peace movements emerged during the 1930s. The American League Against War and Fascism attracted many Communist sympathizers and workers in opposition to European Fascism. The Emergency Peace Campaign opposed both Fascist aggression and Communist agitation and tended to attract members of the middle and upper classes. Although both of these groups denounced Fascism, they advocated a nonaggressive course of action.

The cynicism many felt over participation in World War I compounded America's revulsion to war. In addition to the ire raised by the continued squabbling of European powers, a 1935 Senate committee headed by Senator Gerald Nye of Colorado charged that corporate interests had influenced Wilson's decision to go to war in an effort to safeguard their overseas investments. The Neutrality Acts of 1935, 1936, and 1937 codified the isolationist impulse by prohibiting the shipment of war materials to any belligerents.

Not surprisingly, when war broke out again in Europe in 1939, the majority of Americans favored inaction. The most vocal Americans calling for U.S. abstention from the war were not pacifists but those claiming that it was not in America's interests to fight. The America First Committee (AFC), headed by General Robert E. Wood and with notable members such as Senator Nye and Charles Lindbergh, argued that America should arm itself only to defend its own borders and refrain from overseas combat. But the Japanese attack on Pearl Harbor on December 7, 1941, quickly snuffed out any momentum gained by peace movements. This one act of aggression caused America to go to war more unified, perhaps, than at any other time before or since. The AFC voluntarily disbanded on December 11, 1941. Thereafter, opposition to the war effort tended to be expressed through individual acts of conscience rather than through any broad-based movement.

BIBLIOGRAPHY

Adams, David. *The American Peace Movements.* New Haven, CT: Advocate Press, 1985.

Beisner, Robert. *Twelve against Empire: The Anti-Imperialists, 1898–1900*. New York: McGraw-Hill, 1968.

Cole, Wayne S. *America First: The Battle Against Intervention, 1940–1941*. Madison: University of Wisconsin Press, 1953.

Early, Frances H. *A World without War: How U.S. Feminists and Pacifists Resisted World War I*. Syracuse, NY: Syracuse University Press, 1997.

Kennedy, David. M. *Over Here: The First World War and American Society*. New York: Oxford University Press, 1980.

Kennedy, David M. *Freedom from Fear: The American People in Depression and War, 1929–1945*. New York: Oxford University Press, 1999.

Tompkins, E. Berkley. *Anti-Imperialism in the United States: The Great Debate, 1890–1920*. (University of Pennsylvania Press, 1970).

Mark Boulton

See also: **Addams, Jane; Propaganda, War; Public Opinion.**

PEARL HARBOR INVESTIGATION

On Sunday, December 7, 1941, Japanese naval and air forces attacked the United States Pacific Fleet and nearby army installations in and around Pearl Harbor, Hawaii. The Japanese attack killed over 2,400 people, sank four battleships, damaged ten other warships and destroyed almost 200 warplanes.

Two days after the Japanese attack, the first formal inquiry into the disaster began when Navy Secretary Frank Knox flew to Hawaii to see the damage firsthand. While noting that neither the army nor the navy had adequately prepared for a carrier-borne assault, Knox credited the disaster to superior Japanese planning rather than negligence on the part of American commanders. A second committee, chaired by Supreme Court Justice Owen Roberts, blamed Admiral Husband E. Kimmel, Commander of the Pacific Fleet, and General Walter C. Short, Commander of the Hawaiian Department, when it issued its findings in January 1942. While exonerating senior leaders, including Secretary of State Cordell Hull, Secretary of War Henry Stimson, and Army Chief of Staff George C. Marshall, the Roberts Commission concluded that Kimmel and Short received adequate warning of a possible Japanese attack but failed to act accordingly. Both Short and Kimmel were demoted and relieved of command. Both men subsequently retired from the military within months.

While Kimmel and Short received the bulk of the blame in 1942, subsequent investigations spread fault more evenly. In June 1944, Congress ordered concurrent army-navy hearings into the Pearl Harbor disaster. The army hearing, which concluded in October 1944, noted, for example, that Hull's decision to effectively terminate talks with the Japanese on November 26 ran counter to the military's goal of delaying hostilities for as long as possible. The committee also rebuked General Marshall for neither clarifying his orders to General Short nor contacting him on December 6 to notify him that Japan would soon sever relations with the United States. For its part, the Navy Court of Inquiry, which also adjourned in October 1944, found significant fault with top Navy officials. In particular, the inquiry found fault with Chief of Naval Operations Harold Stark's failure to keep Admiral Kimmel fully informed of the latest intelligence.

The Joint Congressional Committee on the Investigation of the Pearl Harbor Attack, the final official investigation into the attack, concluded in 1946 that Kimmel and Short made "errors of Judgment [and] not derelictions of duty" (U.S. Congress, p. 252). The report, however, mirroring the earlier army and navy hearings, cast a wider net when it concluded that "high authorities in Washington" failed to adequately inform Kimmel and Short of the immediacy of war and the possibility of a Japanese strike at Pearl Harbor. The Committee also noted that military intelligence analysts consistently underestimated Japanese capabilities and intentions and therefore discounted the likelihood of a strike against Hawaii.

At the same time that the various hearings rebuked Kimmel, Short, and leading figures in Washington, rumors surfaced of a conspiracy reaching all the way to the Oval Office that sought to bring on a Japanese attack in order to pave the way for American entry into the Second World War. The conspiracy theory clearly originated from the search for a plausible explanation for the greatest military disaster in American history and was no doubt fed by the findings of the final Congressional hearing. Given that most Americans deprecated Japanese military capabilities in December 1941, many could not fathom that Japanese skill and training, rather than duplicity on the part of senior leaders, led to the debacle. There is no doubt that many of President Franklin D. Roosevelt's domestic opponents sought to link the commander in chief to the disaster. Moreover, isolationists, who had long charged that Roosevelt's polices would lead to war, saw proof of their own prescience in the Japanese attack. The conspiracy theory persisted long after the death of President Roosevelt and the end of the war. Since the 1948 publication of Charles Beard's book *President Roosevelt and the Coming of the War, 1941*, in which the author argued that the president hoped to use foreign policy crises to divert attention away from the failure of the New Deal, myriad historians have attempted, with limited success,

The USS *Arizona* burning in Pearl Harbor, December 7, 1941. AP/WIDE WORLD PHOTOS

to connect the president to the destruction at Pearl Harbor.

The Pearl Harbor disaster continues to hold America's attention. In 1999 the spotlight once again shone on the leading actors in the Pearl Harbor drama when the House voted to posthumously reverse the wartime demotions of Admiral Kimmel and General Short, and the latest conspiracy history, Robert Stinnett's *Day of Deceit*, hit the shelves the following year.

BIBLIOGRAPHY

Beard, Charles. *President Roosevelt and the Coming of the War, 1941*. New Haven, CT: Yale University Press, 1948.

Prange, Gordon; Goldstein, Donald; and Dillon, Katherine. *Pearl Harbor: The Verdict of History*. New York: McGraw-Hill, 1986.

Stinnett, Robert. *Day of Deceit: The Truth about FDR and Pearl Harbor*. New York: Free Press, 2000.

U.S. Congress. Joint Congressional Committee on the Investigation of the Pearl Harbor Attack. *Investigation of the Pearl Harbor Attack: Report of the Joint Congressional Committee*, part V. Washington, DC: U.S. Government Printing Office, 1946.

Internet Resource

History Associates Incorporated. "The Pearl Harbor Attack Hearings." Available from <http://www.ibiblio.org/pha/pha/invest.html>.

Sidney L. Pash

See also: **Propaganda, War; Roosevelt, Franklin Delano.**

PHOTOGRAPHY, WORLD WAR I

The images now associated with World War I—of the slaughter in the trenches, of the disillusionment of the soldiers mired in the muck—did not emerge in the still photographs published during the conflict, thanks in large measure to the stifling censorship. No photographs were published during the war of sodden heaps of the American dead, nor the glazed eyes of the shell-shocked, nor even of the troops vaulting desperately out of the trenches. "At the end of one week's continuous fight [at Chateau-Thierry], in which the American troops were brilliantly engaged, only 24 still photographs had been received at the photographic laboratory from the various units on the fighting front," noted one of the censors at the time. "Even these pictures were very poor and did not indicate in any way that they were taken in a combat zone." What seems so disappointing about the World War I photographs is the near-total absence of either a sense of the horror or the thrill of the danger. With few exceptions—and those often turned out to be faked or staged pictures—the photographs that were allowed to pass the censor were mundane and uninspired.

MILITARY PHOTOGRAPHY: TRAINING AND EQUIPMENT

The official photography of the war was largely the work of the Army Signal Corps, although the navy and the Marine Corps also appointed military photographers. The Signal Corps Photographic Section was created in July 1917, three months after the United States entered the war. By the end of the conflict in November 1918, 6,500 students were enrolled at the land and aerial photography schools, but few had completed their photography course and their one-month army training in time to be sent overseas before the Armistice. By that November there were 54 officers and 418 enlisted military photographers in France; most had already been photographers before the war, so had been able to be expedited through the process.

The standard still camera issued to the field units was the revolutionary 4 x 5-inch single-lens reflex Graflex. Introduced at the turn of the century, it made possible fast exposures and control over focus. Others carried 4 x 5-inch Speed Graphics. Depending on the available light, both could either be handheld or mounted on a tripod. Civilian photographers often traveled lighter with smaller 3 ¼ x 5 ½-inch roll-film cameras.

The Signal Corps photographic units took pictures primarily for military and "educational" use. Aerial photography taken with the fledgling Air Service greatly enhanced the ability of the army to gain information about the enemy lines. Images taken by all the units were pressed into service in the education of the raw recruits and to serve as propaganda for the public.

CENSORSHIP

World War I began in 1914 as a grand pastime and ended four years later as a grand massacre. The censorship echoed that metamorphosis. From August 1914 to June 1915, the journalistic coverage as well as the censorship was cavalierly handled. It was not so much that American correspondents could go anywhere, see anything, and report whatever they wanted, but that the rules to limit the journalists were not always evenly applied or without loopholes. Unscrupulous correspondents and publications also passed on rumors and propaganda—often with the tacit approval of the Allied censors—which resulted in the undermining of the media's reputation for factual and balanced reporting.

By the summer of 1915 the unrelenting butchery in the trenches had already begun, and so came the need for the governments on all sides to hide what was happening. Most journalists were not allowed anywhere near the front, and many American reporters and photographers—who were still neutral, since the United States had not entered the war—went home in frustration. American correspondents who attempted to get to the front by stealth faced severe punishment: the United Press reporter who managed to get to the frontlines in Italy was told when he was taken into custody that he could remain there, "but if you do we'll be forced to shoot you." The famous photographer Jimmy Hare observed that "to so much as make a snapshot without official permission in writing means arrest."

When the United States became a belligerent in April 1917, the focus of the American media naturally shifted to the American role in the conflict. Many reporters and photographers were called home to follow the training of the troops over the spring, summer, and fall. By July 1917, press bases of the American Expeditionary Force (AEF) were established in France. Fifty American, Allied, and neutral journalists were accredited to the AEF—twenty-one were American print reporters, and the remaining twenty-nine were American photographers and artists and the non-American press. That number expanded in the summer of 1918 as the AEF significantly entered the fighting.

Through the AEF, accredited photographers were authorized to travel within the zone of the U.S. Army— a greater flexibility that encouraged many of the major photographic services (including Underwood and Underwood, Keystone View Company, Brown Brothers, Harris and Ewing, and Kadel and Herbert) in the United States to send over representatives. Once the system was in place, the civilian photographers sent home, in total, several hundred pictures a week, and the military sent back fifty or so for publication. In the three months from May to July 1918, the censors approved 1,650 photographs for use by the media.

But the marginally greater latitude, beginning in 1917, to travel to take photographs did not result in any greater candor in the images that emerged. Censors subjected the photographs to two oppressive levels of scrutiny: 1), photographs could not depict any subject that would give the enemy useful information, a limitation that was interpreted to mean that any insignia that could be recognized as belonging to an identifiable outfit and any identifiable locale would prevent a photograph from being passed; and 2), photographs could not depict subjects that would affect the "morale" of either the soldiers or the homefront, which meant that photographs could not depict wounded or dead Americans, wrecked airplanes or other U.S. materiel, or even soldiers in improper uniform.

By 1918 the photographers of World War I had seen too much to remain pro-war, although most continued to back the U.S. war effort. By Armistice, both the glorying in war and the naïve enthusiasm for the coverage of it were irrevocably in the past. Then, in the late 1920s and 1930s, as a new generation worried about war on the horizon, the antiseptic vision of World War I was exposed. Horrific images emerged of the dead in the trenches and the living dead with disfiguring wounds. The documents of what had actually happened at the front served to reinforce Americans' isolationism and made it difficult for President Franklin Roosevelt to argue for U.S. entry into a new European conflict.

Susan Moeller

See also: **Propaganda, War; Visual Arts, World War II.**

PHOTOGRAPHY, WORLD WAR II

During World War II most photographers were "engaged"—they fervently believed in America and in the American cause. Many of the photographers of the war came out of the 1930s tradition of social documentary photography. Documenting soldiers in war was an expansion of the photographers' prewar project of documenting the people of the United States. It was a continuing attempt to reaffirm the nation's democratic ideals and cultural values. During the succeeding wars in Korea and Vietnam, photography was used to challenge American policies and question the nation's values. During World War II, the photography of Americans at war was still an affirmation of the United States as the land of the free, the shining city on a hill, the last best hope for civilization.

MILITARY PHOTOGRAPHY

As a war on five continents, seven seas, and a dozen fronts, World War II posed entirely new problems of personnel, expense, transportation, and communication. Yet, unlike during the First World War, single photographs could be transmitted across oceans by radio and across continents by wire. Long-range airplanes could rapidly deliver rolls of film and thousands of prints. Large-format Speed Graphic cameras that took 4 x 5 inch negatives became supplemented with smaller 2 ¼ x 2 ¼ Rolleiflex

cameras and the even smaller and faster 35mm cameras with telephoto lenses. The challenge amid all this innovation became how to organize the picture-taking so that all the fronts would be covered and all publications would have access to the images.

As in World War I, the army, the navy, the Marines and the Coast Guard each assigned military combat correspondents and photographers to their operations. Most military photography was taken for official reasons. If the still pictures sent back to the United States helped to win the battle for public opinion at home, photographs taken for military purposes helped to win the war at the fronts; it is estimated, for example, that between 80 and 90 percent of all the Allied information about the enemy came from aerial photography taken by U.S. airmen. The navy combat photography group also had a deservedly excellent reputation for its coverage of the war—a direct result of the fact that Edward Steichen, the former chief of the army's photographic section in World War I and subsequently the director of photography for the Museum of Modern Art, headed the naval aviation's photographic unit.

Although the coverage of the army air forces and the navy operations was highly touted, the majority of the military photographers who covered combat were in the Signal Corps. Signal Corps companies consisted of seventy-five men: twenty were still photographers, thirty were motion picture cameramen, twenty were darkroom technicians, two were film recorders, and three were maintenance men. Signal Corps units accompanied U.S. troops from the beginning of U.S. operations abroad, but they did not have a major presence until later in the war. When the American soldiers first landed in Algeria, for example, a sergeant and a private were the only combat photographers with the operation. By 1944, 100 combat photographers covered the Normandy D-Day invasion.

Some of the Signal Corps photography units were assigned to combat areas, others to communications zones. Those photographers stationed in forward areas received two sorts of orders: a general assignment to cover an operation (such as an assault on an island or a town), and a specific assignment (such as to record the effect of enemy tank-destroyer fire on friendly tanks). The photographs these units produced were put to many uses: tactical, for immediate use in the theaters; strategic, for use in planning; training, for the instruction of troops; morale, for the support of troops and civilians at home; public relations, for the media in the United States and abroad; intelligence, for reconnaissance; technical, for the improvement of equipment; historical, for future study; and legal, for war crimes trials.

Over the course of the war, military combat photographers supplied over half a million still pictures to

American infantrymen wading ashore off the ramp of a Coast Guard landing craft during D-Day invasion of the French coast of Normandy on June 6, 1944. AP/WIDE WORLD PHOTOS

the U.S. and British media. Daily official communiqués and a package of photographs were issued from the several theaters and made available to the press.

CIVILIAN PHOTOGRAPHY

Immediately after Pearl Harbor, the War and Navy Departments (soon to be joined by the army) set down strict guidelines under which pictures could be made. One key regulation was that all civilian pictures had to be equally available to all. Therefore all civilian coverage had to operate on a basis of pooled staff. The original participants in the pool were the three chief American picture-gathering agencies—the Associated Press (AP), Acme Newspictures, and International News Photos—and *Life* magazine. Through the pool participants and the various services they supplied, all the daily and weekly newspapers across the United States had access to the photographs.

While the army or navy picked up the bill for transportation and usually billeted and fed the photographers when they were at the front, the pool members paid the salary and expenses of their own representatives. The four pool members spent approximately $400,000 per year for their war pictures.

A year after the inauguration of the Still Photographic War Pool, there were twenty-eight pool photographers in the various theaters. Full-time photographers who had already been on foreign assignment before the war constituted its nucleus. The number of photographers in each theater from the member agencies was subject to mutual agreement. When new assignments opened up, photographers were supplied from each organization by rotation, although *Life* did put more photographers (twenty-one) in the field than the other pool members. Five *Life* photographers were wounded in action, two were torpedoed, one was imprisoned, and a dozen contracted malaria. All told, thirty-seven print and photographic correspondents were killed in the course of the war, 112 were wounded, and fifty were interned in prisoner-of-war camps. The casualty rate for civilian correspondents was four times greater than it was for American soldiers.

Members of the United States Marine Corps raising the American flag on Mount Suribachi on February 23, 1945, after the Battle of Iwo Jima. This photography would be used as the model for the Iwo Jima memorial in Arlington, Virginia. NATIONAL ARCHIVES AND RECORDS ADMINISTRATION (NARA)

CENSORSHIP

General Dwight Eisenhower wrote in a memorandum in the days before the Normandy cross-channel invasion: "Correspondents have a job in war as essential as the military personnel. . . . fundamentally, public opinion wins wars." With that understanding, U.S. government and military officials had from the outset of the conflict actively managed the distribution of the news. Both willingly and grudgingly, the press acquiesced not only in an official censorship but to the government and military's flooding of the news channels with handouts, communiqués, and military photographs.

At the start of the war, the formal censorship mirrored that of the previous world war: publications could publish photographs of the enemy or even the Allied dead, but not of American boys. Even photographs of destruction to "things" American were looked at askance

and released with caution. Censors banned images that portrayed the American military in an unfavorable light, such as those that showed troops openly consorting with prostitutes. In addition, photographs documenting African-American participation in the military were suppressed on a number of occasions.

Then, almost two years into the war, President Franklin Roosevelt and the War Department reversed the regulations. The antiseptic version of the war that had been coming home offered few reasons for the level of sacrifice the American public was being asked to make. By 1943 there remained considerable discord on the homefront, marked by business-labor tensions, including several strikes; by opposition to higher taxation; and by significant patronage of the black market to circumvent rationing. Roosevelt understood that there was a need for those at home to see the casualties. So the new guidelines put in place in September 1943 allowed photographs of American soldiers bleeding, dying, and dead—although censors continued to make sure that the dead or grievously injured could not be identified (no faces were shown, and names on uniforms and division patches, for example, were retouched out). The images that pictured American soldiers bleeding or dead were packaged with captions and text so that the public at home was jarred into a realization that its ideals had to be fought for.

The new candor inspired Americans. The liberalized censorship found that a balance could be made between a modest disclosure of what was happening on the frontlines and the homefront's support for the war. But such a balance was not discovered during the succeeding conflicts in Korea and Vietnam. Perhaps the Second World War had drained Americans of their ability to muster up the financial, logistical, emotional, and moral commitment they had called together. Or perhaps World War II really was, in some defensible way, a "good" war—and so the casualties, however many and however graphically depicted, seemed justified.

Susan Moeller

See also: **Propaganda, War; Visual Arts, World War I.**

PREPAREDNESS

Before 1898, there was almost no serious planning in the United States for a major war. By the time of the Pearl Harbor attack in December 1941, by contrast, the United States was able to draw on a quarter-century of formal planning for mobilization. This rise in readiness helped the United States and its allies win World War II. But it also involved serious struggles over American political and cultural ideals.

PREPAREDNESS AND ANTI–PREPAREDNESS MOVEMENTS

One of the most important military preparedness campaigns in American history began just before World War I. This campaign was led by former president Theodore Roosevelt and his friend Leonard Wood, who had been military governor of Cuba after the Spanish-American War. In 1913, when he was serving as the army's chief of staff, General Wood started a summer military training program for college students. This program served as the foundation for the Plattsburg movement, named after the location of one of the main summer training camps in upstate New York. In the summer of 1915, four Plattsburg-style camps trained some 4,000 men, many of them middle-aged business leaders from Eastern cities. The Plattsburg movement called for "Universal Military Training" (UMT) for American males. They believed that UMT would not only prepare the nation for a future war, but would also create a more disciplined citizenry.

During the Progressive Era and World War I, the preparedness question divided Americans. Wood and Roosevelt were supported by organizations such as the Military Training Camp Association, the National Security League, and the American Defense Society. Such groups, whose influence peaked in 1916, were opposed by pacifist organizations such as Jane Addams' Women's Peace Party and the American Union Against Militarism.

After the United States entered World War I in 1917, a draft mobilized 4 million soldiers in under two years. But when the war ended, Congress and President Woodrow Wilson rejected the idea of instituting a peacetime draft or UMT; instead, they returned the nation to the former system, consisting of a small, volunteer regular army and a National Guard. It was only after a new draft starting in 1940, which put 1.6 million soldiers in uniform by the eve of Pearl Harbor, that the United States returned to a compulsory service program.

INDUSTRIAL MOBILIZATION PLANNING

Military-industrial cooperation in modern America was pioneered by the U.S. Navy, which by the 1880s had already begun to construct new steel battleships. By the eve of World War I, the U.S. Navy had a world-class fleet. Although Congress did not fund it fully during the years between World War I and World War II, the navy continued to modernize. Thus the navy and its industrial base remained at a relatively high level of mobilization throughout this period, even if they did not fully anticipate the stresses of a future war.

Planning for an industrial mobilization that would support a large army began just before the U.S. entered World War I. By 1915, when American companies were already supplying arms to European nations, calls for economic mobilization planning were coming from the U.S. Chamber of Commerce and private citizens such as Wall Street financier Bernard Baruch. By 1916, Washington was home to a new "Committee on Industrial Preparedness," comprised of business executives who conducted surveys of American industrial capacity. During the war itself, the most important economic coordination agency was the War Industries Board (WIB), led by Baruch.

After World War I, the military planned for economic mobilization through a variety of new institutions. The National Defense Act of 1920 created an Office of the Assistant Secretary of War, which became responsible for military-industrial planning. The Army-Navy Munitions Board (created in 1922) and the Army Industrial College (1924) also promoted cooperation between the military and key industries.

Meanwhile, some Americans, aware of the high profits enjoyed by some military contractors in World War I, expressed concerns about military-industrial connections. Throughout the interwar period, the American Legion and other groups tried to secure legislation that would limit contractors' profits in future wars. In the mid–1930s, pacifists helped to create the Nye Committee, a special Senate body that used its powers to curtail alleged profiteering and warmongering among munitions suppliers.

Despite the public opposition, however, military strategists planned to harness the economy for war. In the 1930s, they published a series of Industrial Mobilization Plans (IMPs) that imagined a mobilization coordinated by a WIB-style central civilian authority. Although the IMP model was not followed exactly by President Franklin Roosevelt, many of the military-industrial connections and policy recommendations cultivated by the interwar planners were used in World War II.

STRATEGIC PLANNING

Although much of the American public was wary of war, small groups of military planners created scenarios for future wars. Such preparations were promoted by increasing specialization within the armed services. The Naval War College (established in 1884) and the Army War College (1900), which offered advanced training to officers, were both interested in strategic planning. During the first decades of the twentieth century, the war colleges imagined a frightening array of conflicts with potential enemies all over the world.

The foresight of these strategic planners should not be exaggerated. Plans for wars against Mexico or Britain sat on the shelf. The speed of German advances in 1940, along with the Pearl Harbor attack in 1941, were not anticipated. Nevertheless, strategic planners did prepare for World War II. Plans for a war against Japan in the Pacific, color-coded "Orange" by the military, had developed over a period of forty years before they were actually used. In the 1930s, the U.S. military was anticipating global coalition warfare; in 1940, American strategic planners had drafted a "Rainbow" plan that called for defeating Germany first, and then Japan. This strategy was used successfully during World War II.

Although the United States did not enter a state of high peacetime military mobilization until the Cold War, the first half of the twentieth century had seen significant efforts to plan for war. During those years, some Americans inside and outside the military viewed preparedness as an important way of promoting national security; others, however, wondered if such planning might actually make war more likely. This debate would continue into the future.

BIBLIOGRAPHY

Finnegan, John Patrick. *Against the Specter of a Dragon: The Campaign for American Military Preparedness, 1914–1917.* Westport, CT: Greenwood Press, 1974.

Gole, Henry G. *The Road to Rainbow: Army Planning for Global War, 1934–1940.* Annapolis, MD: Naval Institute Press, 2003.

Koistinen, Paul A.C. *Mobilizing for Modern War: The Political Economy of American Warfare, 1865–1919.* Lawrence: University Press of Kansas, 1997.

Koistinen, Paul A.C. *Planning War, Pursuing Peace: The Political Economy of American Warfare, 1920–1939.* Lawrence: University Press of Kansas, 1998.

Pearlman, Michael. *To Make Democracy Safe for America: Patricians and Preparedness in the Progressive Era.* Urbana: University of Illinois Press, 1984.

Ross, Steven T. *American War Plans, 1890–1939.* London: Frank Cass, 2002.

Mark R. Wilson

See also: **Addams, Jane; Roosevelt, Theodore.**

PRISONER OF WAR CAMPS, UNITED STATES

In both World Wars, despite questions about the validity of the respective Hague (1907) and Geneva (1929) Conventions, the United States generally treated prisoners of war according to the standards set by these agreements. Although the same issues of prisoner treatment occurred in both wars, the vastly expanded scale of the POW system in World War II left a much greater impact on the American war experience than had World War I.

WORLD WAR I

When the United States entered World War I, officials disagreed as to whether the Army should house captured soldiers within America itself. Many advocated the plan as a way to offset labor shortages and assure the protection of returning troop ships from submarines. However, General Pershing's appeal to the government to fill labor shortages in France and Belgium persuaded the Army to keep captured German soldiers in Europe. By November 1918, about 48,000 German soldiers were in the custody of the American Expeditionary Force.

Although captured soldiers remained in Europe, the Army did hold approximately 6,000 naval prisoners, merchant seamen, and civilian internees at four locations within the United States: Forts Oglethorpe and McPherson in Georgia, Fort Douglas in Utah, and in Hot Springs, North Carolina. Of the 6,000 detainees, only

1,346 naval prisoners could be utilized for work not related to their own care, in accordance with the Hague Convention. Officials initially refused requests to employ prisoners outside the camps, but by the end of the war German POWs were working for government organizations such as the Forestry Service and the Department of Agriculture. Limited employment by private individuals and firms also took place, but prisoners' small numbers prevented the formation of any widespread programs.

WORLD WAR II

American entry into World War II necessitated a rapid expansion of the previous war's system. The Provost Marshal General (PMG), now responsible for enemy prisoners, decided to transport them to the United States to prevent escapes and to keep them out of harm's way. Following the transfer of 50,000 German POWs from the British in September 1942, the PMG secured the use of Civilian Conservation Corps camps to house the first arrivals, and continued constructing camps throughout the war. By mid-1945, the American POW camp system consisted of 155 base camps in 44 states, Alaska, and Hawaii. At its height, the system held 371,683 German, 50,571 Italian, and 5,413 Japanese POWs.

According to the 1929 Geneva Convention, American camp officials could require enlisted prisoners to work, if the work was not dangerous and did not directly aid the military. Officer POWs received monthly pay and were not required to work, while NCOs could only work as supervisors. As in World War I, enemy prisoners worked for the government, but they also worked for private employers on a larger scale, primarily in the agricultural and lumber industries. The generally amiable relationship between POW laborers and their employers was the most common form of contact between prisoners and the public, and it undoubtedly contributed to the labor program's success. By the end of the war, the prisoners contributed an estimated 34,219,185 man-days of labor to the American economy.

In addition to working, prisoners formed sports teams, created artwork, published newspapers, read, watched films, and attended classes. In German camps, educational systems incorporated the "reeducation" program of the Special Projects Division (SPD), whose goal was to present prisoners with a positive view of democracy. The project's leadership, which included a number of German POWs, conducted surveys, distributed films, and produced a pro-democracy newspaper, *Der Ruf*. The project's overall effectiveness was questionable, however, because the German intellectuals in the program were generally unrepresentative of the general prisoner population.

Most Americans' only knowledge of the POW camps came from news bulletins about short-lived escape attempts. Towards the end of the war, however, news of poor conditions for American POWs in Germany caused many to question the American system's lax treatment of Germans, and African-American communities resented the preferential treatment given to prisoners in stores and on public transportation. In November 1944, a growing wave of resentment convinced the House Military Affairs Committee to investigate whether German POWs were living too comfortably. The Committee concluded that the American camp system adhered to the Geneva Convention, and that most complaints about excessive comforts were based on hearsay. Government officials declared their intention to adhere to the Convention regardless of conditions in Germany, emphasizing the value of humane treatment in convincing more Axis troops to surrender.

Shortly after the Italian capitulation in September 1943, the U.S. government declared Italian prisoners to be "co-belligerents" and kept only the most ardent fascists under strict confinement. The others received great freedom, including permission to interact with Italian-American communities. Many joined Italian Service Units, which performed labor roles for the American military. The increasing visibility of Italian prisoners fostered indignation among some Americans, including soldiers who resented interactions between Italians and American women. In response, the government reminded the public of the prisoners' "co-belligerent" status, while simultaneously reducing the extent of Italians' contact with the public.

Ideological and racial differences complicated the American relationships with Japanese POWs. Captures were less frequent in the Pacific, as many Japanese soldiers fought to the death, committed suicide, or were killed by their captors. Once in American camps, however, the Japanese received treatment on par with that of other prisoners. Contact with the public was much more limited for Japanese prisoners, because of smaller numbers, and presumably because of greater public hostility towards all Japanese individuals, as seen in the demand for internment of Japanese-Americans.

POSTWAR

After the war, although many POWs wanted to stay, the U.S. government made repatriation mandatory. There were several delays in their departure, however, because of the persistent labor shortage. After several extensions of POW labor contracts, President Truman eventually set a deadline of June 1946 for the removal of all prisoners from the United States. The Allies utilized many prisoners for reconstruction in Western Europe, but protests among the public and the POWs brought about the American withdrawal from the program in early 1947.

German prisoners of war in 1945 at Camp Mackall, North Carolina.

The most important effect of the POW program in the Second World War was the ability of American civilians to come face-to-face with enemy soldiers. Although a number of Americans protested the prisoners' general level of comfort, those who dealt directly with German laborers or Italian "co-belligerents" usually gained a favorable impression of these "enemies." Likewise, German and Italian prisoners tended to have positive memories of their experiences, as is evident in the fact that many returned to live in the United States after the war.

BIBLIOGRAPHY

Keefer, Louis E. *Italian Prisoners of War in America, 1942–1946: Captives or Allies?* New York: Praeger, 1992.

Krammer, Arnold. *Nazi Prisoners of War in America.* New York: Stein and Day, 1979.

Lewis, George, and Mewha, John. *History of Prisoner of War Utilization by the United States Army, 1776–1945.* Washington, D.C.: Department of the Army Pamphlet 20–213, June 1955.

Mackenzie, S.P. "The Treatment of Prisoners of War in World War II." *The Journal of Modern History* 66:3 (September 1994), 487–520.

Robin, Ron. *The Barbed Wire College: Reeducating German POWs in the United States During World War II.* Princeton, NJ: Princeton University Press, 1995.

Gregory Kupsky

See also: **Enemy, Images of.**

PROFITEERING

How much profit is reasonable in time of war? This question lies at the heart of concerns about war profiteering between the period 1898 to 1945. Antiwar advocates believed that eliminating profit from war would prevent wars from beginning. Government officials were more concerned about limiting private profits to control the ultimate cost of warfare. The patriotic emphasis on unity and sacrifice during both World War I and World War II helped the government gain public support for regulating war profiteering. In both periods, however, the government only had mixed success holding down illicit wartime earnings, leading to postwar recriminations against American business. The Wilson and Roosevelt administrations were less concerned about how arms dealing led to war, and more interested in controlling prices once their respective wars were under way. During both world wars, the administration tried to ensure that it paid "reasonable" prices for war-related goods and limited corporations to "reasonable" profits.

The three-month Spanish-American War in 1898 was too short for much controversy to emerge over war profiteering. The biggest scandal involved large quantities of canned beef that spoiled quickly in the tropical heat. Critics accused the manufacturer of knowingly selling the military rotten meat. Complaints about shoddy uniforms, obsolete weapons, and costly lumber for army cantonments also surfaced. Lack of preparedness, rather than deliberate attempts by manufactures to bilk the government, was the more probable reason for high costs and supply shortages during the war.

WORLD WAR I

Concerns about profiteering were the strongest before, during, and after the First World War. The "Merchants of Death" theory, accusing arms dealers of working behind the scenes to encourage war, was popularized by progressives and isolationists active in the antiwar movement prior to America's entry into the war. In the 1930s, evidence collected by the Senate committee headed by Senator Gerald Nye showed only that munitions dealers were quick to take advantage of the new markets that the outbreak of war in Europe created in 1914. Some American companies made truly staggering profits supplying the Allies. Du Pont, which manufactured smokeless gunpowder, doubled its price in 1915 and saw its annual profits skyrocket from $5 million to $82 million. The J. P. Morgan banking firm earned $30 million for its work as purchasing agent for the British. When the Allies ran short of cash in 1915, they began to borrow money from American banks to purchase American-manufactured goods. Postwar critics charged that the United States entered the war in 1917 to guarantee repayment of these loans.

In 1918 the War Industries Board relied on cost-plus contracting that allowed companies to earn a ten percent profit. Many companies found inventive ways to increase their profits by artificially elevating their costs with lavish executive salaries and bonuses. Controlling costs, therefore, required constant vigilance from government auditors. Taxes on excess profits and luxury taxes on goods used primarily by the rich were also intended to limit the accumulation and spending of war profits. Not all corporations used the war to increase their bottom line, however. The Ford Company, for instance, had a contract with the government to manufacture helmets

for thirty-one cents each. When Ford discovered that it could make them for ten cents each, the company returned nearly $200,000 to the government.

WORLD WAR II

Profiteering remained a potent political issue in the interwar period. In the 1920s, the American Legion and both political parties proposed that the government use a universal draft (conscripting soldiers, workers, and capital) to limit profiteering in the next war. The Nye Committee hearings popularized the notion that trading with warring Europe had set the neutral United States on the path for war. To avoid a repeat of the past, Congress passed a series of Neutrality Laws from 1935 to 1939 that limited or barred loans and sales to warring nations.

When the United States entered World War II, the government tried once again to curb profiteering. The government enacted price controls and instituted an excess profits tax, but Congress was unwilling to authorize an executive salary cap. Rationing consumer goods opened up new profiteering opportunities by creating black markets for nearly all items. Businesses also found legal ways to bolster their war profits by taking advantage of lavish tax incentives designed to stimulate production. Overall, corporation earnings rose between forty-one and seventy-seven percent during the war.

War profiteering contradicted the democratic ethos of both world wars. Instead of sacrificing for the general good, many businesses and individuals used the war to accumulate vast fortunes. These immoral gains helped create a sense of disillusionment in American society after each war, and raised important ethical questions about how the United States waged war.

Jennifer D. Keene

BIBLIOGRAPHY

Brandes, Stuart D. *Warhogs: A History of War Profits in America.* Lexington: University Press of Kentucky, 1997.

Kaufman, Richard F. *The War Profiteers.* Indianapolis, IN: Bobbs-Merrill Co., 1970.

See also: **Economy, World War I; Economy, World War II; Labor, World War I; Labor, World War II; Rationing.**

PROPAGANDA, 1898–1945

With the notable exception of Pearl Harbor, the United States was neither invaded, attacked nor seriously threatened between 1898 and 1945. Yet during that time Americans sent their troops to fight and die in all corners of the world. Without the immediate threat of invading armies or imminent danger, the American people needed to be convinced that the sacrifice of so many men and women was justified. Therefore, during the Spanish-American War of 1898, World War I, and World War II the U.S. government, along with elements of the private sector, waged its own war for the American mind. These propaganda messages helped unify the country during wartime and also helped define the meaning of U.S. intervention in each war.

SPANISH-AMERICAN WAR OF 1898

Although public officials and eminent figures cited a variety of reasons for America's intervention in Cuba in 1898, newspapers were responsible for the most notorious propaganda during the Spanish-American War. So-called "Yellow press" journalists convinced millions of the need for U.S. intervention by highlighting the barbarity of Spain's colonial rule and the humanitarian obligation to alleviate the suffering of the Cuban people.

The Cuban revolt against Spanish colonial rule in 1895 occurred at a time when America's leading newspapers were locked in a battle for preeminence. Events in Cuba promised the kind of dramatic stories that would attract new readers. Consequently, William Randolph Hearst's *New York Journal* and Joseph Pulitzer's *World* sent journalists to Cuba in search of sensational material (although many composed their stories from secondhand accounts without ever leaving Florida). Demonizing the Spanish colonial authorities became a key component of "yellow-press" propaganda. In 1896 the *World* cast Valeriano Weylan, Spain's governor of Cuba, as one of a succession of "narrow minded military dictators whose pusillanimous rigor in dealing with the defenseless cost Spain her colonies." The paper went on to claim that "the old, the young, the weak, the crippled—all are butchered without mercy. . . . Is there no nation wise enough, brave enough to aid this blood-smitten land?"

The press's handling of two events in 1898 ensured that public outrage against Spain reached fever pitch. In February, Hearst's *Journal* exposed a letter sent by Spanish minister Dupuy Du Lome in which he derided President McKinley as "weak." The explosion of the battleship *Maine* in Havana harbor a few weeks later proved even more inflammatory. Though no one knew the true cause of the explosion, both the *World* and the *Journal* left their readers convinced that it was no accident. The *World* carried the headline "Maine Explosion Caused by Bomb or Torpedo" above claims that a correspondent overheard a plot to blow up the ship. The *Journal* offered a reward of $50,000 to find the perpetrators. Suggestions of Spanish culpability convinced many of the need for military intervention in Cuba. Rallying around the cry

"Remember the Maine, to Hell with Spain!" the public demanded action. Soon after, McKinley delivered his war message to Congress.

Although newspapers alone did not cause America's war with Spain and the subsequent war in the Philippines, they, more than any other source contributed to the sense of outrage against Spain and the clamor for action that led to the conflict. Though conducted mainly for commercial reasons, the "yellow press" propaganda helped infuse American intervention with a crusading zeal. Moreover, the techniques of demonizing the enemy and highlighting the moral, humanitarian element proved very influential on propagandists of World War I.

WORLD WAR I

Whereas newspapers took the lead in espousing propaganda during the Spanish-American war, the federal government disseminated the majority of propaganda during World War I. Before 1917, few Americans saw the need to get involved in a European war that seemed of little concern to U.S. interests. Widespread peace movements as well as Woodrow Wilson's election as a "peace" candidate testified to the pervasive mood in America. The presence of over eight million people of German descent in the United States further diminished public support for intervention. But as events compelled him to move toward war in 1917, Wilson acted quickly to unify the country behind the war effort.

On April 13, 1917, Wilson created by executive order the Committee on Public Information (CPI). The CPI represented a concerted effort on the part of the government to persuade the American public of the urgent need to go to war with Germany. To head the organization, Wilson chose friend and supporter George Creel, a former "muckraking" or scandal-seeking journalist. The CPI was subdivided into numerous divisions to circulate information to such areas as the press, the movie industry, and education. As a result, Creel successfully flooded almost every medium of public communication with prowar messages and images. For example, the Division of Films promoted such cinematic fare as *Beast of Berlin*, *Pershing's Crusaders*, and *The Prussian Cur*. The Division of Civic and Educational Cooperation encouraged teachers to preach the gospel of Wilsonian internationalism while denouncing Prussian autocracy.

In a further effort to encourage a unified homefront, the CPI sent bilingual agents into ethnic communities to monitor potentially subversive foreign literature. The CPI also sent out over 75,000 volunteers to give brief patriotic talks in movie theaters and other public places. These "Four-Minute Men" spoke widely on such matters as the need to buy war bonds. Some of the stirring titles of their lectures included "Why We Are Fighting," "Onward to

Victory," and "The Danger to Democracy." As in the Spanish-American War, these propaganda messages helped sell the public on the lofty idealism behind intervention. The CPI also employed the same demonizing techniques against the Germans that the "yellow press" had used so successfully against the Spanish. One of the "Four-Minute Men" lectures charged that in occupied Belgium "the wives and children of 40 men were forced to witness the execution of their fathers and husbands."

Other sectors of society aided the CPI in promoting Wilson's war message and his vision of a postwar world. Business interests encouraged the CPI's gospel of unity in the hopes of dispelling labor unrest. CPI posters tried to persuade workers that the war was not being fought for capitalist interests while cautioning that strike action during wartime might threaten the war effort. Civic groups such as Sunday schools, settlement houses, and the Red Cross helped distribute some of the seventy-five million pamphlets produced by the CPI. The Boy Scouts of America sold war bonds and saving stamps in addition to growing food and gathering war material.

Wilson promptly terminated the CPI on November 12, 1918, the day after cessation of hostilities. But despite its successes in papering over some of the cracks in American society, the CPI contributed to some of the more unpleasant aspects of the homefront experience. In particular, the CPI's tendency to debase all things German in its propaganda contributed to the acceptance of attacks against German Americans and their culture. Perhaps due to these excesses, the next federal attempts at wartime propaganda never quite reached the magnitude of those in World War I.

WORLD WAR II

Although the attack on Pearl Harbor caused the United States to enter World War II far more unified than it had been in World War I, sustaining this unity through such a long and destructive conflict necessitated another propaganda effort. At first, the private sector took the lead. Long before Pearl Harbor, organizations such as the Committee on National Morale warned of the dangers of Nazi aggression. Others, such as the Institute for Propaganda Analysis, studied the utility of propaganda in an attempt to both counter Nazi propaganda and lay the groundwork for America's own propaganda offensive. The movie industry weighed in with such films as *Confessions of a Nazi Spy* (1939) and the antipacifist *Sergeant York* (1941). Through the remainder of the war, films such as *Bataan* (1943) and *The Fighting SeaBees* (1944) promoted messages of ethnic harmony and Allied valor on screen.

The government's propaganda assault had also begun before Pearl Harbor. In October, 1941 the Office of Facts and Figures (OFF), under Archibald MacLeish,

began distributing pamphlets and information on the foreseen conflict. With America's entry into the war, the government saw the need for an increased propaganda offensive. A number of federal agencies contributed to the propaganda effort. The Office of Strategic Services promoted propaganda abroad, while the War Department sponsored such domestic fare as Frank Capra's *Why We Fight* film series. But by far the most effective propaganda agency of the war was the Office of War Information (OWI), created by President Roosevelt by executive order in June, 1942.

Headed by Indiana-born broadcaster Elmer Davis, the OWI attempted to coordinate information on the progress of the war and on the United States' wider war aims. Similar to the CPI, the OWI was subdivided into different bureaus to coordinate propaganda through pamphlets, posters, movies, and radio broadcast, etc. One pamphlet, *Negroes and the War*, attempted to solidify black support for the war by warning of the racial violence inherent in Nazi ideology. Others emphasized the resilience of European allies and the need for sacrifice on the homefront through purchasing war bonds and accepting higher taxes. Though Davis never enjoyed the close relationship with Roosevelt that Creel had enjoyed with Wilson, critics of the OWI accused it of being too partisan in promoting Roosevelt's domestic and foreign policy agenda. In 1943, a coalition of Republicans and Southern Democrats slashed the agency's domestic funding. However, the CPI continued to perform an important role in spreading propaganda overseas.

The foreign branch of the OWI remained active throughout the war. The agency dropped propaganda leaflets on the enemy in the European and Pacific theaters, including an intensive leaflet drop on German positions in the months leading up to D-Day. The OWI also emphasized America's commitment to the "Four Freedoms" throughout Allied countries. When he finally ended it on August 31, 1945, President Truman praised the OWI for its "outstanding contribution to victory."

In America's three major wars from 1898 to 1945, the propaganda produced by the government and private sector helped to unify the country and to clarify the principles for which America fought. These propaganda efforts promoted the ideas of America as a nation dedicated to freedom and justice. They reveal how participation in war forces Americans to define their very identity as a nation and the ideals for which they stand.

BIBLIOGRAPHY

Blum, John Morton. *V Was for Victory: Politics and American Culture During World War II*. New York: Harcourt Brace Jovanovich, 1976.

Kennedy, David M. *Over Here: The First World War and American Society*. New York: Oxford University Press, 1980.

Laurie, Clayton D. *The Propaganda Warriors: America's Crusade Against Nazi Germany*. Lawrence: University of Kansas Press, 1996.

Mock, James R., and Larson, Cedric. *Words that Won the War: The Story of the Committee on Public Information, 1917–1919*. Princeton, NJ: Princeton University Press, 1939.

Wilkerson, Marcus M. *Public Opinion and the Spanish American War: A Study in War Propaganda*. New York: Russell and Russell, 1967.

Winkler, Allan M. *The Politics of Propaganda: The Office of War Information, 1942–1945*. New Haven, CT, and London: Yale University Press, 1978.

Mark Boulton

See also: Journalism, Spanish-American War; Journalism, World War I; Journalism, World War II; Motion Pictures, World War I and World War II.

PUBLIC OPINION

The nature of American democracy has created an inextricable link between public opinion and foreign policy. From the earliest days of the republic, the makers of foreign policy have found their ability to make war constrained by public opinion, and the public has often found itself the target of myriad groups seeking to manipulate its views for or against war.

THE SPANISH AMERICAN WAR

In the run-up to war with Spain in 1898, public opinion exercised a decisive influence. The yellow press biased public opinion against Spain, as did the publication of the de Lôme letter, an intercepted correspondence by the Spanish Minister ridiculing President William McKinley, and the destruction of the USS *Maine* in the harbor at Havana, Cuba, with the loss of 266 lives. The heady mixture of indignation and outrage created by these incidents overwhelmed McKinley and forced him to bow to congressional pressure for $50 million in military appropriations and the issuance of an ultimatum that left Madrid little choice but to declare war on the United States on April 24, 1898.

WORLD WAR I

During World War I, America's next major military confrontation, public opinion once again played a major, if very different role. Considerable support among German and Irish Americans for the Triple Alliance, for example, influenced President Woodrow Wilson's early policy of neutrality. Although support for Germany and its allies gradually narrowed throughout 1915 and 1916 following tragedies such as the sinking of the British pas-

senger ship *Lusitania*, considerable opposition to intervention continued among Progressives of both parties, who rallied to weaken the Wilson administration's military preparedness campaign.

As public opinion slowly shifted to favor the Triple Entente and the government pursued limited preparedness, the nation drifted inexorably to war with the Triple Alliance. In the winter of 1917, a series of events, eerily similar to those of the winter of 1898, unleashed a flood of nationalism and indignation that galvanized the majority of Americans against Germany and swept aside the final barriers to U.S. intervention. On February 1, 1917, Germany violated a pledge to end attacks on civilian ships and resumed unrestricted submarine warfare. Later that month, British authorities passed on an intercepted telegram from German Foreign Minister Arthur Zimmerman to the German Embassy in Mexico City, instructing the ambassador to arrange for a German-Mexican military alliance against the United States. With the public now supporting war against Germany, Wilson easily overcame congressional opposition to entering the conflict. On April 4 and 6, the Senate and then the House overwhelmingly approved a declaration of war.

INTERWAR YEARS

In the aftermath of American intervention in Europe, the nation turned inward as Americans sought to escape foreign entanglements. This isolationist impulse contributed to the Senate's rejection of the Versailles Treaty and America's decision to reject membership in the new League of Nations. Isolationism, however, did not prevent an active role in disarmament and Asian affairs. During the 1921–1922 Washington Conference, the United States led the way in reducing naval arms spending and securing an agreement among the great powers respect to Chinese sovereignty and to aid in that country's development. Along with limited isolation from world affairs, Americans increasingly embraced pacifism during the interwar period. This desire to banish war forever found its clearest expression in 1928, when the United States and France led sixty-two nations to "renounce . . . [war] as an instrument of national policy"(Patterson, et al., 124). Reflecting the nation's prevailing antiwar sentiment, the Senate approved the Kellogg-Briand Pact outlawing war by a vote of 85 to 1.

After 1935, when the Gallup organization unveiled the first modern public opinion poll, public opinion began to influence critical foreign policy issues ever more clearly. Public opinion in the 1930s opposed involvement that could lead to war and isolationists used polls to push four neutrality acts through Congress between 1935 and 1939 and to block aggressive aid to China and the use of economic sanctions against Japan after the onset of the Second Sino-Japanese War in 1937.

WORLD WAR II

But if polling data restrained President Franklin Delano Roosevelt from pursuing a more assertive foreign policy, it did allow the administration to embark on a vast preparedness program prior to December 1941. In 1939, the president secured over $500 million in appropriations for the army and additional money for the new Civilian Pilot Training Program, which was designed to increase the number of aviators. Between May and October 1940, as Germany struck west, bringing France to its knees and preparing for an invasion of England, the president secured some $17 billion for the armed forces, of which the army gained $8 billion, enough money to equip over 1.2 million men by October 1941.

Like the Nazi victories in Europe, the Japanese decision to join the Axis Alliance on September 27, 1940, galvanized public opinion against Japan and paved the way for an American deterrence policy that included increased economic sanctions and the redeployment of American forces to Hawaii and the Philippines. By autumn 1941, however, as the president sought a way to avoid war with Japan, opinion polls supported an uncompromising American position, including the maintenance of a full trade embargo, which helped bring about war in the Pacific. The attack on Pearl Harbor on December 7, 1941, followed by Germany's declaration of war against the United States, swept away the last remnants of isolationism and mobilized public opinion in support of war.

As Americans looked forward to the postwar world, they continued to influence the conduct of U.S. foreign policy. Internationalism replaced isolationism and pacifism, and when President Truman moved to resurrect Wilson's vision of cooperative diplomacy he did so with the public's overwhelming approval. With a vast popular mandate, the Senate embraced internationalism when it approved the United Nations Charter on July 28, 1945, by a vote of 89 to 2.

Public opinion has not always facilitated a wise or even consistent foreign policy. Upsurges of nationalism, isolationism, and pacifism have often swept aside the voice of reason, but in a democracy the people will always have their say. From decisions made on election day to the expression of personal opinion about the government's most solemn obligation—the maintenance of peace and the defense of the nation in war—the people will continue, as they have since the dawn of the republic, to influence the conduct of American foreign policy.

BIBLIOGRAPHY

Bagby, Wesley M. *America's International Relations since World War I.* New York: Oxford University Press, 1999.

Dallek, Robert. *Franklin D. Roosevelt and American Foreign Policy, 1932–1945.* New York: Oxford University Press, 1979.

LaFeber, Walter. *The New Empire: An Interpretation of American Expansion, 1860–1898.* Ithaca, NY: Cornell University Press, 1963.

Link, William A., and Link, William S. *American Epoch: A History of the United States Since 1900.* New York: McGraw Hill, 1993.

May, Ernest R. *Imperial Democracy: The Emergence of America as a Great Power.* New York: Harcourt, 1961.

O'Neill, William L. *A Democracy at War: America's Fight at Home and Abroad in World War II.* New York: Free Press, 1993.

Patterson, Thomas, et. al. *American Foreign Relations: A History since 1895.* Boston: Houghton Mifflin, 2000.

Sidney L. Pash

See also: **Journalism, Spanish American War; Journalism, World War I; Journalism, World War II; Propaganda, War.**

RADIO AND THE POWER OF BROADCASTING

Although wireless technology developed prior to World War I, only experimental broadcasting occurred prior to 1920. World War I army and navy training introduced thousands of men to radio's technology and applications. Pooling (sharing) of patents allowed the manufacture of the best radio equipment. By World War II, radio broadcasting had become an established mass medium and contributed strongly to the war effort. After World War II, television replaced radio as the source of news for most Americans.

RADIO AND WORLD WAR I

Radio played only a limited role in the First World War. Telegraph and telephone were more important on the battlefield, and newspapers, magazines, and film communicated war news to the homefront. The few experimental broadcasters closed down from 1917 to 1919. Because the military needed trained personnel, thousands of men (and a few women) learned radio's technology. To meet military demand, manufacturers such as Westinghouse and General Electric (GE) were encouraged to share ("pool") their patents during the emergency, thus allowing both to create vastly improved radio transmitters and receivers—and demonstrating the cooperation that would be needed after the war. Inventor Edwin Howard Armstrong, serving in the army, developed improved receiver circuits that would be used for years.

Westinghouse and GE converted their military capacity to manufacture civilian radios in 1920–1921 and initiated some of the first broadcast stations to encourage people to buy receivers. With other firms they created a postwar commercial patent pool, allowing more rapid production of better radios than would otherwise have been possible. As radio broadcasting developed in the 1920s, men trained during the war played a central role.

RADIO AND WORLD WAR II

Radio played a far larger homefront role in the Second World War. By 1941 most homes owned at least one radio and listening to both news and entertainment was a national pastime. Wartime priorities eliminated manufacture of civilian products—including radios and the tubes to power them—in 1942, and receiver repair and sharing blossomed. Industry-trained personnel flocked to military service.

Edward R. Murrow (center) is considered one of the most influential broadcast journalists in American history. He began his career during the London blitzkrieg, was one of the first to report on the horrors from a Nazi concentration camp, and was instrumental in bringing about the end of the reign of McCarthyism. © CORBIS

Radio programs reflected the war, especially the growing number of network and local station newscasts. Listeners sought breaking news from radio rather than newspapers. Americans heard Edward R. Murrow and other network reporters from European and Pacific fighting fronts, thanks to the use of short-wave transmission and recordings of broadcasts. A federal Office of Censorship eliminated radio weather forecasts and man-on-the-street radio interviews (the latter might be used for secret messages), but otherwise radio networks and stations operated under a voluntary code of censorship. A federal Office of War Information, under the direction of former radio commentator Elmer Davis, was the chief government source of military news, although President Franklin D. Roosevelt remained by far the most effective single communicator.

Radio strongly promoted wartime patriotism in its entertainment programs as well. Radio dramas featured war-related stories and people; even comedy shows helped to further the nation's wartime aims. Variety and music programs, such as those of the comedian Bob Hope and the Glen Miller Band, were broadcast live from military camps filled with thousands of soldiers or sailors. Radio's stars and its reporters helped to tie the country together, especially in the difficult early months of wartime losses. Some of radio's finest writing came from Norman Corwin and others celebrating the war's end.

During World War II radio proved to be a powerful tool in the United States, as in other countries, to promote patriotism, to raise morale among civilians and soldiers, and for propaganda. Radio showed the influence of mass communications in mobilizing the nation and shaping public opinion, a role now largely played by television.

BIBLIOGRAPHY

Barnouw, Erik. "Crusade." In *The Golden Web: A History of Broadcasting in the United States, 1933–1953*. New York: Oxford University Press, 1968.

Cloud, Stanley, and Olson, Lynne. *The Murrow Boys: Pioneers on the Front Lines of Broadcast Journalism*. Boston: Houghton Mifflin, 1996.

Dryer, Sherman H., ed. *Radio in Wartime*. New York: Greenberg, 1942.

Kirby, Edward M., and Harris, Jack W. *Star-Spangled Radio*. Chicago: Ziff-Davis, 1948.

Sterling, Christopher H., and Kittross, John M. "Radio Goes to War (1941–1945)." In *Stay Tuned: A History of American Broadcasting*, 3d edition. Mahwah, NJ: Lawrence Erlbaum Associates, 2002.

Christopher H. Sterling

See also: Journalism, World War I; Journalism, World War II; Propaganda, War.

RATIONING

In the nineteenth and twentieth centuries, warfare changed from seasonal campaigns and battlefield conflicts that involved only military personnel to what has been term "total war." Total wars not only make civilians targets of warfare, as they were during the bombing of cities in World War II, but engage the entire population in sacrificing for the war effort. The purpose of imposing civilian sacrifices, such as rationing food and consumer goods, is not only to increase war production but also to forge unity between soldiers and civilians in winning the war. In this way modern warfare has both material and psychological effects on the home front that have long-term effects on society and culture.

WORLD WAR I

During the First and Second World Wars, the United States sent millions of men into battle overseas. They left the farms for the front lines. Many factories switched to making munitions rather than consumer goods. Exotic foods (such as pineapple) that required shipment over the ocean were in short supply. Fats found in popular foods were needed to make glycerin, a key component in wartime explosives. The metal used to can food was more urgently needed for the war effort. Rubber was needed to make jeep tires and tank tracks for vehicles that rolled

through hundreds of miles of terrain in Africa and Europe. Massive quantities of gasoline were needed to fuel these vehicles.

For all of these reasons, the United States government found it necessary to limit the consumption of these and other critical items in order to prevent hoarding and severe shortages. During World War I, a voluntary policy of food conservation was devised by the United States Food Administration, headed by Herbert Hoover. Rationing of foods such as sugar, meat and flour were suggested, not mandated. "Meatless Mondays" and "Wheatless Wednesdays" were recommended. Americans were also encouraged to grow their own food and eat less to ensure a steady food supply.

WORLD WAR II

The more intense and longer American involvement during World War II meant stricter rationing policies. President Roosevelt created the Office of Price Administration (OPA) in early 1942 to oversee rationing and the rules of wartime product pricing. A system was established under which all families were given ration books filled with coupons that they could use for certain foods such as sugar, butter, meat, and canned goods. Each food had a certain point value per unit. Different cuts of meat were valued according to their rarity; ground beef was seven points while steak was twelve points. There were also ration coupons for shoes.

Once the coupons for the month were used up, the family was not entitled to buy any more rationed goods until the next month. Cookbooks of the time responded to rationing with suggestions for "extending" rationed items such as butter and meat and for substituting similar non-rationed foods. One 1943 pamphlet was titled "Your Share" and focused on telling housewives how to use their share of America's food to best advantage. The booklet explained how to make the most of meat by knowing point values and by storing and cooking meat properly. Many American households were already used to limiting their food intake due to the decade of the Depression that preceded the war.

Gasoline and tires were rationed according to a four-tiered government system of classification that rated a consumer's need to drive. The wartime speed limit was set at thirty-five miles per hour to keep tires from wearing out too quickly and to maximize fuel efficiency. In a way, automobiles were also rationed; new cars were not produced at all between early 1942 and 1945—only war-related vehicles were made.

Coupled with rationing was a system of price ceilings set up by the government to ensure that prices of rare items remained stable. Of course, this system led to a black market for some rationed goods. There were two

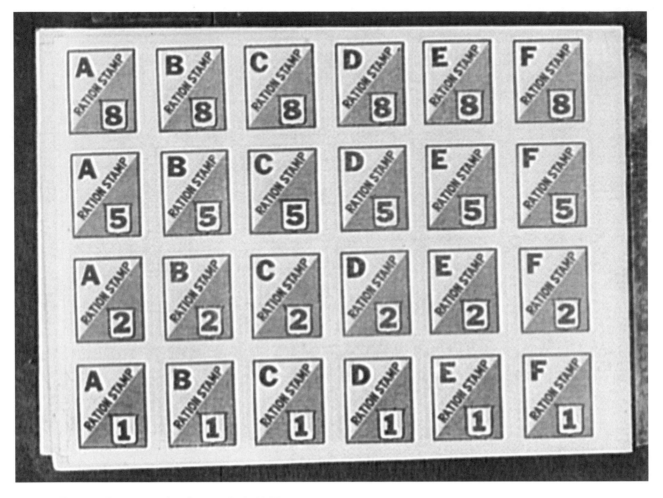

World War II ration stamp book, ca. 1940–1946.

forms of black market transactions—selling rationed items to people without ration coupons, and selling items at more than the ceiling price. It is estimated that as much as twenty-five percent of the supply of some rationed goods was sold through the black market. The OPA received thousands of complaints about price violations during the course of the war.

Public response to rationing was mostly favorable. Despite complaints, rationing was seen as a way to help the United States defeat the enemy. Wartime posters issued by the government played on the public's sentiment. "Be patriotic, sign your country's pledge to save the food," a World War I posted explained, while another told the public to "Eat less and let us be thankful that we have enough to share with those who fight for freedom." World War II posters were similar in sentiment; "Do with less—so they'll have enough," a 1943 poster exclaimed, depicting a smiling GI holding a cup of coffee.

Rationing was also closely connected with scrap drives. Americans were encouraged to save fat drippings, and to collect and turn in metal items for use in the war effort. Another response to wartime rationing was the creation of millions of backyard "Victory Gardens." These gardens were a good source of fruit and vegetables that helped ease the hardship of rationing, especially by reducing the need for canned foods and taking some pressure off of farmers.

Whereas many of these activities, such as scrap drives, may not have contributed much of material value to the war effort, they were very effective in sustaining morale on the home front by allowing citizens to make their own contribution to winning the war. The effect was profound, as civilians and soldiers during World War II have been celebrated by their descendents as "The Greatest Generation," marking an iconic period in American culture and identity as a society.

BIBLIOGRAPHY

Auerbach, Alfred. *OPA and Its Pricing Policies.* New York: Fairchild Publishing, 1945.

The Home Front: America During World War II. Compiled by Mark Jonathan Harris, Franklin D. Mitchell and Steven J. Schechter. New York: Putnam, 1984.

Lawson, Don. *An Album of World War II Home Fronts.* New York: Franklin Watts, 1980.

Panchyk, Richard. *World War II for Kids: A History with 21 Activities.* Chicago: Chicago Review Press, 2002.

Your Share. (pamphlet) Minneapolis: General Mills, 1943.

Internet Resources

"America from the Great Depression to World War Two." American Memory Website of the Library of Congress. Available from <http://memory.loc.gov/ammem/fsahtml/fahome.html>.

"Herbert Hoover Biography: U.S. Food Administrator." U.S. National Archives and Records Administration. Available from <http://www.ecommcode.com/hoover/hooveronline/hoover_bio/food.htm>.

Richard Panchyk

RED CROSS, AMERICAN

The American Red Cross traces its origins to 1864, when the first Geneva Convention established the International Committee of the Red Cross, whose charter obligates member organizations to provide volunteer aid to the sick and wounded of armies in time of war and to carry on a peacetime program of national and international relief during disasters caused by either nature or human actions. Clara Barton founded the American chapter of the Red Cross on May 21, 1881, and it first served the United States military in 1898, during the Spanish-American War.

Initially the organization distributed relief supplies to the several hundred thousand Cubans suffering from the Spanish re-concentration policy, which held individuals in concentration camps. When the United States declared war on Spain on April 25, 1898, the American Red Cross directed its efforts toward assisting the poorly supplied volunteer army regiments in camps located in the Southern United States. The Red Cross provided them with items such as toothbrushes, sleeping apparel, cots, canned goods, and even ambulances. When the army launched its overseas expeditionary forces to the Philippines, Cuba, and Puerto Rico, the American Red Cross followed, providing the forces with nurses and supplies not issued by the army, including mosquito netting, bedding, blankets, and towels.

Clara Barton, who arrived in Cuba aboard the relief ship *City of Texas,* was often seen unloading supplies and helping care for sick and wounded soldiers. When the Spanish-American War ended in August 1898 and the soldiers returned to the United States for demobilization, many of them were suffering from malaria and the Red Cross provided kitchens and emergency hospitals at the various debarkation points, including Jacksonville, Florida, and Montauk Point, New York.

During World War I, the American Red Cross once again provided assistance on the homefront and overseas, mostly in the area of medical and health services. The Red Cross operated fifty-eight domestic and overseas hospitals for the military, staffing them with doctors, nurses, and administrative personnel, and provided ambulances and trucks. On the homefront, the Red Cross set up a Home Service to help solve personal and family problems for veterans and their next of kin. Overseas, the Red Cross was in France by June of 1917, and by the time of the armistice in 1918, more than 8,000 America Red Cross workers were in Europe providing medical, recreational, and welfare services. General Pershing expressed his gratitude to the Red Cross when he said, "No organization since the world began has done such great constructive work with the efficiency, dispatch, sympathy, and understanding with which the Red Cross has accomplished its work" (American Red Cross, p. 15).

World War II created an even greater need for the American Red Cross than had earlier wars. During the war, the Red Cross had 7.5 million volunteers, and 39,000 paid employees The organization undertook a major recruiting drive for nurses and established blood donor services throughout the United States, receiving 134,000,000 pints of blood for military use. To assist veterans far from home, it offered financial assistance and recreational facilities near training camps and it distributed books, magazines, birthday gifts, stationery, and other essential items. Red Cross volunteers responded to 100,000 letters per week from relatives and friends of veterans who were seeking their whereabouts. Among its more noteworthy efforts was the weekly distribution of packaged supplies for American prisoners of war held in Europe. By the end of the war, more than 28,000,000 food, medical, and other POW parcels had been distributed by the International Red Cross, and public contributions totaled 784,000,000 dollars. Similar efforts in Japan were less successful because the Japanese government refused to let neutral vessels enter waters controlled by its military. One of the more memorable American Red Cross programs were the Club Mobiles—converted jeeps, ambulances, command cars, or weapons carriers that operated just behind the advancing front lines and distributed doughnuts and coffee. In August 1945, the American Red Cross began assisting Veterans Adminis-

American Red Cross motorcyclists called the "Flying Squadron," who prided themselves on being able to get under way within three minutes of receiving a call, in Great Britain, ca. 1918.

tration (VA) hospitals by providing 40,000 volunteers and staff members.

After World War II, the American Red Cross shifted its emphasis, helping more than one million veterans and their families with disability claims that had been challenged by the Veterans Administration. American Red Cross workers were also assigned to VA hospitals to run recreational programs and to serve as nurses' aides.

The impact of the American Red Cross during wartime was unprecedented. It was able to fill a void that federal agencies did not have the resources for. The American Red Cross continues to serve the military and public. Its success and secure place in American society reflect the volunteer spirit and humanitarian impulses that are deeply embedded in American culture.

BIBLIOGRAPHY

American Red Cross. *The Red Cross Activities of the American People during 75 Years, 1881–1955.* Washington, DC: American Red Cross, 1955.

Dulles, Foster Rhea. *The American Red Cross: A History.* New York: Harper, 1950.

Mitchell Yockelson

See also: **Medicine, World War I; Medicine, World War II.**

RED SCARE

President Woodrow Wilson's World War I pledge to make the world safe for democracy was severely compromised on the home front by the red scare of 1919–1920. With its xenophobia, attacks on labor, radical witch hunts, and insistence on one hundred percent Americanism, the red scare had deep roots in the American past, but it also triggered a growing American paranoia about an increasingly dangerous and chaotic world.

WORLD WAR I AND THE BOLSHEVIK REVOLUTION

Many factors precipitated this first red scare: World War I had called for a peremptory patriotism that brooked no dissent. Former journalist George Creel, who headed President Wilson's committee on public safety, reinforced this demand for total loyalty, and the 1918 Sedition Act made it a crime to criticize by speech or in writing the government or the Constitution. Also significant was the successful Russian Revolution, and its leaders' subsequent withdrawal of Russia from World War I and their exporting of Marxist ideology westward. In addition, Americans' increasing disillusionment with President Wilson's peace proceedings also bred a suspicion, if not hostility, toward any kind of internationalism.

The emergence of two domestic Communist parties in 1919 alarmed many Americans. Although their combined membership totaled only 70,000, or less than one-tenth of 1 percent of the total population, their impact was considerably greater than their numbers, especially after Communists from around the world called for worldwide revolution at their meeting of the Third International. Some 500 radical periodicals were published within the United States, and although their circulation and readership were limited, some did advocate the violent overthrow of capitalism. Finally, there was a growing distrust of labor unions, which having held the line on wages during the war were now demanding higher wages, the right to organize, and safer working conditions. A series of strikes, followed by numerous unsolved bombings and general urban and racial unrest, helped convince the press, as well as many political figures and millions of everyday Americans, that revolution was imminent. On January 16, 1919, the *New York Times* published "The Red Menace," a poem which warned that Reds "running riot under freedom's name, seek to destroy what they cannot enjoy."

SEATTLE, BOSTON, CENTRALIA

The Seattle General Strike of February 1919 earned national notoriety for Seattle Mayor Ole Hanson, who insisted that the Industrial Workers of the World (better known as the IWW or Wobblies) were trying to use 35,000 shipyard strikers to overthrow democracy and set up a Bolshevik state. Similarly, the Boston Police Strike, which began on September 9, advanced the political career of Governor Calvin Coolidge when he announced, "There is no right to strike against the public safety by anybody, anywhere, anytime." (Allen, *Only Yesterday*) In the fall of 1919, more than 400,000 coal miners struck against U.S. Steel. In every case, after corporate and political leaders and the press branded strikers as reds, the workers were forced to return to their jobs with no concessions.

Fueled by inflammatory reporting, the red scare quickly spread to other segments of the population. Superpatriotic organizations flourished, including the National Security League, the American Defense Society, and especially the American Legion, which was founded on May 8, 1919, to, among other things, foster and perpetuate one hundred percent Americanism. By the end of the year, the Legion claimed more than a million members. On Armistice Day, November 11, the Legion chapter in Centralia, Washington, sacked the local IWW headquarters in what became known as the Centralia Massacre. When the Wobblies defended themselves, four Legionnaires were killed. Among the Wobblies arrested was Wesley Everest, who was summarily lynched.

BOMBINGS AND THE PALMER RAIDS

A rash of unsolved bombings further fanned the flames of intolerance and rage. On April 28, a bomb targeted Ole Hanson, and another the next day injured the housekeeper of U.S. Senator Thomas W. Hartwick. On April 30, an alert New York City postal employee discovered sixteen bombs being held for insufficient postage. On June 2, eight bombs went off almost simultaneously in eight different cities, including one that exploded on Attorney General A. Mitchell Palmer's front porch.

On November 7, 1919, the attorney general launched the first of his so-called Palmer Raids against foreign radicals. This first raid led to the arrest of Emma Goldman, dubbed the Anarchist Queen by the press, and 248 other foreign-born radicals, all of whom were deported aboard the *Buford,* or the Red Ark, as it was referred to in the press.

Other raids followed in January 1920, with more than 6,000 arrests in over thirty American cities. Those arrested were often held without specific charges or legal counsel, and most were guilty of little more than having been born in foreign lands. Nevertheless, Palmer announced to a gullible public, "Out of the sly and crafty eyes of many of them leap cupidity, cruelty, insanity, and crime; from their lopsided faces, sloping brows, and misshapen features may be recognized the unmistakable criminal type." (Murray, *Red Scare*)

AFTERMATH

The red scare abated in 1920 almost as quickly as it had begun. The spread of Bolshevism in Europe had slowed down, and many domestic radicals had given up their fight or gone underground. Palmer, who clearly had presidential ambitions, overstepped his authority and frightened growing numbers of prominent political, legal, and intellectual figures. The American public had also become tired of crusades, even against Bolsheviks, especially after they realized that the threat had been wildly exaggerated. Presidential candidate Warren G. Harding summed up changing popular sentiment when he called for the country to return to normalcy.

Nevertheless, exploiting the nativist sentiment that had been unleashed by the red scare, the Ku Klux Klan greatly increased its membership by turning its attention to immigrants, especially Catholics and Jews. By 1924, the Klan had become such a powerful political force that its resolution to burn a cross at the Democratic National Convention was only narrowly defeated.

The red scare may have burned itself out, but its long term effects were profound. Organized labor was badly damaged when employers seized the opportunity to introduce the open shop, now called the American Plan, which forbid mandatory union membership. Social and economic reformers were thoroughly discredited, and the xenophobia of the era contributed to the anti-immigration laws of the 1920s. The sacrifice of civil liberties in the name of national security also had long-term repercussions, especially in times of war. Above all, the red scare showed how tenuous was Americans' appreciation and understanding of their own democracy and its constitutional ideals.

BIBLIOGRAPHY

Allen, Frederick Lewis. *Only Yesterday: An Informal History of the 1920s.* New York: Harper & Brothers, 1931.

Coben, Stanley. *A Study in Nativism: The American Red Scare of 1919–20.* New York: Irvington, 1991.

Feuerlicht, Roberta Strauss. *America's Reign of Terror: World War I, the Red Scare, and the Palmer Raids.* New York: Random House, 1971.

Gengarelly, W. Anthony. *Distinguished Dissenters and Opposition to the 1919–1920 Red Scare.* New York: Edwin Mellen, 1996.

Murray, Robert K. *Red Scare: A Study in National Hysteria, 1919–1920.* Minneapolis: University of Minnesota Press, 1955.

Schmidt, Regin. *Red Scare: FBI and the Origins of Anti-Communism in the United States.* Copenhagen: Museum Tusculanum Press, 2000.

Lewis H. Carlson

See also: American Legion; Americanization; Dissent, World War I and World War II; Civil Liberties, World War I; Labor, World War I.

REGIONAL MIGRATION, WORLD WAR I AND WORLD WAR II

The most basic concept to understand when examining regional migration is the fact that industrialization has always developed unevenly. Because jobs were never on a geographic parity with workers, workers have been forced to pack up and move themselves to areas were jobs were plentiful. Wartime mobilization heightened this phenomenon.

WORLD WAR I

American industrialists had long exploited the unevenness of worldwide economic development by employing immigrants, many of whom they recruited directly to their factories. By 1915, however, World War I had stopped the flow of immigrant labor. As a result, new opportunities for industrial employment opened for Americans living in rural poverty and for blacks and other minorities in the South. As war orders from England and France rose, and especially after the United States entered the war in 1917 and mobilized, the need to find new sources of industrial labor became a national crisis that threatened the American war effort. The war, which depleted the traditional pool of labor, increased the need to recruit minorities already living in the United States from farms to factories.

"The Great Migration" of black Americans out of the South and into the North is one of the best-known results of wartime migration. Although industrialists welcomed (at least temporarily) black workers, one should not ignore the other factors that pushed workers northward, including the crop losses due to the boll weevil, falling cotton prices, natural disasters, and, especially, a long history of racial oppression. The war turned black northern migration from a trickle to a flood. Historian James Grossman in *Land of Hope* writes that the migration "drew upon black southerners who looked to urban life and the industrial economy for the social and economic foundation of full citizenship and its perquisites" (p. 19). But the Great Migration cannot be seen solely in economic terms. Historians have argued that black Americans moved not just for jobs but for good schools, equal rights, and equal access to public facilities.

The stories associated with such a migration are rich, filled with both anticipation and frustration, particularly as migrants believed northern cities, such as Chicago, Detroit, and Cleveland, offered a racial paradise that could actually be seen when crossing the Mason-Dixon Line. One young man recalled that he expected to see the Mason-Dixon Line, perhaps marked by a row of trees. Although disappointed, he quickly moved into another car and took a seat next to a white man when someone reported that they were now in the North. Chicago and other northern cities were never quite the racial paradise, free from segregation and discrimination, that some envisioned, but kinship made the adjustment to northern culture easier. In Chicago, for example, friends and relatives and even churches helped newcomers find shelter on Chicago's South Side. The black community was also a source of comfort when conditions were tough, as they were during the summer race riot in Chicago in 1919.

Mexican Americans also moved from rural to urban areas to work in industry. Historian Dionicio Nodín Valdés in *Barrios Norteños* argues that Mexicans entered the northern United States "en masse as a reserve labor army" whose purpose was to work in the most "unstable, unpleasant, and seasonal" fields, factories, and railroads. Unlike African Americans, who often moved as family units, the Mexican experience was largely a "man's world"; families were seldom welcomed by American society during the early period of migration.

Southern whites were the third group to be affected by wartime opportunity. An entire generation of southerners came to see World War I as the benchmark for social change. As Kentuckian Zeke Jett explained after the war, "people went to going out of here for public works, and plants started up over the country. And they could make a better living, and so a greater part of them moved out. Now, when you hear tell of some elderly person like me be deceased, well, they'll give the names. . . . They'll have boys and girls in California, Michigan, New York, and all over the country. Whereas, I'd say, thirty years before that time, everybody was right in that same creek—never had gone out. But things changed after World War I in this country where there were more works and they could make a better living [in the North] . . . and they moved out" (Berry, p. 16). The war had uprooted millions of Americans and changed the composition of many Northern cities.

After World War I, regional migration networks grew, particularly through the 1920s, as new generations of workers left home to pursue new opportunities. The Great Depression created a dilemma for those who had recently migrated: stay and try to tough out conditions in northern and western cities, or return to their homes of origin. African Americans for the most part decided to stay in northern areas, having long given up on the South. Mexican Americans who were not American citizens often had no choice; their tenuous presence after World War I made them particularly vulnerable to nativist sentiment such as Herbert Hoover's "Hire Ameri-

can" campaign. The government embarked on a drive to deport those who entered the country illegally and even urged U.S. citizens of Mexican descent to leave the country. White Southern Americans also participated in a back-to-the-land movement. Denver Mattingly was one of thousands who left Detroit for his eastern Kentucky home because he was working less than twenty hours per week. Those who did leave northern industry waited until prosperity would again call them.

WORLD WAR II

Prosperity returned as the country mobilized for World War II. Eight months before the bombing of Pearl Harbor, the Tolan Committee investigating the migration of destitute citizens changed its name to the Committee on National Defense Migration. It went from a committee preventing people from migrating to one worried that not enough people would migrate to fill the jobs required by defense mobilization. Preparation for war generated a new wave of migration.

The South, with a glut of surplus labor, provided workers to the industrialized Midwest and an industrializing West. Most defense industries were located in the North and West, thus wasting a rare opportunity to change the course of southern social and economic life. The Willow Run bomber plant, constructed by Henry Ford near Detroit, attracted a flood of new laborers from other regions despite the urging of Office of Production Management to build defense plants in areas with labor surpluses, such as the South.

California became a magnet for regional migration. Historian James N. Gregory explains in *American Exodus*, "the effects were particularly stunning in California, which received more federal defense dollars than any other state, some ten percent of total war-era expenditures." All of those defense dollars attracted a mammoth migration of 621,000 people from Oklahoma, Arkansas, Texas, and Missouri that dwarfed the number of people who left these states during the 1930s Dust Bowl, an ecological disaster that ruined agriculture. And increasing numbers of African Americans from the South gave California its first significant black population.

CULTURAL IMPACT OF MIGRATION

As migrant people always do, wartime newcomers brought their cultural traditions with them. They tended to settle in neighborhoods filled with people just like them. They brought their preferences for music and food with them. Southern whites, for example, could tune in to northern radio stations and hear "country" music from the Grand Ole Opry whose themes of migration, Mom and Dad, and the old home place tugged at the hearts of migrant listeners; no better example is Danny Dill's and Mel Tillis's show "Detroit City." Mexican, southern, and

African-American foods could be found wherever critical masses of migrants ventured; tortillas, dumplings, and collards dispersed throughout the country. And finally, migrants transplanted their churches wherever they moved. Older ethnic Catholic parishes became Mexican in northern urban barrios, and southern whites spread their evangelical churches throughout the North and West. All the children of newcomers had to adjust in various ways to the differences in schools, while their parents and grandparents struggled to hold on to traditional culture in the face of rapid change.

Thus, World War I and World War II, in addition to the Great depression of the 1930s, helped to transform American society and culture. Because industrial capitalism did not develop in a systematic, uniform way, areas of labor shortages and labor surplus resulted in regional migration to address the imbalances, and the exigencies of wartime exacerbated migration adjustments for native populations and newcomers. Regional migration in the twentieth century altered the landscape and the people in numerous and long-lasting ways, scattering as it did regional peoples across an increasingly homogenized country.

BIBLIOGRAPHY

Berry, Chad. *Southern Migrants, Northern Exiles.* Urbana: University of Illinois Press, 2000.

Gregory, James N. *American Exodus: The Dust Bowl Migration and Okie Culture in California.* New York: Oxford University Press, 1989.

Grossman, James R. *Land of Hope: Chicago, Black Southerners, and the Great Migration.* Chicago: University of Chicago Press, 1989.

Valdés, Dionicio Nodín. *Barrios Norteños: St. Paul and Midwestern Mexican Communities in the Twentieth Century.* Austin: University of Texas Press, 2000.

Chad Berry

See also: **African Americans, World War I; African Americans, World War II; Economy, World War I; Economy, World War II.**

RELIGION, WORLD WAR II

The devastation of World War I loomed in the background for Americans when war began in Europe in September 1939 and when the United States moved to assist Britain prior to entering the war in December 1941. Many members of the clergy realized in the wake of World War I that they had been duped by propaganda, and they recognized that the lofty principles over which the war was fought were never achieved. Making pledges

to resist all wars, they cried, "never again," even when the shadow of Nazism fell over Europe. Religious groups resisted American entry into the war. That resistance set off a wide and intense debate about intervention. The Christian theologian Reinhold Niebuhr and his colleagues encouraged intervention, but they were the minority. Most mainline Christian groups opposed entry. Fundamentalists, meanwhile, looked to see if this would lead to the end of history. However, the attack on Pearl Harbor made the debate irrelevant.

Religious groups rallied to support the Allied cause during World War II, as they had during World War I. They sent their sons and daughters into the military, accepted shortages as a matter of course, worked in industries that fueled the war machine, and prayed for safety and victory. If anything, Americans were confident that the Allied cause was right and that the enemy was wrong. God would therefore vindicate them.

Yet religious groups responded to the war with surprising reservation and ambivalence, too. In deliberate contrast to the zealous, jingoistic support they had displayed during World War I, American religious organizations were careful to hold fast to the ideals of peace, justice, and humanitarianism during World War II, even if it meant criticizing the American government. They ministered to the spiritual needs of the nation and supported the war effort, yet without abandoning their commitment to religious principles that transcended the war effort. They exhibited a cautious patriotism.

Still, American entry into the war did not mitigate the concerns that many religious groups had about the war itself. They tried to walk a fine line between support and criticism, cooperation and resistance. For example, Christians, Jews, and Buddhists entered the military in unprecedented numbers. Like their fellow citizens, they proudly joined the military and fought the enemy. Religious groups also sponsored some 10,000 military chaplains and initiated various ministries in and around military bases. But they also advocated the rights of conscientious objectors, whether or not they belonged to the historic peace churches.

During the war religious groups also expressed concern about human rights. Some religious leaders, especially from mainstream churches, protested the segregation of blacks in the military, even joining the "Double V" campaign to secure victory for civil rights at home as America fought for victory abroad. They argued that a war to protect democracy should also advance the cause of democracy on America's soil. As a result of this protest, the military did begin to desegregate, as did war-related industries. Religious groups criticized the government for the unjust internment of Japanese Americans on the West Coast, however unsuccessfully, and they also initiated

HOW RELIGIOUS GROUPS SERVED TROOPS IN WORLD WAR I

During World War I religious groups were responsible for meeting not only the spiritual needs of the troops in training camps and overseas, but their recreational needs as well. Their aim was to foster the comfort and morale of servicemen and to keep them away from negative influences such as prostitution and gambling by providing social activities, entertainment, and "a home away from home." The major organizations involved in this work were the Young Men's Christian Association (YMCA), the Knights of Columbus, the Jewish Welfare Board, and the Salvation Army. The programs conceived and developed by these organizations had a major impact on the well-being of American soldiers, sailors, and marines.

The YMCA, which had been serving troops since the Civil War, provided 90 percent of all social services (then called "welfare") to the American Expeditionary Forces in Europe, using nearly 13,000 men and women workers in France alone. In addition to conducting religious services and counseling, it established Rest and Recreation (R&R) facilities, canteens and post exchanges for battle-weary servicemen, conducted athletic programs, and mobilized entertainers to perform overseas. Several thousand huts and tents were operated by the YMCA as well as twenty-six R&R leave centers in France and over forty factories for the production of candy and baked goods. The YMCA also advised and entertained men aboard transport ships and did humanitarian work among prisoners of war.

On a smaller scale, similar work was done by the Knights of Columbus, a fraternal Catholic organization, which provided chaplains to Catholics and offered recreational services to all members of the armed forces regardless of race or religion. The motto of its clubhouses, both in the United States and abroad, was "Everyone welcome, everything free." Many of these clubs featured ballfields and boxing rings, and major sports figures were brought in to work there.

Social and recreational services for Jewish servicemen were provided by the Jewish Welfare Board, which was established by the Young Men's Hebrew Association (YMHA) during its effort to enlist rabbis for service at military posts. Its workers were welcomed by the YMCA to assist in conducting general religious services.

Although the Salvation Army sent relatively few workers overseas, it won recognition for the quality and efficiency of its service there. Its four hundred huts, some on the front lines, offered home-cooked cakes, pies, and especially doughnuts, and the women officers provided a clothes-mending service. Like the YMCA, it operated a system through which men could send money home to their families.

After the war, it became apparent that the work done by the religious groups was an indispensable element of military operations, and much of it was taken over by the military itself. In World War II, the civilian volunteers who provided social and recreational services to the troops did so through the United Service Organizations for National Defense (USO), a private charitable organization that was created under the leadership of six groups, some religious and some secular, to serve as a link between the military and the American people.

Sylvia Engdahl

ministries in those camps to relieve the suffering. A number of Japanese-American students attended church-related colleges during the war as a result of this initiative.

Military strategy also came under scrutiny. There was widespread debate over the policy of saturation or obliteration bombing, though without sufficient force to alter the military's policy. The debate heated up when America used the atomic bomb, raising questions about whether the possibility of a just war had become a historic relic. The Holocaust only reinforced this sentiment. Religious leaders, like the public at large, were suspicious of the reports about the genocide against the Jews, assuming that no civilized nation could conceive of doing such a thing. Instead, they thought such reports were just another example of Allied propaganda. Then the truth was discovered for all to see. Suddenly the cost of war became apparent, which only reinforced the importance of making future wars less likely.

American religious leaders did not want to be caught off guard at the end of the war as they had been during World War I, assuming America could once more return to business as usual. Even before Pearl Harbor, they had begun to talk about "a just and durable peace." Religious groups organized committees, often chaired by high-profile leaders like future Secretary of State John Foster Dulles, to study and propose peace plans for the postwar world. The Methodist Church included over one million of its members in study groups to explore this issue.

This intense commitment to a just peace had a positive outcome. Religious groups supported plans for a United Nations and massive aid to rebuild Europe and Japan. They also developed new programs that would revitalize religious faith in America and around the world. The assumption was that democracy could not survive without a vital religious faith and a strong church. Thus religious groups started campaigns to reach nonreligious people, both at home and abroad. The postwar boom in religion is evidence of that effort.

World War II provided religious groups with an opportunity to express both their patriotism and their commitment to religious principles. War, however, often produced tensions between these two ideals. American religious groups supported the war, but not at the expense of their commitment to human rights, a just peace, and a renewed church.

BIBLIOGRAPHY

Fox, Richard Wightman. *Reinhold Niebuhr: A Biography.* New York: Harper and Row, 1985.

Marty, Martin E. *Under God, Indivisible, 1941–1960.* Chicago: University of Chicago Press, 1996.

Ross, Robert W. *So It Was True: The American Protestant Press and the Nazi Persecution of the Jews.* Minneapolis: University of Minnesota Press, 1973.

Sittser, Gerald L. *A Cautious Patriotism: The American Churches and the Second World War.* Chapel Hill: University of North Carolina Press, 1997.

Toulouse, Mark G. *The Transformation of John Foster Dulles: From Prophet of Realism to Priest of Nationalism.* Macon, GA: Mercer University Press, 1985.

Gerald L. Sittser

ROOSEVELT, ELEANOR

(b. October 11, 1884; d. November 7, 1962) First Lady from 1933 to 1945, during the administration of Franklin Delano Roosevelt; one of the most important public figures of the twentieth century.

Anna Eleanor Roosevelt was a First Lady, social reformer, diplomat, and one of the most important public figures of the twentieth century. Throughout her political life she was a powerful advocate for human rights, international peace, and race and gender equality. She devoted herself to the underprivileged, disenfranchised, and downtrodden of the nation and the world.

Eleanor Roosevelt was born in New York City to a wealthy and politically active family. At the age of ten, following the death of her parents, Eleanor Roosevelt went to live with her grandparents and later attended boarding school in England. It was after she finished school that she first became active in the social reform movement, where she worked to better the working and living conditions of the urban poor, and performed settlement house work. In 1905 she married Franklin Delano Roosevelt, her fifth cousin once removed and the future four-term president of the United States. During the United States' participation in World War I, Eleanor Roosevelt coordinated activities at a Red Cross canteen in Washington, D.C., worked with wounded soldiers recovering in area hospitals, spoke at patriotic rallies, and performed other duties at home to aid the war effort abroad.

In the years leading up to World War II, Eleanor Roosevelt became more active in the social reform movement on an increasingly large scale. During the period between the World Wars she reversed her opposition to women's suffrage and became active in the League of Women Voters, the Women's International League for Peace and Freedom, and other political groups. After Franklin was elected president, Eleanor became the first politically active first lady in the history of American democracy. She stepped outside the role of the "politician's wife" and created her own distinct political identity. Eleanor Roosevelt effectively lobbied to enhance the role women played at all levels of American government. She worked with her husband and congress to ensure that women were not neglected in the New Deal programs of the 1930s. She tried to use her influence to focus public attention on injustice and racial inequality, publicly resigning from the Daughters of the American Revolution to protest racism in the organization in 1939. She also presented her social and political views through radio programs, lectures, political writings, and her nationally syndicated daily newspaper column "My Day."

Prior to the outbreak of World War II, Eleanor Roosevelt publicly supported the use of international economic pressure, rather than arms, to fight fascism overseas. She changed her mind in the years immediately preceding U.S. entry into the war, however, as she gradually developed a belief that Adolf Hitler and other Fascist leaders could not be stopped without the use of military force. During the war itself, Eleanor Roosevelt continued to champion the rights of oppressed citizens. She worked toward justice and equality for African Americans, consistently objecting to the hypocrisy of American political discourse that criticized Nazi racism abroad while condoning racism towards African Americans at home. She also attempted to work with the U.S. State Department, both during and after the war, to find a safe haven for Jewish refugees who managed to flee persecution in Europe. Eleanor Roosevelt was an outspoken opponent of Japanese interment, and an outspoken supporter of conscientious objectors who opposed compulsory armed service.

Eleanor Roosevelt (center left) talking to patients at a field hospital in Guadalcanal, Solomon Islands, on September 25, 1943. AP/WIDE WORLD PHOTOS

At the onset of American participation in World War II, Eleanor Roosevelt served as codirector of the Office of Civilian Defense during the early stages of its development. In that capacity she was responsible for administering an agency that provided American citizens with protection in the event of enemy attack, until her resignation amid controversy over her physical fitness program in 1942. She influenced women to support the war effort by encouraging them to enlist, support the activities of the Red Cross, and work in war related industries. She carried on an active correspondence with soldiers in the field and with their family members who remained at home, as well as visiting troops in the European and Pacific theaters.

Following her husband's death and the end of the war, Eleanor Roosevelt emerged as a powerful figure inside the Democratic Party. She eschewed offers to run for elected office in order to continue her political activities independently. She gained an avid interest in veterans' issues, and publicly supported such measures as the GI Bill and full employment legislation that was designed to provide soldiers with jobs once they returned to civilian life. In 1946 President Harry Truman appointed her to the United States delegation to the United Nations, where she navigated the troubled waters of Cold War international diplomacy, lead the committee that drafted the International Declaration of Human Rights, championed democracy abroad, and tirelessly worked to maintain international peace.

BIBLIOGRAPHY

Black, Allida M. *Casting Her Own Shadow: Eleanor Roosevelt and the Shaping of Postwar Liberalism.* New York: Columbia University Press, 1996.

Black, Allida M. *Courage in a Dangerous World: The Political Writings of Eleanor Roosevelt.* New York: Columbia University Press, 1999.

Hoff-Wilson, Joan, and Lightman, Majorie. *Without Precedent: The Life and Career of Eleanor Roosevelt.* Bloomington: Indiana University Press, 1984.

Lash, Joseph P. *Eleanor and Franklin: The Story of their Relationship Based on Eleanor Roosevelt's Personal Papers.* New York: W.W. Norton & Company, 1971.

Lash, Joseph P. *Eleanor Roosevelt: The Years Alone.* New York: W.W. Norton & Company, 1972.

Scharf, Lois. *Eleanor Roosevelt: First Lady of American Liberalism.* Boston: Twayne Publishers, 1987.

Thomas I. Faith

See also: Holocaust, American Response to; New Deal; Red Cross, American; Roosevelt, Franklin Delano.

ROOSEVELT, FRANKLIN DELANO

(b. January 30, 1882; d. April 12, 1945) Thirty-second president of the United States (1933–1945).

Franklin Delano Roosevelt led the nation through its worst depression and greatest world war. As president, he championed his New Deal and other social programs, some that endure into the twenty-first century.

EARLY CAREER

Roosevelt was born in Hyde Park, New York, graduated from Harvard College in 1904, studied at Columbia University's School of Law, and gained admission to the bar in 1907. He served one term, 1911 to 1913, in the New York Senate, and was assistant secretary of the navy from 1913 until 1920, when he became the Democratic vice presidential nominee. Roosevelt lost the election, but enhanced his reputation by waging a vigorous campaign.

Roosevelt contracted polio the following year, which cost him the use of his legs but not his political future. He served two terms as governor of New York, winning the office in 1928 and reelection in 1930. His efforts to ease the suffering of New Yorkers caused by the Great Depression gained him the Democratic presidential nomination in 1932. He crushed President Herbert Hoover, who received only 59 electoral votes to Roosevelt's 472. Roosevelt failed to end the depression but saved the banking system, restored public confidence in democracy and capitalism, and persuaded Congress to enact a host of bills providing jobs and other benefits to millions of people. His New Deal laid the groundwork for the nation that is America today. Roosevelt easily won reelection in 1936 and ran for an unprecedented third term in 1940.

OUTBREAK OF WORLD WAR II

By then Roosevelt had focused his attention on the developing world crisis. In East Asia, Japan had seized Manchuria and large parts of China. In 1938, in his famous Quarantine speech, he proposed that peaceful nations stop aggressors like Japan by cutting off their trade. This proposal fell on deaf ears. Nazi Germany dominated Europe after defeating France and its allies in June 1940. Of the great powers, Britain alone remained at war with Hitler. At first, Roosevelt apparently hoped that the United States could remain neutral. But with the collapse of France, American aid to Britain become imperative, for if the island nation fell, or made peace with Germany, all the world would be at risk of Nazi domination.

Before his election, Roosevelt's hands were tied as polls showed most Americans still favored neutrality at all costs, a doctrine known as isolationism that Republicans exploited to the hilt. In order to win a third term, Roosevelt, out of necessity, misrepresented himself as opposed to any steps that might lead America into war. Even so, taking a chance, he persuaded Congress to enact the first peacetime military draft in American history.

Once safely reelected, Roosevelt asked Congress for a plan to aid Britain, which he disingenuously called Lend-Lease; the theory being that America would somehow be repaid after the war. Thus sugarcoated, the bill passed, despite much ranting by isolationists. At first America had little to lend or lease as rearmament lagged far behind need, which became all the greater in June 1941 when Germany attacked the Soviet Union. In the fall of 1941, Roosevelt tried to provoke a German declaration of war by ordering U.S. warships to escort convoys and fire upon U-boats. Despite considerable provocation, Hitler failed to comply.

WAR LEADER

America actually went to war because of Japan rather than Germany. While America fought an undeclared war in the Atlantic, Japan, frustrated by its inability to defeat China, was planning to conquer Southeast Asia to secure needed raw materials and cut off Nationalist China from American aid. Efforts at negotiating a compromise failed because Roosevelt insisted that Japan withdraw from China. Since the Japanese would not give up China, they decided on war instead. On December 7, 1941 Japanese carrier planes attacked Hawaii, destroying military installations and sinking the navy's battleship fleet in Pearl Harbor. Japan then went on to seize other American possessions, notably the Philippines, and all of Southeast Asia. Germany declared war on the United States four days after Pearl Harbor, at last giving Roosevelt the war America had to fight.

President Franklin D. Roosevelt signs the declaration of war following the Japanese attack on Pearl Harbor, December 8, 1941. AP/WIDE WORLD PHOTOS

With both the Soviets and the Americans allied against Germany, its fate was sealed, as was that of Japan. But victory seemed far from certain in the early months of the war. Having been attacked, Americans achieved a unity never seen before nor since. Congress appropriated more money than could be spent at first. The nation's idled or underused factories converted quickly to full production of military goods. In June 1942, the Pacific Fleet defeated a much stronger Japanese carrier force near Midway Island, ending Japan's relentless advance and throwing it onto the strategic defensive.

At about the same time, Roosevelt made one of his most important decisions. Instead of building up strength in England for an invasion of France in 1943 as the Joint Chiefs wanted, he ordered that French North Africa be taken in 1942. This delayed the invasion of France by a year, which could not be helped. Americans hated the Japanese so much because of Pearl Harbor that a real danger existed that the Pacific War would get top priority, even though Germany had to be beaten first since it posed the greater danger. Roosevelt wanted American forces engaged in battle with Germans to draw attention away from the Pacific. So it transpired that American troops began the liberation of Europe by invading North Africa in November 1942. Two months later the remnants of Germany's Sixth Army surrendered to the Soviets at Stalingrad. Germany was now forced onto the strategic defensive as well.

FDR AND THE SOVIETS

Although many bloody battles remained to be fought because neither Germany nor Japan would concede defeat, Roosevelt spent the rest of the war planning how to establish a lasting peace (he won a fourth term on the fly in 1944). Germany and Japan would be occupied for as long as it took to make them democratic. The Soviets would receive a large sphere of interest, chiefly in Eastern Europe. Because the Soviets were going to seize this region in any case, accepting that fact might enable the Grand Alliance of America, Britain, and the Soviet Union to outlast the war. If the Soviets proved troublesome, Roosevelt retained certain options. He did not tell Stalin about the atomic bombs America had under development. He refused to allow the Soviets any part in the occupation of

Japan. And he declined to promise the Soviets much-needed American aid in the postwar era. The velvet glove he extended to Stalin concealed an iron fist.

LEGACY

Roosevelt died before the Axis powers gave up, but Germany had been largely overrun and Japan's defeat was imminent. Roosevelt had his failings as a war leader. Secretive and devious, he put off decisions as long as he could and kept everyone around him guessing. But the power of his oratory lifted the spirits of Americans in their darkest hours, and his belief in the inevitable victory became the people's as well. Sometimes petty and wrong about smaller issues, he seldom erred on the big ones. Roosevelt linked America's values to its foreign policy in his January 1941 proclamation that the United States not only opposed tyranny but also sought to secure "the four essential freedoms" for all of mankind—freedom of speech, freedom of religion, freedom from want, and freedom from fear. His position as the greatest president of the twentieth century remains secure.

BIBLIOGRAPHY

Burns, James MacGregor. *Roosevelt: The Lion and the Fox.* New York: Harcourt Brace Jovanovich, 1956.

Burns, James MacGregor. *Roosevelt: The Soldier of Freedom.* New York: Harcourt Brace Jovanovich, 1970.

Ward, Geoffrey C. *Before the Trumpet: Young Franklin Roosevelt, 1882–1905.* New York: Harper & Row, 1985.

Ward, Geoffrey C. *A First-Class Temperament: The Emergence of Franklin Roosevelt.* New York: Harper & Row, 1989.

William L. O'Neill

See also: **New Deal; Roosevelt, Eleanor.**

ROOSEVELT, THEODORE

(b. October 27, 1858, d. January 6, 1919) Twenty-fifth president of the United States (1901–1909).

Theodore Roosevelt led the United States into the front ranks of the world's imperial powers at the turn of the twentieth century. He pushed for war with Spain during the 1890s and then served in the Spanish-American War. As president from 1901 to 1909, Roosevelt promoted American overseas interests and modernized U.S. military forces. After World War I erupted in Europe, he argued for American military preparedness and intervention, and hoped to serve his country again on the battlefield.

Roosevelt was born into one of the richest families in New York City. Although asthma and physical frailty plagued him in his youth, he enjoyed a life of privilege.

His formal education consisted chiefly of private tutors, studies in Germany, and a degree from Harvard College. Throughout the 1880s and 1890s, he served in various governmental positions, but his major impact on national and international affairs started only after President William McKinley appointed him assistant secretary of the navy in 1897.

Roosevelt claimed that a large navy was essential for the United States to be a great power. He believed even more strongly that imperial struggles were essential for encouraging "frontier virtues" such as courage, self-reliance, and physical hardiness. With the American West now settled, the pursuit of overseas interests, he asserted, would help preserve those qualities in an increasingly urbanized and industrialized country. Roosevelt argued for war with Spain, in particular, because of reports of Spanish brutality in suppressing a revolt in its colony of Cuba. Even as he urged American intervention in Cuba, he prepared the navy for possible battle, which included orders for possible action against Spain's colony in the Philippines. When the U.S.S. *Maine*, sent to Cuba to observe conditions there, exploded in Havana harbor in early 1898, Roosevelt blamed the Spaniards. After President McKinley called for war, Roosevelt resigned his Navy Department post and gained an appointment as lieutenant colonel in the First United States Volunteer Cavalry, nicknamed the Rough Riders. Composed of men from the wilds of the West and elite colleges in the East, this diverse and colorful unit captured national attention. By June 1898 the Rough Riders sailed as part of an army expedition to Cuba.

The Spanish-American conflict was brief. American warships swiftly destroyed Spanish naval forces in the Philippines at the Battle of Manila bay. In Cuba, small engagements climaxed in battles to take the hills overlooking Santiago de Cuba, where a Spanish naval force lay anchored. On July 1, 1898, Roosevelt led his troops first up Kettle Hill, and then on to San Juan Hill, as part of coordinated American attacks. These charges were the defining moment of Roosevelt's national political career and of American imperialism. Reporters made him the hero of the day, and the public thrilled to read of the success of the expedition, which in reality suffered from supply and medical problems. Roosevelt returned home to become governor of New York and then the vice president when McKinley ran for a second term in 1900. McKinley's assassination elevated Roosevelt to the presidency in 1901.

Roosevelt made military matters one of his top priorities as president. A naval building program increased the fleet to twenty battleships by 1909, and to demonstrate American sea power he sent this force on a round-the-world cruise from 1907 to 1909. Roosevelt also supported reform of the National Guard, and signed legislation creating an army general staff to provide better planning and command. He imposed a physical test on army and navy officers to make them models of physical fitness and sponsored new technologies. Roosevelt became an enthusiast for submarines after a voyage on the U.S.S. *Plunger* and also promoted the military potential of aviation. His greatest military and diplomatic interest was, however, the construction of an interoceanic canal in Central America to speed the transit of the navy, and trade, between the Atlantic and Pacific Oceans. To accomplish this goal, Roosevelt attempted, but failed to reach, an agreement with Colombia for a route through its province of Panama. Construction began only after Roosevelt encouraged a revolt in Panama and then used the U.S. Navy to support it. The canal opened in 1914, and Roosevelt considered it one of the country's greatest achievements, a symbol of American know-how and power. Reflecting the racial attitudes of his era, he dismissed the Colombians' bitterness over his actions.

In 1914 Roosevelt also focused on the outbreak of World War I in Europe. Although no longer in office, he still urged American military readiness and supported civilian training camps such as the one at Plattsburgh, New York, to prepare for any future mobilization. He also became increasingly outspoken in his support of Britain and France and in 1915 argued for war against Germany after 128 Americans died in the sinking of the British passenger liner *Lusitania*. Upon United States entry into the war in 1917, Roosevelt offered to raise a division to fight in France. President Woodrow Wilson declined the request, and Roosevelt instead could only send his four sons to war. Three survived, but the youngest, Quentin, died in combat in 1918. Roosevelt himself died soon after in January 1919.

Throughout his political career, Roosevelt rejected America's traditional isolationism to embrace a new role for the United States as a world power and colonial nation. Both roles were bitterly debated at the turn of the twentieth century. In particular America's war against insurgents in the Philippines who opposed U.S. rule was denounced by critics as abandoning the nation's traditional values and democratic principles. Despite entry into World War I, which Roosevelt favored, Americans later turned their backs on internationalism by rejecting Woodrow Wilson's dream of a League of Nations. America returned to isolationism until forced into war by the Japanese attack on Pearl Harbor on December 7, 1941, and Germany's declaration of war on the United States a few days later.

BIBLIOGRAPHY

Brands, H. W. *T.R.: The Last Romantic*. New York: Basic Books, 1997.

Theodore "Teddy" Roosevelt (center) with members of the Rough Riders, 1898. AP/WIDE WORLD PHOTOS

Dalton, Kathleen. *Theodore Roosevelt: A Strenuous Life*. New York: Knopf, 2002.

Morris, Edmund. *The Rise of Theodore Roosevelt*. New York: Coward, McCann and Geoghegan, 1979.

Morris, Edmund. *Theodore Rex*. New York: Random House, 2001.

Reckner, James R. *Teddy Roosevelt's Great White Fleet*. Annapolis, MD: Naval Institute Press, 1988.

Roosevelt, Theodore. *The Rough Riders*. New York: Scribner, 1902; reprint, New York: Da Capo Press, 1990.

Matthew M. Oyos

See also: **Imperialism; Journalism, Spanish American War; Wilson, Woodrow.**

ROSIE THE RIVETER

With some 16.3 million men in the military, employment opportunities for women expanded at unparalleled rates during World War II. Rosie the Riveter became the

Poster depicting Rosie the Riveter, declaring "We Can Do It!" to World War II women.

national symbol of the millions of women who took on new and challenging jobs created by the nation's expanded wartime economy. Songwriters Redd Evans and John Jacob Loeb first popularized the term in a 1942 song that heralded the contributions of a dedicated riveter named Rosie. Newspapers and magazines regularly published stories about strong, powerful women in overalls and hardhats performing "men's jobs" in behalf of the war effort. This image was reinforced early in 1943 when a recruitment poster, commissioned by the U.S. War Production Commission, featured a resolute female worker, with upraised muscular arm, that included the caption, "We Can Do It!" The May 29, 1943, issue of the *Saturday Evening Post* drew further attention to wartime working women when it published on its cover an extraordinary painting by Norman Rockwell that depicted an imposing and self-assured riveter, clad in overalls with her shirtsleeves rolled up to reveal commanding, muscular arms. Rosie the Riveter has now become a generic term used to describe all women workers in the United States during World War II.

In sharp contrast to the Depression years of the 1930s, when working women were often harshly criticized for taking jobs away from men, the woman worker of World War II was highly lauded. Responding to the unprecedented demand for war workers, the number of employed women grew by 6.5 million. The proportion of women in the work force rose from 25 percent at the beginning of the war to 36 percent at war's end; an increase greater than the previous four decades combined. Just as important, growing numbers of married and older women joined the work force. More than 3 million of the new female war workers were married. Married women over the age of thirty-five were far more likely to seek employment than younger mothers with children. Public disapproval of working mothers, coupled with woefully inadequate childcare programs, discouraged young mothers from working. In contrast to earlier eras, when the typical female worker was young and single, women workers during World War II were much more likely to be older and married. This changing profile continued into the postwar era.

The largest gain in female employment occurred in manufacturing, with more than 3 million women employed in defense industries. While defense work paid better than most other jobs available to women, such as service and office work, the wages of female industrial workers equaled only 60 percent of what men received. This discrepancy reflected the fact that women were concentrated in lower-paying, less skilled positions; rarely did they qualify for skilled work.

New opportunities in manufacturing enabled African-American women to leave low-paying domestic work for better paying factory jobs. In fact, the number of black women employed as domestics declined by 15 percent while their participation in factory work more than doubled. Yet black industrial women were usually relegated to the lowest-paying jobs, such as janitors and sweepers, and they suffered even more discrimination than their white counterparts. Still, even these factory jobs were preferable to domestic work.

At the conclusion of the war, as the nation shifted its production from a wartime to a peacetime economy, female industrial workers were laid off from their jobs at nearly double the rates of men. By 1947, the percentage of women in the work force had declined to 27 percent. While the labor participatimon rate of women began to climb in the years after 1947, women discovered that jobs in heavy industry were now cut off to them. Instead, they were forced to accept less-prestigious, lower-paying jobs in areas such as retail trade and service. Moreover, the decade of the 1950s witnessed a renewed interest in motherhood and traditional family life that resulted in wage-earning women placing family needs above work.

Historians continue to debate the impact of World War II on the lives of working women. For some, the Second World War represented a major turning point for women as they eagerly supported the war effort by engaging in new and challenging jobs that had previously been denied them. Other historians have emphasized that the changes wrought by World War II were only temporary, pointing out that immediately after the war women were expected to return to their traditional roles as wives and mothers. A third group of historians has emphasized how the long-range significance of the changes brought about by the war provided the foundation for the rejuvenation of the contemporary women's movement in the late 1960s and early 1970s as the daughters of the wartime generation demanded greater equality for women in the workplace and in society at large.

BIBLIOGRAPHY

Campbell, D'Ann. *Women at War with America: Private Lives in a Patriotic Era*. Cambridge, MA: Harvard University Press, 1984.

Gluck, Sherna. *Rosie the Riveter Revisited: Women, the War and Social Change*. Boston: Twayne, 1987.

Hartmann, Susan M. *The Home Front and Beyond: American Women in the 1940s*. Boston: Twayne, 1982.

Kessler-Harris, Alice. *Out to Work: A History of Wage-Earning Women in the United States*. New York: Oxford University Press, 1982.

Litoff, Judy Barrett, and David C. Smith. *Since You Went Away: World War II letters from American Women on the Home Front*. New York: Oxford University Press, 1991

Internet Resources

"Rosie the Riveter Trust." Available from <http://www
.rosietheriveter.org>

Judy Barrett Litoff

See also: **Feminism; Propaganda, War; Sexual Behavior; Women,
Employment of; Women, World War I; Women, World
War II.**

SEXUAL BEHAVIOR

Traditionally puritanical about sexual matters, Americans have seldom wanted to confront openly the controversial issue of sexuality. Wars, however, by loosening communal bonds and creating new pressures, often have forced Americans to deal with questions of acceptable sexual behavior. The Spanish American War, World War I, and World War II all compelled Americans to reexamine their sexual practices and mores, creating changed sexual conditions for the country.

Americans in the late nineteenth century had anxieties about sex even before the Spanish American War. Anonymity, brought on by the growth of cities, allowed the numbers of brothels and prostitutes and the extent of sexual activity among the unmarried to increase. Social purity advocates sought to eradicate these behaviors and restore the old Victorian moral code. They pushed the Comstock Act of 1873 through Congress, making it illegal to circulate information on contraception, and they persuaded several states to outlaw the sale of condoms and diaphragms as well as the practice of abortion. Laws, however, could not make sex unpopular, and by the late 1890s cases of venereal disease, especially gonorrhea and syphilis, were on the rise. Even without war, these circumstances might have prompted crusaders to step up campaigns aimed at restoring America's virtue, but war gave added impetus and urgency to the cause.

SPANISH AMERICAN WAR

The Spanish American War, like all wars, drew large numbers of young men away from home and traditional courtship patterns. Overseas, soldiers hungered for companionship, or, more bluntly, for sex. For the U.S. military, these needs presented a practical problem—to both satisfy and preserve the health of soldiers in the field. By 1900, rumors that the U.S. Army in the Philippines had actually established houses of prostitution for the soldiers, to be maintained and supervised by the United States, began circulating stateside. These accounts triggered outrage among many Americans and also stirred up prewar debates over whether prostitution should be regulated or outlawed. With the Spanish American War, public morality resurfaced as a national issue.

WORLD WAR I

By the eve of World War I, arguments over prostitution and American sexuality had reached a fever pitch. Some Progressives had adopted the purity crusade as their own,

THE ENEMY IS SYPHILIS

Enlist employees in a campaign against it

MADE BY ILLINOIS WPA ART PROJECT-CHICAGO

Public health poster from 1940 which states, "The Enemy Is Syphilis. Enlist employees in a campaign against it."

cities across America wiped out their red-light districts, and many more imposed curfews on women or required them to carry letters written by their parents permitting them to accompany soldiers. Many municipalities allowed known or suspected prostitutes or even suspected venereal disease carriers to be detained and examined by health officials. Those found to be diseased, and sometimes even those who were not, could be imprisoned, committed to a juvenile reformatory, or placed in isolation. Eventually, federal legislation caught up to these local customs. In 1918 Congress passed the Chamberlain-Kahn Act, officially giving local boards of health the authority to force any suspected carrier of venereal disease to be detained and examined. As a result, some 18,000 women were quarantined in federally supported institutions during the war.

For its part, the Army declared many infected men unfit for service, but soldiers who contracted a venereal disease had only to check into an army clinic within twenty-four hours to avoid penalty. In order to protect the war machine, America became a nation willing to regulate private sex lives at the expense of women's civil rights. World War I resulted in a governmentally supported standard of morality; for a while the national Public Health Service monitored citizens through a special Division of Venereal Disease, and many states required blood tests before marriage and mandatory reporting of confirmed cases of venereal disease.

WORLD WAR II

Wartime anxieties eventually did cool, and in 1923 the Chamberlain-Kahn Act expired without notice. By 1941 society had changed dramatically, with American youth becoming increasingly promiscuous. When World War II came, the military still worried about soldiers contracting venereal disease, but this time they laid much of the blame not on prostitutes but on "victory girls" or "khaki wackies" who wanted to send the boys off with something to remember. Communities made every effort to deprive soldiers of sex, closing down remaining red-light districts and threatening potential partners, and the military tried to frighten men into abstinence with propaganda. In the end, more practical methods of disease control had to be devised. Of the first two million inductees to the military, forty-eight of every one thousand had syphilis. Despite some protest, the military established prophylactic stations in the United States to clinically treat men after intercourse, and it passed out fifty million condoms a month.

Also during the Second World War, the U.S. Military for the first time systematically sought to exclude homosexuals from service. As part of the induction process, each enlistee received a psychiatric examination designed to screen out homosexual servicemen and

but a growing number of literary and social radicals called for new sexual mores, including relaxed divorce laws or even "free love." In the midst of this, muckrakers (journalists who looked for and exposed scandals) insisted that young white girls were being kidnapped and forced into prostitution on a fairly regular basis. By the outbreak of war in 1917, these pressures, along with a high rate of venereal disease among draft-age men, caused near hysteria in American society. Naturally, the war effort reflected these fears, and rhetoric began to link antiprostitution and American morality to the meaning of the war itself.

As keeping the men "fit to fight" became the homefront mantra, prostitutes and promiscuous women found themselves targeted as public enemies. Sympathetic prewar depictions of victims of the white slave trade disappeared, replaced by propaganda portraying prostitutes as harmful and disease-ridden. Hundreds of towns and

women. Despite the official policy of exclusion, however, a significant number of gays and lesbians continued to serve in all branches of the military. Often, official policies of intolerance were modified or circumvented in order to fill the need for trained men and women.

World War II also caused a loosening of American morality simply by causing a loosening of the social bonds that had served to keep sexuality under control. As women moved away from family into cities and war jobs, they experienced a new sense of freedom. Others, too, reacted to the anonymity that movement brought. In places like Denver and Kansas City, gay bars opened for the first time. A homosexual subculture developed, and it did not disappear at war's end. For those who chose not to participate in the marriage boom that solved the sexual crisis of so many, World War II produced a climate more tolerant of promiscuity and sexual differences. The war left America more open to discussions about sex, whether through the Kinsey report on male sexual behavior or the homoerotic poetry of Beatniks like Allen Ginsberg.

The Spanish American War publicized debate over prostitution, but World War I gave moralists the ammunition to control how far Americans could go and in what context sex was acceptable—not far and only within marriage. World War II revolutionized this World War I order, opening the door for what would become the sexual revolution of the next generation.

BIBLIOGRAPHY

Chambers, John Whiteclay II. *The Tyranny of Change: America in the Progressive Era, 1890–1920*. New York: St. Martin's, 1992.

D'Emilio, John, and Freedman, Estelle B. *Intimate Matters: A History of Sexuality in America*. New York: Harper and Row, 1988.

Hobson, Barbara Meil. *Uneasy Virtue: The Politics of Prostitution and the American Reform Tradition*. Chicago: University of Chicago Press, 1990.

Link, William A., and Link, Arthur S. *American Epoch: A History of the United States Since 1900*, Vol. I: *War, Reform, and Society, 1900–1945*, 6th edition. New York: McGraw Hill, 1987.

May, Henry. *The End of American Innocence: A Study of the First Years of Our Own Time, 1912–1917*. New York: Alfred A. Knopf, 1959.

O'Neill, William L. *A Democracy at War: America's Fight at Home and Abroad in World War II*. Cambridge, MA: Harvard University Press, 1997.

Internet Resources

Blackwell, Henry B. "Prostitution Licensed in the Philippines." *The Woman's Journal* 31 (Sept. 1, 1900). Available from <http://www.boondocksnet.com/ai>.

Melinda Lee Pash

See also: **Feminism; Medicine, World War I; Medicine, World War II; Women and World War I; Women and World War II.**

SPORTS, WORLD WAR I

Although sports and military preparedness have been intertwined throughout human history, armed combat between 1914 and 1919 made federally financed sports and athletics central components of morale and military preparedness for the first time in American history. American soldiers had participated in various sports and athletic contests between the Civil War and World War I, but no formal policy existed and few commanders were interested in promoting an athletic component as an antidote to saber exercises, revolver practice, line skirmishes, and mounted drills. By the turn of the twentieth century, a new generation of officers maintained that physical training should precede all specifically military activities—an idea incorporated in the mandatory physical training regimen instituted by Lieutenant H. J. Koehler of West Point. Prior to World War I, surveys reported that between one-third and one-half of all military recruits were physically unfit; military leaders and physical educators waged prewar preparedness crusades that linked the strenuous life to military readiness, patriotism, manliness, morals, honor, ethnic assimilation, and national physical vitality.

In 1916 the military turned to sports as an antidote to the drinking and soliciting of prostitutes with which enlisted men tended to fill their leisure time. General John J. Pershing summoned the assistance of public and private organizations such as the Young Men's Christian Association (YMCA), the Knights of Columbus, the Playground and Recreation Association of America, and the American Library Association to assist the Commission on Training Camp Activities in developing healthy living and social arrangements for the 75 percent of troops who spent time in the thirty-two training camps at ports of entry, aviation camps, training camps, combat zones, convalescent camps, and leave areas. Physical educator James Naismith, who invented basketball in 1891, served as the YMCA's sex education instructor, lecturing enlisted men on the evils of venereal disease.

The war experience heightened interest in the dominant American sports of baseball, football, and boxing, which were covered in the pages of the weekly armed forces paper, the *Stars and Stripes*. World War I strengthened the bond between the military and football when Army-Navy football games (begun in 1890) became a grand showcase and patriotic tradition. Football's popularity derived from the numerous enlisted men who had been collegiate players and coaches, and college and intercamp teams played each other in major stadiums. Boxing became a popular respite from military drilling at the training camps and proved to be an effective educational tool for hand-to-hand combat. Professional boxers taught the fundamentals and most states repealed their prohibitions against boxing, which became a major commercial success during the 1920s and after.

After the war, policymakers frightened by the threat of Bolshevism in postwar Europe, were unwilling to bring troops home immediately and used organized sports to occupy them. The YMCA organized an ambitious series of competitions that led to the American Expeditionary Forces championship, which flowed into a wider crusade to convert Europeans to American athletic and sporting sensibilities. The U.S. Army, working with the YMCA, invited the military officials of twenty-nine nations, colonies, and dependencies to participate in Inter-Allied Games, led by the American Expeditionary Forces. Held at the newly built Pershing Stadium near Paris, the stadium was consecrated with the words "may the cherished bonds of friendship between France and America, forged anew on the common field of battle, be tempered and made enduring on the friendly field of sport." Watched by hundreds of thousands of spectators, the games were promoted by and covered extensively in the U.S. and Allied-friendly European press. Nearly 1,500 athletes representing eighteen Allied nations or dominions participated. Never before had so much information about a sports event reached so many publications in so many countries.

The wartime sporting experience heightened the national awareness of fitness and organized athletics, fostering the sports boom of the 1920s. Burgeoning physical education programs linked fitness and athleticism to patriotic virtue and inspired millions to participate. The war experience brought sports into the elementary, high school, and college curriculums. Between 1919 and 1921, seventeen states passed physical education legislation; by 1930, thirty-six had done so. In sum, the World War I trinity of sports, the military, and national preparedness validated the various strands of early twentieth-century Progressivism in a way none of its various activists and spokespeople could have envisioned.

BIBLIOGRAPHY

Allen, Edward Frank. *Keeping Our Fighters Fit for War and After.* New York: Century, 1918.

Gorn, Elliott, and Goldstein, Warren. *A Brief History of American Sports.* New York: Hill and Wang, 1993.

Lewis, Guy. "World War I and the Emergence of Sport for the Masses." In *Maryland Historian* 2 (1973): 109–22.

Pope, S. W. *Patriotic Games: Sporting Traditions in the American Imagination, 1876–1926.* New York: Oxford University Press, 1997.

Wakefield, Wanda E. *Playing to Win: Sports and the American Military, 1898–1945.* Albany: State University of New York Press, 1997.

Whyte, Major G., et al. *The Inter-Allied Games, Paris, 22nd June to 6th July 1919.* Paris, 1919.

S. W. Pope

See also: **Sports, World War II.**

SPORTS, WORLD WAR II

The relationship between sports and the American armed forces reached a climax during World War II. The military broadened its athletic regimen, established during World War I, and thereby reproduced a patriotic sporting culture that soldiers had known as civilians. The armed services provided equipment, training, and personnel rather than rely on private agencies, as had been done in World War I. The entry of numerous prominent athletes into military service represented a public relations boon for the Department of War and cemented a bond between professional sports, athletes, and patriotism. On the homefront, President Franklin D. Roosevelt declared that all sports, professional and amateur, should continue during wartime given their inherent "morale benefits." Military athletic prowess was widely celebrated as an affirmation of national identity and patriotic fortitude.

Sports reputedly reflect nationally specific sporting temperaments and styles of play. Many Americans distinguished between "their" sports and those national sports of the Allies as well as the opposing Axis powers. Within this nationalistic, militaristically charged context, American football was glorified as everything masculine and befitting the U.S. military experience. As organized sports became even more closely linked with fitness, morale, and patriotism, both within the ranks and on the homefront, football became a fixture on military bases at home and abroad. Football was the favored sport among the military brass, as Generals George Marshall, Dwight Eisenhower, Douglas MacArthur, and Omar Bradley all thought that football produced the best soldiers. Army and Navy were the two leading collegiate football powers during the war (Army was unbeaten from 1944 to 1946) and their games were broadcast over Armed Forces Radio. High school and collegiate coaches encouraged their players to join the service. Within five months after the bombing of Pearl Harbor, 32 percent of the NFL's professional players had enlisted and many more joined the war effort thereafter, which caused the League to shrink from ten to eight teams. By 1950 the Navy counted eighty former players as admirals, the Army, ninety-eight generals. One such former general, Robert Neyland, coached the University of Tennessee while on active duty with the Army for twenty years. He brought military organization and discipline to his highly ranked teams and compared football to war.

World War II broke the traditional recruiting pattern in college sports. After the war most coaches went far beyond their own territories to hunt for service-team vets and other prime military athletic prospects. After the war, 2.2 million vets went to college on the GI Bill, and thousands with football experience went to colleges with teams, making up 50 percent of collegiate players. More than three times as many colleges and universities fielded teams in 1946 than in 1945.

WOMEN IN SPORTS

World War II mobilized women to make further inroads into the male-dominated domain of sports. Working-class women played basketball and softball in public and industrial leagues, as well as leagues formed by the Young Women's Christian Association (YWCA), the Catholic Youth Organization (CYO), and the Amateur Athletic Union (AAU). Middle- and upper-class women embraced tennis, golf, and skiing at private clubs and resorts. Black female athletes competed in intercollegiate track and field during the late 1930s and early 1940s and dominated post-World War II Olympic competitions. Enlisted women participated in military service sports and competed against civilian teams to demonstrate that military personnel were just like the woman next door.

Women's sports were constricted by sexist notions that female athleticism ought to foster femininity and sexual attractiveness. As such, sports often provided a venue for sexual entertainment, with female athletes participating in beauty contests to demonstrate their sex appeal as well as athletic ability. Nowhere were these assumptions more in evidence than in the All-American Girls Baseball League (AAGBL). Founded in 1942 by Chicago magnate Philip K. Wrigley, the AAGBL (which at its peak operated in ten cities and drew nearly a million annual spectators) championed women's baseball as a spectacle of feminine "nice girls" who could "play like men."

BASEBALL

As the national pastime, baseball was a prominent component of the wartime experience both at home and in the European theater of war. One month after the attack on Pearl Harbor, Major League Baseball Commissioner Kenesaw Mountain Landis wrote President Roosevelt to inquire if games should be played during American involvement in the war. Roosevelt responded in a "green light letter" that "it would be best for the country to keep baseball going. Everybody will work longer hours and harder than ever before. And they ought to have a chance for . . . taking their minds off their work even more than before." Ninety-five percent of players on Major League rosters in 1941 served in some capacity in the war effort. Many of the game's star players, such as Ted Williams, Joe DiMaggio, Hank Greenberg, Stan Musial, Warren Spahn, and Yogi Berra, forfeited seasons in the prime of their careers.

Baseball's war-depleted Major League rosters prompted several owners to recruit players of color—beginning first with Latin American players and, after the war, veterans of the Negro Leagues. The military was in the vanguard in utilizing black athletes—recognizing that in the war against Fascism and racism, the appearance of American racial harmony on the playing field (or arena) contributed to racial harmony. On the other hand, the military adhered to segregated training camps, relegating black soldiers to labor or service units and denying blacks access to naval positions. The War Department and the Office of War Information (OWI), however, exploited the celebrity status of prominent black athletes so as to defuse the escalating "Negro problem" inherent in the military's segregationist policies.

No individual athlete played a greater role in war morale and American propaganda than the heavyweight boxer Joe Louis. Louis became a potent symbol who simultaneously represented heroism, patriotism, and black military involvement; but his persona was severed from racial issues. Louis was neither a black nationalist who spoke on behalf of racial equality nor a pawn of the white establishment. Rather, as one who understood race relations as a gradual process for white acceptance, he boosted troop morale as a patriotic American who symbolized black potential but who did not threaten the racialized views of armed black men that prevailed on the homefront.

BIBLIOGRAPHY

Oriard, Michael. *King Football: Sport and Spectacle in the Golden Age of Radio and Newsreels, Movies and Magazines, the Weekly and the Daily Press.* Chapel Hill: University of North Carolina Press, 2001.

Sklaroff, Lauren Rebecca. "Constructing G.I. Joe Louis: Cultural Solutions to the 'Negro Problem' during World War II." *Journal of American History* 89 (December 2002).

Wakefield, Wanda Ellen. *Playing to Win: Sports and the American Military, 1898–1945.* Albany: State University of New York Press, 1997.

S. W. Pope

See also: **Sports, World War I; USO.**

STEWART, JIMMY

(b. May 20, 1908; d. July 7, 1997) Actor, pilot, and Colonel in Army Air Force in World War II; served as Brigadier General in Air Force Reserves.

Jimmy Stewart is one of America's most beloved movie stars, playing common men in heroic roles in classics such as *It's a Wonderful Life* and *Mr. Smith Goes to Washington*. But he also was a courageous patriot in real life, actively seeking wartime service during World War II in the Army Air Force (AAF) and eventually achieving the rank of Brigadier General in the U.S. Air Force Reserves.

James Maitland Stewart was born in Indiana, Pennsylvania. His family had military roots: both grandfathers had fought in the Civil War, and his father had served during both the Spanish-American War and World War I. Jimmy considered his father to be the biggest influence on his life, so it is not surprising that when another war came, another Stewart would be in uniform.

Though Jimmy had already won an Oscar for *The Philadelphia Story* and was recognized as one of Hollywood's top leading men, he never considered trying to evade his 1940 draft notice. He called the draft "the only lottery I ever won." While many other prominent people were coming up with reasons to avoid active service, he became the first major movie star to wear a uniform.

But it was not easy. The AAF had strict height and weight requirements for new recruits, and Jimmy was five pounds under the standard. To get up to 148 pounds, he enlisted the help of Metro-Goldwyn-Mayer's muscle man, Don Loomis, who was legendary for his ability to add or subtract pounds in his studio gymnasium. But he failed with Jimmy, who was rejected for being underweight. Refusing to accept that verdict, he persuaded the AAF enlistment officer to run new tests, this time skipping the weigh-in. Jimmy passed this evaluation, earning a new job with a salary that was $12,000 a month less than he was paid by his movie contract.

Jimmy loved to fly, having gained his pilot's license in 1935. Though early in the war he narrated documentaries for the Office of War Information and hosted some radio shows to support the military, he actively sought a combat role as a pilot. He worked his way from boot camp to flight school, earning his officer's commission and pilot's wings. In November 1943, he flew to Europe with the 445th Bomb Group (Heavy) of the Eighth Air Force.

For his leadership and flying skills, Major Stewart was given command of the bomb group's 703rd Squadron. He flew a score of combat missions and earned six Bat-

Lieutenant James "Jimmy" Stewart of the U.S. Army Air Corps on February 20, 1942. AP/WIDE WORLD PHOTOS

tle Stars. Like many flyers he admitted praying a lot, but he didn't pray for himself. His main request to the Lord was to avoid any mistakes that might cost the lives of his men. His wartime decorations included the Distinguished Flying Cross with Oak Leaf Cluster and the French Croix de Guerre with Palm. By the time the war ended, he had been promoted to Colonel and become Chief of Staff of the 2nd Combat Wing of the 2nd Division, Eighth Air Force.

After 1945 Stewart continued to serve the Air Force on the screen and in uniform. He hosted tributes to servicemen during the Korean War and starred in the movie *Strategic Air Command* in 1955, a film designed to glorify that organization in the eyes of the American public and to inspire recalled reservists to resume military careers. His own love of flying was very evident in the passion displayed by his character of Tom Hamilton, who gives up his stardom in professional baseball in order to pilot new jet bombers. Stewart continued his own career in the Air Force Reserves, achieving the rank of Brigadier General in 1959. When he retired in 1968, he received the Distinguished Service Medal.

The Stewart family tradition of courageous military service was carried on by his stepson Ronald, who was tragically killed as a Marine in Vietnam in 1969, earning a Silver Star. Jimmy received one final recognition from a grateful nation in 1985, when he was awarded the Presidential Medal of Freedom. When he died, the United States lost one of its greatest actors and finest citizens.

BIBLIOGRAPHY

Amory, Cleveland. "The Man Even Hollywood Likes." *Parade* (October 21, 1984): 4–9.

Crane, Conrad. *Bombs, Cities, and Civilians: American Airpower Strategy in World War II.* Lawrence: University Press of Kansas, 1993.

Crane, Conrad. *American Airpower Strategy in Korea.* Lawrence: University Press of Kansas, 2000.

Internet Resource

The James M. Stewart Museum website. Available from <http://www.jimmy.org>

Conrad C. Crane

See also: **Motion Pictures, World War I and World War II; Wayne, John.**

TOKYO ROSE

(b. July 4, 1916) Radio Tokyo broadcaster during World War II.

In October 1945, General Douglas MacArthur's Tokyo headquarters arrested Iva Ikuko Toguri d'Aquino, a program host on Radio Tokyo, which broadcast Japanese propaganda to Allied troops during World War II. Ambitious and at times unscrupulous reporters referred to her as "Tokyo Rose," the name given by American soldiers to all female broadcasters for Radio Tokyo. The name has since been associated primarily with her. D'Aquino spent the next year in jail, treated as a Japanese national despite her American citizenship. Her ensuing legal journey highlights both the continuing prejudice faced by Japanese Americans after the war and the paranoia concerning disloyalty in the United States during the early years of the Cold War (1946–1991).

Toguri had traveled to Japan in 1941 to visit a dying aunt and to see her parents' native land. She left the United States without a passport, a decision that would cause insuperable problems when she attempted to return home before and during World War II. Trapped in Japan after hostilities commenced, Toguri found work in Radio Tokyo's business office. At Radio Tokyo, two Allied prisoners of war, Major Charles Cousens of Australia and Major Ted Ince of the United States, asked Toguri to read scripts for a radio program called *Zero Hour*. In wartime Japan, such a "request" was in reality an order. Thus Toguri became "Orphan Ann," host of the program. Cousens and Ince secretly assured her that their program would focus on entertainment in an attempt to soften anti-American propaganda. Toguri, who had been providing Allied prisoners of war with food and accurate news, refused persistent pressure from the Japanese secret police throughout the war to renounce her United States citizenship and even maintained her American citizenship after marrying Felipe J. d'Aquino, a Japanese-Portuguese with Portuguese citizenship, in 1945.

Although thirteen other female announcers had broadcast in English during the war, only d'Aquino was arrested as the fictitious "Tokyo Rose." Both the Army and the Justice Department initially decided not to pursue treason charges after lengthy investigations determined that d'Aquino had only introduced music on the program. In 1947, however, d'Aquino's plans to return to the United States prompted protests from the popular radio personality Walter Winchell, the American Legion, and the Native Sons of the Golden West. These

Tokyo Rose being interviewed by correspondents in 1945.

protests convinced Attorney General Tom Clark to reopen the case. Bowing to public pressure, Clark eventually decided to prosecute d'Aquino, despite reports from subordinates that recommended dropping the case and the fact that Ince was never tried.

Tom DeWolfe, a Justice Department lawyer, presented the government's case, a task made more difficult by the perjury of a key prosecution witness. Wayne Collins, an advocate for many Japanese Americans involved in key World War II cases, represented d'Aquino. The trial took place in the context of the "fall" of China and the Soviet Union's successful testing of an atomic device. After three months of testimony, an all-white jury convicted d'Aquino of one of the eight charges of overt acts of treason she faced. The judge then stripped her of her citizenship, sentenced her to ten years in jail, and fined her $10,000. With the help of Collins, d'Aquino successfully contested a deportation order upon her early release for good behavior in 1956.

Japanese Americans largely ignored d'Aquino's story until the early 1970s, when Dr. Clifford I. Uyeda and later the Japanese American Citizens League and Senator S. I. Hayakawa of Hawaii campaigned for a pardon that had been rejected by the Eisenhower and Nixon administrations. Positive media coverage of d'Aquino's case, most prominently on the television program *60 Minutes*, added to the growing support for a pardon. President Gerald R. Ford granted d'Aquino a pardon on January 19, 1977, his last day in office.

The story of "Tokyo Rose" highlights Cold War paranoia and racism. D'Aquino's trial and conviction resulted largely from the Truman administration's concern to avoid appearing soft on disloyalty. Public pressure from influential individuals and groups in addition to, as Stanley Kutler puts it, "bureaucratic inertia, timidity, and, at times, chicanery" exacerbated these concerns (*The American Inquisition*, p. 29). Furthermore, the Japanese-American community's reaction to d'Aquino's case reveals the continued existence of racism in the postwar United States. The trial demonstrated that Japanese Americans, victims of exile and incarceration during the war, continued to face postwar prejudice. Japanese Americans provided scant support for d'Aquino during the trial, perhaps preoccupied with rebuilding their lives after their wartime losses or fearful that the trial might add to their already considerable problems. The increasing willingness of Japanese Americans to support d'Aquino in the 1970s, on the other hand, suggests an increasing psychological comfort on the part of Japanese Americans, who no longer sought to avoid the subject of World War II and its effects on their lives and community.

BIBLIOGRAPHY

Daniels, Roger. *Asian America: Chinese and Japanese in the United States Since 1850*. Seattle: University of Washington Press, 1988.

Duus, Masayo. *Tokyo Rose: Orphan of the Pacific*, translated by Peter Duus. New York: Kodansha International, 1979.

Kutler, Stanley I. *The American Inquisition: Justice and Injustice in the Cold War*. New York: Hill and Wang, 1982.

Yoo, David K. *Growing Up Nisei: Race, Generation, and Culture among Japanese Americans of California, 1924–1949*. Urbana: University of Illinois Press, 2000.

Uyeda, Clifford I. "The Pardoning of 'Tokyo Rose': A Report on the Restoration of American Citizenship to Iva Ikuko Toguri." *Amerasia Journal* 5 (1978): 69–94.

Allan W. Austin

See also: **Enemy, Images of; Japanese Americans, World War II.**

UNITED NATIONS

The United Nations, headquartered in New York City, is an international organization established to preserve world peace and security and to develop friendly relations among all peoples. It was created in the aftermath of the Second World War and officially came into existence on October 24, 1945.

At the end of World War I, President Woodrow Wilson was instrumental in convincing the victorious Allied powers to establish a League of Nations. Despite Wilson's pivotal role, the U.S. Senate failed to ratify American membership in the League. Both within the Senate and among the general public there were significant fears concerning the League's charter limiting national sovereignty and congressional authority to make war, although a few U.S. leaders continued to embrace the idea of an international organization aimed at keeping peace. The failure of the United States to join played an important role in the League's inability to meet the growing threats posed by Nazi Germany's and Japan's aggression in the 1930s. Although the League of Nations continued to exist during the Second World War, it was a doomed body and it formally dissolved itself in 1946.

The Japanese attack on Pearl Harbor galvanized American support for entering the Second World War and dealt a crippling blow to isolationism. In contrast to the view that had prevailed after the First World War, a consensus developed within the United States regarding the need to establish and join an international organization to maintain collective security. The term "United Nations" was proposed by President Franklin D. Roosevelt as the formal name for the anti-Nazi alliance. On January 1, 1942, the United States was one of twenty-six states to sign the Declaration of the United Nations. Unlike Wilson, FDR supported an organization structured to stress the primacy of the major powers in maintaining international stability.

Within the State Department, planning for the United Nations began in earnest in 1942 and Roosevelt, Soviet premier Joseph Stalin, and British prime minister Winston Churchill agreed at the Tehran Conference (November 1943) on the general outlines for this new world body. At the Dumbarton Oaks Conference in Washington, D.C. (August–October, 1944), diplomats from China, the Soviet Union, the United Kingdom, and the United States established the basic outlines of the organization, designating the Security Council as the principal body to preserve peace and security. This council would

A 1943 United Nations promotional poster by Leslie Ragan. © SWIM INK/CORBIS

be dominated by the Big Four: the United States, Britain, the Soviet Union, and China. A general assembly would include representatives from all member states. Ultimately, at the USSR's insistence, the major powers would have absolute veto power over Security Council resolutions.

The formal drafting of the UN Charter took place in San Francisco in 1945. In its final form, the United Nations Security Council consisted of five permanent members with veto power (France joined the Big Four) and six (later raised to ten) other nations elected for two-year terms. The General Assembly represented the interests of all nations and a smaller Economic and Social Council promoted international cooperation in these areas. The Charter also established a Secretariat and since the organization's founding, several Secretary Generals have been significant figures on the world stage. An International Court of Justice was established and headquartered in the Hague.

Ratification of the United Nations charter, in contrast to that of the League of Nations, sailed through the U.S. Senate. In the early years of the UN, the United States often dominated the body, especially in the General Assembly. The Cold War seriously hampered the ability of the UN to preserve international peace and the Soviet veto on resolutions of the Security Council often paralyzed this body. Nonetheless, the UN did endorse collective action in 1950 to repel the North Korean invasion of South Korea. Beginning in 1956 the United Nations created international "peacekeeping" forces contributed by member states to patrol the cease-fire line between Egypt and Israel. Despite Soviet-U.S. competition, the UN was successful in mediating several regional conflicts, often deploying UN peacekeepers, especially to the Middle East.

The end of the Cold War in 1991 appeared to invigorate the UN and strengthen its ability to preserve international peace and stability. In 1990–1991, the United States and a broad alliance took military action under a Security Council mandate to intervene in Kuwait and expelled the invading Iraqi forces. But in 2003, the UN failed to sanction the Anglo-American war against Iraq. Although its record has been uneven in the area of peace and war, the UN has played an important role in encouraging economic and social development through the Economic and Social Council as well as through specialized agencies, most notably the World Health Organization and the United Nations International Children's Fund. For instance, the World Health Organization coordinated a major campaign in the 1970s to totally eliminate polio.

Born of a wartime alliance between the Great Powers in World War II, but also reflecting a genuine desire by the American people to build a better world free of war, American support for the UN has waxed and waned. In more than one instance, especially in the early 1980s and in 2002, the UN was written off as ineffective. Despite these periods of disillusionment, the United States has often seen the United Nations as a valuable institution for advancing American national interests.

BIBLIOGRAPHY

Hoopes, Townsend and Brinkley, Douglas. *FDR and the Creation of the U.N.* New Haven, CT: Yale University Press, 1997.

Meisler, Stanley. *United Nations: The First Fifty Years.* New York: Atlantic Monthly Press, 1995.

Scott, George. *The Rise and Fall of the League of Nations.* New York: Macmillan, 1974.

Internet Resources

"Milestones in United Nations History." United Nations Department of Public Information. Available from <www.un.org/aboutun/milestones.htm>

"United Nations." Wikipedia. Available from <www.worldhistory/wiki/U/United-Nations.htm>

Corinne J. Naden and Rose Blue

See also: **Allies, Images of; Isolationism; Public Opinion; Roosevelt, Eleanor; Roosevelt, Franklin Delano; Wilson, Woodrow.**

USO

Throughout World War II, the United Service Organizations (USO) provided entertainment for enlisted servicemen and women in the United States during their off-duty hours and entertained American troops overseas and in hospitals through its subsidiary, USO-Camp Shows. Massive population shifts caused by the military's mobilization of troops and the need for industrial workers throughout the country led to inadequate off-duty housing and recreation options in American communities for people in the military service. As a civilian, volunteer organization, USO attempted to ease this problem.

It is likely that many servicemen and women spent their entire wartime experiences in the vicinity of a USO club or canteen. Of the 16 million individuals who served in the military, 25 percent remained in the United States throughout the war, and many of them frequented

USO establishments. By September 1942, an average of 4,500,000 servicepersons visited USO clubs on a monthly basis. These numbers increased greatly as the war progressed. By July 1944, 22,740,431 people had visited USO clubs.

In anticipation of the United States' entrance into the war, the Young Men's and Young Women's Christian Associations, the Salvation Army, the Jewish Community Centers Association, the National Catholic Community Service, and the Traveler's Aid Association of America combined to form the USO in February 1941. This marked the first time that the country's key religious organizations had joined for a common purpose on the national level. These agencies operated their own clubs and canteens under the auspices of the USO and offered spiritual guidance to servicepersons of all faiths.

Servicemen and women of all racial backgrounds relied on the USO to alleviate the boredom, loneliness, and

Bob Hope (1903–2003) entertaining the troops in New Caledonia, South Pacific, during one of his famous USO shows, 1944. AP/WIDE WORLD PHOTOS

tension of military life. USO clubs gave them—and a smaller number of industrial workers—free coffee, meals, lodging, and mailing services. It also entertained them with dances, ping-pong, board games, picnics, art classes, and other amusements. Servicemen and hostesses made USO dances with big band music and jitterbugging a Saturday night mainstay throughout the war.

Between 1941 and 1945, the American people donated $200,000,000 to the USO. The organization was spending $4,000,000 a month by the war's end. At the war's height, in 1944, the USO operated 3,035 clubs and canteens, which assisted a million people each day. The USO operated 178 clubs in places such as Hawaii, Panama, and the Philippines. One and a half million Americans had volunteered for the USO by the end of the war in 1945.

The United States military sanctioned USO-Camp Shows, and it became the only organization to entertain troops overseas, bringing 4,900 performers to perform in 300,000 shows for troops stationed abroad and in 192 hospitals stateside. Famous actors, singers, and musicians volunteered at the American Theatre Wing's Stage Door Canteens in New York, Cleveland, Hollywood, and elsewhere. The comedian Bob Hope began entertaining troops in May 1941 and after the war began led USO tours in Europe and Africa. Mobile USO units also distributed religious material and stationery and showed popular movies to servicepeople on maneuvers in the United States.

Although both men and women volunteered for the organization, women coordinated most USO activities and their labor kept the clubs open throughout the war. The senior hostesses were married women, usually over thirty-five, who acted as surrogate mothers to servicemen. They talked with them during informal counseling sessions, baked cookies for club cookie jars, and made sandwiches by the dozen. They mended uniforms and sewed on chevrons, and they chaperoned contact between junior hostesses and the servicemen who attended USO functions.

The USO counted on junior hostesses, usually women between the ages of eighteen and twenty-five to lift servicemen's morale by dancing with them, playing board games, and engaging them in light conversation. While policies varied from club to club, for the most part senior hostesses did not allow juniors to leave USO premises with servicemen. The USO put this rule in place to safeguard the reputations of its female volunteers and to maintain the what it promoted as the organization's wholesome character. The army and navy, along with USO leaders, hoped that participation in USO activities would reduce the military's high rates of venereal disease and alcohol consumption. Junior hostesses volunteered for the USO to fulfill what they considered their patriotic duty and to socialize with servicemen in a positive environment.

USO hostesses fulfilled the symbolic roles of mother and sweetheart in the lives of servicemen. Their service contrasted with that of women who took on new and sometimes controversial roles as a result of the war, such as soldier or industrial worker. The USO was a home away from home for servicemen and women and helped them to maintain their ties to civilian life and their humanity during a time of crisis.

BIBLIOGRAPHY

Adams, Michael, C. C. *The Best War Ever: America and World War II.* Baltimore, MD: Johns Hopkins University Press, 1994.

Coffey, Frank. *Always Home: 50 Years of USO—the Official Photographic History.* Washington D.C.: Brassey's (U.S.), 1991.

Lovelace, Maryann. "Facing Change in Wartime Philadelphia: The Story of the Philadelphia USO." *Pennsylvania Magazine of History and Biography* 123 (July 1999): 143–175.

United Service Organizations, Inc. *USO, Five Years of Service: Report of the President.* New York: author, 1946.

Meghan Kate Winchell

See also: **Music, World War II; Red Cross, American; Sexual Behavior.**

VETERANS BENEFITS

Between 1890 and 1945, the United States modernized its system of veterans' benefits and expanded the rewards of military service. The culmination of these efforts was the landmark Servicemen's Readjustment Act of 1944, popularly known as the GI Bill of Rights. The GI Bill revolutionized how the nation provided for its returning soldiers. It also shifted government's obligation to veterans from provision of pensions to benefits that eased the return to civilian life, stimulated economic growth, promoted the expansion of the middle class, and helped to transform American higher education.

CIVIL WAR THROUGH SPANISH AMERICAN WAR

By 1890, the Civil War pension system had become a major source of political power and government entitlement. What had once been a program to provide for disabled veterans expanded into pensions for elderly veterans, their spouses and children, and widows. In 1902, nearly a million war veterans and their dependents received pensions at a cost of over $140 million, one-third of the national budget. The following year, President Theodore Roosevelt signed an executive order to expand war pension eligibility to cover old age. In 1912, Congress expanded pension eligibility once again.

Veterans of the Spanish American War followed suit in pressing for access to veterans' benefits. Over 300,000 soldiers had served in the war in Cuba and during the Philippine Insurrection. These veterans sought bonuses for their service and disability pensions for the nearly two thousand injured. Congress extended coverage of the general pension system of 1862 to disabled veterans of the war. In 1913, the two largest Spanish War veterans' organizations merged to create Veterans of Foreign Wars. That year, more than 29,000 of these veterans, widows, and dependents were on the pension rolls; in 1920, pension eligibility was extended to Spanish American War veterans over age sixty-two.

WORLD WAR I

With the possibility of American entry into the First World War, critics of the military pension system did not want to extend "the pension racket" to a new cohort of veterans. With nearly five million soldiers in the wartime army, progressive reformers wanted to limit the economic and political consequences for the country. The cost of Civil War pensions was already over five billion dollars in 1917. Following this lead, Congress created a new program for the armed forces. Called War Risk Insurance, it was a voluntary and contributory insurance in which soldiers paid small premiums for life and disability coverage that could be transferred to civilian life.

While the war lasted, War Risk Insurance remained the major program for returning soldiers. By war's end, however, there were unforeseen problems facing veterans. There was little provision for the over 300,000 veterans needing medical care. In 1919, Congress passed a bill making the U. S. Public Health Service responsible for veterans with service-related injuries and diseases. This bill opened the twenty marine hospitals to returning servicemen and leased other hospital facilities from the army and navy, but it still was inadequate. In 1921, Congress passed the Langley Act, which authorized $18.6 million for the construction of new veterans' hospitals.

Peace brought with it high unemployment and new political pressures to aid veterans. In response, Congress granted returning soldiers a readjustment allowance of $60. It also passed the Sweet Act of 1921 to create the Veterans Bureau. The new bureau administered pensions and services for disabled veterans. The early years of the bureau were marked by the graft and corruption of its first director, Charles Forbes. The ensuing scandal left many veterans with an embittered view of the government's concern for its citizen-soldiers. The Bureau's new director, Brigadier General Frank T. Himes, greatly improved the hospitals, vocational training, and rehabilitation efforts.

The Veterans Bureau was only one aspect of the protracted campaign to expand benefits to World War I veterans. The Veterans of Foreign Wars, the American Legion, and the Disabled American Veterans proposed a program of "adjusted compensation," known as the Soldiers' Bonus, in 1919. The bill's sponsors argued that it was time to make good on the nation's obligations to those who served. After five years of debate, Congress passed the Soldiers' Adjusted Compensation Act over a presidential veto. Designed to compensate individual soldiers for income lost during their service, the bonus was issued in twenty-year insurance certificates payable in 1945.

From 1918 to 1941, the cost of benefits for World War I ex-servicemen, including disability, insurance allotments, and health care, equaled $14 billion dollars. In the 1920s, annual cost had escalated to $650 million a year, nearly 20 percent of the national budget. At the same time, veterans' organizations continued to lobby for early payment of the bonus. They used the massive unemployment of the 1930s to highlight the question of why the government postponed paying its debt of honor.

Unemployed veterans joined the Bonus March of 1932 to solicit Congress's aid. Some saw this "Bonus Expeditionary Army" as a greedy special interest group; others protested that the government had an obligation to those who had served their country.

The coming of the New Deal might have silenced these demands. Government relief, public works, and other programs gave new resources and hope to the unemployed. The 1933 National Economy Act, however, cut veterans' pension payments and called for an investigation of the Veterans' Bureau. Outraged, Congressman John Rankin of Mississippi, joined by Wright Patman of Texas and others, sponsored legislation to restore existing pensions and grant early payment of the Bonus. Despite the administration's opposition, Congress paid the bonus in 1936 at a cost of $3.9 billion, nearly half that year's national budget.

WORLD WAR II: GI BILL

The political struggle between New Dealers and the veterans' lobby was the context in which the most generous government program for veterans in United States emerged. Faced with another war, the Roosevelt administration preferred to address future veterans' needs within a broader plan for the postwar economy. Veterans' advocates in Congress, however, used wartime exigencies to shape a new program. The Selective Service and Training Act of 1940, the Veterans' Preference Act of 1944, and the Servicemen's Readjustment Act of 1944 established the priority of veterans' needs in the postwar world.

The centerpiece of the program was the GI Bill of Rights. Drafted by the American Legion, the bill guaranteed reemployment rights, life insurance, and mustering-out pay. It also expanded the scope of veterans' benefits. World War II veterans received preference in employment; the opportunity for tuition, books, and living allowances for college or vocational school; and loans for homes, farms, and businesses. These programs constituted the largest package of veterans' benefits in American history. Between 1944 and 1949 alone, they cost American taxpayers over $12 billion dollars. World War I veterans often bitterly complained that they had been promised their jobs back on returning home. Veterans of the next generation were able to draw on the promise of the GI Bill of Rights to grant them unprecedented economic opportunities.

BIBLIOGRAPHY

Bennett, Michael J. *When Dreams Came True: The GI Bill and the Making of Modern America*. Washington, DC: Brasseys, 1996.

Boedinger, Robert George. "Soldiers' Bonuses: A History of Veterans Benefits in the United States, 1776–1967." Ph.D. diss., Pennsylvania State University, 1971.

Keene, Jennifer. *Doughboys, the Great War, and the Remaking of America.* Baltimore, MD: Johns Hopkins University Press, 2001.

Kelly, Patrick J. *Creating a National Home: Building the Veterans' Welfare State, 1860–1900.* Cambridge, MA: Harvard University Press, 1997.

Pencak, William. *For God and Country: The American Legion, 1919–1941.* Boston: Northeastern University Press, 1989.

Ross, Davis R. B. *Preparing for Ulysses: Politics and Veterans During World War II.* New York: Columbia University Press, 1969.

Skocpol, Theda. *Protecting Soldiers and Mothers: The Political Origins of Social Policy in the United States.* Cambridge, MA: Belknap Press of Harvard University Press, 1992.

Elizabeth Faue

See also: **American Legion; Bonus March; Demobilization; Economy, World War I; Economy, World War II; GI Bill of Rights; Veterans of Foreign Wars.**

VETERANS OF FOREIGN WARS

Since the late nineteenth century veteran organizations have influenced the nation's domestic, defense, and foreign policies. They have lobbied for benefits and have been engaged in political debates over America's preparedness for war. Moreover, veteran organizations, such as the American Legion and the Veterans of Foreign Wars (VFW) have seen themselves as privileged to define America's cultural values, in particular the meaning of patriotism, because of their members' defense of America through military service.

The VFW traces its roots to 1899 when veterans of the Spanish-American War and the Philippine Insurrection formed local organizations to assist them in securing medical care and other benefits. Some of the groups banded together and in 1914, formed the VFW, which received a congressional charter in 1936. From the beginning, the organization limited its membership to officers and enlisted men (and later women) honorably discharged from the military who had served in any foreign war, insurrection, or expedition in the service of the United States. The major original purposes of the VFW were to promote comradeship among its members, to perpetuate the memory of the dead, and to assist the widows and orphans of veterans. In 1925, the organization established a National Home for Veterans' Orphans.

One of the VFW's more noteworthy efforts resulted in the passage of the 1924 World War Veterans Adjusted Compensation Act, also known as "the Soldier's Bonus." This act granted World War I veterans a deferred payment, due in 1945, as compensation for wages that were lost due to wartime service. In 1932 a spontaneous gathering of 15,000 unemployed veterans in Washington, D.C. demanded early payment of that bonus. Congress's refusal to grant payment and the violent dispersal of the so-called "Bonus Army" increased social and political tensions during the depths of the Great Depression. The VFW opposed the (President Franklin) Roosevelt administration's cuts in veterans' benefits in the Economy Act of 1933. It also played a crucial role, along with the American Legion, in lobbying for an earlier payment of the bonus. Congress in 1936 overrode Roosevelt's veto of legislation providing that payment.

In the early 1930s, the VFW supported a series of neutrality laws that sought to prevent America from entering another overseas war. After the Munich Pact of 1938, isolationist sentiment within the organization waned. Upon the United States' entry into World War II, the VFW's first official act was to lobby Congress to provide for immediate life insurance coverage for all service personnel. Through its efforts Congress approved a bill that would award a $5000 policy to every member of the service and his or her dependents.

The VFW's main contribution to the war effort was in the area of civilian defense. This included promoting a physical fitness campaign and recruiting auxiliary police and firefighters to replace those who had joined the service. The VFW also established an Aviation Cadet Committee to test and drill men eighteen to twenty-six years of age so they could qualify for the Air Corps. The VFW successfully recruited 75,000 men for the Air Corps and another 45,000 for other branches of service.

The greatest accomplishment of the VFW, along with its chief rival, the more politically powerful American Legion, was the effort that led to passing of the GI Bill of Rights in 1944. Initially, the VFW remained lukewarm to the GI Bill and feared a recurrence of the postwar backlash against veterans' benefits by big business that had occurred in the 1920s and early 1930s. But in the end, the VFW embraced the GI Bill of Rights and played a crucial role in its passage. In contrast to the World War I bonus, the GI Bill was widely hailed as one of the great pieces of legislation passed by Congress in the twentieth century.

In addition to its main aim of aiding veterans, the VFW sought from its beginning to promote patriotism among Americans. For example, it placed emphasis on respect for the American flag; as early as the 1920s it distributed nearly a million copies of a booklet, "Etiquette of the Stars and Stripes," to schools and other organizations. One of its achievements was a lobbying campaign that in 1931 led Congress to officially designate "The Star-Spangled Banner" as America's national anthem.

BIBLIOGRAPHY

Bottoms, Bill. *The VFW: An Illustrated History of the Veterans of Foreign Wars of the United States.* Bethesda, MD: Woodbine House, 1991.

Mason, Herbert Molloy, Jr. *VFW: Our First Century, 1899–1999.* Lenexa, KS: Addax Publishing, 1999.

Ortiz, Stephen R. "Soldier-Citizens: The Veterans of Foreign Wars and Veteran Political Activism from the Bonus March to the GI Bill." Ph.D. dissertation, University of Florida, 2004.

Internet Resources

"Americanism Program." Ventura, California: VFW Post No. 1679. Available from <http://vfw1679.tripod.com/vfwamer.htm>.

"The Official Site of Veterans of Foreign Wars of the United States." Available from <http://www.vfw.org>.

Mitchell Yockelson and Steve R. Ortiz

See also: **GI Bill of Rights; National Anthem; Patriotism.**

VISUAL ARTS, WORLD WAR I

During World War I, the visual arts in America were an important part of the war effort. Both the government and the private sector used cartoons, poster art, film, and even individual artists as part of this orchestrated effort. In 1917, less than a week after the United States entered the war, President Woodrow Wilson created a Committee on Public Information, which included a Films Division, a News Division, and a Division of Pictorial Publicity.

The Division of Pictorial Publicity used the most talented advertising illustrators and cartoonists of the time. These artists worked closely with the Advertising Division, which induced magazines and newspapers to donate advertising space to help the war effort. For the first time, the United States government specifically commissioned eight artists, mostly experienced magazine illustrators, to go to the front to produce patriotic images of the American Expeditionary Forces in France. By the end of the war, these artists had produced almost 500 pieces of art. Charles Dana Gibson, America's most popular illustrator, was also an ardent supporter of the war. He recruited his artist friends to design posters for the Committee on Public Information.

Donating their time and work, famous illustrators such as James Montgomery Flagg, Joseph Pennell, and N. C. Wyeth created images to promote causes as diverse as food conservation, the purchase of Liberty Bonds, and armed forces enlistment. This campaign was so successful that more than twenty million people pledged to re-duce consumption of wheat, meat, and eggs, while the Treasury Department's Liberty Loan bond drive netted over $23 billion to help the war effort. As part of this effort, over the next eighteen months, the Division of Pictorial Publicity produced over 1,400 posters seen on billboards all over the country.

The most famous poster was James Montgomery Flagg's "I Want You," an image of Uncle Sam pointing his finger at the viewer. Other images demonized the enemy. One circus-type poster portrayed a gorilla with a club carrying off a half-naked woman, declaiming "Destroy This Mad Brute, Enlist U.S. Army." The most compelling Red Cross poster featured a Red Cross nurse cradling a wounded soldier, evocative of Michelangelo's *Pieta*, a Renaissance sculpture of Mary holding Jesus. More than sixteen million Americans subsequently joined the Red Cross during a weeklong Christmas campaign.

Both the government and Hollywood aided the war campaign by making patriotic films. Pro-war films (*The Battle Cry for Peace*) and pacifist films (*Civilization*) appeared in 1915 and 1916, but by 1917 American films showed mainly German brutality and depicted the war as a struggle between good and evil. The Committee on Public Information had its own division of films to create short documentaries, but, along with Hollywood, it put out feature-length dramas mixing fact and fiction as well. The private movie industry produced a number of "Kaiser" films (*To Hell with the Kaiser, The Kaiser, the Beast of Berlin,* and *The Kaiser's Finish,* among others). Celebrities such as Mary Pickford, Tom Mix, and Charlie Chaplin aided the war effort by starring in patriotic films. One critically acclaimed work, D. W. Griffith's *Hearts of the World,* was released just before the Armistice, but Griffith made a one-reel short to aid a Liberty Loan drive and served as chairman of the Motion Picture War Service Association during the war.

In the private sector, artists like Childe Hassam, the Impressionist painter, celebrated the American entry into World War I with a series of festive flag paintings (*Allied Flags, 1917, Allies Day, May 1917*). John Singer Sargent, most famous as a society portrait painter, produced a commemorative work, *Gassed 1918–19,* for the Hall of Remembrance in London. However, some artists were pacifists or largely ignored the war effort. European avant-garde artists carried on transatlantic exchanges during the war, helping to encourage a uniquely American modernism that was divorced from the wartime atmosphere.

On November 12, 1918, the activities of the Committee for Public Information ended. Critics of the organization claimed that artists and the visual arts had been used to promote censored and dishonest messages during the war. Some writers claimed that hatred for the

Germans became hatred for the Bolsheviks, resulting in the repressive "Red Scare" hysteria of 1919 and fueling later Cold War (1946–1991) rhetoric. Techniques used by wartime professionals were successfully transferred to the advertising industry for peacetime use. The legacy of the first large-scale national propaganda effort involving the visual arts continues up to this time.

BIBLIOGRAPHY

Cork, David. *A Bitter Truth: Avant-Garde Art and the Great War*. New Haven: Yale University Press, 1994.

Corn, Wanda A. *The Great American Thing: Modern Art and National Identity, 1915–1935*. Berkeley: University of California Press, 1999.

Paret, Peter; Lewis, Beth Irwin; and Paret, Paul. *Persuasive Images: Posters of War and Revolution from the Hoover Institution Archives*. Princeton, NJ: Princeton University Press, 1992.

Rogers, W. A. *America's Black and White Book: One Hundred Pictured Reasons Why We Are at War*. New York: Cupples and Leon Co., 1917.

Ross, Stewart Halsey. *Propaganda for War: How the United States Was Conditioned to Fight the Great War of 1914–1918*. Jefferson, NC: McFarland and Co., 1996.

Schickel, Richard. *D. W. Griffith: An American Life*. New York: Simon and Schuster, 1984.

Mary W. Blanchard

See also: **Monuments, Cemeteries, World War I; Motion Pictures, World War I and World War II; Photography, World War I.**

VISUAL ARTS, WORLD WAR II

Although their contributions might not seem as obvious as those of war industry workers, nurses, and servicemen and -women, American painters, sculptors, graphic designers, illustrators, and photographers lent their talents to the war effort in numerous and important ways. Whether serving in military or civilian positions, artists not only helped to create an extensive pictorial record of World War II, but they also aided local and national campaigns to boost morale, promote conservation, sell war bonds, and encourage national unity among all Americans. Depictions of the battlefield and home front incorporated icons of American culture and reinforced the nation's identity as a patriotic, virtuous, and democratic people.

Thanks to New Deal programs such as the Federal Art Project (FAP, 1935–1943), a close working relationship between the federal government and American artists already existed when the United States entered World War II. Designed to put the nation's artists back to work during the Depression, the FAP sponsored the creation of thousands of public artworks that celebrated regional identities and themes from American history. In 1940, however, FAP projects shifted from uplifting the spirits of Americans hard hit by the economic ruin of the 1930s to helping the nation prepare for war. The art historian Jonathan Harris estimates that by "the end of 1941, 80 percent of Project work was being produced for the National Defense Program" (p. 150). Instead of painting murals and running community art centers, federally employed artists were designing camouflage, illustrating military manuals, producing maps, and decorating canteens.

Although some artists worked directly for the government through programs like the FAP, many more artists served the war effort by creating images that boosted morale and reminded the American public what they were fighting for. Even before the United States entered the war, the regionalist painter Grant Wood called upon his fellow artists "to awaken the public to what it stood to lose" while offering his own works depicting the beauty of everyday American life (Haskell, p. 311). Heeding Grant's call, thousands of artists banded together to create works that would aid national defense and spur the nation to victory. In 1942 twenty-three separate art organizations were consolidated into the Artists for Victory group, which served as the principal liaison between the federal government and the more than ten thousand artists who joined the group. Throughout the war, the group sponsored several important exhibitions, including the Museum of Modern Art's "Road to Victory" show, which paired inspiring photographs with text by the poet Carl Sandburg to boost public morale after the defeat at Pearl Harbor, and the 1943 traveling exhibit "America and the War," which brought war-themed artwork to twenty-six cities across the nation.

Perhaps the most important way in which artists aided the war effort was by allowing various government agencies and corporations to reproduce their works in posters. Norman Rockwell's depictions of the "Four Freedoms" outlined in President Franklin D. Roosevelt's 1941 State of the Union address, for example, became the focus of an enormously successful 1943 War Bond campaign. Originally commissioned by *The Saturday Evening Post*, Rockwell's paintings were reproduced by the Office of War Information on four million posters, which encouraged war bond purchases and reminded the public of core American values. Other artists like Thomas Hart Benton and Ben Shahn inspired wartime participation by dramatizing the threat posed by the Axis nations. Benton's eight-part series of paintings, *The Year of Peril*, imagined the widespread devastation that a Fascist victory might bring to the United States.

Shahn's 1942 work *This Is Nazi Brutality* informed viewers about specific Nazi atrocities committed in Lidice, Czechoslovakia. Reproduced by the millions on posters, stamps, stickers, and booklets, Benton's and Shahn's images, along with those by other popular artists like N. C. Wyeth and James Montgomery Flagg, became effective instruments of U.S. propaganda.

Although most artists remained in the United States recording life on the home front and producing artwork in the name of national defense, some artists went overseas to capture the realities of combat and war's aftermath. Serving in all branches of the armed forces, hundreds of combat artists, working in a variety of styles and mediums, created an extraordinary visual account of both the war's heroes and its many victims—the dead, the wounded, prisoners of war, refugees, and civilians in war-torn lands. By the war's end combat artists had produced more than twelve thousand drawings and paintings for military magazines, art shows, and government archives. Civilian photographers and other artists, meanwhile, filled the pages of *Life*, *Time*, and other periodicals with dramatic images in an effort to bring the war home for people in America. More than mere snapshots of events, Robert Capa's photographs of the invasion at Normandy, Margaret Bourke-White's photographs of Nazi concentration camps, and Alfred Eisenstaedt's images of VJ-Day (the day of victory over Japan) celebrations captured both the emotional complexity and historical significance of their subjects.

In addition to its profound effects on the lives and work of American artists, World War II also prompted the geographical center of the art world to shift from Paris to New York. Following the Nazi occupation of Paris in June 1940, many famous artists such as Piet Mondrian, Max Ernst, Salvador Dalí, Walter Gropius, and Marc Chagall moved to the United States, bringing the European vanguard with them. The European Surrealists, with their emphasis on the irrational and the interior landscapes of dreams, had an especially important influence on the New York art scene. Taking Surrealism's automatism, energy, and emphasis on the unconscious to new levels, American artists like Jackson Pollock, David Smith, and Clyfford Still played leading roles in the Abstract Expressionist movement, further reinforcing New York's position as the hub of the art world.

In response to World War II, some American artists served government and military agencies by creating art to celebrate American history and culture in the name of defense. Others bore witness to more universal themes by depicting the war's victories, injustices, and devastation. The painters Edward Hopper and Jacob Lawrence reacted to war's horrors by creating chilling scenes "of existential solitude" (Haskell, p. 343), whereas others turned to both past and future—reviving ancient myths and inventing new forms of expression—to unite humanity in a terrifying atomic age. Ultimately, the visual arts in America were fundamentally transformed as the United States took a prominent role on the global stage.

BIBLIOGRAPHY

Arnason, H. H. *History of Modern Art: Painting, Sculpture, Architecture, Photography*, 3d edition, revised by Daniel Wheeler. New York: Harry N. Abrams, 1986.

Harris, Jonathan. *Federal Art and National Culture: The Politics of Identity in New Deal America*. Cambridge, U.K.: Cambridge University Press, 1995.

Haskell, Barbara. *The American Century: Art and Culture, 1900–1950*. New York: Whitney Museum of Art, 1999.

Henkes, Robert. *World War II in American Art*. Jefferson, NC: McFarland and Company, 2001.

Lanker, Brian, and Newnham, Nicole. *They Drew Fire: Combat Artists of World War II*. New York: TV Books, 2000.

Christina Jarvis

See also: **Monuments, Cemeteries, World War II; Photography, World War II; Propaganda, War.**

WAYNE, JOHN
(b. May 26, 1907; d. June 11, 1979) Actor.

Born Marion Michael Morrison in Winterset, Iowa, John Wayne moved to California at a young age. After an undistinguished football career at the University of Southern California, Wayne entered the movie world changing props for Fox studio before playing roles in a number of unremarkable films. It was not until the 1939 film *Stagecoach* that Wayne gained star status in Hollywood. *Stagecoach* marked the first of his many successful collaborations with director John Ford and contributed to the long association of John Wayne with Western films.

The advent of World War II transformed Wayne's career. While many of Hollywood's leading men, such as Clark Gable, Henry Fonda, and Jimmy Stewart, entered the armed forces, Wayne chose to advance his career at home. The dearth of leading men allowed Wayne's star to rise during the war. Although apologists for Wayne claim that he could not enlist due to an old football injury, family obligations, or his age, many of Hollywood's royalty in similar circumstances gave up their crowns to serve their country. It is with no small amount of irony, therefore, that the other major impact of WWII on Wayne's career was that it allowed him to cultivate an image of himself as the embodiment of the American fighting man on screen.

Without exception, Wayne's WWII characters displayed bravery and patriotism. His cocksure walk and menacing aura (crafted in Western roles) combined with the values of self-sacrifice and necessary violence to sanitize his image of the American soldier. He fought the Japanese as an airman in *The Flying Tigers* (1942), as a construction worker in *The Fighting Seabees* (1944), as an Army colonel in *Back to Bataan* (1945), and on a PT boat in *They Were Expendable* (1945). However, the apogee of Wayne's idealized military character came in the 1949 film, *Sands of Iwo Jima*. In *Sands*, Wayne played the hardheaded Marine Sergeant John M. Stryker whose courage and discipline guide his men though the brutal landings at Tarawa and Iwo Jima. Though Wayne continued to play WWII roles in later films, most notably *The Longest Day* (1962), his Stryker character remains his most memorable depiction of the American serviceman.

Wayne's WWII characters offered a new definition of American military conduct. General Douglas A. Macarthur told Wayne, "you represent the American serviceman better than the American serviceman himself"

John Wayne as Tom Doniphon in the movie, *The Man Who Shot Liberty Valance*. GETTY IMAGES

(Slotkin, p. 514). In 1971, the Marine Corps League hailed Wayne as "the man who best exemplifies the word 'American'" (Eyles, p.11). The attitudes of many Vietnam combatants reveal the impact of Wayne's characterizations on American perceptions of the military. Ron Kovic, in his memoir *Born on the Fourth of July*, recalled how the promise of glory suggested by Wayne's WWII characters influenced his decision to enlist. Cultural historian Richard Slotkin even suggests that many Vietnam servicemen suffered from a "John Wayne syndrome" that left them feeling guilty at their inability to recreate the heroics of Wayne's WWII characters (Slotkin, p. 519–520).

Wayne carried his bellicose, patriotic screen persona into the public arena with right-wing political activism. He made frequent calls for a harder line against communists at home and abroad, and backed up his rhetoric by joining the Hollywood witch-hunt against communists in the 1950s. Wayne also made hawkish statements in support of the Vietnam War. Wayne melded his political views with his heroic military persona in the 1968 film, *The Green Berets*. Though released after the Tet Offensive when popular support for the war was rapidly waning, the movie unashamedly regurgitates official government claims about communist barbarity and American altruism. Wayne's character, Colonel Mike Kirby, displays compassion and sympathy toward the South Vietnamese while maintaining a steely determination to vanquish the enemy, reminiscent of his John Stryker character. Despite its crude and simplistic nature, the film found a ready audience among America's "silent majority" and became one of Wayne's most commercially successful films.

By the time of his death in June 1979, Wayne's outspoken political views earned him almost as many detractors as fans. But in a 1995 Harris poll, the American people named him their all-time favorite male actor (Davis, p. xi). For many, his name remains synonymous with a set of values such as honor, duty, patriotism, and strength. Without exception, his military roles displayed these qualities. For over forty years, they offered a superlative image of the American military and in particular, had a profound impact on how America viewed the WWII serviceman. Today, WWII veterans are routinely lauded as the "greatest generation." The characters created by John Wayne contributed to this sentiment.

BIBLIOGRAPHY

Davis, Ronald L. *Duke: The Life and Image of John Wayne*. Norman: University of Oklahoma Press, 1998.

Eyles, Allen. *John Wayne and the Movies*. South Brunswick: A.S. Barnes, 1976.

Kovic, Ron. *Born on the Fourth of July*. New York: McGraw-Hill, 1976.

Levy, Emmanuel. *John Wayne: Prophet of the American Way of Life*. Metuchen, NJ: Scarecrow Press, 1998.

Roberts, Randy; and James S. Olsen. *John Wayne: American*. New York: Free Press, 1995.

Slotkin, Richard. *Gunfighter Nation: The Myth of the Frontier in Twentieth-Century America*. New York: Atheneum, 1992.

Wills, Garry. *John Wayne's America: The Politics of Celebrity*. New York: Simon & Schuster, 1997.

Mark Boulton

See also: **Motion Pictures, World War I & World War II; Stewart, Jimmy.**

WIDOWS AND ORPHANS

America's involvement in the Spanish-American War, World War I, and World War II left a population of widows and orphans in its wake. Faced with rebuilding their lives alone, many wives and mothers confronted great emotional and financial hardship. War orphans found their situation equally difficult as they faced growing up without their fathers. There were ways, however, in which these victims of war coped with their unique situation through self-determination, aid from family, and government assistance.

EMOTIONAL TOLL

Widows blunted the emotional hardship in a variety of ways. Many sought comfort by moving in with family members. Others remarried soon after their husbands' deaths in order to bring some sense of normalcy to their lives. Those with children found that remarriage also eased the financial and emotional strains associated with single parenthood. In extreme cases, widows overwhelmed with grief succumbed to alcoholism, suffered severe bouts of depression, or committed suicide.

The children of soldiers killed in battle also experienced difficult periods of adjustment. In World War II alone, government records show that 183,000 children lost their fathers during their service overseas. Many young children had no recollection of their fathers and thus depended on family stories, mementos, pictures, and letters to provide a link that memory could not. Children's ability to cope with their father's death varied considerably: some experienced a short-term loss of security whereas others endured long-term psychological disorders.

With little assistance from public organizations, children's ability to cope with a father's death depended greatly on family response. As William Tuttle points out in *Daddy's Gone to War*, psychologists during World War

II commonly advised mothers assisting grieving children that "if you can take it, your children can" (Tuttle p. 45). Furthermore, families often helped children in the grieving process by restructuring their daily routines to accommodate the absence of their fathers. Memorials in the home and larger community also helped children to adjust to a father's death by providing them with an emotional outlet. The presence of a stepfather in the home, however, often complicated children's ability to cope. Some war orphans reported a troubled home life caused by a neglectful mother or an abusive stepfather, but others recalled that the presence of a stepfather helped fill the emotional void left by the father's death.

FINANCIAL COST

The financial costs of losing a husband or father added to the hardships of war widows and orphans. Between 1898 and 1945, society generally embraced men as breadwinners and the heads of their households. During wartime, soldiers' wives continued to rely on their husbands' income. Although women during the two world wars found new job opportunities in war industries, they received lower pay than men and had fewer chances for advancement. Given popular attitudes toward women in the workforce, war widows confronted hardships adjusting to the loss of their husbands' income. In the aftermath of the Spanish American War and World War I, many widows moved in with their fathers, brothers, or other male relatives who could assume primary responsibility for supporting their families. Widows did have the option of assuming the role of breadwinner and working outside the home, but inequalities in pay and lack of public childcare made it difficult for women to work while raising a family. During World War II, however, increasing numbers of women joined the workforce as jobs in areas such as industry and clerical work increased and the government took steps to provide childcare for working mothers. Yet some mothers grew frustrated with the financial demands of maintaining a family without the income of a spouse and placed their children in orphanages.

FEDERAL ASSISTANCE

The federal government recognized the need to provide these victims of war with financial assistance. Since the passage of the first widows' pension act in 1836, war widows and orphans received some form of government aid. World War I prompted the government to liberalize benefits to accommodate the growing population of widows and orphans as well as to meet yearly increases in the cost of living. Assistance to wives and children varied according to the war in which their husbands or fathers had served.

During World War I, the government initiated new forms of veterans' benefits that affected aid to war widows and orphans. Under the War Risk Insurance Act of 1917, the government provided monthly payments to the wives and dependents of soldiers who died in battle and allowed soldiers to take out life insurance payable to their families in the event of their death. In 1920 and 1926, legislators approved benefits for widows of the Spanish American war that provided monthly payments based on family size. The government likewise addressed the needs of war orphans. Traditionally, a child received benefits until the age of eighteen, but in 1928 Congress raised the age to twenty-one for those attending college. As the United States entered the Great Depression, the government removed a number of widows who had remarried from their roster and reduced the annual allotment of pensions; but by the late 1930s legislators again raised pension payments to help families recover from the financial crisis. Legislators continued to expand benefits to wives and children as America entered World War II. A federal law in 1944, for example, allowed benefit payments to the dependents of soldiers missing in action upon confirmation of their death by the secretary of war or secretary of the navy.

Between 1898 and 1945, the number of war widows and orphans in the United States rose considerably. The wives and children of deceased soldiers found a variety of ways to cope with financial and emotional hardships. Many developed a sense of self-reliance that allowed them to adapt to the loss of a spouse or father, whereas others turned to the help of family members. Government officials also recognized the growing number of widows and orphans and took steps to provide financial assistance. Although the experiences of war widows and orphans varied, all found a degree of solace in the private and public sectors of American society.

BIBLIOGRAPHY

Dillingham, William Pyrle. *Federal Aid to Veterans, 1917–1941*. Gainesville: University of Florida Press, 1952.

Levitan, Sar A. and Cleary, Karen A. *Old Wars Remain Unfinished: The Veterans Benefits System.* Baltimore, MD: Johns Hopkins University Press, 1973.

Christman, Calvin L., ed. *Lost in the Victory: Reflections of American War Orphans of World War II.* Denton: University of North Texas Press, 1998.

Tuttle, William M., Jr. *Daddy's Gone to War: The Second World War in the Lives of America's Children.* New York: University of Oxford Press, 1993.

Victoria E. Ott

See also: **Veterans' Benefits; Women and World War I; Women and World War II.**

WILSON, WOODROW

⭐ (b. December 28, 1856; d. February 3, 1924) Twenty-eighth president of the United States (1913–1921); presidency marked by substantial use of military, president during World War I; enunciated Fourteen Points as American war aims and helped forge the Treaty of Versailles/League of Nations, but the treaty was rejected by Senate.

Woodrow Wilson was born in Staunton, Virginia, the son of a Presbyterian minister, and graduated from Princeton University in 1879. With a doctorate from the Johns Hopkins University, he taught history and political science at Bryn Mawr, Wesleyan, and Princeton. He became president of Princeton in 1902. A Democrat, Wilson was elected governor of New Jersey in 1910 and president of the United States in 1912, being reelected in 1916.

Although Wilson came to the presidency emphasizing a progressive domestic agenda and instituted many reforms in office, his presidency was marked by substantial use of military force, including the massive U.S. intervention in World War I. Wilson believed that the use of force was sometimes necessary to achieve foreign policy goals, although as a liberal internationalist, he preferred diplomacy, moral suasion, and international law to promote democracy, commerce, and peaceful relations among nations. Wilson justified his use of the armed forces on such idealistic grounds.

He used the military most frequently in Latin America. In April 1914, U.S. forces temporarily occupied the Mexican port of Vera Cruz. In July 1915, they occupied Haiti and in May 1916, the Dominican Republic. In summer 1916, Wilson dispatched a punitive expedition deep into northern Mexico when revolutionaries raided across the U.S. border.

At the outbreak of the European War in 1914, Wilson declared neutrality, but by 1916, the vastly expanded American trade with the Allies and German submarine warfare threatened to draw the United States into the war. When a U-boat sank the British liner *Lusitania* in May 1915 with the loss of 1,198 lives, including 128 Americans, Wilson had responded with personal diplomacy that by 1916 led to suspension of U-boat warfare. In the 1916 election year, under cross pressures regarding the need to increase the U.S. armed forces, Wilson endorsed a compromise expansion of the U.S. Army and National Guard, including the creation of a Reserve Officer Training Corps (ROTC), and supported a major building program for the navy.

Still, the president sought to avoid being drawn into the European war. In May 1916, he praised the idea of a postwar league to enforce peace. After his reelection in

Woodrow Wilson (right) with British Prime Minister Lloyd George (left) and French Prime Minister Georges Clemenceau (center) at a peace conference in Paris, 1919. GETTY IMAGES

November 1916, he sought to mediate an end to the war. This failed, and in January 1917, he announced his own vision of a peace without vengeance and territorial gains, a "Peace without Victory."

When the Germans, in a desperate gamble, instituted unrestricted submarine warfare in February 1917, Wilson, recognizing the sharp divisions among Americans, considered armed neutrality but ultimately chose full belligerency. His war message in April emphasized German violations of neutral rights and his desire to end autocracy and encourage democracy. He also wanted to shape a liberal, internationalist peace based on postwar cooperation and collective security.

During the war, Wilson proved a forceful wartime commander in chief. He pressured a reluctant Democratic Congress to adopt the modern selective draft, which became the model for raising the majority of America's soldiers in most of the nation's wars in the twentieth century. To mobilize the economy and public opinion, Wilson created a host of powerful ad hoc agencies that were later replicated in World War II. However, extensive wartime violations of civil liberties at all levels left a dark legacy and, in reaction, resulted in the postwar founding of the American Civil Liberties Union (ACLU).

Militarily, Wilson gave Gen. John J. Pershing, commander of the American Expeditionary Forces, maximum freedom in maintaining and directing an American army in France. But in October 1918, when a desperate German government asked Wilson for an armistice based on his liberal "Fourteen Points" peace plan of January 1918, the president forced Pershing and the Allied military leaders to abandon plans for an invasion of Germany and accept an armistice and the Fourteen Points as the basis for negotiations.

In 1919, Wilson became the first serving U.S. President to go to Europe. At the Paris peace talks, he conceded a number of the Fourteen Points to obtain his larger aim—participation in The League of Nations. But when he submitted the Treaty of Versailles to a Republican controlled Senate in July 1919, it failed, a victim of partisan politics, fears of loss of American sovereignty, discontentment with concessions, and the intransigence of a president handicapped by a massive stroke in October 1919.

The United States did not join the League of Nations, and a period of renewed unilateralism ensued. But the Wilsonian vision of collective security linked to liberal ideals would reemerge as a dominant aspect of U.S. policy during World War II and the second half of the twentieth century.

BIBLIOGRAPHY

Chambers II, John Whiteclay. *The Tyranny of Change: America in the Progressive Era, 1890–1920*, 2d ed., updated. New Brunswick, NJ: Rutgers University Press, 2000.

Clements, Kendrick A. *The Presidency of Woodrow Wilson*. Lawrence: University Press of Kansas, 1992.

James, D. Clayton and Wells, Anne Sharp. *America and the Great War, 1914–1920*. Wheeling, IL: Harlan Davidson, 1998.

Knock, Thomas J. *To End All Wars: Woodrow Wilson and the Quest for a New World Order*. New York: Oxford University Press, 1992.

Link, Arthur S.; and Chambers, John Whiteclay, II. "Woodrow Wilson as Commander in Chief." In *The United States Military under the Constitution of the United States, 1789–1989*, edited by Richard H. Kohn, (pp. 317–375). New York: New York University Press, 1991.

Thompson, John A. *Woodrow Wilson*. London: Longman, 2002.

John Whiteclay Chambers II

See also: **Conscription, World War I; Economy, World War I; Financing, World War I.**

WOMEN AND WORLD WAR I

The status of women had risen so high by 1917 that public opinion for the first time recognized a women's voice in public affairs. Two main themes were central. The suffrage movement was building rapidly, pushing eastward from its base in California and the western states. Carrie Chapman Catt, as president of the National American Woman Suffrage Association, was a key leader, as the suffragists organized in hundreds of cities in every state. The second main theme was pacifism. Jane Addams, the Chicago social worker, was perhaps the foremost spokesperson for opposition to war, as head of the International Congress of Women for Permanent Peace. Pressures toward war proved irresistible. President Woodrow Wilson deliberately appealed to the pacifist vision by promising this would be a war to end all wars. The one woman in Congress, Representative Jeanette Rankin, Democrat of Montana, voted against the war resolution, an action she would repeat after Pearl Harbor.

All the home front war agencies made special efforts to enlist the support of women. This was especially notable in the case of the Food Administration. Under the direction of Herbert Hoover, it made a systematic appeal to housewives to conserve meat and fats by eating more fish and grain, and by minimizing waste around the home. The draft laws proved largely successful because American mothers supported the war effort and made no organized effort to persuade their men to resist the draft. Volunteer work was of central importance to middle class women. Much of the organization was handled by the YWCA, women's clubs, and especially by the Red Cross, a private relief organization whose appeal resonated strongly with women. It exploded from 267 local chapters in early 1917 to 2300 by summer. Eight million women labored, without machinery, to make medical and clothing supplies for soldiers. Others volunteered in canteens, as drivers, and as aides at military camps and assembly points.

The closure of immigration created serious labor shortages in the munitions industries. Millions of women were already working in factories, such as clothing and textiles, that directly supported the war effort. Others took jobs in munitions factories. A relatively small number did temporary service (replacing men who had been drafted) in jobs such as streetcar conductors. The Army Nurse Corps and Nurse Corps Reserve (both all-female organizations) expanded from 400 women before the war to more than 21,000. Several hundred nurses, on loan to the British, went to France in the summer of 1917. The Red Cross facilitated young women enlisting and serving in hospitals both on the home front and in Europe.

Among the three million soldiers sent to France with the American Expeditionary Force (AEF) were 16,000 women. They served in a variety of roles, all of which had been dominated or monopolized on the home front by women. These women became nurse's aids, physical therapists, dieticians, relief workers, file clerks and librarians. Ten thousand served the AEF as Army nurses. The Navy, creating a new category of service, Yeoman (F), enlisted over 11,000 women to handle clerical jobs stateside. They enjoyed equal status and equal pay to sailors, but were all deactivated in 1919. The Army, by contrast, refused to countenance any official uniformed role for women beyond that of nurse. General Pershing nevertheless demanded women telephone operators, so a contingent of 223 civilian women served under contract with the Signal Corps in France. Later other civilian contract women worked with the Quartermaster Corps. Civilian agencies such as the Red Cross and Salvation Army brought over some 6,000 additional women, especially to handle welfare and canteen work among American soldiers, and perhaps distract them from red light districts. About 300 women died in service; some when a hospital was shelled, most in the influenza epidemic of 1918.

The unexpectedly enthusiastic outpouring of women volunteers profoundly affected American attitudes toward the role of women. The women were obviously not helpless nor unpatriotic: they were fighting in essential ways for American values. The experience guaranteed overwhelming support for the suffrage movement. The growing strength of women also materially aided the passage of the 18th Amendment to impose prohibition. Male politicians exaggerated the likely impact of woman suffrage, and to get ahead of the crowd, started supporting "women's issues" in the early 1920s rather more readily than women themselves. Pacifism and prohibition thus had strong support in the immediate aftermath of the war, in considerable part as recognition for the involvement of women. The peace issue waxed strong throughout the 1920s. It was no longer possible for militarists to dismiss women as inadequate who hindered the war effort; instead people came to see that the dream of women such as Addams and Emily Balch in heading off future wars was a worthy goal.

BIBLIOGRAPHY

Ebbert, Jean, and Hall, Mary-Beth. *The First, The Few, The Forgotten: Navy and Marine Corps Women in World War I.* Annapolis, MD: Naval Institute Press, 2002.

Gavin, Lettie. *American Women in World War I: They Also Served.* Niwot, CO: University Press of Colorado, 1997.

Godson, Susan H. *Serving Proudly: A History of Women in the U.S. Navy.* Annapolis, MD: U.S. Naval Institute, 2002.

Hewitt, Linda J. *Women Marines in World War I.* Washington, DC: United States Marines Corps, History and Museums Division, 1974.

Schneider, Dorothy, and Schneider, Carl J. *Into the Breach: American Women Overseas in WWI.* New York: Viking Press, 1991

Steinson, Barbara. *American Women's Activism in World War I.* New York: Garland, 1982.

Zeiger, Susan. *In Uncle Sam's Service: Women Workers with the American Expeditionary Force, 1917-1919.* Ithaca, NY: Cornell University Press, 1999.

D'Ann Campbell

See also: **Addams, Jane; Catt, Carrie Chapman; Feminism; Women, Employment of; Women's Suffrage Movement.**

WOMEN AND WORLD WAR II

Making women soldiers was the most radical experiment ever undertaken in American gender roles. World War II was a total war, which required full utilization of womanpower. The American way of warfare was based on elaborate managerial systems; as a consequence, one-fourth of those in the military were assigned to paperwork duty. The generals wanted men to fight in combat, not "waste" their time in clerical work. The British had already successfully mobilized more of their resources than any other nation; they drafted women, assigning some to munitions factories and putting others (including Princess Elizabeth) into Army uniforms.

MOBILIZATION

The American high command followed the British model in 1942. In May, the Women's Army Auxiliary Corps (WAAC) was created with an ambiguous status, half in and half out of the Army. In July the Navy by-passed the auxiliary stage and created the Women Accepted for Voluntary Emergency Service (WAVES), granting the same status as reservist men. By November the Coast Guard had created the SPARS (Latin motto: Semper Paratus); the women Marines began in February, 1943. In June, 1943 the WAAC became the Women's Army Corps (WAC) and gained full military status. In 1942, society women and women college administrators worked with Congress and the Pentagon to secure necessary legislation; they pointed to thousands of patriotic young women anxious to serve their country in non-combat roles. Indeed, almost all women who enlisted cited patriotism as their primary reason for volunteering.

WOMEN AT WAR

The military hired many civilians but did not fully trust them. They wanted secrets confined to soldiers under military discipline. They wanted to be able to move people around whenever and wherever urgency demanded,

Major Charity Adams reviewing her troops, the first African-American WACs to go overseas during World War II.

no matter how long the hours or how unpleasant the conditions. They wanted no one to quit. At first, the main objective was to replace men working the typewriters, mimeograph machines, and telephones. In contrast to the media image of women as pilots or mechanics doing "men's work," in practice the overwhelming majority served in jobs traditionally labeled as "women's work" on the home front. Confounding the myth that women were unsuited for military life, they mastered military language and customs, thrived at marching, accepted the discipline, excelled at their jobs and enjoyed the experiences.

The most supportive unit was the Army Air Force, using women in the largest numbers and in the greatest variety of jobs. Women were concentrated in the Chemical Corps and Signal Corps, but were not used as extensively elsewhere. The Army Ground Forces, which operated training camps in the States, asked that its allocation of 5,000 WACs clericals be reduced to 3,600. The Air Force employed 1000 women in the Women's Auxilliary Service Pilots (WASP), technically with civil-

ian status, which ferried bombers and towed practice targets, but which never had a combat role. Directed by flamboyant Jacqueline Cochran, WASP avoided any affiliations with the WAC.

Servicewomen provided about a tenth of the office-power the military needed, as well as highly appreciated nursing skills. As the quantity and quality of available manpower ran thin, the senior commanders came to realize that women were not just emergency substitutes for men, but valuable performers in a multitude of roles. General Dwight D. Eisenhower was an early convert, calling on WAC commander Colonel Oveta Culp Hobby for thousands of reinforcements for his London headquarters. He played a key role in making the WAC permanent in 1948. The Adjutant General optimistically estimated that 1.5 million WACs could be used in 406 of the 628 Army military occupations. The Navy had much the same learning curve. In the Twelfth Naval District, by September, 1945, over 8,000 WAVES held 30 different rates and performed 130 different activities; they were restricted to the continental United States. Women comprised six out of seven of the enlisted personnel in the Marine Corps Headquarters and over half of the uniformed Navy staff in the Pentagon.

Soldiers and civilians both welcomed nurses, a profession with a highly favorable image, but one controlled by doctors and the Red Cross. During the war, the women nurses took control, making their field a true profession. Nurses began to do tasks commonly reserved only for doctors stateside and ventured into new fields such as psychological nursing. Often a major civilian hospital would set up an entire general military hospital of doctors and nurses, mobilized as a team. The entire group was then sent to the European theater or to the South Pacific. Nearly half of the eligible civilian nurses in the country joined the Army or Navy Nurse Corps, the highest service rate by far of any occupational group, male or female. Another 150,000 were in pre-induction training in the Cadet Nurse Corps as the war ended.

Public opinion turned negative in 1943, led by soldiers who feared large numbers of servicewomen would take over the safe jobs and ship them off to combat. They circulated false rumors to the effect that many women were lesbians, sexually loose, or otherwise unwholesome. In reality, the women were much less sexually active than the men. Recruiting plunged and in the end only 350,000 women served. At peak strength there were about 100,000 WACs, 47,000 Army nurses, 11,000 Navy Nurses, 86,000 WAVES, 10,000 SPARS and 23,000 Marines. The segregated Army set a ceiling of 10 percent black women in the WAAC/WACs but never reached over 6 percent. The Army Nurse Corps allowed a few black women. The Navy rejected black WAVES and nurses until 1945, when President Roosevelt demanded that token numbers be admitted.

LEGACY

Instead of disliking regimentation, women discovered systematic, rigidly enforced discipline produced soaring morale. They became more mature, more realistic, more open-minded, more independent, assertive, and interested in learning and in travel. The military gave them a rare opportunity to learn and practice leadership and management skills. Veterans said their military experience enabled them to better manage time, relate to people, and juggle multiple assignments whether working inside or outside the home. They found life-time friends and, often, husbands as well. Looking back, most veterans recalled their service with pride and satisfaction. Wartime service had transformed the lives of hundreds of thousands of women and their families. It had elevated the status of women in society as patriots. Their legacy would inspire future generations of women to advance the cause of equality in society and in the armed services.

Women fighter pilots of the twenty first century stand on the shoulders of World War II's service women.

BIBLIOGRAPHY

Campbell, D'Ann. *Women at War With America: Private Lives in a Patriotic Era.* Cambridge, MA: Harvard University Press, 1984.

Godson, Susan H. *Serving Proudly: A History of Women in the U.S. Navy.* Annapolis, MD: Naval Institute Press, 2001.

Holm, Jeanne. *Women in the Military: An Unfinished Revolution.* Novato, CA: Presido Press, 1982.

Meyer, Leisa D. *Creating G. I. Jane: Sexuality and Power in the Women's Army Corps during World War II.* New York: Columbia University Press, 1996.

Treadwell, Mattie. *The Women's Army Corps.* In the series *U.S. Army in World War II: Special Studies*, Washington, DC: Office of the Chief of Military History, Dept. of the Army, 1954.

D'Ann Campbell

See also: **Cochran, Jackie; Feminism; Roosevelt, Eleanor; Rosie the Riveter; Women, Employment of.**

WOMEN, EMPLOYMENT OF

The involvement of the United States in major wars between 1898 and 1945 presented new and challenging employment opportunities, both civilian and military, for women. Expanding war economies and the departure of large numbers of men from civilian jobs to military duty created labor shortages that led to the employment of women in untraditional jobs usually denied to them during peacetime. At war's end, women were encouraged to return to traditional work patterns and ways of life. However, the long-term consequences of women's war work have been substantial.

SPANISH-AMERICAN WAR

The Spanish-American War of 1898 was a relatively short war, lasting only three months. Yet this brief war propelled the United States into the position of a great world power. Despite its global significance, the impact of this war on the American home front was negligible. Casualty rates were low, rationing was unnecessary, shortages did not exist, and there was simply not enough time to convert to a large wartime economy.

With the exception of nurses, the Spanish-American War had little impact on America's working women, who made up about 18 percent of the labor force. However, over 1500 nurses were contracted by the government to help care for the 200,000 troops who volunteered to fight in the war. Working for the U.S. Army, these nurses were stationed in the United States, Cuba, Puerto Rico, Hawaii, and the Philippines, and on three ships as well. Nurses assigned to stateside duty mostly cared for soldiers suffering from typhoid, malaria, yellow fever, and dysentery. At the conclusion of the war, the number of nurses under contract to the government was quickly reduced. Nonetheless, recognition of the important work of these nurses paved the way for the establishment of the Army Nurse Corps in 1901 and the Navy Nurse Corps in 1908 as permanent organizations within the Army and Navy.

WORLD WAR I: CIVILIAN WOMEN

The entry of the United States into World War I in April 1917 had a much more profound impact on the lives of working women. During the fall of 1917, as increasing numbers of young men were drafted for military service, the U.S. Employment Service launched a campaign to recruit women to work in war industries. Government posters, carrying messages such as "Will you have a part in Victory?" implored women to join the war effort. Yet the government emphasized that these job opportunities would last only "for the duration." At the end of the war, women would be expected to return to their former activities.

Approximately 400,000 women, out of a female labor force of 8 million, joined the work force for the first time. More significantly, millions of working women switched to better, higher-paying jobs in steel mills, railway yards, oil refineries, chemical plants, automobile factories, and many other war-related industries. In addition, some 15,000 women joined the Women's Land Army of America to replace farmers who had been drafted. To protect their new status as war workers, women joined labor unions and worked with middle-class "allies" in the National Women's Trade Union League. However, many men resented the presence of women on the shop floor and supported union women only in gender-segregated circumstances.

For African-American women, the situation was far more troubling. Doubly exploited because of their gender and race, they found far fewer job opportunities available to them than their white counterparts. African-American women became part of the "great migration" of southern blacks that left the rural South for cities of the North during the early decades of the twentieth century in search of better employment opportunities. Unfortunately, many black women were disappointed to discover that the only positions available to them in the North were the same type of domestic jobs that they had left behind. In fact, the percentage of black women domestics in the North increased by 7 percent between 1910 and 1920.

Only 1.2 percent of African-American women were employed in manufacturing during World War I. Most of these women were concentrated in the tobacco and food processing industries. Black women also worked in the garment trades, government arsenals, and the railroad industry. Segregated from white workers, the wartime employment opportunities available to African-American women did not equal that of white women. However, when compared with the drudgery and demands of domestic work, the minority of black women who secured relatively good-paying jobs in factories experienced marked improvements in their lives.

WORLD WAR I: MILITARY WOMEN

World War I also opened up new opportunities for women to serve in the military. Following the U.S. entry into the war, the recently established Army and Navy Nurse Corps immediately began recruitment campaigns. At peak strength, the Army Nurse Corps totaled approximately 21,000 members, about half of whom served stateside. Some 1500 nurses served in the Navy Nurse Corps. Of this number, approximately 200 served in the United States. Throughout the war, the status of military nurses remained unclear. Neither commissioned nor enlisted, they had no rank or status. In June 1920, the Army granted nurses relative rank, meaning the women had the pay of officers but not full command authority of officers. Not until July 1942 did Navy nurses gain relative rank. In 1944, both Army and Navy nurses were finally granted full officer status.

Under the Naval Appropriations Act of 1916, the Navy recruited over 11,000 women to serve as Yeomen (F). Receiving the same pay and allowances as their male counterparts, Yeomen (F) served in all naval districts and at training stations and navy yards across the nation where they performed crucial clerical skills. In addition, they worked as telephone operators, fingerprint experts, cable decoders, translators, medical technologists, and in munitions factories and torpedo plants. A few of these women served overseas. Joining the Yeomen (F) were 305 women Marines who performed valuable clerical services in Washington, D.C. area offices and at recruiting stations around the country. Opportunities for African-American women in the Navy were severely limited; only 14 of the 11,000 enlisted women have been identified as black. Following their discharge at the end of the war, Navy and Marine women achieved veteran status that entitled them to certain benefits. However, Yeomen (F) received a crushing blow when, with the exception of nurses, the Naval Reserve Act of 1925 specifically limited membership in the Naval Reserve to men. An additional 233 women served as bilingual communications specialists for the U.S. Army Signal Corps in France. Affectionately known as the "Hello Girls," these women finally received military status retroactively in the late 1970s.

Whether employed in military or civilian jobs, women were expected to return to their prior activities at the end of the war. Nonetheless, women took advantage of the wartime emergency to seek out jobs that had previously been closed to them. In the process, their self-worth as workers and as women was significantly enhanced. In partial recognition of women's war efforts, the 19th Amendment to the Constitution, the woman's suffrage amendment, was ratified in 1920.

WORLD WAR II: CIVILIAN WOMEN

When the United States entered World War II in December 1941, women made up 25 percent of the work force. As increasing numbers of men were drafted or volunteered for the military, it became clear that women were needed as war workers. Using World War I as a model, the government launched a vigorous campaign to recruit women into the industrial and agricultural labor force. Posters depicting strong, muscular women as workers appeared across the nation. The largest gain occurred in the defense industries where 3 million women were employed as welders, riveters, and in other "men's jobs." Despite continued discrimination and prejudice, the participation of African-American women in factory work more than doubled, and the number of black women employed as domestics dropped by 15 percent. Heeding the call of the government that "raising food is a real war job," millions of women joined the Women's Land Army or found farm work on their own. By the end of the war, women made up 36 percent of the civilian work force.

WORLD WAR II: MILITARY WOMEN

Another 350,000 women found work as members of one of the women's branches of the Army, Navy, Coast Guard, or Marines or in the Army or Navy Nurse Corps. While most of these women were assigned to stateside posts, members of the Women's Army Corps (WAC) and the Army and Navy Nurse Corps were assigned overseas, sometimes close to the front lines of battle. Another thousand women served in the United States with the Women Airforce Service Pilots (WASP), a quasi-military organization loosely affiliated with the Army Air Forces. Women also served overseas with the American Red Cross where they drove clubmobiles to isolated posts, organized Red Cross clubs for American troops, and worked as recreational staff for military hospitals. While opportunities for African-American women to serve in the military increased substantially compared to the World War I years, most military units were segregated and black women were often assigned to menial jobs such as cooking and cleaning.

At the end of the war, female civilian war workers, especially those employed in defense industries, were laid off from their jobs at about double the rate of men. African-American women, who had been the last to be hired, were the first to be fired. Women in the military were also speedily discharged. Yet women war workers, whether civilian or military, developed a new sense of themselves and their capabilities, and they emerged from World War II as much stronger individuals because of their wartime experiences.

LEGACY

World War I and World War II, and to a far lesser extent the Spanish American War, provided expanded job opportunities for working women that had both an immediate and long-range impact on the role and status of women in society. Building on the experiences of their foremothers, each generation of women was better equipped to confront the challenges of war. While the immediate economic gains experienced by women war workers were only "for the duration," many women emerged from the war with a new sense of empowerment that had significant and long-term consequences for them and for the nation.

Historians continue to debate the larger meaning of the World War II experience for working women. Some have emphasized how expanding wartime job opportunities represented a watershed for women. Others have argued that these changes were temporary and only "for the duration." A third group of historians has asserted that the long-term effects of the war were quite profound. They note that recognition of the important role played by military women during World War II led to the passage of the 1948 Women's Armed Services Integration Act, a law that gave women permanent military status. They also maintain that the war provided the foundation for the rejuvenation of the woman's movement of the 1960s and 1970s as the daughters of the wartime generation drew upon the experiences of their mothers to demand better treatment of women in the work force and in society at large.

BIBLIOGRAPHY

Campbell, D'Ann. *Women at War With America: Private Lives in a Patriotic Era*. Cambridge, MA: Harvard University Press, 1984.

Ebbert, Jean; and Hall, Marie-Beth. *The First, the Few, the Forgotten: Navy and Marine Corps Women in World War I*. Annapolis, MD: Naval Institute Press, 2002.

Gluck, Sherna. *Rosie the Riveter Revisited: Women, the War and Social Change*. Boston: Twayne Publishers, 1987.

Godson, Susan H. *Serving Proudly: A History of Women in the U.S. Navy*. Annapolis, MD: Naval Institute Press, 2001.

Greenwald, Maurine Weiner. *Women, War, and Work: The Impact of World War I on Women Workers in the United States.* Westport, CT: Greenwood Press, 1980.

Hartman, Susan. *The Home Front and Beyond: American Women in the 1940s.* Boston: Twayne Publishers, 1982.

Kennedy, David M. *Over Here: The First World War and American Society.* New York: Oxford University Press, 1980.

Kessler-Harris, Alice. *Out to Work: A History of Wage-Earning Women in the United States.* New York: Oxford University Press, 1982.

Litoff, Judy Barrett, and Smith, David C. *We're In This War Too: World War II Letters from American Women in Uniform.* New York: Oxford University Press, 1994.

Piemonte, Robert V., and Gurney, Cindy, eds. *Highlights in the History of the Army Nurse Corps.* Washington, DC: U.S. Army Center of Military History, 1987.

Schneider, Dorothy, and Schneider, Carl J. *Into the Breach: American Women Overseas in World War I.* New York: Viking, 1991.

Judy Barrett Litoff

See also: **African Americans, World War I; African Americans, World War II; Feminism; Labor, World War I; Labor, World War II; Regional Migration, World War I and World War II; Rosie the Riveter; Women, World War I; Women, World War II.**

WOMEN'S SUFFRAGE MOVEMENT

American women's efforts to win the vote were significantly influenced by both the Civil War and World War I. The organized suffrage movement was in its beginning stages in 1861 when the pressures of the Civil War forced activists such as Elizabeth Cady Stanton and Susan B. Anthony to choose between concentrating their energies on such activities as organizing fundraisers to support Union troops or focusing on suffrage laws and property rights for married women. In World War I the choice was the same, although the context and the response were different. In August 1920, the Nineteenth Amendment was ratified. Partly as a result of the war, all American women finally received the right to vote.

NINETEENTH-CENTURY EFFORTS

Before the Civil War, the idea of women voting was a radical concept that threatened the traditional male role as head of the household. In 1848, at the Seneca Falls Convention in New York, activists from the Northeast began a seventy-year struggle for what seemed to them a natural right of all Americans. In the document written for this meeting by Elizabeth Cady Stanton, "The Declaration of Rights and Sentiments," women laid claim to the need for judicial, religious, and civil equality with men. The most controversial of the resolutions held that men had denied them their "inalienable" right to the franchise and that women had a duty to seek the right to vote. By the 1850s, suffragists, sometimes affiliated with antislavery and temperance groups, were actively lobbying at the state level for constitutional changes at the same time that they traveled throughout the United States giving speeches to raise the women's consciousness of the importance of the vote. Connecting freedom for slaves with their own civic emancipation, women had great hopes for the postwar period.

These hopes were not realized. Instead, women were not included in the postwar settlement that included the ratification of the Fourteenth and Fifteenth amendments. The courts continued to deny that citizenship included the right to vote, although as women activists such as Stanton and Anthony noted that their conditional citizenship included the obligation to pay taxes. Another argument used by opponents was that women did not serve in the military and hence did not merit the vote.

By the end of the nineteenth century, four Western states—Idaho, Colorado, Utah, and Wyoming—had enfranchised women, in most cases after elaborate, expensive campaigns by the suffrage associations at the state level.

TWENTIETH-CENTURY MOVEMENTS

In the twentieth century, the focus turned to a crusade by the National American Woman's Suffrage Association to pass a national amendment, the Susan B. Anthony Amendment authorizing suffrage, which had been presented to Congress annually from 1870 on, but until 1914 the resolution never had sufficient support for an affirmative vote, much less the requisite two-thirds majority.

Inspired by the radical tactics used by women in Great Britain, a group of younger American women led by Alice Paul and Lucy Burns formed the National Woman's Party in 1915. They emphasized attention-getting parades and other forms of publicity as well as pressure tactics that made women's suffrage an unavoidable topic even for those who opposed it. When World War I began in April 1917, the more conservative National American Woman's Suffrage Association for a time submerged its suffrage activities in war work. The association supported war work and efforts to inspire female patriotism even at the cost of suffrage efforts. Women who had little to do with the suffrage campaign were drawn into wartime work outside the home, and their contributions became an important part of the suffragists' argument that women deserved the vote.

Suffragettes marching in front of the White House, 1918. AP/WIDE WORLD PHOTOS

Meanwhile, Paul and her activists challenged Woodrow Wilson's government. Beginning in 1917, these women made the case, often using President Wilson's own words on their banners, that the war was being fought for democracy. Quoting Wilson, a favorite banner read, "We shall fight for the right of those who submit to authority to have a voice in their own governments." The National Woman's Party stationed pickets outside the White House until embarrassed officials began arresting and imprisoning them on frivolous charges such as impeding access to sidewalks. In prison, Alice

Paul insisted that they were political prisoners. When privileges such as writing letters and not wearing prison uniforms were denied, the Paul and other women in jail began hunger strikes, which, in an overreaction by the government, led to their being force-fed. Still, Wilson— who believed that suffrage was a state and not a federal issue—withheld his support from a national amendment. Finally, in early 1918, under pressure from both of the suffrage associations, he urged a compliant Congress to pass what became, when it was ratified in the summer of 1920, the Nineteenth Amendment.

World War I provided a necessary boost to the organized suffrage movement. Not only had the wartime activities of women in factories and businesses, on farms and in stores, made the denial of the franchise an absurdity given women's patriotic service and the purpose of the war to make the world safe for democracy, but the connection between the international goal of democracy that Wilson articulated and the organized crusade of women's suffrage changed the opinions of both lawmakers and ordinary Americans.

BIBLIOGRAPHY

Baker, Jean H., ed. *Votes for Women: The Struggle for Suffrage Revisited.* New York: Oxford University Press, 2001.

DuBois, Ellen Carol. *Feminism and Suffrage: The Emergence of an Independent Women's Movement in America, 1848–1869.* Ithaca, NY: Cornell University Press, 1978.

Flexner, Eleanor. *Century of Struggle: The Woman's Rights Movement in the United States.* Cambridge, MA: Belknap Press of Harvard University Press, 1959.

Stanton, Elizabeth Cady, et al., eds. *History of Woman Suffrage,* 6 vols. Rochester, NY: Source Book Press 1881–1922.

Jean Harvey Baker

See also: **Anthony, Susan B.; Catt, Carrie Chapman; Feminism; Stanton, Elizabeth Cady; Wilson, Woodrow; Women and World War I.**

YORK, ALVIN CULLUM

(b. December 13, 1887; d. September 2, 1964) World War I hero and recruiting figure during World War II.

Alvin C. York was born the third child of eleven to William and Mary Brooks York in Pall Mall, Tennessee. York's family eked out an existence in a two-room cabin. York was raised as a country boy who had only attended school for nine months. In 1917, York's world was changed forever when he was drafted into the American Army. York resisted because of religious beliefs; his Church of Christ in Christian Union denounced killing. But because his church was not recognized by the draft board as a legitimate denomination, York could not be excused from service as a conscientious objector.

Sergeant Alvin C. York's amazing exploit near Chatel-Chehery in the Argonne Forest during World War I captured American imagination. On the foggy, rain soaked morning of October 8, 1918, York and seventeen doughboys received daunting orders to secure the Decauville Railroad in an attempt to disrupt German supply lines. Things went terribly awry, however, and the soldiers from Company G, 328th infantry, of the 82nd Division, found themselves behind enemy lines pinned down by withering machine-gun fire. York's best friend, Murray Savage, and eight other Americans lay dead. Acting Sergeant Bernard Early, suffering from multiple gunshot wounds, ordered York to silence the machine-gun nest. Armed only with his rifle, pistol, and a profound belief that God would protect him, Alvin C. York used his formidable skills as a marksman to take out the gun. When the smoke cleared, York and the seven survivors captured 132 German prisoners and delivered them to U.S. authorities. News of the event made York a household name and the most popular American hero of the war.

While the near mythic feat is worthy of awe and respect, it is not the way "Big 'un," the redheaded mountaineer from Pall Mall, Tennessee, wanted to be remembered. York's life, though defined for most by Gary Cooper's Academy Award winning portrayal in the Warner Bros. film *Sergeant York* (1941), was more interesting than the film character, especially after the war. When York returned to New York in May, 1919, he found himself the object of the city's attention. A ticker tape parade down Fifth Avenue and a suite of rooms at the Waldorf Astoria awaited him. Influential people offered him outstanding sums of money for endorsements of products, public appearances, and shoot-

Alvin York. AP/WIDE WORLD PHOTOS

other great American hero, Charles Lindbergh. The two men squared off against each other through 1940 and 1941, representing the two poles of American thought regarding the war in Europe. Lindbergh argued that the Nazis posed no threat to the United States. Lindbergh claimed that the British, Hollywood, and Jews were agitating for war. York argued that the Nazis threatened freedom, democracy, and the American way of life.

When the U.S. entered World War II, Sergeant York was used as a recruiting tool. The movie about his World War I heroics won two Academy Awards. York tried to reenlist, but was prevented by poor health. Instead, he worked in the Signal Corps to boost American morale. He visited training camps, demonstrated his shooting skills, and signed autographs. York also had a weekly newspaper column, "Sergeant York Says," and broadcast a weekly radio program, "Tennessee Americans," over the Mutual Broadcasting System throughout the war. He reinforced his image as hero and patriot to the war effort.

When the war ended, troubles awaited him. His mythic image did not shield him from the Internal Revenue Service, which demanded taxes on revenue from the movie. Obesity, stress, and other factors led to a stroke in 1948, the first in a series of several strokes that would leave York, still hounded by the IRS, bedridden for the last ten years of his life. Friends, neighbors, and the American Legion launched a campaign to bail him out of his debt. In 1963, President John F. Kennedy persuaded the IRS to reduce his debt, take a portion of the money raised, and allow the Sergeant to live out the remainder of his life in dignity. Less than a year later, a frail and exhausted York died. He was buried in the cemetery of the Wolf Creek Methodist Church with full military honors.

ing demonstrations, all of which York turned down because he believed no one should profit from taking the lives of others. He returned home intent on two things: marrying Gracie Williams, and improving education in his region. As events heated up in the Europe during the 1930s, York initially spoke out against American intervention. He joined the Emergency Peace Campaign organized by the eminent churchman Harry Emerson Fosdick. From 1936 to 1939, York traveled the country condemning the first World War while promoting Progressive reforms. His stance changed, however, as a result of his relationship with Warner Bros., a Hollywood film company. In 1940, he agreed to have Warner Bros. make a film of his life.

Through his association with Warner Bros., York became a member of the Fight For Freedom Committee (FFF) created in direct opposition to the isolationist (and some would say pro-Nazi) America First Committee. In his capacity as a spokesman for the FFF, York found himself diametrically opposed to the stance of an-

BIBLIOGRAPHY

Birdwell, Michael E. *Celluloid Soldiers: Warner Bros. Campaign Against Nazism.* New York: New York University Press, 1999.

Cooke, James J. *The All-Americans at War: The 82nd Division in the Great War, 1917–1918.* West Port, Connecticut: Praeger, 1999.

Lee, David D. *Sergeant York: An American Hero.* Lexington: University Press of Kentucky, 1985.

Michael E. Birdwell

See also: **Heroes; Perception of; Isolationism; Motion Pictures, World War I & World War II; Peace Movements.**

Abolitionist: In the United States, anyone who campaigned against the continued practice of slavery during the eighteenth and nineteenth centuries.

Allies: The nations, including Great Britain, France, and the United States, among others, aligned against the Central Powers during World War I and against the Axis during World War II.

American Anti-Slavery Society: Abolitionist organization found in 1833 by William Lloyd Garrison and Arthur Tappan. Frederick Douglass was one of the group's most prominent members.

Americanization Movement: During the early part of the twentieth century, a social trend, partly driven by fear, towards pressuring recent immigrants to adopt American styles, values, and language.

(Anti)Rent War: An uprising in New York state in which disgruntled tenants resisted attempts by local sheriffs to evict them. Governor Silas Wright involved the state militia in 1845, and the violent phase of the anti-rent movement came to an end.

Antisuffragist: Anyone who opposed the right of women to vote.

Baltimore Riots: On April 19, 1861, a pitched battle between a mob of secessionists and a group of Union soldiers on its way through Baltimore. Four soldiers and twelve civilians were killed. Scores more were wounded. The encounter is often considered to be the first blood drawn in the American Civil War.

Barbary Coast: Common name for the waterfront area of San Francisco, California, in the years following the Gold Rush of 1849, when the area was famous for prostitution, gambling, crime, and a surfeit of notorious characters.

Barbary States: From the sixteenth to the nineteenth century, collective name of the North African countries of Morocco, Tunisia, Algeria, and Tripoli, and used especially to denote a time and an area in which ocean piracy was common.

Bedouin: A desert nomad, especially an Arab in the Middle East or North Africa.

Berber: Of or belonging to any of a number of Muslim North African tribes. Also, the language of those tribes.

Berlin airlift: In 1948 and 1949, the massive air transport into post-war Berlin of food, fuel, and other necessities by the Allies in response to a Soviet blockade of the divided city. By the end of the operation, more than two million tons of goods had been delivered.

Berlin blockade: In 1948, an attempt by the Soviet Union to force the United States and its allies out of Berlin by blocking access to their occupied territories. Following the success of the Berlin airlift, however, the Soviets were forced to abandon their plan and reopen the borders in May 1949.

Berlin Wall: Constructed in 1961 by the East German government, a wall to separate West Berlin from East Berlin. Among the most visible symbols of the Cold War, the Berlin Wall kept East Germans from crossing over into the west until November 1989 when a series of bureaucratic miscommunications led the government of East Germany to once again begin issuing visas. The wall was soon demolished.

Bey: In the Ottoman Empire, a denotation of rank or superior status. A provincial governor there.

Black Codes: Laws passed by former Confederate states to restrict the personal freedoms of recently freed slaves. Among their many notorious proscriptions were the segregation of places of public access and restrictions on the right to own property.

British Crown: The monarchy of Great Britain and the United Kingdom.

Bumppo, Natty: The hero of the so-called Leatherstocking Tales by James Fenimore Cooper (1789–1851), Bumppo was a tracker, a trapper, and an all-around outdoorsman. A voluntary outcast from his own society, Bumppo lived among Native Americans and was known by several nicknames, among them Hawkeye, Pathfinder, Leatherstocking, and Deerslayer.

Carte De Visite: Literally, a visiting card. One's photographic likeness, printed on a card for use as proof of identity.

Central Powers: During World War I, Germany and its military allies, including Bulgaria and the Ottoman Empire.

Civil Rights Movement: In the United States, the popular movement among African Americans and their supporters during the 1950s and 1960s to secure equal treatment under the law and to defeat segregation and other forms of institutionalized racism.

Committee On Public Information: Established in 1917 during World War I, the Committee spread propaganda to help increase support for the war in the United States.

Communism: A political ideology in which property and industry belong to the citizenry, rather than to individuals.

Constitution: Established in 1787 at the constitutional convention in Philadelphia, the foundational document of the United States. Originally consisting of a preamble and seven articles, the Constitution has been amended twenty-seven times.

Defense Plant Corporation: Organized in 1940, a government agency responsible for overseeing the production and finance of the facilities utilized by private defense contractors and manufacturers.

Department of the Treasury: Established in 1789, an arm of the federal executive branch charged with minting currency, advising the President on fiscal matters, and collecting taxes. The treasury department also administers the Secret Service.

Détente: A period or state of relaxed tensions between two military powers.

Dey: During the reign of the Ottoman Empire, the title given to the governor of Algiers.

Don't Ask, Don't Tell: Adopted in 1993 during the administration of President Bill Clinton, a policy on homosexuals in the United States military in which commanders agree to not attempt to learn a soldier's sexual orientation ("don't ask") as long as the soldier does not volunteer it ("don't tell").

Dred Scott Case: In 1857, a case before the United States Supreme Court. Dred Scott, a slave, argued that since he had lived for four years in a free territory that he should be declared free. The court disagreed, declaring that Scott was property and therefore could not seek status as a citizen of the United States.

E-mail: A method of communication whereby correspondence is instantaneously transmitted from one computer to another. Also, a communication sent or received by this method.

Euro-American: A citizen of the United States of European descent.

Federal: Denotes a system of government in which several regions or states agree to defer certain rights and responsibilities to a centralized authority.

First Lady: The wife of the president of the United States or of one of its state governors.

Founding Fathers: A collective name for the men who signed the Declaration of Independence and who helped to compose the Constitution of the United States.

Freedpeople: Slaves freed after or during the American Civil War.

G.I.: In military parlance, general issue, or that provided by the United States military to its soldiers. By extension, a soldier in that military.

Gorbachev, Mikhail: Soviet political leader (b. 1931), responsible for many pro-democratic reforms and the liberalization of Soviet society, Gorbachev was instrumental in improving relations with the United States and in helping to end the Cold War. Gorbachev resigned in 1991.

Gross National Product (GNP): The accumulated value of goods and services produced by the citizenry of a country within a year. Often used as an indicator of a country's economic health.

Gulf War: From January to February 1991, a military conflict between Iraq and a United States-led coalition of more than thirty countries. The war erupted after Iraq invaded Kuwait, its oil-rich neighbor, on 2 August 1990. Hostilities came to an end on 28 February with the rout of Iraqi forces during a short-lived ground war.

Habeas Corpus: A legal writ issued to order the physical production of a detained person as well as appropriate evidence of the necessity of continued detention. Literally, you should have the body.

House of Representatives: In the United States, the lower house of Congress.

Image-Maker: An individual or organization employed to help create a positive public image for another individual or organization, especially in politics and the entertainment industry.

Indian Wars: Collective term for a number of violent clashes between Native Americans and Europeans or people of European descent at various times during American history.

Internet: A global network connecting computers for the purpose of information exchange and communication through a variety of specialized servers, such as e-mail, bulletin boards, and the World Wide Web of on-line sites, magazines, newspapers, stores, and entertainment venues.

Jamestown colony: Founded in 1607, the first English settlement in North America. Jamestown was named for King James I.

Kansas–Nebraska Act: A law passed by Congress in 1854 that created the western territories of Kansas and Nebraska. In the end, the Act, which legalized slavery in the new territories in defiance of the Missouri Compromise, led to the rise of the Republican party.

Know-Nothings: During the 1850s, nickname for members of the American Party, nativists who opposed the holding of public office by immigrants and Roman Catholics. The name derived from the party's notorious secrecy and its unwillingness to answer questions about its activities.

Lame Duck: An elected official serving out his or her term after having been defeated or having decided not to seek another term. A figure of powerlessness.

Lend-Lease Act: Legislation passed in 1941 by the Congress, the Lend-Lease Act gave the president the discretion to sell, lease, or lend supplies and necessities during wartime to countries believed to be vital to the security of the United States.

Lopez de Santa Anna: General of the Armies of Mexico, politician, dictator, and twice President. Santa Anna (1794–1876) had a remarkable, often brutal, capricious, and mystifying career in his various roles. His most infamous military achievement was the capture of the Alamo and the slaughter of Texas revolutionaries in 1836. In and out of public favor his entire life, Santa Anna was twice exiled from Mexico, but at last allowed to return in 1874.

Lost Cause: During the American Civil War, another name for the cause of the Confederate states.

Manifest Destiny: A belief among many Americans of the nineteenth century, whereby the United States was thought to possess, by the grace of God, the right to expand to fill the whole of the North American continent.

Mexican War: From 1846 to 1848, military conflict between the United States and Mexico. Growing tensions between the two nations erupted into war with the United States' decision to annex Texas in December of 1845. In the negotiated peace, the United States won some two–fifths of Mexico's territory as well as $15 million in compensation.

Military-Industrial Complex: So called by President Dwight D. Eisenhower (1890–1969), a cautionary description of the relationship between the military and the industrial forces responsible for manufacturing military equipment. Eisenhower warned that such a collaboration might one day endanger the republic.

Militia: An army of civilians with military training who can be called upon to serve in time of war or national emergency.

Naiveté: A quality of excessive trustworthiness or belief in the fundamental goodness of human nature, often among the very young or inexperienced.

National American Woman's Suffrage Association: Organization of suffragettes that in 1920 became the League of Women Voters.

National Security Council Paper 68 (NSC #68): Ordered by President Harry S. Truman (1884–1972), an examination and reassessment of both the relative strengths of the Soviet Union and of the United States' strategy in containing or stopping the spread of Communism. Considered a seminal Cold War document, NSC #68 led to a massive military buildup and to increased tensions between the two global superpowers.

National Women's Party: Organization of suffragettes founded in 1916.

Nativists: Members of the American Party, known for its anti-immigration, anti-Catholic positions, and its belief that only "native born" Americans had the right to hold public office.

Nemattanew: Powhatan warrior and mystic. His murder by the English in 1622 led the Powhatan chief Opechancanough to make war against the English colonies, killing more than three hundred of the colonists.

Newburgh Conspiracy: In 1783, a plot by members of the Continental Army of the United States, stationed in Newburgh, New York, to overthrow the Congress by coup. A speech given by George Washington was instrumental in convincing the officers to set aside their plans.

Neoconservative: A political ideology in the United States that embraced the conservative policies and ideas of the Republican party, favored an active and robust military, and believed in the spread of democracy through armed intervention in undemocratic societies.

Opechancanough: Native American chief, and brother to Powhatan, Opechancanough (c. 1545–1644) was responsible for the capture of the English Captain, John Smith, and, indirectly, for Captain Smith's introduction to Opechancanough's niece, Pocahontas.

Pasha: Title used in Turkey and various Middle Eastern countries during the reign of the Ottoman Empire to denote a high-ranking official.

Patriot Missiles: A guided surface-to-air missile designed primarily to shoot down incoming missiles before they reach their targets. First widely deployed during the Gulf War in 1991, the Patriot Missile system, though at first reported to be successful, in fact shot down none of its intended targets and may have been responsible for firing on friendly Coalition aircraft.

Patriots: Before and during the Revolutionary War, the colonists who supported independence from Great Britain. Generally, anyone who proudly defends the actions or culture of his or her own country.

Policymakers: Those responsible for creating or crafting public policy, as legislators, politicians, or other elected or appointed officials.

Postwar: The period following the end of a military conflict.

Progressives: From 1900 to 1920, a political and social movement inside the United States that called for, among other things, a graduated income tax, direct election of the United States Senate, and government action to break up industrial monopolies.

Radical Republicans: Members of the Republican party during and after the American Civil War who advocated harsh Reconstruction measures as a way of punishing the former Confederate states.

Reconstruction Acts: Passed on May 31, 1870, February 28, 1870, and April 20, 1871, laws designed to curb illegal activity, such as that perpetrated by the Ku Klux Klan, in parts of the South after the end of hostilities in the Civil War. Among other things, the Reconstruction Acts levied harsh penalties against anyone who attempted to prevent recently freed slaves from voting.

Redcoats: Informal or derisive name given to British soldiers, especially those in the colonies before and during the American Revolutionary War.

Red Scare: Following the end of World War I and brought about largely by the onset of the Russian Revolution, a period of general suspicion and paranoia regarding the political beliefs of recent immigrants, a few hundred who were arrested and deported. A second scare occurred in the late 1940s as Americans began to fear that communists had infiltrated the highest levels of government and the entertainment industry.

Revolutionary War: From 1775 to 1781, the war of American independence, fought between the colonies in the New World and the forces of the British Crown.

SCUD Missiles: Short-range ballistic missiles used by the Iraqi military, especially during the Gulf War of 1991.

Senate: In the United States, the highest house of Congress.

Slaughterhouse Cases: A number of cases heard by the United States Supreme Court in 1873 involving the legality of a twenty-five year monopoly granted by the Louisiana state legislature to a single slaughterhouse operator in New Orleans for the purpose of protecting the public health. The court ruled that the state had not violated the 14th amendment, as had been charged.

Slave-Power Conspiracy: Before the American Civil War, a belief among many northerners, to some degree perpetuated by the Republican Party and abolitionist groups, that the South planned to marginalize the North by extending slavery into the western territories and Central America.

Spanish American War: In 1898, a military conflict between the United States and Spain on behalf of Cuba. Its victory increased the standing of the United States as a legitimate world power.

Sunset Laws: Laws designed with a specific date of termination.

Supreme Court: The highest federal court in the United States, composed of a chief justice and eight associate judges. The Supreme Court was established by Article 3 of the United States Constitution. Its justices are appointed by the President and serve for life.

Texas Revolution: Beginning in 1835, Texas' war of independence from Mexico. The conflict involved the famous battle at the Alamo and ended in 1836 when Samuel Houston defeated Santa Anna and forced him to recognize the independence of Texas.

Three-Fifths Compromise: An agreement reached during the Constitutional Convention of 1787. As proposed by James Madison, the Three-Fifths Compromise sought to solve the divisive issue of how to count the slaves for the purpose of establishing representation in the new Congress. Madison's compromise was that each slave would be counted as three-fifths of a free white. The 14th Amendment to the United States Constitution later repealed the Compromise.

Unionist: One who supported the Northern or Union cause during the Civil War.

Vietcong: Any supporter or member of the Communist-supported armed forces of the so-called National Liberation Front, which fought to reunite South Vietnam with North Vietnam during the Vietnam War (1954–1976).

Whig Party: Political party founded in the 1830s to oppose the Democrats. Notable Whigs include Daniel Webster (1782–1852) and William Henry Harrison (1773–1841).

Women's Rights Movement: The populist activity that aimed to secure social, economic, and political equality for women.

Zacatecas: A state in north central Mexico. Also, the capital of that state.

PRIMARY SOURCE DOCUMENTS

ACTS OF CONGRESS

Selective Service Act (1917)

Commentary

When the United States entered World War I, the nation's armed forces consisted of about 200,000 volunteers. To address the manpower shortage, Congress passed the Selective Service Act in May 1917. The act authorized the President to increase temporarily the size of the military and required all men between the ages of twenty-one and thirty to register for the wartime draft. At its peak in 1918, the U.S. Army numbered 3.7 million soldiers, 2.8 million of whom had been drafted.

To authorize the President to increase temporarily the Military Establishment of the United States.

Be it enacted by the Senate and House of Representatives of the United States of America in Congress assembled, That in view of the existing emergency, which demands the raising of troops in addition to those now available, the President be, and he is hereby, authorized—

First. Immediately to raise, organize, officer, and equip all or such number of increments of the Regular Army provided by the national defense Act approved June third, nineteen hundred and sixteen, or such parts thereof as he may deem necessary; to raise all organizations of the Regular Army, including those added by such increments, to the maximum enlisted strength authorized by law. Vacancies in the Regular Army created or caused by the addition of increments as herein authorized which can not be filled by promotion may be filled by temporary appointment for the period of the emergency or until replaced by permanent appointments or by provisional appointments made under the provisions of section twenty-three of the national defense Act, approved June third, nineteen hundred and sixteen, and hereafter provisional appointments under said section may be terminated whenever it is determined, in the manner prescribed by the President, that the officer has not the suitability and fitness requisite for permanent appointment.

Second. To draft into the military service of the United States, organize, and officer, in accordance with the provisions of section one hundred and eleven of said national defense Act, so far as the provisions of said section may be applicable and not inconsistent with the terms of this Act, any or all members of the National Guard and of the National Guard Reserves, and said members so drafted into the military service of the United States shall serve therein for the period of the existing emergency unless sooner discharged: Provided, That when so drafted the organizations or units of the National Guard shall, so far as practicable, retain the State designations of their respective organizations.

Third. To raise by draft as herein provided, organize and equip an additional force of five hundred thousand enlisted men, or such part or parts thereof as he may at any time deem necessary, and to provide the necessary officers, line and staff, for said force and for organizations of the other forces hereby authorized, or by combining organizations of said other forces, by ordering members of the Officers' Reserve Corps to temporary duty in accordance with the provisions of section thirty-eight of the national defense Act approved June third, nineteen hundred and sixteen; by appointment from the Regular Army, the Officers' Reserve Corps, from those duly qualified and registered pursuant to section twenty-three of the Act of Congress approved January twenty-first, nineteen hundred and three (Thirty-second Statutes at Large, page seven hundred and seventy-five), from the members of the National Guard drafted into the service of the United States, from those who have been graduated from educational institutions at which military instruction is compulsory, or from those who have had honorable service in the Regular Army, the National Guard, or in the volunteer forces, or from the country at large; by assigning retired officers of the Regular Army to active duty with such force with their rank on the retired list and the full pay and allowances of their grade; or by the appointment of retired officers and enlisted men, active or retired, of the Regular Army as commissioned officers in such forces: Provided, That the organization of said force shall be the same as that of the corresponding organizations of the Regular Army: Provided further, That the President is authorized to increase or decrease the number of organizations prescribed for the typical brigades, divisions, or army corps of the Regular Army, and to prescribe such new and different organizations and personnel for army corps, divisions, brigades, regiments, battalions, squadrons, companies, troops, and batteries as the efficiency of the service may require: Provided further, That number of organizations in a regiment shall not be increased nor shall the number of regiments be decreased: Provided further, That the President in his discretion may organize, officer, and equip for each Infantry and Cavalry brigade three machine-gun companies, and for each Infantry and Cavalry division four machine-gun companies, all in addition to the machine-gun companies comprised in organizations included in such brigades and divisions: Provided further, That the President in his discretion may organize for each division one armored motor-car machine-gun company.

The machine-gun companies organized under this section shall consist of such commissioned and enlisted personnel and be equipped in such manner as the President may prescribe: And Provided further, That officers with rank not above that of colonel shall be appointed by the President alone, and officers above that grade by the President by and with the advice and consent of the Senate: Provided further, That the President may in his discretion recommission in the Coast Guard persons who have heretofore held commissions in the Revenue-Cutter Service or the Coast Guard and have left the service honorably, after ascertaining that they are qualified for service physically, morally, and as to age and military fitness.

Fourth. The President is further authorized, in his discretion and at such time as he may determine, to raise and begin the training of an additional force of five hundred thousand men organized, officered, and equipped, as provided for the force first mentioned in the preceding paragraph of this section.

Fifth. To raise by draft, organize, equip, and officer, as provided in the third paragraph of this section, in addition to and for each of the above forces, such recruit training units as he may deem necessary for the maintenance of such forces at the maximum strength.

Sixth. To raise, organize, officer, and maintain during the emergency such number of ammunition batteries and battalions, depot batteries and battalions, and such artillery parks, with such numbers and grades of personnel as he may deem necessary. Such organizations shall be officered in the manner provided in the third paragraph of this section, and enlisted men may be assigned to said organizations from any of the forces herein provided for or raised by selective draft as by this Act provided.

Seventh. The President is further authorized to raise and maintain by voluntary enlistment, to organize, and equip, not to exceed four infantry divisions, the officers of which shall be selected in the manner provided by paragraph three of section one of this Act: Provided, That the organization of said force shall be the same as that of the corresponding organization of the Regular Army: And provided further, That there shall be no enlistments in said force of men under twenty-five years of age at time of enlisting: And provided further, That no such volunteer force shall be accepted in any unit smaller than a division.

Sec. 2. That the enlisted men required to raise and maintain the organizations of the Regular Army and to complete and maintain the organizations embodying the members of the National Guard drafted into the service of the United States, at the maximum legal strength as by this Act provided, shall be raised by voluntary enlistment, or if and whenever the President decides that they can not effectually be so raised or maintained, then by selective draft; and all other forces hereby authorized, except as provided in the seventh paragraph of section one, shall be raised and maintained by selective draft exclusively; but this provision shall not prevent the transfer to any force of training cadres from other forces. Such draft as herein provided shall be based upon liability to military, service of all male citizens, or male persons not alien enemies who have declared their intention to become citizens, between the ages of twenty-one and thirty- years, both inclusive, and shall take place and be maintained under such regulations as the President may prescribe not inconsistent with the terms of this Act. Quotas for the several States, Territories, and the District of Columbia, or subdivisions thereof, shall be determined in proportion to the population thereof, and credit shall be given to any State, Territory, District, or subdivision thereof, for the number of men who were in the military service of the United States as members of the National Guard on April first, nineteen hundred and seventeen, or who have since said date entered the military service of the United States from any such State, Territory, District, or subdivision, either as members of the Regular Army or the National Guard. All persons drafted into the service of the United States and all officers accepting commissions in the forces herein provided for shall, from the date of said draft or acceptance, be subject to the laws and regulations governing the Regular Army, except as to promotions, so far as such laws and regulations are applicable to persons whose permanent retention in the military service on the active or retired list is not contemplated by existing law, and those drafted shall be required to serve for the period of the existing emergency unless sooner discharged: Provided , That the President is authorized to raise and maintain by voluntary enlistment or draft, as herein provided, special and technical troops as he may deem necessary, and to embody them into organizations and to officer them as provided in the third paragraph of section one and section nine of this Act. Organizations of the forces herein provided for, except the Regular Army and the divisions authorized in the seventh paragraph of section one, shall, as far as the interests of the service permit, be composed of men who come, and of officers who are appointed from, the same State or locality.

Sec. 3. No bounty shall be paid to induce any person to enlist in the military service of the United States; and no person liable to military service shall hereafter be permitted or allowed to furnish a substitute for such service; nor shall any substitute be received, enlisted, or enrolled in the military service of the United States; and no such person shall be permitted to escape such service or to be discharged therefrom prior to the expiration of his term of service by the payment of money or any other valuable thing whatsoever as consideration for his release from military service or liability thereto.

Sec. 4. That the Vice President of the United States, the officers, legislative, executive, and judicial, of the United States and of the several States, Territories, and the District of Columbia, regular or duly ordained ministers of religion, students who at the time of the approval of this Act are preparing for the ministry in recognized theological or divinity schools, and all persons in the military and naval service of the United States shall be exempt from the selective draft herein prescribed; and nothing in this Act contained shall be construed to require or compel any person to serve in any of the forces herein provided for who is found to be a member of any well-recognized religious sect or organization at present organized and existing and whose existing creed or principles forbid its members to participate in war in any form and whose religious convictions are against war or participation therein in accordance with the creed or principles of said religious organizations, but no person so exempted shall be exempted from service in any capacity that the President shall declare to be noncombatant; and the President is hereby authorized to exclude or discharge from said selective draft and from the draft under the second paragraph of section one hereof, or to draft for partial military service only from those liable to draft as in this Act provided, persons of the following classes: County and municipal officials; customhouse clerks; persons employed by the United States in the transmission of the mails; artificers and workmen employed in the armories, arsenals, and navy yards of the United States, and such other persons employed in the service of the United States as the President may designate; pilots; mariners actually employed in the sea service of any citizen or merchant within the United States; persons engaged in industries, including agriculture, found to be necessary to the maintenance of the Military Establishment or the effective operation of the military forces or the maintenance of national interest during the emergency; those in a status with respect to persons dependent upon them for support which renders their exclusion or discharge advisable; and those found to be physically or morally deficient. No exemption or exclusion shall continue when a cause therefor no longer exists: *Provided,* That notwithstanding the exemptions enumerated herein, each State, Territory, and the District of Columbia shall be required to supply its quota in the proportion that its population bears to the total population of the United States.

The President is hereby authorized, in his discretion, to create and establish throughout the several States and subdivisions thereof and in the Territories and the District of Columbia local boards, and where, in his discretion, practicable and desirable, there shall be created and established one such local board in each county or similar subdivision in each State, and one for approximately each thirty thousand of population in each city of thirty thousand population or over, according to the last census taken or estimates furnished by the Bureau of Census of the Department of Commerce. Such boards shall be appointed by the President, and shall consist of three or more members, none of whom shall be connected with the Military Establishment, to be chosen from among the local authorities of such subdivisions or from other citizens residing in the subdivision or area in which the respective boards will have jurisdiction under the rules and regulations prescribed by the President. Such boards shall have power within their respective jurisdictions to hear and determine, subject to review as hereinafter provided, all questions of exemption under this Act, and all questions of or claims for including or discharging individuals or classes of individuals from the selective draft, which shall be made under rules and regulations prescribed by the President, except any and every question or claim for including or excluding or discharging persons or classes of persons from the selective draft under the provisions of this Act authorizing the President to exclude or discharge from the selective draft "Persons engaged in industries, including agriculture, found to be necessary to the maintenance of the Military Establishment, or the effective operation of the military forces, or the maintenance of national interest during the emergency."

The President is hereby authorized to establish additional boards, one in each Federal judicial district of the United States, consisting of such number of citizens, not connected with the Military Establishment, as the President may determine, who shall be appointed by the President. The President is hereby authorized, in his discretion, to establish more than one such board in any Federal judicial district of the United States, or to establish one such board having jurisdiction of an area extending into more than one Federal judicial district.

Such district boards shall have review on appeal and affirm, modify, or reverse any decision of any local board having jurisdiction in the area in which any such district board has jurisdiction under the rules and regulations prescribed by the President. Such district boards shall have exclusive original jurisdiction within their respective areas to hear and determine all questions or claims for including or excluding or discharging persons or classes of persons from the selective draft, under the provisions of this Act, not included within the original jurisdiction of such local boards.

The decisions of such district boards shall be final except that, in accordance with such rules and regulations as the President may prescribe, he may affirm, modify or reverse any such decision.

Any vacancy in any such local board or district board shall be filled by the President, and any member of any such local board or district board may be removed and another appointed in his place by the President, whenever he considers that the interest of the nation demands it.

The President shall make rules and regulations governing the organization and procedure of such local boards and district boards, and providing for and governing appeals from such local boards to such district boards, and reviews of the decisions of any local board by the district board having jurisdiction, and determining and prescribing the several areas in which the respective local boards and district boards shall have jurisdiction, and all other rules and regulations necessary to carry out the terms and provisions of this section, and shall provide for the issuance of certificates of exemption, or partial or limited exemptions, and for a system to exclude and discharge individuals from selective draft.

Sec. 5. That all male persons between the ages of twenty-one and thirty, both inclusive, shall be subject to registration in accordance with regulations to be prescribed by the President; and upon proclamation by the President or other public notice given by him or by his direction stating the time and place of such registration it shall be the duty of all persons of the designated ages, except officers and enlisted men of the Regular Army, the Navy, and the National Guard and Naval Militia while in the service of the United States, to present themselves for and submit to registration under the provisions of this Act; and every such person shall be deemed to have notice of the requirements of this Act upon the publication of said proclamation or other notice as aforesaid given by the President or by his direction; and any person who shall willfully fail or refuse to present himself for registration or to submit thereto as herein provided, shall be guilty of a misdemeanor and shall, upon conviction in the district court of the United States having jurisdiction thereof, be punished by imprisonment for not more than one year, and shall thereupon be duly registered: *Provided,* That in the call of the docket precedence shall be given, in courts trying the same, to the trial of criminal proceedings under this Act: *Provided further,* That persons shall be subject to registration as herein provided who shall have attained their twenty-first birthday and who shall not have attained their thirty-first birthday on or before the day set for the registration, and all persons so registered shall be and remain subject to draft into the forces hereby authorized, unless exempted or excused therefrom as in this Act provided: *Provided further,* That in the case of temporary absence from actual place of legal residence of any person liable to registration as provided herein such registration may be made by mail under regulations to be prescribed by the President.

Sec. 6. That the President is hereby authorized to utilize the service of any or all departments and any or all officers or agents of the United States and of the several States, Territories, and the District of Columbia, and subdivisions thereof, in the execution of this Act, and all officers and agents of the United States and of the several States, Territories, and subdivisions thereof, and of the District of Columbia, and all persons designated or appointed under regulations prescribed by the President whether such appointments are made by the President himself or by the governor or other officer of any State or Territory to perform any duty in the execution of this Act, are hereby required to perform such duty as the President shall order or direct, and all such officers and agents and persons so designated or appointed shall hereby have full authority for all acts done by them in the execution of this Act by the direction of the President. Correspondence in the execution of this Act may be carried in penalty envelopes bearing the frank of the War Department. Any person charged as herein provided with the duty of carrying into effect any of the provisions of this Act or the regulations made or directions given thereunder who shall fail or neglect to perform such duty; and any person charged with such duty or having and exercising any authority under said Act, regulations, or directions, who shall knowingly make or be a party to the making of any false or incorrect registration, physical examination, exemption, enlistment, enrollment, or muster; and any person who shall make or be a party to the making of any false statement or certificate as to the fitness or liability of himself or any other person for service under the provisions of this Act, or regulations made by the President thereunder, or otherwise evades or aids another to evade the requirements of this Act or of said regulations, or who, in any manner, shall fail or neglect fully to perform any duty required of him in the execution of this Act, shall, if not subject to military law, be guilty of a misdemeanor, and upon conviction in the district court of the United States having jurisdiction thereof, be punished by imprisonment for not more than one year, or, if subject to military law, shall be tried by court-martial and suffer such punishment as a court-martial may direct.

Sec. 7. That the qualifications and conditions for voluntary enlistment as herein provided shall be the same as those prescribed by existing law for enlistments in the Regular Army, except that recruits must be between the ages of eighteen and forty years, both inclusive, at the time of their enlistment; and such enlistments shall be for the period of the emergency unless sooner discharged. All enlistments, including those in the Regular Army Reserve, which are in force on the date of the approval of this Act and which would terminate during the emergency shall continue in force during the emergency unless sooner discharged; but nothing herein contained shall be construed to shorten the period of any existing enlistment: *Provided,* That all persons enlisted or drafted under any of the provisions of this Act shall as far as practicable be grouped into units by States and the political subdivisions of the same: *Provided further,* That all persons who have enlisted since April first, nineteen hundred and seventeen, either in the Regular Army or in the National Guard, and all persons who have enlisted in the National Guard since June third, nineteen hundred and sixteen, upon their application, shall be discharged upon the termination of the existing emergency.

The President may provide for the discharge of any of all enlisted men whose status with respect to dependents renders such discharge advisable; and he may also authorize the employment on any active duty of retired enlisted men of the Regular Army, either with their rank on the retired list or in higher enlisted grades, and such retired enlisted men shall receive the full pay and allowances of the grades in which they are actively employed.

Sec. 8. That the President, by and with the advice and consent of the Senate is authorized to appoint for the period of the existing emergency such general officers of appropriate grades as may be necessary for duty with brigades, divisions, and higher units in which the forces provided for herein may be organized by the President, and general officers of appropriate grade for the several Coast Artillery districts. In so far as such appointments may be made from any of the forces herein provided for, the appointees may be selected irrespective of the grades held by them in such forces. Vacancies in all grades in Regular Army resulting from the appointment of officers thereof to higher grades in the forces other than the Regular Army herein provided for shall be filled by temporary promotions and appointments in the manner prescribed for filling temporary vacancies by section one hundred and fourteen of the national defense Act approved June third, nineteen hundred and sixteen; and officers appointed under the provisions of this Act to higher grades in the forces other than the Regular Army herein provided for shall not vacate their permanent commissions nor be prejudiced in their relative or lineal standing in the Regular Army.

Sec. 9. That the appointments authorized and made as provided by the second, third, fourth, fifth, sixth, and seventh paragraphs of section one and by section eight of this Act, and the temporary appointments in the Regular Army authorized by the first paragraph of section one of this Act, shall be for the period of the emergency, unless sooner terminated by discharge or otherwise. The President is hereby authorized to discharge any officer from the office held by him under such appointment for any cause which, in the judgment of the President, would promote the public service; and the general commanding any division and higher tactical organization or territorial department is authorized to appoint from time to time military boards of not less than three nor more than five officers of the forces herein provided for to examine into and report upon the capacity, qualification, conduct, and efficiency of any commissioned officer within his command other than officers of the Regular Army holding permanent or provisional commissions therein. Each member of such board shall be superior in rank to the officer whose qualifications are to be inquired into, and if the report of such board be adverse to the continuance of any such officer and be approved by the President, such officer shall be discharged from the service at the discretion of the President with one month's pay and allowances.

Sec. 10. That all officers and enlisted men of the forces herein provided for other than the Regular Army shall be in all respects on the same footing as to pay, allowances, and pensions as officers and enlisted men of corresponding grades and length of service in the Regular Army; and commencing June one, nineteen hundred and seventeen, and continuing until the termination of the emergency, all enlisted men of the Army of the United States in active service whose base pay does not exceed $21 per month shall receive an increase of $15 per month; those whose base pay is $24, an increase of $12 per month; those whose base pay is $30, $36, or $40, an increase of $8 per month; and those whose base pay is $45 or more, an increase of $6 per month: *Provided,* That the increases of pay herein authorized shall not enter into the computation of continuous-service pay.

Sec. 11. That all existing restrictions upon the detail, detachment, and employment of officers and enlisted men of the Regular Army are hereby suspended for the period of the present emergency.

Sec. 12. That the President of the United States, as Commander in Chief of the Army, is authorized to make such regulations governing the prohibition of alcoholic liquors in or near military camps and to the officers and enlisted men of the Army as he may from time to time deem necessary or advisable: *Provided,* That no person, corporation, partnership, or association shall sell, supply, or have in his or its possession any intoxicating or spirituous liquors at any military station, cantonment, camp, fort, post, officers' or enlisted men's club, which is being used at the time for military purposes under this Act, but the Secretary of War may make regulations permitting the

sale and use of intoxicating liquors for medicinal purposes. It shall be unlawful to sell any intoxicating liquor, including beer, ale, or wine, to any officer or member of the military forces while in uniform, except herein provided. Any person, corporation, partnership, or association violating the provisions of this section of the regulations made thereunder shall, unless otherwise punishable under the Articles of War, be deemed guilty of a misdemeanor and be punished by a fine of not more than $1,000 or imprisonment for not more than twelve months, or both.

Sec. 13. That the Secretary of War is hereby authorized, empowered, and directed during the present war to do everything by him deemed necessary to suppress and prevent the keeping or setting up of houses of ill fame, brothels, or bawdy houses within such distance as he may deem needful of any military camp, station, fort, post, cantonment, training, or mobilization place, and any person, corporation, partnership, or association receiving or permitting to be received for immoral purposes any person into any place, structure, or building used for the purpose of lewdness, assignation, or prostitution within such distance of said places as may be designated, or shall permit any such person to remain for immoral purposes in any such place, structure, or building as aforesaid, or who shall violate any order, rule, or regulation issued to carry out the object and purpose of this section shall, unless otherwise punishable under the Articles of War, be deemed guilty of a misdemeanor and be punished by a fine of not more than $1,000, or imprisonment for not more than twelve months, or both.

Sec. 14. That all laws and parts of laws in conflict with the provisions of this Act are hereby suspended during the period of this emergency.

Approved, May 18, 1917.

Sedition Act of 1918

Commentary

In May 1918, Attorney General Thomas W. Gregory (1861–1933) won increased authority to crack down on critics of the Wilson administration through amendments to the Espionage Act of June 15, 1917. The Espionage Act allowed imprisonment for up to twenty years and/or a fine of up to $10,000 for individuals found guilty of aiding the enemy, obstructing military recruitment, or causing insubordination, disloyalty, or a refusal to serve in the armed forces. Arguing that the language of that act was too narrow, Gregory insisted on more sweeping language in the 1918 amendments, which became known as the Sedition Act.

The Sedition Act included vague and general language that went beyond prosecution of those hampering national security. Provisions of the act made it a crime to "utter, print, write, or publish any disloyal, profane, scurrilous or abusive language" about the form of government of the United States, the U.S. Constitution, the armed forces, the flag, or military uniforms. It also made it illegal for anyone "by word or act [to] support or favor the cause of any country with which the United States is at war or by word or act to oppose the cause of the United States." Under the Espionage and Sedition acts, more than 1,500 citizens were prosecuted and more than 100 were convicted. In several cases decided after the war, the U.S. Supreme Court ruled that both acts were constitutional.

Sedition Act of May 16, 1918

Be it enacted by the Senate and House of Representatives of the United States of America in Congress assembled, That section three of title one of the Act entitled, "An Act to punish acts of interference with the foreign relations, the neutrality, and the foreign commerce of the United States, to punish espionage, and better to enforce the criminal laws of the United States, and for other purposes," approved June fifteenth, nineteen hundred and seventeen, be, and the same is hereby, amended so as to read as follows:

"Sec. 3. Whoever, when the United States is at war, shall willfully make or convey false reports or false statements with intent to interfere with the operation or success of the military or naval forces of the United States, or to promote the success of its enemies, or shall willfully make or convey false reports or false statements, or say or do anything except by way of bona fide and not disloyal advice to an investor or investors, with intent to obstruct the sale by the United States of bonds or other securities of the United States or the making of loans by or to the United States, and whoever, when the United States is at war, shall willfully cause or attempt to cause, or incite or attempt to incite, insubordination, disloyalty, mutiny, or refusal of duty, in the military or naval forces of the United States, or shall willfully obstruct or attempt to obstruct the recruiting or enlistment service of the United States, and whoever, when the United States is at war, shall willfully utter, print, write, or publish any disloyal, profane, scurrilous, or abusive language about the form of government of the United States, or the Constitution of the United States, or the military or naval forces of the United States, or the flag of the United States, or the uniform of the Army or Navy of the United States, or any language intended to bring the form of government of the United States, or the Constitution of the United States, or the military or naval forces of the United States, or the flag of the United States, or the uniform of the Army or Navy of the United States into contempt, scorn, contumely, or disrepute, or shall willfully utter, print, write, or publish any language intended to incite, provoke, or encourage resistance to the United States, or to promote the cause of its enemies, or shall willfully display the flag of any foreign enemy, or shall willfully by utterance, writing, printing, publication, or language spoken, urge, incite, or advocate any curtailment of production in this country of any thing or things, product or products, necessary or essential to the prosecution of the war in which the United States may be engaged, with intent by such curtailment to cripple or hinder the United States in the prosecution of the war, and whoever shall willfully advocate, teach, defend, or suggest the doing of any of the acts or things in this section enumerated, and whoever shall by word or act support or favor the cause of any country with which the United States is at war or by word or act oppose the cause of the United States therein, shall be punished by a fine of not more than $10,000 or imprisonment for not more than twenty years, or both. . . .

Title XII of the said Act of June fifteenth, nineteen hundred and seventeen, be, and the same is hereby, amended by adding thereto the following section:

"Sec. 4. When the United States is at war, the Postmaster General may, upon evidence satisfactory to him that any person or concern is using the mails in violation of any of the provisions of this Act, instruct the postmaster at any post office at which mail is received addressed to such person or concern to return to the postmaster at the office at which they were originally mailed all letters or other matter so addressed, with the words 'Mail to this address undeliverable under Espionage Act' plainly written or stamped upon the outside thereof, and all such letters or other matter so returned to such postmasters shall be by them returned to the senders thereof under such regulations as the Postmaster General may prescribe."

Approved, May 16, 1918.

Neutrality Act (1935)

Commentary

The Joint Resolution passed on August 31, 1935, offers an example of one of the Neutrality Acts that Congress passed during the 1930s in an attempt to keep the United States out of the growing conflict in Europe. A committee headed by Senator Gerald P. Nye (1892–1971) convinced a majority of the American public and many congressional leaders that the way to avoid U.S. involvement in a future war demanded passing a series of laws designed to prevent the very issues that had led the United States into World War I. The Neutrality Act, included here, banned arms exports to belligerent states. It responded directly to the criticism that the Nye Committee aimed at munitions makers.

49 stat. 1081; 22 U.S.C. 441 note

Providing for the prohibition of the export of arms, ammunition, and implements of war to belligerent countries; the prohibition of the transportation of arms, ammunition, and implements of war by vessels of the United

States for the use of belligerent states; for the registration and licensing of persons engaged in the business of manufacturing, exporting, or importing arms, ammunition, or implements of war; and restricting travel by American citizens on belligerent ships during war.

Resolved by the Senate and House of Representatives of the United States of America in Congress assembled, That upon the outbreak or during the progress of war between, or among, two or more foreign states, the President shall proclaim such fact, and it shall thereafter be unlawful to export arms, ammunition, or implements of war from any place in the United States, or possessions of the United States, to any port of such belligerent states, or to any neutral port for transshipment to, or for the use of, a belligerent country.

The President, by proclamation, shall definitely enumerate the arms, ammunition, or implements of war, the export of which is prohibited by this Act.

The President may, from time to time, by proclamation, extend such embargo upon the export of arms, ammunition, or implements of war to other states as and when they may become involved in such war.

Whoever, in violation of any of the provisions of this section, shall export, or attempt to export, or cause to be exported, arms, ammunition, or implements of war from the United States, or any of its possessions, shall be fined not more than $10,000 or imprisoned not more than five years, or both, and the property, vessel, or vehicle containing the same shall be subject to the provisions of sections 1 to 8, inclusive, title 6, chapter 30, of the Act approved June 15, 1917 (40 Stat. 223–225; U. S. C., title 22, secs. 238–245).

In the case of the forfeiture of any arms, ammunition, or implements of war by reason of a violation of this Act, no public or private sale shall be required; but such arms, ammunition, or implements of war shall be delivered to the Secretary of War for such use or disposal thereof as shall be approved by the President.

When in the judgment of the President the conditions which have caused him to issue his proclamation have ceased to exist he shall revoke the same and the provisions hereof shall thereupon cease to apply.

Except with respect to prosecutions committed or forfeitures incurred prior to March 1, 1936, this section and all proclamations issued thereunder shall not be effective after February 29, 1936.

Sec. 2. That for the purpose of this Act—

(a) The term "Board" means the National Munitions Control Board which is hereby established to carry out the provisions of this Act. The Board shall consist of the Secretary of State, who shall be chairman and executive officer of the Board; the Secretary of the Treasury; the Secretary of War; the Secretary of the Navy; and the Secretary of Commerce. Except as otherwise provided in this Act, or by other law, the administration of this Act is vested in the Department of State;

(b) The term "United States" when used in a geographical sense, includes the several States and Territories, the insular possessions of the United States (including the Philippine Islands), the Canal Zone, and the District of Columbia;

(c) The term "person" includes a partnership, company, association, or corporation, as well as a natural person.

Within ninety days after the effective date of this Act, or upon first engaging in business, every person who engages in the business of manufacturing, exporting, or importing any of the arms, ammunition, and implements of war referred to in this Act, whether as an exporter, importer, manufacturer, or dealer, shall register with the Secretary of State his name, or business name, principal place of business, and places of business in the United States, and a list of the arms, ammunition, and implements of war which he manufactures, imports, or exports.

Every person required to register under this section shall notify the Secretary of State of any change in the arms, ammunition, and implements of war which he exports, imports, or manufactures; and upon such notification the Secretary of State shall issue to such person an amended certificate of registration, free of charge, which shall remain valid until the date of expiration of the original certificate. Every person required to register under the provisions of this section shall pay a registration fee of $500, and upon receipt of such fee the Secretary of State shall issue a registration certificate valid for five years, which shall be renewable for further periods of five years upon the payment of each renewal of a fee of $500.

It shall be unlawful for any person to export, or attempt to export, from the United States any of the arms, ammunition, or implements of war referred to in this Act to any other country or to import, or attempt to import, to the United States from any other country any of the arms, ammunition, or implements of war referred to in this Act without first having obtained a license therefor.

All persons required to register under this section shall maintain, subject to the inspection of the Board, such permanent records of manufacture for export, importation, and exportation of arms, ammunition, and implements of war as the Board shall prescribe.

Licenses shall be issued to persons who have registered as provided for, except in cases of export or import licenses where exportation of arms, ammunition, or implements of war would be in violation of this Act or any other law of the United States, or of a treaty to which the United States is a party, in which cases such licenses shall not be issued.

The Board shall be called by the Chairman and shall hold at least one meeting a year.

No purchase of arms, ammunition, and implements of war shall be made on behalf of the United States by any officer, executive department, or independent establishment of the Government from any person who shall have failed to register under the provisions of this Act.

The Board shall make an annual report to Congress, copies of which shall be distributed as are other reports transmitted to Congress. Such report shall contain such information and data collected by the Board as may be considered of value in the determination of questions connected with the control of trade in arms, ammunition, and implements of war. It shall include a list of all persons required to register under the provisions of this Act, and full information concerning the licenses issued hereunder.

The Secretary of State shall promulgate such rules and regulations with regard to the enforcement of this section as he may deem necessary to carry out its provisions.

The President is hereby authorized to proclaim upon recommendation of the Board from time to time a list of articles which shall be considered arms, ammunition, and implements of war for the purposes of this section.

This section shall take effect on the ninetieth day after the date of its enactment.

Sec. 3. Whenever the President shall issue the proclamation provided for in section 1 of this Act, thereafter it shall be unlawful for any American vessel to carry any arms, ammunition, or implements of war to any port of the belligerent countries named in such proclamation as being at war, or to any neutral port for transshipment to, or for the use of, a belligerent country.

Whoever, in violation of the provisions of this section, shall take, attempt to take, or shall authorize, hire, or solicit another to take any such vessel carrying such cargo out of port or from the jurisdiction of the United States shall be fined not more than $10,000 or imprisoned not more than five years, or both; and, in addition, such vessel, her tackle, apparel, furniture, equipment, and the arms, ammunition, and implements of war on board shall be forfeited to the United States.

When the President finds the conditions which have caused him to issue his proclamation have ceased to exist, he shall revoke his proclamation, and the provisions of this section shall thereupon cease to apply.

Sec. 4. Whenever, during any war in which the United States is neutral, the President, or any person hereunto authorized by him, shall have cause to believe that any vessel, domestic or foreign, whether requiring clearance or not, is about to carry out of a port of the United States, or its possession, men or fuel, arms, ammunition, implements of war, or other supplies to any warship, tender, or supply ship of a foreign belligerent nation, but the evidence is not deemed sufficient to justify forbidding the departure of the vessel as provided for by section 1, title V, chapter 30, of the Act approved June 15, 1917 (40 Stat. [221[22]]; U. S. C. title 18, sec. 31), and if, in the President's judgment, such action will serve to maintain peace between the United States and foreign nations, or to protect the commercial interests of the United States and its citizens, or to promote the security of the United States, he shall have the power and it shall be his duty to require the owner, master, or person in command thereof, before departing from a port of the United States, or any of its possessions, for a foreign port, to give a bond to the United States, with sufficient sureties, in such amount as he shall deem proper, conditioned that the vessel will not deliver the men, or the cargo, or any part thereof, to any warship, tender, or supply ship of a belligerent nation; and, if the President, or any person thereunto authorized by him, shall find that a vessel, domestic or foreign, in a port of the United States, or one of its possessions, has previously cleared from such port during such war and delivered its cargo or any part thereof to a warship, tender, or supply ship of a belligerent nation, he may prohibit the departure of such vessel during the duration of the war.

Sec. 5. Whenever, during any war in which the United States is neutral, the President shall find that special restrictions placed on the use of the ports and territorial waters of the United States, or of its possessions, by the submarines of a foreign nation will serve to maintain peace between the United States and foreign nations, or to protect the commercial interests of the United States and its citizens, or to promote the security of the United States, and shall make proclamation thereof, it shall thereafter be unlawful for any such submarine to enter a port or the territorial waters of the United States or any of its possessions, or to depart therefrom, except under such conditions and subject to such limitations as the President may prescribe. When, in his judgment, the conditions which have caused him to issue his proclamation have ceased to exist, he shall revoke his proclamation and the provisions of this section shall thereupon cease to apply.

Sec. 6. Whenever, during any war in which the United States is neutral, the President shall find that the maintenance of peace between the United States and foreign nations, or the protection of the lives of citizens of the United States, or the protection of the commercial interests of the United States and its citizens, or the security of the United States requires that the American citizens should refrain from traveling as passengers on the vessels of any belligerent nation, he shall so proclaim, and thereafter no citizen of the United States shall travel on any vessel of any belligerent nation except at his own risk, unless in accordance with such rules and regulations as the President shall prescribe: Provided, however, That the provisions of this section shall not apply to a citizen travelling on the vessel of a belligerent whose voyage was begun in advance of the date of the President's proclamation, and who had no opportunity to discontinue his voyage after that date: And provided further, That they shall not apply under ninety days after the date of the President's proclamation to a citizen returning from a foreign country to the United States or to any of its possessions.

When, in the President's judgment, the conditions which have cause him to issue his proclamation have ceased to exist, he shall revoke his proclamation and the provisions of this section shall thereupon cease to apply.

Sec. 7. In every case of the violation of any of the provisions of this Act where a specific penalty is not herein provided, such violator or violators, upon conviction, shall be fined not more than $10,000 or imprisoned not more than five years, or both.

Sec. 8. If any of the provisions of this Act, or the application thereof to any person or circumstance, is held invalid, the remainder of the Act, and the application of such provision to other persons or circumstances, shall not be affected thereby.

Sec. 9. The sum of $25,000 is hereby authorized to be appropriated, out of any money in the Treasury not otherwise appropriated, to be expended by the Secretary of State in administering this Act.

Approved, August 31, 1935.

Executive Order 8802 (1941)

Commentary

On June 28, 1941, President Franklin Delano Roosevelt (1882–1945) issued Executive Order 8802, desegregating the nation's defense industries and establishing the Fair Employment Practices Commission. The order was issued in response to the call by the labor leader A. Philip Randolph for a march on Washington to protest discrimination in defense work.

Whereas it is the policy of the United States to encourage full participation in the national defense program by all citizens of the United States, regardless of race, creed, color, or national origin, in the firm belief that the democratic way of life within the Nation can be defended successfully only with the help and support of all groups within its borders; and

Whereas there is evidence that available and needed workers have been barred from employment in industries engaged in defense production solely because of considerations of race, creed, color, or national origin, to the detriment of workers' morale and of national unity:

Now, Therefore, by virtue of the authority vested in me by the Constitution and the statutes, and as a prerequisite to the successful conduct of our national defense production effort, I do hereby reaffirm the policy of the United States that there shall be no discrimination in the employment of workers in defense industries or government because of race, creed, color, or national origin, and I do hereby declare that it is the duty of employers and of labor organizations, in furtherance of said policy and of this order, to provide for the full and equitable participation of all workers in defense industries, without discrimination because of race, creed, color, or national origin;

And it is hereby ordered as follows:

1. All departments and agencies of the Government of the United States concerned with vocational and training programs for defense production shall take special measures appropriate to assure that such programs are administered without discrimination because of race, creed, color, or national origin;

2. All contracting agencies of the Government of the United States shall include in all defense contracts hereafter negotiated by them a provision obligating the contractor not to discriminate against any worker because of race, creed, color, or national origin;

3. There is established in the Office of Production Management a Committee on Fair Employment Practice, which shall consist of a chairman and four other members to be appointed by the President. The Chairman and members of the Committee shall serve as such without compensation, but shall be entitled to actual and necessary transportation, subsistence, and other expenses incidental to performance of their duties. The Committee shall receive and investigate complaints of discrimination in violation of the provisions of this order and shall take appropriate steps to redress grievances which it finds to be valid. The Committee shall also recommend to the several departments and agencies of the Government of the United States and to the President all measures which may be deemed by it necessary or proper to effectuate the provisions of this order.

White House, June 25, 1941

Lend–Lease Act (1941)

Commentary

Following the Destroyers for Bases Agreement in September 1940, U.S. President Franklin Delano Roosevelt worked quickly to dismantle the Neutrality Acts and provide increased aid to nations fighting the Nazis and Japanese. Three months after the president's arsenal of democracy radio address, Congress passed the Lend Lease Act on March 11, 1941. A careful look at its stipulations indicated that Roosevelt had convinced Congress and the American people to grant the administration its all-aid-short-of-war requirements. The public still hoped that Roosevelt's policies would prevent the United States from direct military involvement in World War II, but that would not be the case.

AN ACT

Further to promote the defense of the United States, and for other purposes.

Be it enacted by the Senate add House of Representatives of the United States of America in Congress assembled, That this Act may be cited as "An Act to Promote the Defense of the United States".

Sec. 2. As used in this Act—

(a) The term "defense article" means—

(1) Any weapon, munition, aircraft, vessel, or boat;

(2) Any machinery, facility, tool, material, or supply necessary for the manufacture, production, processing, repair, servicing, or operation of any article described in this subsection;

(3) Any component material or part of or equipment for any article described in this subsection;

(4) Any agricultural, industrial or other commodity or article for defense.

Such term "defense article" includes any article described in this subsection: Manufactured or procured pursuant to section 3, or to which the United States or any foreign government has or hereafter acquires title, possession, or control.

(b) The term "defense information" means any plan, specification, design, prototype, or information pertaining to any defense article.

Sec. 3. (a) Notwithstanding the provisions of any other law, the President may, from time to time. when he deems it in the interest of national defense, authorize the Secretary Of War, the Secretary of the Navy, or the bead of any other department or agency of the Government—

(1) To manufacture in arsenals, factories, and shipyards under their jurisdiction, or otherwise procure, to the extent to which funds are made available therefor, or contracts are authorized from time to time by the Congress, or both, any defense article for the government of

any country whose defense the President deems vital to the defense of the United States.

(2) To sell, transfer title to, exchange, lease, lend, or otherwise dispose of, to any such government any defense article, but no defense article not manufactured or procured under paragraph (1) shall in any way be disposed of under this paragraph, except after consultation with the Chief of Staff of the Army or the Chief of Naval Operations of the Navy, or both. The value of defense articles disposed of in any way under authority of this paragraph, and procured from funds heretofore appropriated, shall not exceed $1,300,000,000. The value of such defense articles shall be determined by the head of the department or agency concerned or such other department, agency or officer as shall be designated in the manner provided in the rules and regulations issued hereunder. Defense articles procured from funds hereafter appropriated to any department or agency of the Government, other than from funds authorized to he appropriated under this Act. shall not be disposed of in any way under authority of this paragraph except to the extent hereafter authorized by the Congress in the Acts appropriating such funds or otherwise.

(3) To test, inspect, prove, repair, outfit, recondition, or otherwise to place in good working order, to the extent to which funds are made available therefor, or contracts are authorized from time to time by the Congress, or both, any defense article for any such government, or to procure any or all such services by private contract.

(4) To communicate to any such government any defense information pertaining to any defense article furnished to such government under paragraph (2) of this subsection.

(5) To release for export any defense article disposed of in any way under this subsection to any such government.

(b) The terms and conditions upon which any such foreign government receives any aid authorized under subsection (a) shall be those which the President deems satisfactory, and the benefit to the United States may he payment or repayment in kind or property, or any other direct or indirect benefit which the President deems satisfactory.

(c) After June 30, 1943, or after the passage of a concurrent resolution by the two Houses before June 30, 1943, which declares that the powers conferred by or pursuant to subsection (a) are no longer necessary to promote the defense of the United States, neither the President nor the head of any department or agency shall exercise any of the powers conferred by or pursuant to subsection (a) except that until July 1, 1946, any of such powers may be exercised to the extent necessary to carry out a contract or agreement with such a foreign government made before July 1,1943, or before the passage of such concurrent resolution, whichever is the earlier.

(d) Nothing in this Act shall be construed to authorize or to permit the authorization of convoying vessels by naval vessels of the United States.

(e) Nothing in this Act shall be construed to authorize or to permit the authorization of the entry of any American vessel into a combat area in violation of section 3 of the neutrality Act of 1939.

Sec. 4. All contracts or agreements made for the disposition of any defense article or defense information pursuant to section 3 shall contain a clause by which the foreign government undertakes that it will not, without the consent of the President, transfer title to or possession of such defense article or defense information by gift, sale, or otherwise, or permit its use by anyone not an officer, employee, or agent of such foreign government.

Sec. 5. (a) The Secretary of War, the Secretary of the Navy, or the head of any other department or agency of the Government involved shall when any such defense article or defense information is exported, immediately inform the department or agency designated by the President to administer section 6 of the Act of July 2, 1940 (54 Stat. 714). of the quantities, character, value, terms of disposition and destination of the article and information so exported.

(b) The President from time to time, but not less frequently than once every ninety days, shall transmit to the Congress a report of operations under this Act except such information as he deems incompatible with the public interest to disclose. Reports provided for under this subsection shall be transmitted to the Secretary of the Senate or the Clerk of the House of representatives, as the case may be, if the Senate or the House of Representatives, as the case may be, is not in session.

Sec. 6. (a) There is hereby authorized to be appropriated from time to time, out of any money in the Treasury not otherwise appropriated, such amounts as may be necessary to carry out the provisions and accomplish the purposes of this Act.

(b) All money and all property which is converted into money received under section 3 from any government shall, with the approval of the Director of the Budget. revert to the respective appropriation or appropriations out of which funds were expended with respect to the defense article or defense information for which such consideration is received, and shall be available for expenditure for the purpose for which such expended funds were appropriated by law, during the fiscal year in which such funds are received and the ensuing fiscal year; but in no event

shall any funds so received be available for expenditure after June 30, 1946.

Sec. 7. The Secretary of War, the Secretary of the Navy, and the head of the department or agency shall in all contracts or agreements for the disposition of any defense article or defense information fully protect the rights of all citizens of the United States who have patent rights in and to any such article or information which is hereby authorized to he disposed of and the payments collected for royalties on such patents shall be paid to the owners and holders of such patents.

Sec. 8. The Secretaries of War and of the Navy are hereby authorized to purchase or otherwise acquire arms, ammunition, and implements of war produced within the jurisdiction of any country to which section 3 is applicable, whenever the President deems such purchase or acquisition to be necessary in the interests of the defense of the United States.

Sec. 9. The President may, from time to time, promulgate such rules and regulations as may be necessary and proper to carry out any of the provisions of this Act; and he may exercise any power or authority conferred on him by this Act through such department, agency, or officer as be shall direct.

Sec. 10. Nothing in this Act shall be construed to change existing law relating to the use of the land and naval forces of the United States, except insofar as such use relates to the manufacture, procurement, and repair of defense articles, the communication of information and other noncombatant purposes enumerated in this Act.

Sec. 11. If any provision of this Act or the application of such provision to any circumstance shall be held invalid, the validity of the remainder of the Act and the applicability of such provision to other circumstances shall not be affected thereby.

Approved, March 11, 1941.

Bracero Agreement (1942)

Commentary

The manpower needs of the United States during World War II created continuous shortages. The mobilization of more than 12 million men and women forced a rethinking of labor resources. Nowhere were the consequences more extensive than in agriculture. Not only Americans but vast numbers of American allies were dependent on American farm production. In the highly productive regions of the Southwest and California, a significant dependence on *braceros*, seasonal contract workers, already existed. These Mexican farm workers harvested almost half of all vegetables, fruits, nuts, and other consumer crops. Furthermore, they picked much of the cotton crop of Texas, Arizona, and California. Their status was a question that commanded the highest levels of diplomatic interest between the United States and Mexico. The existing patterns of discrimination familiar to Mexicans made it imperative that the Mexican government be included in both defining and enforcing new regulations to govern increased numbers of braceros working in the United States during World War II. A unique feature was the knowledge that the braceros remained Mexicans and most likely would return to Mexico.

Agreement between the United States of America and Mexico respecting the temporary migration of Mexican agricultural workers. Effected by exchange of notes signed August 4, 1942.

The Mexican Minister of Foreign Affairs to the American Ambassado

DEPARTMENT OF FOREIGN RELATIONS UNITED MEXICAN STATES MEXICO CITY

No. 312 Mexico, D.F., *August 4, 1942.*
Mr. Ambassador:

I have the honor to refer to the matter presented by the Embassy worthily in Your Excellency's charge regarding the possibility that the Government of Mexico authorize the departure of Mexican workers for the United States and the conditions under which such emigration can be affected.

This Department considers itself under the obligation, first of all, of pointing out the importance for the country at the present moment of conserving intact its human material, indispensable for the development of the program of continental defense to which the Government of Mexico is jointly obligated and in which, by very urgent recommendation of the Head of the Executive Power, the intensification of activities and especially agricultural production take first rank. Nevertheless, the need for workers which exists on some parts of the United States having been laid before the President of the Republic himself, and the First Magistrate, being desirous of not scanting the cooperation which he has been offering to the Government worthily represented by Your Excellency in the measure that the Nation's resources permit, has been pleased to decide that no obstacles be placed in the way of the departure of such nationals as desire to emigrate, temporarily, for the performance of the tasks in which their services may be required and that no other essential conditions be fixed than those which are required by circumstances and those established by legal provisions in force in the two countries.

For the purpose of determining the scope of this matter it was agreed, as Your Excellency is aware, to treat it as a matter between States, and in order to examine it in all its aspects, it was deemed necessary to hold a meeting of Mexican and American experts, who have just completed their task, having already submitted the recommendations which they formulated and which, duly signed, are sent enclosed with this communication.

The conclusions in reference have been examined with all care, and the Government of Mexico gives them its full approval. I beg Your Excellency to be good enough to take steps that the Government of the United States of America may, if it sees fit, do likewise, in order that this matter may be concluded and that the proper instructions may be issued, consequently, to the various official agencies which are to intervene therein, and in this way the arrangement which has been happily arrived at may be immediately effective.

I avail myself of the opportunity to renew to Your Excellency the assurances of my highest and most distinguished consideration.

E. Padilla

His Excellency George S. Messersmith,
*Ambassador Extraordinary and Plenipotentiary
of the United States of America, City*

*The American Ambassador to the Mexican Minister
of Foreign Affairs*

Embassy of the United States of America Mexico,
August 4, 1942
No. 503
Excellency:

I have the honor to acknowledge the receipt of Your Excellency's Note No. 312 of August 4, 1942, regarding the temporary migration of Mexican workers to the United States to engage in agricultural work, the subject matter of which was presented by the Embassy some days ago.

Due note has been taken of the considerations expressed in Your Excellency's Note under acknowledgment with respect to the maintenance of indispensable labor within the Republic of Mexico for the development of the Continental Defense Program, especially agricultural production, to which the Government of Mexico is committed. My Government is fully conscious of these commitments and at the same time is deeply appreciative of the attitude of His Excellency President Manuel Avila Camacho for the sincere and helpful manner in which he has extended the cooperation of the Government of Mexico within the resources of the nation of permit Mexican nationals temporarily to emigrate to the United States for the purpose of aiding in our own agricultural production.

In order to determine the scope of the conditions under which Mexican labor might proceed to the United States for the purpose set forth above, it was agreed that the negotiations should be between our two Governments, and Your Excellency was kind enough to arrange for the meeting of Mexican and American representatives to submit recommendations which they have duly completed. Your Excellency was good enough to enclose a copy of these recommendations in the Spanish with your Note under reference.

My Government accepts these recommendations as a satisfactory arrangement, and I am authorized to inform Your Excellency that my Government will place this arrangement in effect immediately, and in confirmation thereof I attach hereto the English of the arrangement as agreed upon.

Accept, Excellency, the renewed assurances of my highest and most distinguished consideration.

George S. Messersmith

Enclosure.

His Excellency
Senor Lic. Ezequiel Padilla *Minister for Foreign Affairs, Mexico.*

[Enclosure]

In order to effect a satisfactory arrangement whereby Mexican agricultural labor may be made available for use in the United States and at the same time provide means whereby this labor will be adequately protected while out of Mexico, the following general provisions are suggested:

1) It is understood that Mexicans contracting to work in the United States shall not be engaged in any military service.

2) Mexicans entering the United States as a result of this understanding shall not suffer discriminatory acts of any kind in accordance with the Executive Order No. 8802 issued at the White House June 25, 1941.

3) Mexicans entering the United States under this understanding shall enjoy the guarantees of transportation, living expenses and repatriation established in Article 29 of the Mexican Labor Law.

4) Mexicans entering the United States under this understanding shall not be employed to displace other workers, or for the purpose of reducing rates of pay previously established.

In order to implement the application of the general principles mentioned above the following specific clauses are established.

(When the word "employer" is used hereinafter it shall be understood to mean the Farm Security Administration of the Department of Agriculture of the United States of America; the word "sub-employer" shall mean the owner or operator of the farm or farms in the United States on which the Mexican will be employed; the word "worker" hereinafter used shall refer to the Mexican farm laborer entering the United States under this understanding.)

CONTRACTS

a. Contracts will be made between the employer and the worker under the supervision of the Mexican Government. (Contracts must be written in Spanish.)

b. The employer shall enter into a contract with the sub-employer, with a view to proper observance of the principles embodied in this understanding.

ADMISSION

a. The Mexican health authorities will, at the place whence the worker comes, see that he meets the necessary physical conditions.

TRANSPORATION

a. All transportation and living expenses from the place of origin to destination, and return, as well as expenses incurred in the fulfillment of any requirements of a migratory nature shall be met by the employer.

b. Personal belongings of the workers up to a maximum of 35 kilos per person shall be transported at the expense of the employer.

c. In accord with the intent of Article 29 of the Mexican Federal Labor Law, it is expected that the employer will collect all or part of the cost accruing under (a) and (b) of transportation from the sub-employer.

WAGES AND EMPLOYMENT

a. (1) Wages to be paid the worker shall be the same as those paid for similar work to other agricultural laborers in the respective regions of destination; but in no case shall this wage be less than 30 cents per hour (U.S. currency); piece rates shall be so set as to enable the worker of average ability to earn the prevailing wage.

a. (2) On the basis of prior authorization from the Mexican Government salaries lower than those established in the previous clause may be paid those emigrants admitted into the United States as members of the family of the worker under contract and who, when they are in the field, are able also to become agricultural laborers but who, by their condition of age or sex cannot carry out the average amount of ordinary work.

b. The worker shall be exclusively employed as an agricultural laborer for which he has been engaged; any change from such type of employment shall be made with the express approval of the worker and with the authority of the Mexican Government.

c. There shall be considered illegal any collection by reason of commission or for any other concept demanded of the worker.

d. Work for minors under 14 years shall be strictly prohibited, and they shall have the same schooling opportunities as those enjoyed by children of other agricultural laborers.

e. Workers domiciled in the migratory labor camps or at any other place of employment under this understanding shall be free to obtain articles for their personal consumption, or that of their families, wherever it is most convenient for them.

f. Housing conditions, sanitary and medical services enjoyed by workers admitted under this understanding shall be identical to those enjoyed by the other agricultural workers in the same localities.

g. Workers admitted under this understanding shall enjoy as regards occupational diseases and accidents the same guarantees enjoyed by other agricultural workers under United States legislation.

h. Groups of workers admitted under this understanding shall elect their own representatives to deal with the employer, but it is understood that all such representatives shall be working members of the group. The Mexican consuls in their respective jurisdiction shall make every effort to extend all possible protection to all these workers on any questions affecting them.

i. For such time as they are unemployed under a period equal to 75% of the period (exclusive of Sundays) for which the workers have been contracted they shall receive a subsistence allowance at the rate of $3.00 per day.

For the remaining 25% of the period for which the workers have been contracted during which the workers may be unemployed they shall receive subsistence on the same bases that are established for farm laborers in the United States.

Should the cost of living rise this will be a matter for reconsideration.

The master contracts for workers submitted to the Mexican Government shall contain definite provisions for computation of subsistence and payments under this understanding.

j. The term of the contract shall be made in accordance with the authorities of the respective countries.

k. At the expiration of the contract under this understanding, and if the same is not renewed, the authorities of the United States shall consider illegal, from an immigration point of view, the continued stay of the worker in the territory of the United States, exception made of cases of physical impossibility.

SAVINGS FUND

a) The respective agency of the Government of the United States shall be responsible for the safekeeping of the sums contributed by the Mexican workers toward the formation of their Rural Savings Fund, until such sums are transferred to the Mexican Agricultural Credit Bank which shall assume responsibilities for the deposit, for their safekeeping and for their application, or, in the absence of these, for their return.

b) The Mexican Government through the Banco de Credito Agricola will take care of the security of the savings of the workers to be used for payment of the agricultural implements, which may be made available to the Banco de Credito Agricola in accordance with exportation permits for shipment to Mexico with the understanding that the Farm Security Administration will recommend priority treatment for such implements.

NUMBERS

As it is impossible to determine at this time the number of workers who may be needed in the United States for agricultural labor employment, the employer shall advise the Mexican Government from time to time as to the number needed. The Government of Mexico shall determine in each case the number of workers who may leave the country without detriment to its national economy.

GENERAL PROVISIONS

It is understood that, with reference to the departure from Mexico of Mexican workers, who are not farm laborers, there shall govern in understandings reached by agencies of the respective Governments the same fundamental principles which have been applied here to the departure of farm labor.

It is understood that the employers will co-operate with such other agencies of the Government of the United States in carrying this understanding into effect whose authority under the laws of the United States are such as to contribute to the effectuation of the understanding.

Either government shall have the right to renounce this understanding, giving appropriate notification to the other Government 90 days in advance.

This understanding may be formalized by an exchange of notes between the Ministry of Foreign Affairs of the Republic of Mexico and the Embassy of the United States of America in Mexico.

Mexico City, the 23rd of July 1942.

MEXICAN COMMISSIONERS

E. Hidalgo
acting as representative of the Foreign Office.

Abraham J. Navas
acting as representative of the Department of Labor and Social Provision

AMERICAN COMMISSIONERS

J F McGurk
Counselor of the American Embassy in Mexico.

John O Walker
Assistant Administrator Farm Security Administration. (Department of Agriculture).

David Meeker
Assistant Director Office of Agricultural War Relations. (Department of Agriculture)

Executive Order 9066 (1942)

Commentary

When the Japanese navy attacked Pearl Harbor, Hawaii, on December 7, 1941, the United States was plunged into World War II (1939–1945). In the aftermath of the surprise attack, residents of the West Coast of the United States and commanders of military installations there were fearful of another early-morning assault. Their attention was quickly turned to Japanese Americans, who were suspected of sympathy with Japan despite a lack of evidence that they were anything but loyal Americans.

The resulting public-policy directive, Executive Order 9066, issued by President Franklin D. Roosevelt (1882–1945) on February 19, 1942, set the stage for the forced removal of Japanese Americans from the West Coast. They were to be detained in camps for the duration of the war.

In fact, Executive Order 9066 did not specifically name Japanese Americans as a threat to national security. Instead, Secretary of War Henry L. Stimson and Lieutenant General John L. DeWitt (1880–1962) were given responsibility for designating military areas from which any person could be excluded during the "national emergency." These military areas were later defined as the coastal regions of Washington, Oregon, and California and the southern portion of Arizona.

Approximately 110,000 Americans of Japanese descent were removed from the West Coast and relocated in concentration camps—euphemistically called internment camps—throughout the West and Midwest. A few Germans and Italians were removed from the military areas and from other regions, but their numbers were so small as to be lost in the great tide of Japanese who were uprooted and forced into the camps.

In 1980, Congress established the Commission on Wartime Relocation and Internment of Civilians (CWRIC) to investigate the circumstances of Executive Order 9066. The commission concluded that the presidential order to exclude Japanese Americans without individual hearings was not justified by military necessity but was an act of racial prejudice. By an act of law in 1988, the United States formally apologized and offered redress in the form of a $20,000 monetary compensation to anyone who had been incarcerated under Executive Order 9066.

Whereas the successful prosecution of the war requires every possible protection against espionage and against sabotage to national-defense material, national-defense premises, and national-defense utilities as defined in Section 4, Act of April 20, 1918, 40 Stat. 533, as amended by the Act of November 30, 1940, 54 Stat. 1220, and the Act of August 21, 1941, 55 Stat. 655 (U.S.C., Title 50, Sec 104):

Now, Therefore, by virtue of the authority vested in me as President of the United States, and Commander in Chief of the Army and Navy, I hereby authorize and direct the Secretary of War, and the Military Commanders whom he may from time to time designate, whenever he or any designated Commander deems such action necessary or desirable, to prescribe military areas in such places and of such extent as he or the appropriate Military Commander may determine, from which any or all persons may be excluded, and with respect to which, the right of any person to enter, remain in, or leave shall be subject to whatever restrictions the Secretary of War or the appropriate Military Commander may determine, from which any or all persons may be excluded, and with respect to which, the right of any person to enter, remaining, or leave shall be subject to whatever restrictions the Secretary of War or the appropriate Military Commander may impose in his discretion. The Secretary of War is hereby authorized to provide for residents of any such area who are excluded therefrom, such transportation, food, shelter, and other accommodations as may be necessary, in the judgment of the Secretary of War or the said Military Commander, and until other arrangements are made, to accomplish the purpose of this order. The designation of military areas in any region or locality shall supersede designations of prohibited and restricted areas by the Attorney General under the Proclamations of December 7 and 8, 1941, and shall supersede the responsibility and authority of the Attorney General under the said Proclamations in respect of such prohibited and restricted areas.

I hereby further authorize and direct the Secretary of War and said Military Commanders to take such other Commander to take such other steps as he or the appropriate Military Commander may deem advisable to enforce compliance with the restrictions applicable to each Military area hereinabove authorized to be designated, including the use of Federal troops and other Federal Agencies, with authority to accept assistance of state and local agencies.

I hereby further authorize and direct all Executive Departments, independent establishments and other Federal

Agencies, to assist the Secretary of War or the said Military Commanders in carrying out this Executive Order, including the furnishing of medical aid, hospitalization, food, clothing, transportation, use of land, shelter, and other supplies, equipment, utilities, facilities, and services.

This order shall not be construed as modifying or limiting in any way the authority heretofore granted under Executive Order No. 8972, dated December 12, 1941, nor shall it be construed as limiting or modifying the duty and responsibility of the Federal Bureau of Investigation, with respect to the investigation of alleged acts of sabotage or the duty and responsibility of the Attorney General and the Department of Justice under the Proclamations of December 7 and 8, 1941, prescribing regulations for the conduct and control of alien enemies, except as such duty and responsibility is superseded by the designation of military areas hereunder.

Franklin D. Roosevelt

The White House, February 19, 1942.

Servicemen's Readjustment Act of 1944

Commentary

The Servicemen's Readjustment Act of 1944, more commonly known as the G.I. Bill of Rights, provided a solution to the problem of the eventual return of 16 million returning veterans who would need to be reintegrated into the civilian economy without causing massive unemployment. The act provided for tuition, fees, books, and monthly subsistence payments for veterans in school as well as the chance to set up their own businesses, buy their own homes, and receive other financial aid. These provisions addressed fears that massive numbers of veterans returning to civilian life could have economic effects, including another depression. The act was also seen as a way to help compensate veterans for their service during the war. The excerpt below defines health-related benefits. The bill was signed by President Franklin D. Roosevelt on June 22, 1944. In 1947, the program's peak year, veterans accounted for 49 percent of U.S. college enrollments, with slightly more than half of eligible veterans participating.

To provide Federal Government aid for the readjustment in civilian life of returning World War II veterans.

Be it enacted by the Senate and House of Representatives of the United States of America in Congress assembled, That this Act may be cited as the "Servicemen's Readjustment Act of 1944".

TITLE I

CHAPTER I—HOSPITALIZATION, CLAIMS, AND PROCEDURES

Sec. 100. The Veterans' Administration is hereby declared to be an essential war agency and entitled, second only to the War and Navy Departments, to priorities in personnel, equipment, supplies, and material under any laws, Executive orders, and regulations pertaining to priorities, and in appointments of personnel from civil-service registers the Administrator of Veterans' Affairs is hereby granted the same authority and discretion as the War and Navy Departments and the United States Public Health Service: Provided, That the provisions of this section as to priorities for materials shall apply to any State institution to be built for the care or hospitalization of veterans.

Sec. 101. The Administrator of Veterans' Affairs and the Federal Board of Hospitalization are hereby authorized and directed to expedite and complete the construction of additional hospital facilities for war veterans, and to enter into agreements and contracts for the use by or transfer to the Veterans' Administration of suitable Army and Navy hospitals after termination of hostilities in the present war or after such institutions are no longer needed by the armed services; and the Administrator of Veterans Affairs is hereby authorized and directed to establish necessary regional offices, sub-offices, branch offices, contact units, or other subordinate offices in centers of population where there is no Veterans' Administration facility, or where such a facility is not readily available or accessible : Provided, That there is hereby authorized to be appropriated the sum of $500,000,000 for the construction of additional hospital facilities.

Sec. 102. The Administrator of Veterans' Affairs and the Secretary of War and Secretary of the Navy are hereby granted authority to enter into agreements and contracts for the mutual use or exchange of use of hospital and domiciliary facilities, and such supplies, equipment, and material as may be needed to operate properly such facilities, or for the transfer, without reimbursement of appropriations, of facilities, supplies, equipment, or material necessary and proper for authorized care for veterans, except that at no time shall the Administrator of Veterans' Affairs enter into any agreement which will result in a permanent reduction of Veterans' Administration hospital and domiciliary beds below the number now established or approved, plus the estimated number required to meet the load of eligibles under laws administered by the Veterans' Administration, or in any way subordinate or transfer the operation of the Veterans' Administration to any other agency of the Government.

Nothing in the Selective Training and Service Act of 1940, as amended, or any other Act, shall be construed to prevent the transfer or detail of any commissioned, appointed or enlisted personnel from the armed forces to the Veterans Administration subject to agreements between the Secretary of War or the Secretary of the Navy and the Administrator of Veterans' Affairs: Provided, That no such detail shall be made or extend beyond six months after the termination of the war.

Sec.103. The Administrator of Veterans' Affairs shall have authority to place officials and employees designated by him in such Army and Navy installations as may be deemed advisable for the purpose of adjudicating disability claims of, and giving aid and advice to, members of the Army and Navy who are about to be discharged or released from active service.

Sec. 104. No person shall be discharged or released from active duty in the armed forces until his certificate of discharge or release from active duty and final pay, or a substantial portion thereof, are ready for delivery to him or to his next of kin or legal representative; and no person shall be discharged or released from active service on account of disability until and unless he has executed a claim for compensation, pension, or hospitalization, to be filed with the Veterans' Administration or has signed a statement that he has had explained to him the right to file such claim: Provided, That this section shall not preclude immediate transfer to a veterans' facility for necessary hospital care, nor preclude the discharge of any person who refuses to sign such claim or statement: And provided further, That refusal or failure to file a claim shall be without prejudice to any right the veteran may subsequently assert.

Any person entitled to a prosthetic appliance shall be entitled, in addition, to necessary fitting and training, including institutional training, in the use of such appliance, whether in a Service or a Veterans' Administration hospital, or by out-patient treatment, including such service under contract.

Sec. 105. No person in the armed forces shall be required to sign a statement of any nature relating to the origin, incurrence, or aggravation of any disease or injury he may have, and any such statement against his own interest signed at any time, shall be null and void and of no force and effect. . . .

Executive Order 9835 (1947)

Commentary

Executive Order 9835 (March 21, 1947) laid out procedures for a loyalty program for government employees, which included the establishment of a loyalty review board to conduct investigations of persons applying for and already holding government jobs. The loyalty program was a response to American distrust and fear of the Soviet Union. Although that country was an ally during the war, the Soviet post-war aggressions against Eastern Europe and spying against the United States, including the theft of atomic bomb building information, created conditions that helped lead to Executive Order 9835 and the second "Red Scare." The program did not find many communists. Loyalty oaths did result in the firing of some Quakers and others who did not believe in forced displays of loyalty.

PRESCRIBING PROCEDURES FOR THE ADMINISTRATION OF AN EMPLOYEES LOYALTY PROGRAM IN THE EXECUTIVE BRANCH OF THE GOVERNMENT

Whereas each employee of the Government of the United States is endowed with a measure of trusteeship over the democratic processes which are the heart and sinew of the United States; and

Whereas it is of vital importance that persons employed in the Federal service be of complete and unswerving loyalty to the United States; and

Whereas, although the loyalty of by far the overwhelming majority of all Government employees is beyond question, the presence within the Government service of any disloyal or subversive person constitutes a threat to our democratic processes; and

Whereas maximum protection must be afforded the United States against infiltration of disloyal persons into the ranks of its employees, and equal protection from unfounded accusations of disloyalty must be afforded the loyal employees of the Government:

Now, Therefore, by virtue of the authority vested in me by the Constitution and statutes of the United States, including the Civil Service Act of 1883 (22 Stat. 403), as amended, and section 9A of the act approved August 2, 1939 (18 U.S.C. 61i), and as President and Chief Executive of the United States, it is hereby, in the interest of the internal management of the Government, ordered as follows:

PART I,—INVESTIGATION OF APPLICANTS

1. There shall be a loyalty investigation of every person entering the civilian employment of any department or agency of the executive branch of the Federal Government.
   a. Investigations of persons entering the competitive service shall be conducted by the Civil Service Commission, except in such cases as are covered by a special agreement between the Commission and any given department or agency.
   b. Investigations of persons other than those entering the competitive service shall be conducted by the employing department or agency. Departments and agencies without investigative organizations shall utilize the investigative facilities of the Civil Service Commission.

2. The investigations of persons entering the employ of the executive branch may be conducted after any such person enters upon actual employment therein, but in any such case the appointment of such person shall be conditioned upon a favorable determination with respect to his loyalty.

   a. Investigations of persons entering the competitive service shall be conducted as expeditiously as possible; provided, however, that if any such investigation is not completed within 18 months from the date on which a person enters actual employment, the condition that his employment is subject to investigation shall expire, except in a case in which the Civil Service Commission has made an initial adjudication of disloyalty and the case continues to be active by reason of an appeal, and it shall then be the responsibility of the employing department or agency to conclude such investigation and make a final determination concerning the loyalty of such person.

3. An investigation shall be made of all applicants at all available pertinent sources of information and shall include reference to:

   a. Federal Bureau of Investigation files.
   b. Civil Service Commission files.
   c. Military and naval intelligence files.
   d. The files of any other appropriate government investigative or intelligence agency.
   e. House Committee on un-American Activities files.
   f. Local law-enforcement files at the place of residence and employment of the applicant, including municipal, county, and State law-enforcement files.
   g. Schools and colleges attended by applicant.
   h. Former employers of applicant.
   i. References given by applicant.
   j. Any other appropriate source.

4. Whenever derogatory information with respect to loyalty of an applicant is revealed a full investigation shall be conducted. A full field investigation shall also be conducted of those applicants, or of applicants for particular positions, as may be designated by the head of the employing department or agency, such designations to be based on the determination by any such head of the best interests of national security.

PART II—INVESTIGATION OF EMPLOYEES

1. The head of each department and agency in the executive branch of the Government shall be personally responsible for an effective program to assure that disloyal civilian officers or employees are not retained in employment in his department or agency.

   a. He shall be responsible for prescribing and supervising the loyalty determination procedures of his department or agency, in accordance with the provisions of this order, which shall be considered as providing minimum requirements.
   b. The head of a department or agency which does not have an investigative organization shall utilize the investigative facilities of the Civil Service Commission.

2. The head of each department and agency shall appoint one or more loyalty boards, each composed of not less than three representatives of the department or agency concerned, for the purpose of hearing loyalty cases arising within such department or agency and making recommendations with respect to the removal of any officer or employee of such department or agency on grounds relating to loyalty, and he shall prescribe regulations for the conduct of the proceedings before such boards.

   a. An officer or employee who is charged with being disloyal shall have a right to an administrative hearing before a loyalty board in the employing department or agency. He may appear before such board personally, accompanied by counsel or representative of his own choosing, and present evidence on his own behalf, through witnesses or by affidavit.
   b. The officer or employee shall be served with a written notice of such hearing in sufficient time, and shall be informed therein of the nature of the charges against him in sufficient detail, so that he will be enabled to prepare his defense. The charges shall be stated as specifically and completely as, in the discretion of the employing department or agency, security considerations permit, and the officer or employee shall be informed in the notice (1) of his right to reply to such charges in writing within a specified reasonable period of time, (2) of his right to an administrative hearing on such charges before a loyalty board, and (3) of his right to appear before such board personally, to be accompanied by counsel or representative of his own choosing, and to present evidence on his behalf, through witness or by affidavit.

3. A recommendation of removal by a loyalty board shall be subject to appeal by the officer or employee affected, prior to his removal, to the head of the employing department or agency or to such person or persons as may be designated by such head, under such regulations as may be prescribed by him, and the decision of the department or agency concerned

shall be subject to appeal to the Civil Service Commission's Loyalty Review Board, hereinafter provided for, for an advisory recommendation.

4. The rights of hearing, notice thereof, and appeal therefrom shall be accorded to every officer or employee prior to his removal on grounds of disloyalty, irrespective of tenure, or of manner, method, or nature of appointment, but the head of the employing department or agency may suspend any officer or employee at any time pending a determination with respect to loyalty.

5. The loyalty boards of the various departments and agencies shall furnish to the Loyalty Review Board, hereinafter provided for, such reports as may be requested concerning the operation of the loyalty program in any such department or agency.

PART III—RESPONSIBILITIES OF CIVIL SERVICE COMMISSION

1. There shall be established in the Civil Service Commission a Loyalty Review Board of not less than three impartial persons, the members of which shall be officers or employees of the Commission.

   a. The Board shall have authority to review cases involving persons recommended for dismissal on grounds relating to loyalty by the loyalty board of any department or agency and to make advisory recommendations thereon to the head of the employing department or agency. Such cases may be referred to the Board either by the employing department or agency, or by the officer or employee concerned.

   b. The Board shall make rules and regulations, not inconsistent with the provisions of this order, deemed necessary to implement statutes and Executive orders relating to employee loyalty.

   c. The Loyalty Review Board shall also:
      (1) Advise all departments and agencies on all problems relating to employee loyalty.
      (2) Disseminate information pertinent to employee loyalty programs.
      (3) Coordinate the employee loyalty policies and procedures of the several departments and agencies.
      (4) Make reports and submit recommendations to the Civil Service Commission for transmission to the President from time to time as may be necessary to the maintenance of the employee loyalty program.

2. There shall also be established and maintained in the Civil Service Commission a central master index covering all persons on whom loyalty investigations have been made by any department or agency since September 1, 1939. Such master index shall contain the name of each person investigated, adequate identifying information concerning each such person, and a reference to each department and agency which has conducted a loyalty investigation concerning the person involved.

   a. All executive departments and agencies are directed to furnish to the Civil Service Commission all information appropriate for the establishment and maintenance of the central master index.

   b. The reports and other investigative material and information developed by the investigating department or agency shall be retained by such department or agency in each case.

3. The loyalty Review Board shall currently be furnished by the Department of Justice the name of each foreign or domestic organization, association, movement, group or combination of persons which the Attorney General, after appropriate investigation and determination, designates as totalitarian, fascist, communist or subversive, or as having adopted a policy of advocating or approving the commission of acts of force or violence to deny others their rights under the Constitution of the United States, or as seeking to alter the form of government of the United States by unconstitutional means.

   a. The Loyalty Review Board shall disseminate such information to all departments and agencies.

PART IV—SECURITY MEASURES IN INVESTIGATIONS

1. At the request of the head of any department or agency of the executive branch an investigative agency shall make available to such head, personally, all investigative material and information collected by the investigative agency concerning any employee or prospective employee of the requesting department or agency, or shall make such material and information available to any officer or officers designated by such head and approved by the investigative agency.

2. Notwithstanding the foregoing requirement, however, the investigative agency may refuse to disclose the names of confidential informants, provided it furnishes sufficient information about such informants on the basis of which the requesting department or agency can make an adequate evaluation of the information furnished by them, and provided it advises the requesting department or agency in writing that it is essential to the protection of the informants or to the investigation of other cases that the identity of the informants not be revealed. Investigative agencies shall not use this discretion to decline to reveal sources of information where such action is not essential.

3. Each department and agency of the executive branch should develop and maintain, for the collection and analysis of information relating to the loyalty of its employees and prospective employees, a staff specially trained in security techniques, and an effective security control system for protecting such information generally and for protecting confidential sources of such information particularly.

PART V—STANDARDS

1. The standard for the refusal of employment or the removal from employment in an executive department or agency on grounds relating to loyalty shall be that, on all the evidence, reasonable grounds exist for belief that the person involved is disloyal to the Government of the United States.
2. Activities and associations of an applicant or employee which may be considered in connection with the determination of disloyalty may include one or more of the following:
   a. Sabotage, espionage, or attempts or preparations therefor, or knowingly associating with spies or saboteurs;
   b. Treason or sedition or advocacy thereof;
   c. Advocacy of revolution or force or violence to alter the constitutional form of government of the United States;
   d. Intentional, unauthorized disclosure to any person, under circumstances which may indicate disloyalty to the United States, of documents or information of a confidential or non-public character obtained by the person making the disclosure as a result of his employment by the Government of the United States;
   e. Performing or attempting to perform his duties, or otherwise acting, so as to serve the interests of another government in preference to the interests of the United States.
   f. Membership in, affiliation with or sympathetic association with any foreign or domestic organization, association, movement, group or combination of persons, designated by the Attorney General as totalitarian, fascist, communist, or subversive, or as having adopted a policy of advocating or approving the commission of acts of force or violence to deny other persons their rights under the Constitution of the United States, or as seeking to alter the form of government of the United States by unconstitutional means.

PART VI—MISCELLANEOUS

1. Each department and agency of the executive branch, to the extent that it has not already done so, shall submit, to the Federal Bureau of Investigation of the Department of Justice, either directly or through the Civil Service Commission, the names (and such other necessary identifying material as the Federal Bureau of Investigation may require) of all of its incumbent employees.
   a. The Federal Bureau of Investigation shall check such names against its records of persons concerning whom there is substantial evidence of being within the purview of paragraph 2 of Part V hereof, and shall notify each department and agency of such information.
   b. Upon receipt of the above-mentioned information from the Federal Bureau of Investigation, each department and agency shall make, or cause to be made by the Civil Service Commission, such investigation of those employees as the head of the department or agency shall deem advisable.
2. The Security Advisory Board of the State-War-Navy Coordinating Committee shall draft rules applicable to the handling and transmission of confidential documents and other documents and information which should not be publicly disclosed, and upon approval by the President such rules shall constitute the minimum standards for the handling and transmission of such documents and information, and shall be applicable to all departments and agencies of the executive branch.
3. The provisions of this order shall not be applicable to persons summarily removed under the provisions of section 3 of the act of December 17, 1942, 56 Stat. 1053, of the act of July 5, 1946, 60 Stat. 453, or of any other statute conferring the power of summary removal.
4. The Secretary of War and the Secretary of the Navy, and the Secretary of the Treasury with respect to the Coast Guard, are hereby directed to continue to enforce and maintain the highest standards of loyalty within the armed services, pursuant to the applicable statutes, the Articles of War, and the Articles for the Government of the Navy.
5. This order shall be effective immediately, but compliance with such of its provisions as require the expenditure of funds shall be deferred pending the appropriation of such funds.
6. Executive Order No. 9300 of February 5, 1943, is hereby revoked.

Harry S. Truman

The White House,

March 21, 1947

ARTICLES, SONGS, AND INTERVIEWS

Excerpt from "The War in Its Effect upon Women" (1916)

Source: Swanwick, Helena. "The War in Its Effect upon Women," 1916. Reprinted in *World War I and European Society: A Sourcebook.* Edited by Marilyn Shevin-Coetzee and Frans Coetzee. Lexington, MA: D.C. Heath, 1995.

Commentary

The cost of the Great War (World War I) in Europe was the needless loss of nearly an entire generation of young men, but in many regards, the social conventions of the time, exemplified in the infamous, government concocted "Little Mother" letter, required women to accept their losses quietly. A dedicated pacifist and supporter of universal suffrage, among the most outspoken opponents of Britain's participation in World War I, Helena Swanwick defied this thinking. As active after the war as during it, she later served in the League of Nations Union and was a member of the Empire's delegation to the League in 1929, though she remained always a harsh critic of the watered-down and self-serving Treaty of Versailles. Her many writings, salient, strong, and fiercely argued, would prove a powerful influence on a generation of women across the ocean in the United States, as well as in her native England. Depressed by failing health and the rise of fascism on the continent, she committed suicide in 1939, shortly before the outbreak of World War II.

How has the war affected women? How will it affect them? Women, as half the human race, are compelled to take their share of evil and good with men, the other half. The destruction of property, the increase of taxation, the rise of prices, the devastation of beautiful things in nature and art—these are felt by men as well as by women. Some losses doubtless appeal to one or the other sex with peculiar poignancy, but it would be difficult to say whose sufferings are the greater, though there can be no doubt at all that men get an exhilaration out of war which is denied to most women. When they see pictures of soldiers encamped in the ruins of what was once a home, amidst the dead bodies of gentle milch cows, most women would be thinking too insistently of the babies who must die for need of milk to entertain the exhilaration which no doubt may be felt at "the good work of our guns." When they read of miles upon miles of kindly earth made barren, the hearts of men may be wrung to think of wasted toil, but to women the thought suggests a simile full of an even deeper pathos; they will think of the millions of young lives destroyed, each one having cost the travail and care of a mother, and of the millions of young bodies made barren by the premature death of those who should have been their mates. The millions of widowed maidens in the coming generation will have to turn their thoughts away from one particular joy and fulfilment of life. While men in war give what is, at the present stage of the world's development, the peculiar service of men, let them not forget that in rendering that very service they are depriving a corresponding number of women of the opportunity of rendering what must, at all stages of the world's development, be the peculiar service of women. After the war, men will go on doing what has been regarded as men's work; women, deprived of their own, will also have to do much of what has been regarded as men's work. These things are going to affect women profoundly, and one hopes that the reconstruction of society is going to be met by the whole people—men and women—with a sympathetic understanding of each other's circumstances. When what are known as men's questions are discussed, it is generally assumed that the settlement of them depends upon men only; when what are known as women's questions are discussed, there is never any suggestion that they can be settled by women independently of men. Of course they cannot. But, then, neither can "men's questions" be rightly settled so. In fact, life would be far more truly envisaged if we dropped the silly phrases "men's and women's questions"; for, indeed, there are no such matters, and all human questions affect all humanity.

Now, for the right consideration of human questions, it is necessary for humans to understand each other. This catastrophic war will do one good thing if it opens our eyes to real live women as they are, as we know them in workaday life, but as the politician and the journalist seem not to have known them. When war broke out, a Labour newspaper, in the midst of the news of men's activities, found space to say that women would feel the pinch, because their supply of attar of roses would be curtailed. It struck some women like a blow in the face. When a great naval engagement took place, the front page of a progressive daily was taken up with portraits of the officers and men who had won distinction, and the back page with portraits of simpering mannequins in extravagantly fashionable hats; not frank advertisement, mind you, but exploitation of women under the guise of news supposed to be peculiarly interesting to the feeble-minded creatures. When a snapshot was published of the first women ticket collectors in England, the legend underneath the picture ran "Superwomen"! It took the life and death of Edith Cavell to open the eyes of the Prime Minister to the fact that there were thousands of women giving life and service to their country. "A year ago we did not know it," he said, in the House of Commons. Is that indeed so? Surely in our private capacities as ordinary citizens, we knew not only of the women whose portraits are in the picture papers (mostly pretty ladies of the music hall or of society), but also of the toiling millions upon whose courage and ability and endurance and goodness of heart the great human family rests. Only the politicians did not know, because their thoughts were too much engrossed with faction fights to think humanly; only the journalists would not write of them, because there was more money in writing the columns which are demanded by the advertisers of feminine luxuries. Anyone who has conducted a woman's paper knows the steady commercial pressure for that sort of "copy."

The other kind of women are, through the war, becoming good "copy." But women have not suddenly become patriotic, or capable, or self-sacrificing; the great masses of women have always shown these qualities in their humble daily life. Now that their services are asked for in unfamiliar directions, attention is being attracted to them, and many more people are realising that, with extended training and opportunity, women's capacity for beneficent work would be extended. . . .

"Over There" (1917)

Source: Cohan, George M. "Over There." New York: Leo Feist, 1917.

Commentary
Penned by George M. Cohan during the earliest days of the United States' involvement in the Great War (World War I), "Over There" stands as an artifact of a more innocent time. By 1917, the war in Europe had entered its third year, and the levels of bloodshed and cruel devastation unleashed by this new mechanized conflict had reached unimaginable levels. (During the Battle of the Somme in France, some 60,000 British soldiers were killed in a single day. That was unimaginable, except that another 60,000 had already been killed in April at Ypres, mostly by gas. Tens of thousands more at Loos when the British's own chlorine canisters blew back into their trenches.) But for the so-called doughboys of the United States Army, something like Old World esprit de corps was still possible. "Over There" was the greatest of the wartime propaganda songs, made famous by the singer Noya Bayes, and recorded dozens of times, once by the opera star Enrico Caruso. By 1918, and the end of hostilities in the European theater, more than a hundred thousand Americans had lost their lives. In 1940, President Franklin D. Roosevelt awarded Cohan a special Medal of Honor for his contribution to the cause in World War I.

Johnnie get your gun, get your gun, get your gun,
Take it on the run, on the run, on the run;
Hear them calling you and me;
Every son of liberty.
Hurry right away, no delay, go today,
Make your daddy glad, to have had such a lad,
Tell your sweetheart not to pine,
To be proud her boy's in line.

Chorus:
Over there, over there,
Send the word, send the word over there,

That the Yanks are coming, the Yanks are
   coming,
The drums rum-tumming everywhere.
So prepare, say a prayer,
Send the word, send the word to beware,
We'll be over, we're coming over,
And we won't come back till it's over over there.

Johnnie get your gun, get your gun, get your gun,
Johnnie show the Hun, you're a son-of-a-gun,
Hoist the flag and let her fly,
Like true heroes do or die.
Pack your little kit, show your grit, do your bit,
Soldiers to the ranks from the towns and the tanks,
Make your mother proud of you,
And to liberty be true.

Dedicating the Tomb of the Unknown Soldier (1921)

Source: Simpson, Kirke L. "Associated Press Report on the Dedication of the Tomb of the Unknown Soldier" (11 November 1921).

Commentary
More than 100,000 Americans lost their lives during the United States's two-year involvement in World War I. Three years after the signing of the Treaty of Versailles and the end of hostilities in Europe, in a solemn ceremony President Warren G. Harding dedicated a monument to unidentifiable, "unknown" soldiers killed during the war. For progressives, World War I represented the shattering failure of the ideal of civilized reform and enlightenment. For isolationists, it was the confirmation of their deepest fears, the beginning of a new era of intercontinental mechanized warfare the likes of which the world had never seen. Thousands; ordinary citizens, foreign dignitaries, and American politicians alike attended the dedication described here. Former President Woodrow Wilson, himself instrumental in crafting the peace, was present. Many years later, the unidentified remains of dead soldiers from World War II and the Korean conflict were buried with the monument's original inhabitant. A casualty of the Vietnam War was interred alongside them in 1973, but when advances in forensic science allowed for his identification, his remains were disinterred and turned over to his family. The age of the unknown soldier, it would seem, had come to an end.

Under the wide and starry skies of his own homeland America's unknown dead from France sleeps tonight, a soldier home from the wars.

Alone, he lies in the narrow cell of stone that guards his body; but his soul has entered into the spirit that is America. Wherever liberty is held close in men's hearts, the honor and the glory and the pledge of high endeavor poured out over this nameless one of fame will be told and sung by Americans for all time.

Scrolled across the marble arch of the memorial raised to American soldier and sailor dead, everywhere, which stands like a monument behind his tomb, runs this legend: "We here highly resolve that these dead shall not have died in vain."

The words were spoken by the martyred Lincoln over the dead at Gettysburg. And today with voice strong with determination and ringing with deep emotion, another President echoed that high resolve over the coffin of the soldier who died for the flag in France.

Great men in the world's affairs heard that high purpose reiterated by the man who stands at the head of the American people. Tomorrow they will gather in the city that stands almost in the shadow of the new American shrine of liberty dedicated today. They will talk of peace; of the curbing of the havoc of war.

They will speak of the war in France, that robbed this soldier of life and name and brought death to comrades of all nations by the hundreds of thousands. And in their ears when they meet must ring President Harding's declaration today beside that flag-wrapped, honor-laden bier:

"There must be, there shall be, the commanding voice of a conscious civilization against armed warfare."

Far across the seas, other unknown dead, hallowed in memory by their countrymen, as this American soldier is enshrined in the heart of America, sleep their last. He, in whose veins ran the blood of British forebears, lies beneath a great stone in ancient Westminster Abbey; he of France, beneath the Arc de Triomphe, and he of Italy under the altar of the fatherland in Rome. . . .

And it seemed today that they, too, must be here among the Potomac hills to greet an American comrade come to join their glorious company, to testify their approval of the high words of hope spoken by America's President. All day long the nation poured out its heart in pride and glory for the nameless American. Before the first crash of the minute guns roared its knell for the dead from the shadow of Washington Monument, the people who claim him as their own were trooping out to do him honor. They lined the long road from the Capitol to the hillside where he sleeps tonight; they flowed like a tide over the slopes about his burial place; they choked the bridges that lead across the river to the fields of the brave, in which he is the last comer. . . .

As he was carried past through the banks of humanity that lined Pennsylvania Avenue a solemn, reverent hush held the living walls. Yet there was not so much of sorrow as of high pride in it all, a pride beyond the reach of shouting and the clamor that marks less sacred moments in life.

Out there in the broad avenue was a simpler soldier, dead for honor of the flag. He was nameless. No man knew what part in the great life of the nation he had died as Americans always have been ready to die, for the flag and what it means. They read the message of the pageant clear, these silent thousands along the way. They stood in almost holy awe to take their own part in what was theirs, the glory of the American people, honored here in the honors showered on America's nameless son from France.

Soldiers, sailors, and marines—all played their part in the thrilling spectacles as the cortege rolled along. And just behind the casket, with its faded French flowers on the draped flag, walked the President, the chosen leader of a hundred million, in whose name he was chief mourner at his bier. Beside him strode the man under whom the fallen hero had lived and died in France, General Pershing, wearing only the single medal of Victory that every American soldier might wear as his only decoration.

Then, row on row, came the men who lead the nation today or have guided its destinies before. They were all there, walking proudly, with age and frailties of the flesh forgotten. Judges, Senators, Representatives, highest officers of every military arm of government, and a trudging little group of the nation's most valorous sons, the Medal of Honor men. Some were gray and bent and drooping with old wounds; some trim and erect as the day they won their way to fame. All walked gladly in this nameless comrade's last parade.

Behind these came the carriage in which rode Woodrow Wilson, also stricken down by infirmities as he served in the highest place in the nation, just as the humble private riding in such state ahead had gone down before a shell of bullet. For the dead man's sake, the former President had put aside his dread of seeming to parade his physical weakness and risked health, perhaps life, to appear among the mourners for the fallen.

There was handclapping and a cheer here and there for the man in the carriage, a tribute to the spirit that brought him to honor the nation's nameless hero, whose commander-in-chief he had been.

After President Harding and most of the high dignitaries of the government had turned aside at the White House, the procession, headed by its solid blocks of soldiery and the battalions of sailor comrades, moved on with Pershing, now flanked by secretaries Weeks and Denby, for the long road to the tomb. It marched on, always between the human borders of the way of victory the nation had made for itself of the great avenue; on over the old bridge that spans the Potomac, on up the long hill to Fort Myer, and at last to the great cemetery beyond, where soldier and sailor folk sleep by the thousands. There the lumbering guns of the artillery swung aside, the cavalry drew their horses out of the long line and left to the foot soldiers and the sailors and marines the last stage of the journey.

Ahead, the white marble of the amphitheater gleamed through the trees. It stands crowning the slope of the hills that sweep upward from the river, and just across was Washington, its clustered buildings and monuments to great dead who have gone before, a moving picture in the autumn haze.

People in thousands were moving about the great circle of the amphitheater. The great ones to whom places had been given in the sacred enclosure and the plain folk who had trudged the long way just to glimpse the pageant from afar, were finding their places. Everywhere within the pillared enclosure bright uniforms of foreign soldiers appeared. They were laden with the jeweled order of rank to honor an American private soldier, great in the majesty of his sacrifices, in the tribute his honors paid to all Americans who died.

Down below the platform placed for the casket, in a stone vault, lay wreaths and garlands brought from England's King and guarded by British soldiers. To them came the British Ambassador in the full uniform of his rank to bid them keep safe against that hour.

Above the platform gathered men whose names ring through history—Briand, Foch, Beatty, Balfour, Jacques, Diaz, and others—in a brilliant array of place and power. They were followed by others, Baron Kato from Japan, the Italian statesmen and officers, by the notables from all countries gathered here for tomorrow's conference, and by some of the older figures in American life too old to walk beside the approaching funeral train.

Down around the circling pillars the marbled box filled with distinguished men and women, with a cluster of shattered men from army hospitals, accompanied by uniformed nurses. A surpliced choir took its place to wait the dead.

Faint and distant, the silvery strains of a military band stole into the big white bowl of the amphitheater. The slow cadences and mourning notes of a funeral march grew clearer amid the roll and mutter of the muffled drums.

At the arch where the choir awaited the heroic dead, comrades lifted his casket down and, followed by the generals and the admirals, who had walked beside him from the Capitol, he was carried to the place of honor. Ahead moved the white-robed singers, chanting solemnly.

Carefully, the casket was placed above the banked flowers, and the Marine Band played sacred melodies until the moment the President and Mrs. Harding stepped to their places beside the casket; then the crashing, triumphant chorus of The Star Spangled Banner swept the gathering to its feet again.

A prayer, carried out over the crowd over the amplifiers so that no word was missed, took a moment or two, then the sharp, clear call of the bugle rang "Attention!" and for two minutes the nation stood at pause for the dead, just at high noon. No sound broke the quiet as all stood with bowed heads. It was much as though a mighty hand had checked the world in full course. Then the band sounded, and in a mighty chorus rolled up in the words of America from the hosts within and without the great open hall of valor.

President Harding stepped forward beside the coffin to say for America the thing that today was nearest to the nation's heart, that sacrifices such as this nameless man, fallen in battle, might perhaps be made unnecessary down through the coming years. Every word that President Harding spoke reached every person through the amplifiers and reached other thousands upon thousands in New York and San Francisco.

Mr. Harding showed strong emotion as his lips formed the last words of the address. He paused, then with raised hand and head bowed, went on in the measured, rolling periods of the Lord's Prayer. The response that came back to him from the thousands he faced, from the other thousands out over the slopes beyond, perhaps from still other thousands away near the Pacific, or close-packed in the heart of the nation's greatest city, arose like a chant. The marble arches hummed with a solemn sound.

Then the foreign officers who stand highest among the soldiers or sailors of their flags came one by one to the bier to place gold and jeweled emblems for the brave above the breast of the sleeper. Already, as the great prayer ended, the President had set the American seal of admiration for the valiant, the nation's love for brave deeds and the courage that defies death, upon the casket.

Side by side he laid the Medal of Honor and the Distinguished Service Cross. And below, set in place with reverent hands, grew the long line of foreign honors, the Victoria Cross, never before laid on the breast of any but those who had served the British flag; all the highest honors of France and Belgium and Italy and Rumania and Czechoslovakia and Poland.

To General Jacques of Belgium it remained to add his own touch to these honors. He tore from the breast of his own tunic the medal of valor pinned there by the Belgian King, tore it with a sweeping gesture, and tenderly bestowed it on the unknown American warrior.

Through the religious services that followed, and prayers, the swelling crowd sat motionless until it rose to join in the old, consoling Rock of Ages, and the last rite for the dead was at hand. Lifted by his hero-bearers from the stage, the unknown was carried in his flag-wrapped, simple coffin out to the wide sweep of the terrace. The bearers laid the sleeper down above the crypt, on which had been placed a little soil of France. The dust his blood helped redeem from alien hands will mingle with his dust as time marches by.

The simple words of the burial ritual were said by Bishop Brent; flowers from war mothers of America and England were laid in place.

For the Indians of America Chief Plenty Coos came to call upon the Great spirit of the Red Men, with gesture and chant and tribal tongue, that the dead should not have died in vain, that war might end, peace be purchased by such blood as this. Upon the casket he laid the coupstick of his tribal office and the feathered war bonnet from his own head. Then the casket, with its weight of honors, was lowered into the crypt.

A rocking blast of gunfire rang from the woods. The glittering circle of bayonets stiffened to a salute to the dead. Again the guns shouted their message of honor and farewell. Again they boomed out; a loyal comrade was being laid to his last, long rest.

High and clear and true in the echoes of the guns, a bugle lifted the old, old notes of taps, the lullaby for the living soldier, in death his requiem. Long ago some forgotten soldier-poet caught its meaning clear and set it down that soldiers everywhere might know its message as they sink to rest:

Fades the light;
And afar
Goeth day, cometh night,
And a star,
Leadeth all, speedeth all,
To their rest.

The guns roared out again in the national salute. He was home, The Unknown, to sleep forever among his own.

Advice to the Unemployed in the Great Depression (1931)

Source: Ford, Henry. "On Unemployment." *Literary Digest* (June 11–18, 1931).

Commentary

The decade before the Great Depression was one of unprecedented economic growth. The rise of new industries, such as automobile manufacturing, created jobs and newfound prosperity for working and middle-class American families. Automobile industry giant Henry Ford (1863–1947), whose company, Ford Motor Company, designed and implemented the first continuously moving assembly line, was a prominent leader in the new industrial order.

The stock market crash of 1929 and the deepening post-war economic crisis overseas devastated the rapidly growing American economy, however, and many industrial workers were forced out of their jobs. Ford regarded himself as a groundbreaking advocate for fair labor management policies, such as the institution, in 1914, of an eight-hour workday, and saw himself as a champion of eco-

nomic independence. In light of these beliefs, in this passage Ford urged the unemployed not to depend upon benefactors or charity for their survival. Hard, self-directed work, he believed, will keep the worker profitably employed until the economic situation turns around.

I have always had to work, whether anyone hired me or not. For the first forty years of my life, I was an employee. When not employed by others, I employed myself. I found very early that being out of hire was not necessarily being out of work. The first means that your employer has not found something for you to do; the second means that you are waiting until he does.

We nowadays think of work as something others find for us to do, call us to do, and pay us to do. No doubt our industrial growth is largely responsible for that. We have accustomed men to think of work that way.

In my own case, I was able to find work for others as well as myself. Outside my family life, nothing has given me more satisfaction than to see jobs increase in number and in profit to the men who handle them. And, beyond question, the jobs of the world today are more numerous and profitable in wages than they were even eighteen year ago.

But something entirely outside the workshops of the nation has affected this hired employment very seriously. The word "unemployment" has become one of the most dreadful words in the language. The condition itself has become the concern of every person in the country.

When this condition arrived, there were just three things to be done. The first, of course, was to maintain employment at the maximum by every means known to management. Employment—hire—was what the people were accustomed to; they preferred it; it was the immediate solution of the difficulty. In our plants we used every expedient to spread as much employment over as many employees as was possible. I don't believe in "make work"—the public pays for all unnecessary work—but there are times when the plight of others compels us to do the human thing even though it be but a makeshift; and I am obliged to admit that, like most manufacturers, we avoided layoffs by continuing work that good business judgment would have halted. All of our nonprofit work was continued in full force and much of the shop work. There were always tens of thousands employed—the lowest point at Dearborn was 40,000—but there were always thousands unemployed or so meagerly employed that the situation was far from desirable.

When all possible devices for providing employment have been used and fall short, there remains no alternative but self-help or charity.

I do not believe in routine charity. I think it a shameful thing that any man should have to stoop to take it, or give it. I do not include human helpfulness under the name of charity. My quarrel with charity is that it is neither helpful nor human. The charity of our cities is the most barbarous thing in our system, with the possible exception of our prisons. What we call charity is a modern substitute for being personally kind, personally concerned, and personally involved in the work of helping others in difficulty. True charity is a much more costly effort than money-giving. Our donations too often purchase exemption from giving the only form of help that will drive the need for charity out of the land.

Our own theory of helping people has been in operation for some years. We used to discuss it years ago—when no one could be persuaded to listen. Those who asked public attention to these matters were ridiculed by the very people who now call most loudly for someone to do something.

Our own work involves the usual emergency relief, hospitalization, adjustment of debt, with this addition—we help people to alter their affairs in commonsense accordance with changed conditions, and we have an understanding that all help received should be repaid in reasonable amounts in better times. Many families were not so badly off as they thought; they needed guidance in the management of their resources and opportunities. Human nature, of course, presented the usual problems. Relying on human sympathy many develop a spirit of professional indigence. But where cooperation is given, honest and self-respecting persons and families can usually be assisted to a condition which is much less distressing than they feared.

One of our responsibilities, voluntarily assumed—not because it was ours but because there seemed to be no one else to assume it—was the care of a village of several hundred families whose condition was pretty low. Ordinarily, a large welfare fund would have been needed to accomplish anything for these people. In this instance, we set the people at work cleaning up their homes and backyards, and then cleaning up the roads of their town, and then plowing up about 500 acres of vacant land around their houses. We abolished everything that savored of "handout" charity, opening instead a modern commissary where personal I O U's were accepted, and a garment-making school, and setting the cobblers and tailors of the community to work for their neighbors. We found the people heavily burdened with debt, and we acted informally as their agents in apportioning their income to straighten their affairs. Many families are now out of debt for the first time in years. There has appeared in this village, not only a new spirit of confidence in life but also a new sense of economic values and an appreciation of economic independence which we feel will not soon be lost.

None of these things could have been accomplished by paying out welfare funds after the orthodox manner. The only true charity for these people was somehow to get under their burdens with them and lend them the value of our experience to show them what can be done by people in their circumstances.

Our visiting staff in city work has personally handled thousands of cases in the manner above described. And while no institution can shoulder all the burden, we feel that merely to mitigate present distress is not enough—we feel that thousands of families have been prepared for a better way of life when the wheels of activity begin turning again.

But there is still another way, a third way, so much better than the very best charitable endeavor that it simply forbids us to be satisfied with anything less. That is the way of Self-Help.

Women and the Changing Times (1940)

Source: Federal Writers' Project. Interview by Daisy Thompson. 1940.

Commentary

The Federal Writers' Project (FWP) was an arm of the New Deal's Works Project Administration (WPA) that gave employment between 1935 and 1939 to some 4,500 American writers. The Folklore Project of the FWP employed writers to record the life histories of Americans throughout the country. One of those writers, Daisy Thompson, captured the life story of Mrs. J. R. Byrd of Augusta, Georgia, on February 8, 1940. An excerpt is reproduced below. The Library of Congress maintains nearly 3,000 life histories from the Folklore Project as part of their American Memory collection.

"I don't think there can be any doubt but that the World War caused the depression. When our country became involved with Europe and our boys went to France, prices soared and salaries went up by leaps and bounds. There were so many positions left open by the boys who went 'Over There,' that there actually seemed to be competition between the heads of businesses as to which one would get the first chance to employ a man and they were not stingy with salaries either.

"People became excited and restless, bought extravagantly and lived entirely beyond their means. Many borrowed money from the banks to buy luxuries they couldn't afford. When things began to level themselves after the close of the war—a depression was inevitable.

"I think President Roosevelt is a wonderful man." She remarked. "I feel that he has done more to help poor people than any other man could have done.

"To my mind one of the greatest accomplishments of the New Deal has been the organization of the Civilian Conservation Camps. The training given the boys will be of lasting benefit. They have changed many a boy from a liability to a valuable asset to his country. They have kept thousands of boys off the roads just idly roaming over the country—hiking and beating rides on freight trains, etc. Many of them have become good citizens.

"We have worked hard and had our ups and downs, but we are very happy and enjoy our home so much. When any of the children get out of work they know they are always welcome to come home and stay until they are on their feet again. It would be a great pleasure to us to keep our [brood?] together at all times but of course that is impossible. Boys, particularly, love to get out and run around and see something of the world.

"I recall one time when one of our boys decided to hitch-hike to Raleigh, North Carolina. It was not nearly so exciting as he had expected.

"He said he only met one man who treated him kindly and he was a person whom he had known before. He obtained employment at a bakery but worked only one night for when the proprietor demanded his straw that broke the camel's back. It was simply disgraceful.

"I have a friend who firmly believed in women's rights and longed for the day when we would have a say-so in our government. The first time she had the opportunity to register she couldn't get there fast enough. The next morning the paper published a list of the would-be woman voters. When her brothers read the paper they were very indignant and for a while made things very uncomfortable for her.

"Today, every woman who is eligible is expected to vote and is considered unpatriotic if she doesn't.

"Now we have women evangelists, lawyers, doctors, nurses, congresswomen and others. Women now practically run the churches and other religious organizations.

"And today we even have ladies flying." She exclaimed, "I wonder what next."

Women Working in World War II (1984)

Source: Terry, Peggy. From an interview in *"The Good War": An Oral History of World War Two.* By Studs Terkel. New York: Pantheon Books, 1984.

Commentary

Since government programs during the Great Depression had concentrated mainly on creating jobs for men, the outbreak of the Second World War brought tremendous labor shortages to the United States. By 1941, huge numbers were abandoning civilian life to serve in the military, leaving women like Peggy Terry to fill their places. For the first time in American history, millions of women took an active role in war, building bombs, planes, and ships in fac-

tories like Henry Ford's massive Willow Run plant outside Detroit which at the height of its production turned out B-24 bombers at the rate of one an hour. Hundreds of thousands more served in women's military auxiliary organizations like the WACs or WASPs. Inspired in part by propaganda posters like the one featuring Rosie the Riveter, a strong, fierce-countenanced factory worker who exhorted her fellow women to "Get The Job Done," the women of the United States responded as no one would have imagined possible. At the beginning of the war, the United States was a third-rate military power, barely mechanized and still cocooned in the separatism brought on by the Great War in Europe, but by 1945, it was a dominant global force, producing more weapons, military vehicles, and ammunition than the rest of the world combined.

The first work I had after the Depression was at a shell-loading plant in Viola, Kentucky. It is between Paducah and Mayfield. They were large shells: anti-aircraft, incendiaries, and tracers.

We painted red on the tips of the tracers. My mother, my sister, and myself worked there. Each of us worked a different shift because we had little ones at home. We made the fabulous sum of thirty-two dollars a week. (Laughs.) To us it was just an absolute miracle. Before that, we made nothing.

You won't believe how incredibly ignorant I was. I knew vaguely that a war had started, but I had no idea what it meant.

Didn't you have a radio?

Gosh, no. That was an absolute luxury. We were just moving around, working wherever we could find work. I was eighteen. My husband was nineteen. We were living day to day. When you are involved in stayin' alive, you don't think about big things like a war. It didn't occur to us that we were making these shells to kill people. It never entered my head.

There were no women foremen where we worked. We were just a bunch of hillbilly women laughin' and talkin'. It was like a social. Now we'd have money to buy shoes and a dress and pay rent and get some food on the table. We were just happy to have work.

I worked in building number 11. I pulled a lot of gadgets on a machine. The shell slid under and powder went into it. Another lever you pulled tamped it down. Then it moved on a conveyer belt to another building where the detonator was dropped in. You did this over and over.

Tetryl was one of the ingredients and it turned us orange. Just as orange as an orange. Our hair was streaked orange. Our hands, our face, our neck just turned orange, even our eyeballs. We never questioned. None of us ever asked, What is this? Is this harmful? We simply didn't think about it. That was just one of the conditions of the job. The only thing we worried about was other women thinking we had dyed our hair. Back then it was a disgrace if you dyed your hair. We worried what people would say.

We used to laugh about it on the bus. It eventually wore off. But I seem to remember some of the women had breathing problems. The shells were painted a dark gray. When the paint didn't come out smooth, we had to take rags wet with some kind of remover and wash that paint off. The fumes from these rags—it was like breathing cleaning fluid. It burned the nose and throat. Oh, it was difficult to breathe. I remember that.

Nothing ever blew up, but I remember the building where they dropped in the detonator. These detonators are little black things about the size of a thumb. This terrible thunderstorm came and all the lights went out. Somebody knocked a box of detonators off on the floor. Here we were in the pitch dark. Somebody was screaming, "Don't move, anybody!" They were afraid you'd step on the detonator. We were down on our hands and knees crawling out of that building in the storm. (Laughs.) We were in slow motion. If we'd stepped on one ...

Mamma was what they call terminated—fired. Mamma's mother took sick and died and Mamma asked for time off and they told her no. Mamma said, "Well, I'm gonna be with my mamma. If I have to give up my job, I will just have to." So they terminated Mamma. That's when I started gettin' nasty. I didn't take as much baloney and pushing around as I had taken. I told 'em I was gonna quit, and they told me if I quit they would blacklist met wherever I would go. They had my fingerprints and all that. I guess it was just bluff, because I did get other work.

I think of how little we knew of human rights, union rights. We knew Daddy had been a hell-raiser in the mine workers' union, but at that point it hadn't rubbed off on any of us women. Coca-Cola and Dr. Pepper were allowed in every building, but not a drop of water. You could only get a drink of water if you went to the cafeteria, which was about two city blocks away. Of course you couldn't leave your machine long enough to go get a drink. I drank Coke and Dr. Pepper and I hated 'em. I hate 'em today. We had to buy it, of course. We couldn't leave to go to the bathroom, 'cause it was way the heck over there.

We were awarded the navy E for excellence. We were just so proud of that E. It was like we were a big family, and we hugged and kissed each other. They had the navy band out there celebrating us. We were so proud of ourselves.

First time my mother ever worked at anything except in the fields—first real job Mamma ever had. It was a big break in everybody's life. Once, Mamma woke up in the middle of the night to go to the bathroom and she saw the bus going down. She said, "Oh my goodness, I've overslept." She jerked her clothes on, throwed her lunch in the bag, and was out on the corner, ready to go, when Boy Blue, our driver, said, "Honey, this is the wrong shift." Mamma wasn't supposed to be there until six in the morning. She never lived that down. She would have enjoyed telling you that.

My world was really very small. When we came from Oklahoma to Paducah, that was like a journey to the center of the earth. It was during the Depression and you did good having bus fare to get across town. The war just widened my world. Especially after I came up to Michigan. My grandfather went up to Jackson, Michigan, after he retired from the railroad. He wrote back and told us we could make twice as much in the war plants in Jackson. We did. We made ninety dollars a week. We did some kind of testing for airplane radios.

Ohh, I met all those wonderful Polacks. They were the first people I'd ever known that were any different from me. A whole new world just opened up. I learned to drink beer like crazy with 'em. They were all very union-conscious. I learned a lot of things that I didn't even know existed.

LETTERS, TELEGRAMS, AND SPEECHES

Lusitania *Note (1915)*

Commentary

The 1914 naval blockade by British forces nearly stopped the flow of supplies to Germany. As a result, in 1915 Germany announced that it would sink any ship found in the waters off Britain. On May 7, 1915, a German submarine sank the British passenger liner *Lusitania*, killing more than one thousand people (including 128 Americans). The American government's indignation was expressed in the following note from Secretary of State William Jennings Bryan (1860–1925), to be delivered to the German minister of foreign affairs.

Washington, May 13, 1915.

Please call on the Minister of Foreign Affairs and after reading to him this communication leave with him a copy.

In view of recent acts of the German authorities in violation of American rights on the high seas which culminated in the torpedoing and sinking of the British steamship *Lusitania* on May 7, 1915, by which over 100 American citizens lost their lives, it is clearly wise and desirable that the Government of the United States and the Imperial German Government should come to a clear and full understanding as to the grave situation which has resulted.

The sinking of the British passenger steamer *Falaba* by a German submarine on March 28, through which Leon C. Thrasher, an American citizen, was drowned; the attack on April 28 on the American vessel *Cushing* by a German aeroplane; the torpedoing on May 1 of the American vessel *Gulflight* by a German submarine, as a result of which two or more American citizens met their death; and, finally, the torpedoing and sinking of the steamship *Lusitania,* constitute a series of events which the Government of the United States has observed with growing concern, distress, and amazement.

Recalling the humane and enlightened attitude hitherto assumed by the Imperial German Government in matters of international right, and particularly with regard to the freedom of the seas; having learned to recognize the German views and the German influence in the field of international obligation as always engaged upon the side of justice and humanity; and having understood the instructions of the Imperial German Government to its naval commanders to be upon the same plane of humane action prescribed by the naval codes of other nations, the Government of the United States was loath to believe—it can not now bring itself to believe—that these acts, so absolutely contrary to the rules, the practices, and the spirit of modern warfare, could have the countenance or sanction of that great Government. It feels it to be its duty, therefore, to address the Imperial German Government concerning them with the utmost frankness and in the earnest hope that it is not mistaken in expecting action on the part of the Imperial German Government which will correct the unfortunate impressions which have been created and vindicate once more the position of that Government with regard to the sacred freedom of the seas.

The Government of the United States has been apprised that the Imperial German Government considered themselves obliged by the extraordinary circumstances of the present war and the measures adopted by their adversaries in seeking to cut Germany off from all commerce, to adopt methods of retaliation which go much beyond the ordinary methods of warfare at sea, in the proclamation of a war zone from which they have warned neutral ships to keep away. This Government has already taken occasion to inform the Imperial German Government that it can not admit the adoption of such measures or such a warning of danger to operate as in any degree an abbreviation of the rights of American shipmasters or of American citizens bound on lawful errands as passengers on merchant ships of belligerent nationality; and that it must hold the Imperial German Government to a strict accountability for any infringement of those rights, intentional or incidental. It does not understand the Imperial German Government to question those rights. It assumes, on the contrary, that the Imperial Government accept, as of course, the rule that the lives of noncombatants, whether they be of neutral citizenship or citizens of one of the nations at war, can not lawfully or rightfully be put in jeopardy by the capture or destruction of an unarmed merchantman, and recognize also, as all other nations do, the obligation to take the usual precaution of visit and search to ascertain whether a suspected merchantman is in fact of belligerent nationality or is in fact carrying contraband of war under a neutral flag.

The Government of the United States, therefore, desires to call the attention of the Imperial German Government with the utmost earnestness to the fact that the objection to their present method of attack against the trade of their enemies lies in the practical impossibility of employing submarines in the destruction of commerce without disregarding those rules of fairness, reason, justice, and humanity which all modern opinion regards as imperative. It is practically impossible for the officers of a submarine to visit a merchantman at sea and examine her papers and cargo. It is practically impossible for them to make a prize of her; and, if they can not put a prize crew on board of her, they can not sink her without leaving her crew and all on board of her the mercy of the sea in her small boats. These facts it is understood the Imperial German Government frankly admit. We are informed that in the instances of which we have spoken time enough for even that poor measure of safety was not given, and in at least two of the cases cited not so much as a warning was received. Manifestly submarines can not be used against merchantmen, as the last few weeks have shown, without an inevitable violation of many sacred principles of justice and humanity.

American citizens act within their indisputable rights in taking their ships and in traveling wherever their legitimate business calls them upon the high seas, and exercise those rights in what should be the well-justified confidence that their lives will not be endangered by acts done in clear violation of universally acknowledged international obligations, and certainly in the confidence that their own Government will sustain them in the exercise of their rights.

There was recently published in the newspapers of the United States, I regret to inform the Imperial German Government, a formal warning, purporting to come from the Imperial German Embassy at Washington, addressed to the people of the United States, and stating, in effect, that any citizen of the United States who exercised his right of free travel upon the seas would do so at his peril if his journey should take him within the zone of waters within which the Imperial German Navy was using submarines against the commerce of Great Britain and France, notwithstanding the respectful but very earnest protest of his Government, the Government of the United States. I do not refer to this for the purpose of calling the attention of the Imperial German Government at this time to the surprising irregularity of a communication from the Imperial German Embassy at Washington addressed to the people of the United States through the newspapers, but only for the purpose of pointing out that no warning that an unlawful and inhumane act will be committed can possibly be accepted as an excuse or palliation for that act or as an abatement of the responsibility for its commission.

Long acquainted as this Government has been with the character of the Imperial German Government and with the high principles of equity by which they have in the past been actuated and guided, the Government of the United States can not believe that the commanders of the vessels which committed these acts of lawlessness did so except under a misapprehension of the orders issued by the Imperial German naval authorities. It takes it for granted that, at least within the practical possibilities of every such case, the commanders even of submarines were expected to do nothing that would involve the lives of noncombatants or the safety of neutral ships, even at the cost of failing of their object of capture or destruction. It confidently expects, therefore, that the Imperial German Government will disavow the acts of which the Government of the United States complains, that they will make reparation so far as reparation is possible for injuries which are without measure, and that they will take immediate steps to prevent the recurrence of anything so obviously subversive of the principles of warfare for which the Imperial German Government have in the past so wisely and so firmly contended.

The Government and people of the United States look to the Imperial German Government for just, prompt, and enlightened action in this vital matter with the greater confidence because the United States and Germany are bound together not only by special ties of friendship but also by the explicit stipulations of the treaty of 1828 between the United States and the Kingdom of Prussia.

Expressions of regret and offers of reparation in the case of the destruction of neutral ships sunk by mistake, while they may satisfy international obligations, if no loss of life results, can not justify or excuse a practice, the natural and necessary effect of which is to subject neutral nations and neutral persons to new and immeasurable risks.

The Imperial German Government will not expect the Government of the United States to omit any word or any act necessary to the performance of its sacred duty of maintaining the rights of the United States and its citizens and of safeguarding their free exercise and enjoyment.

BRYAN.

Against the Declaration of War (1917)

Source: *Congressional Record*, (April 4, 1917) 65th Congress, 1st Session, Vol. 55, pp. 225-34.

Commentary

Two days after President Woodrow Wilson (1856–1924) asked Congress for a formal declaration of war against Germany, Senator Robert M. La Follette (1855–1925), Republican of Wisconsin, gave a speech against U.S. intervention. It is excerpted below. La Follette argued that the war would be fought by poor Americans while benefiting the wealthy. He criticized Wilson's argument that this was a war of American democracy against Prussian (German) autocracy by pointing out that Great Britain is a hereditary monarchy with a landed aristocracy and limited suffrage. He asked Wilson and those supporting American entry to allow a democratic vote to be taken that would let American citizens decide the issue. La Follette also attacked the Wilson administration's bills that would soon become the Espionage Act and the Selective Service Act, which allowed for repression of opponents to the war and the nation's first effective military draft, respectively.

Although the vote in both houses of Congress was overwhelmingly in favor of a declaration of war, a small group of dissenters, including isolationists and independent Progressives in the Midwest such as La Follette, spoke out forcefully, making points that few politicians in favor of the war either addressed or answered fully.

. . . The poor, sir, who are the ones called upon to rot in the trenches, have no organized power, have no press to voice their will upon this question of peace or war; but, oh, Mr. President, at some time they will be heard. I hope and I believe they will be heard in an orderly and a peaceful way. I think they may be heard from before long. I think, sir, if we take this step, when the people to-day who are staggering under the burden of supporting families at the present prices of the necessaries of life find those prices multiplied, when they are raised a hundred percent, or 200 percent, as they will be quickly, aye, sir, when beyond that those who pay taxes come to have their taxes doubled and again doubled to pay the interest on the nontaxable bonds held by Morgan and his combinations, which have been issued to meet this war, there will come an awakening; they will have their day and they will be heard. It will be as certain and as inevitable as the return of the tides, and as resistless, too. . . .

Just a word of comment more upon one of the points in the President's address. He says that this is a war "for the things which we have always carried nearest to our hearts—for democracy, for the right of those who submit to authority to have a voice in their own government." In many places throughout the address is this exalted sentiment given expression.

It is a sentiment peculiarly calculated to appeal to American hearts and, when accompanied by acts consistent with it, is certain to receive our support; but in this same connection, and strangely enough, the President says that we have become convinced that the German Government as it now exists—"Prussian autocracy" he calls it—can never again maintain friendly relations with us. His expression is that "Prussian autocracy was not and could never be our friend," and repeatedly throughout the address the suggestion is made that if the German people would overturn their Government it would probably be the way to peace. So true is this that the dispatches from London all hailed the message of the President as sounding the death knell of Germany's Government.

But the President proposes alliance with Great Britain, which, however liberty-loving its people, is a hereditary monarchy, with a hereditary ruler, with a hereditary House of Lords, with a hereditary landed system, with a limited and restricted suffrage for one class and a multiplied suffrage power for another, and with grinding industrial conditions for all the wageworkers. The President has not suggested that we make our support of Great Britain conditional to her granting home rule to Ireland, or Egypt, or India. We rejoice in the establishment of a democracy in Russia, but it will hardly be contended that if Russia was still an autocratic Government, we would not be asked to enter this alliance with her just the same. Italy and the lesser powers of Europe, Japan in the Orient; in fact, all of the countries with whom we are to enter into alliance, except France and newly revolutionized Russia, are still of the old order—and it will be generally conceded that no one of them has done as much for its people in the solution of municipal problems and in securing social and industrial reforms as Germany.

Is it not a remarkable democracy which leagues itself with allies already far overmatching in strength the German nation and holds out to such beleaguered nation the hope of peace only at the price of giving up their Government? I am not talking now of the merits or demerits of any government, but I am speaking of a profession of democracy that is linked in action with the most brutal and domineering use of autocratic power. Are the people of this country being so well represented in this war movement that we need to go abroad to give other people control of their governments? Will the President and the supporters of this war bill submit it to a vote of the people before the declaration of war goes into

effect? Until we are willing to do that, it illy becomes us to offer as an excuse for our entry into the war the unsupported claim that this war was forced upon the German people by their Government "without their previous knowledge or approval."

Who has registered the knowledge or approval of the American people of the course this Congress is called upon to take in declaring war upon Germany? Submit the question to the people, you who support it. You who support it dare not do it, for you know that by a vote of more than ten to one the American people as a body would register their declaration against it.

In the sense that this war is being forced upon our people without their knowing why and without their approval, and that wars are usually forced upon all peoples in the same way, there is some truth in the statement; but I venture to say that the response which the German people have made to the demands of this war shows that it has a degree of popular support which the war upon which we are entering has not and never will have among our people. The espionage bills, the conscription bills, and other forcible military measures which we understand are being ground out of the war machine in this country is the complete proof that those responsible for this war fear that it has no popular support and that armies sufficient to satisfy the demand of the entente allies can not be recruited by voluntary enlistments. . . .

Excerpt from Wilson Asks Congress for War (1917)

Source: Wilson, Woodrow. "War Message to Congress." 65th Cong., 1st sess. *Congressional Record* (April 2, 1917), vol. 55, pp. 102–4.

Commentary

On the evening of April 2, 1917, President Woodrow Wilson delivered the speech excerpted below to a joint session of Congress. He asked for a declaration of war. He noted that the German government's recent decision to resume unrestricted submarine warfare against Great Britain, France, and its enemies in the Mediterranean Sea marked a departure from previous German restraint in the face of persistent U.S. diplomatic objections to the loss of American lives and property on the high seas. Wilson's strong use of condemnatory language such as "extraordinary," "cruel and unmanly," and "ruthlessly" suggests his anger at what led him to ask Congress, which has the sole power to take the nation into a war, to make such a declaration against Germany. He equated the loss of American lives and property with an assault on "all mankind." He claimed that U.S. entry into the war would be to defend the rights of neutral nations, international law, and all civilized nations.

On the third of February last I officially laid before you the extraordinary announcement of the Imperial German Government that on and after the first day of February it was its purpose to put aside all restraints of law or of humanity and use its submarines to sink every vessel that sought to approach either the ports of Great Britain and Ireland or the western coasts of Europe or any of the ports controlled by the enemies of Germany within the Mediterranean. That had seemed to be the object of the German submarine warfare earlier in the war, but since April of last year the Imperial Government had somewhat restrained the commanders of its undersea craft in conformity with its promise then given to us that passenger boats should not be sunk and that due warning would be given to all other vessels which its submarines might seek to destroy, when no resistance was offered or escape attempted, and care taken that their crews were given at least a fair chance to save their lives in their open boats. The precautions taken were meagre and haphazard enough, as was proved in distressing instance after instance in the progress of the cruel and unmanly business, but a certain degree of restraint was observed. The new policy has swept every restriction aside. Vessels of every kind, whatever their flag, their character, their cargo, their destination, their errand, have been ruthlessly sent to the bottom without warning and without thought of help or mercy for those on board, the vessels of friendly neutrals along with those of belligerents. Even hospital ships and ships carrying relief to the sorely bereaved and stricken people of Belgium, though the latter were provided with safe conduct through the prescribed areas by the German Government itself and were distinguished by unmistakable marks of identity, have been sunk with the same reckless lack of compassion or of principle.

I was for a little while unable to believe that such things would in fact be done by any government that had hitherto subscribed to the humane practices of civilized nations. International law had its origin in the attempt to set up some law which would be respected and observed upon the seas, where no nation had right of dominion and where lay the free highways of the world. By painful stage after stage has that law been built up, with meagre enough results, indeed, after all was accomplished that could be accomplished, but always with a clear view, at least, of what the heart and conscience of mankind demanded. This minimum of right the German Government has swept aside under the plea of retaliation and necessity and because it had no weapons which it could use at sea except these which it is impossible to employ as it is employing them without throwing to the winds all scruples of humanity or of respect for the understandings that were supposed to underlie the intercourse of the world. I am not now thinking of the loss of property involved, immense and serious as that is, but only of the wanton and wholesale destruction of the lives of noncombatants, men, women, and children, engaged in pursuits which have always, even in the darkest periods of modern history, been deemed innocent and legitimate. Property can be paid for; the lives of peaceful and innocent people cannot be. The present German submarine warfare against commerce is a warfare against mankind.

It is a war against all nations. American ships have been sunk, American lives taken, in ways which it has stirred us very deeply to learn of, but the ships and people of other neutral and friendly nations have been sunk and overwhelmed in the waters in the same way. There has been no discrimination. The challenge is to all mankind. Each nation must decide for itself how it will meet it. The choice we make for ourselves must be made with a moderation of counsel and a temperateness of judgment befitting our character and our motives as a nation. We must put excited feeling away. Our motive will not be revenge or the victorious assertion of the physical might of the nation, but only the vindication of right, of human right, of which we are only a single champion. . . .

With a profound sense of the solemn and even tragical character of the step I am taking and of the grave responsibilities which it involves, but in unhesitating obedience to what I deem my constitutional duty, I advise that the Congress declare the recent course of the Imperial German Government to be in fact nothing less than war against the government and people of the United States; that it formally accept the status of belligerent which has thus been thrust upon it; and that it take immediate steps not only to put the country in a more thorough state of defense but also to exert all its power and employ all its resources to bring the Government of the German Empire to terms and end the war. . . .

While we do these things, these deeply momentous things, let us be very clear, and make very clear to all the world what our motives and our objects are. My own thought has not been driven from its habitual and normal course by the unhappy events of the last two months, and I do not believe that the thought of the nation has been altered or clouded by them. I have exactly the same things in mind now that I had in mind when I addressed the Senate on the twenty-second of January last; the same that I had in mind when I addressed the Congress on the third of February and on the twenty-sixth of February. Our object now, as then, is to vindicate the principles of peace and justice in the life of the world as against selfish and autocratic power and to set up amongst the really free and self-governed peoples of the world such a concert of purpose and of action as will henceforth ensure the observance of those principles. Neutrality is no longer feasible or desirable where the peace of the world is involved and the freedom of its peoples, and the menace to that peace and freedom lies in the existence of autocratic governments backed by organized force which is controlled wholly by their will, not by the will of their people. We have seen the last of neutrality in such circumstances. We are at the beginning of an age in which it will be insisted that the same standards of conduct and of responsibility for wrong done shall be observed among nations and their governments that are observed among the individual citizens of civilized states.

We have no quarrel with the German people. We have no feeling towards them but one of sympathy and friendship. It was not upon their impulse that their government acted in entering this war. It was not with their previous knowledge or approval. It was a war determined upon as wars used to be determined upon in the old, unhappy days when peoples were nowhere consulted by their rulers and wars were provoked and waged in the interest of dynasties or of little groups of ambitious men who were accustomed to use their fellow men as pawns and tools. Self-governed nations do not fill their neighbour states with spies or set the course of intrigue to bring about some critical posture of affairs which will give them an opportunity to strike and make conquest. Such designs can be successfully worked out only under cover and where no one has the right to ask questions. Cunningly contrived plans of deception or aggression, carried, it may be, from generation to generation, can be worked out and kept from the light only within the privacy of courts or behind the carefully guarded confidences of a narrow and privileged class. They are happily impossible where public opinion commands and insists upon full information concerning all the nation's affairs.

A steadfast concert for peace can never be maintained except by a partnership of democratic nations. No autocratic government could be trusted to keep faith within it or observe its covenants. It must be a league of honour, a partnership of opinion. Intrigue would eat its vitals away; the plottings of inner circles who could plan what they would and render account to no one would be a corruption seated at its very heart. Only free peoples can hold their purpose and their honour steady to a common end and prefer the interests of mankind to any narrow interest of their own.

Does not every American feel that assurance has been added to our hope for the future peace of the world by the wonderful and heartening things that have been happening within the last few weeks in Russia? Russia was known by those who knew it best to have been always in fact democratic at heart, in all the vital habits of her thought, in all the intimate relationships of her people that spoke their natural instinct, their habitual attitude towards life. The autocracy that crowned the summit of her political structure, long as it had stood and terrible as was the reality of its power, was not in fact Russian in origin, character, or purpose; and now it has been shaken off and the great, generous Russian people have been added in all their naive majesty and might to the forces that are fighting for freedom in the world, for justice, and for peace. Here is a fit partner for a League of Honour.

One of the things that has served to convince us that the Prussian autocracy was not and could never be our friend is that from the very outset of the present war it has filled our unsuspecting communities and even our offices of government with spies and set criminal intrigues everywhere afoot against our national unity of counsel, our peace within and without, our industries and our commerce. Indeed it is now evident that its spies were here even before the war began; and it is unhappily not a matter of conjecture but a fact proved in our courts of justice that the intrigues which have more than once come perilously near to disturbing the peace and dislocating the industries of the country have been carried on at the instigation, with the support, and even under the personal direction of official agents of the Imperial Government accredited to the Government of the United States. Even in checking these things and trying to extirpate them we have sought to put the most generous interpretation possible upon them because we knew that their source lay, not in any hostile feelings or purpose of the German people towards us (who were, no doubt as ignorant of them as we ourselves were), but only in the selfish designs of a Government that did what it pleased and told its people nothing. But they have played their part in serving to convince us at last that that Government entertains no real friendship for us and means to act against our peace and security at its convenience. That it means to stir up enemies against us at our very doors the intercepted note to the German Minister at Mexico City is eloquent evidence.

We are accepting this challenge of hostile purpose because we know that in such a government, following such methods, we can never have a friend; and that in the presence of its organized power, always lying in wait to accomplish we know not what purpose, there can be no assured security for the democratic governments of the world. We are now about to accept gauge of battle with this natural foe to liberty and shall, if necessary, spend the whole force of the nation to check and nullify its pretensions and its power. We are glad, now that we see the facts with no veil of false pretence about them, to fight thus for the ultimate peace of the world and for the liberation of its peoples, the German peoples included; for the rights of nations great and small and the privilege of men everywhere to choose their way of life and of obedience. The world must be made safe for democracy. Its peace must be planted upon the tested foundations of political liberty. We have no selfish ends to serve. We desire no conquest, no dominion. We seek no indemnities for ourselves, no material compensation for the sacrifices we shall freely make. We are but one of the champions of the rights of mankind. We shall be satisfied when those rights have been made as secure as the faith and the freedom of nations can make them. . . . We enter this war only where we are clearly forced into it because there are no other means of defending our rights.

It will be all the easier for us to conduct ourselves as belligerents in a high spirit of right and fairness because we act without animus, not in enmity towards a people or with the desire to bring any injury or disadvantage upon them, but only in armed opposition to an irresponsible government which has thrown aside all considerations of humanity and of right and is running amuck. We are, let me say again, the sincere friends of the German people, and shall desire nothing so much as the early re-establishment of intimate relations of mutual advantage between us,—however hard it may be for them, for the time being, to believe that this is spoken from our hearts. We have borne with their present government through all these bitter months because of that friendship,—exercising a patience and forbearance which would otherwise have been impossible. We shall, happily, still have an opportunity to prove that friendship in our daily attitude and actions towards the millions of men and women of German birth and native sympathy who live amongst us and share our life, and we shall be proud to prove it towards all who are in fact loyal to their neighbours and to the Government in the hour of test. They are, most of them, as true and loyal Americans as if they had never known any other fealty or allegiance. They will be prompt to stand with us in rebuking and restraining the few who may be of a different mind and purpose. If there should be disloyalty, it will be dealt with with a firm hand of stern repression; but, if it lifts its head at all, it will lift it only here and there and without countenance except from a lawless and malignant few.

It is a distressing and oppressive duty, Gentlemen of the Congress, which I have performed in thus addressing you. There are, it may be, many months of fiery trial and sacrifice ahead of us. It is a fearful thing to lead this great peaceful people into war, into the most terrible and disastrous of all wars, civilization itself seeming to be in the balance. But the right is more precious than peace, and we shall fight for the things which we have always carried nearest our hearts, for democracy, for the right of those who submit to authority to have a voice in their own governments, for the rights and liberties of small nations, for a universal dominion of right by such a concert of free people as shall bring peace and safety to all nations and make the world itself at last free. To such a task we can dedicate our lives and our fortunes, every-

thing that we are and everything that we have, with the pride of those who know that the day has come when America is privileged to spend her blood, and her might for the principles that gave her birth and happiness and the peace which she has treasured. God helping her, she can do no other.

Zimmermann Telegraph (1917)

Commentary

On February 23, 1917, British agents intercepted this note from the German foreign secretary, Arthur Zimmermann (1864–1940), to the German ambassador in Mexico. British intelligence turned over the decoded document to American officials in London, who sent it to Washington by the document below. Although the authenticity of the telegram was not established at the time, the American press was told of its existence, and its contents helped to push the United States closer to war with Germany.

London, 24 February 1917, 1 p.m.

For the President and the Secretary of State. Balfour had handed me the text of a cipher telegram from Zimmermann, German Secretary of State for Foreign Affairs, to the German Minister of Mexico, which was sent via Washington and relayed by Bernstorff on 19 January. You can probably obtain a copy of the text relayed by Bernstorff from the cable office in Washington. The first group is the number of the telegram, 130, and the second is 13042, indicating the number of the code used. The last group but two is 97556, which Zimmermann's signature. I shall send you by mail a copy of the cipher text and of the decode into German and meanwhile I give you the English translation as follows:

> We intend to begin on the 1st of February unrestricted submarine warfare. We shall endeavor in spite of this to keep the United States of America neutral. In the event of this not succeeding, we make Mexico a proposal of alliance on the following basis: make war together, make peace together, generous financial support and an understanding on our part that Mexico is to reconquer the lost territory in Texas, New Mexico, and Arizona. The settlement in detail is left to you. You will inform the President of the above most secretly as soon as the outbreak of war with the United States of America is certain and add the suggestion that he should, on his own initiative, invite Japan to immediate adherence and at the same time mediate between Japan and ourselves. Please call the President's attention to the fact that the ruthless employment of our submarines now offers the prospect of compelling England in a few months to make peace. Signed Zimmermann.

The receipt of this information has so greatly exercised the British Government that they have lost no time in communicating it to me to transmit to you, in order that our Government may be able without delay to make such disposition as may be necessary in view of the threatened invasion of our territory.

Early in the war, the British Government obtained possession of a copy of the German cipher code used in the above message and have made it their business to obtain copies of Bernstorff's cipher telegrams to Mexico, amongst others, which are sent back to London and deciphered here. This accounts for their being able to decipher this telegram from the German Government to their representative in Mexico and also for the delay from 19 January until now in their receiving information. This system has hitherto been a jealously guarded secret and is only divulged now to you by the British Government in view of the extraordinary circumstances and their friendly feeling towards the United States. They earnestly request that you will keep the source of your information and the British Government's method of obtaining it profoundly secret, but they put no prohibition on the publication of Zimmermann's telegram itself.

The copies of this and other telegrams were not obtained in Washington but were brought into Mexico.

I have thanked Balfour for the service his Government has rendered us and suggest that a private official message of thanks from our Government to him would be beneficial.

I am informed that this information has not yet been given to the Japanese Government but I think it not unlikely that when it reaches them they may make a public statement on it in order to clear up their position regarding the United States and prove their good faith to their Allies.

America's War Aims: The Fourteen Points (1918)

Commentary

Frustrated by the European Allies' unwillingness to specify their terms for peace in the Great War (later called World War I), President Woodrow Wilson outlined his own plan, later called simply the Fourteen Points, to a joint session of Congress on 8 January 1918. Essentially a foreign policy manifestation of American Progressivism, Wilson's vision of a "Peace Without Victory" articulated modern ideas of free trade, fair dealing, and self-determination, as well as the belief that morality, and not merely self-interest, ought to guide foreign affairs. The speech made Wilson an international hero, a towering figure on a crusade to restore the hope of progressives dashed on the tortured battlefields of the Great War. Unfortunately, the "general association of nations" called for in Wilson's last point was not to be. By 1919, the Congress had become fearful that membership in the League of Nations would subvert its power to declare war and might eventually entrap the United States in another foreign conflict. Wilson's European allies were often as reluctant, and soon the beleaguered president was forced to compromise on point after point. The Treaty of Versailles, which ended hostilities in the Great War, contains little either of the spirit or the matter of Wilson's original vision. Without the support of the United States, the League of Nations failed, and Wilson's fear of another war in Europe, this one more terrible than the last, was a mere twenty years away.

Gentlemen of the Congress:

. . . It will be our wish and purpose that the processes of peace, when they are begun, shall be absolutely open and that they shall involve and permit henceforth no secret understandings of any kind. The day of conquest and aggrandizement is gone by; so is also the day of secret covenants entered into in the interest of particular governments and likely at some unlooked-for moment to upset the peace of the world. It is this happy fact, now clear to the view of every public man whose thoughts do not still linger in an age that is dead and gone, which makes it possible for every nation whose purposes are consistent with justice and the peace of the world to avow now or at any other time the objects it has in view.

We entered this war because violations of right had occurred which touched us to the quick and made the life of our own people impossible unless they were corrected and the world secured once for all against their recurrence. What we demand in this war, therefore, is nothing peculiar to ourselves. It is that the world be made fit and safe to live in; and particularly that it be made safe for every peace-loving nation which, like our own, wishes to live its own life, determine its own institutions, be assured of justice and fair dealing by the other peoples of the world as against force and selfish aggression. All the peoples of the world are in effect partners in this interest, and for our own part we see very clearly that unless justice be done to others it will not be done to us. The program of the world's peace, therefore, is our program; and that program, the only possible program, as we see it, is this:

I. Open covenants of peace, openly arrived at, after which there shall be no private international understandings of any kind but diplomacy shall proceed always frankly and in the public view.

II. Absolute freedom of navigation upon the seas, outside territorial waters, alike in peace and in war, except as the seas may be closed in whole or in part by international action for the enforcement of international covenants.

III. The removal, so far as possible, of all economic barriers and the establishment of an equality of trade conditions among all the nations consenting to the peace and associating themselves for its maintenance.

IV. Adequate guarantees given and taken that national armaments will be reduced to the lowest point consistent with domestic safety.

V. A free, open-minded, and absolutely impartial adjustment of all colonial claims, based upon a strict observance of the principle that in determining all such questions of sovereignty the interests of the populations concerned must have equal weight with the equitable claims of the government whose title is to be determined.

VI. The evacuation of all Russian territory and such a settlement of all questions affecting Russia as will secure the best and freest cooperation of the other nations of the world in obtaining for her an unhampered and unembarrassed opportunity for the independent determination of her own political development and national policy and assure her of a sincere welcome into the society of free nations under institutions of her own choosing; and, more than a welcome, assistance also of every kind that she may need and may herself desire. The treatment accorded Russia by her sister nations in the months to come will be the acid test of their good will, of their comprehension of her needs as distinguished from their own interests, and of their intelligent and unselfish sympathy.

VII. Belgium, the whole world will agree, must be evacuated and restored, without any attempt to limit the sovereignty which she enjoys in common with all other free nations. No other single act will serve as this will serve to restore confidence among the nations in the laws which they have themselves set and determined for the government of their relations with one another. Without this healing act the whole structure and validity of international law is forever impaired.

VIII. All French territory should be freed and the invaded portions restored, and the wrong done to France by Prussia in 1871 in the matter of Alsace-Lorraine, which has unsettled the peace of the world for nearly fifty years, should be righted, in order that peace may once more be made secure in the interest of all.

IX. A readjustment of the frontiers of Italy should be effected along clearly recognizable lines of nationality.

X. The peoples of Austria-Hungary, whose place among the nations we wish to see safe-guarded and assured, should be accorded the freest opportunity of autonomous development.

XI. Rumania, Serbia, and Montenegro should be evacuated; occupied territories restored; Serbia accorded free and secure access to the sea; and the relations of the several Balkan states to one another determined by friendly counsel along historically established lines of allegiance and nationality; and international guarantees of the political and economic independence and territorial integrity of the several Balkan states should be entered into.

XII. The Turkish portions of the present Ottoman Empire should be assured a secure sovereignty, but the other nationalities which are now under Turkish rule should be assured an undoubted security of life and an absolutely unmolested opportunity of autonomous development, and the Dardanelles should be permanently opened as a free passage to the ships and commerce of all nations under international guarantees.

XIII. An independent Polish state should be erected which should include the territories inhabited by indisputably Polish populations, which should be assured a free and secure access to the sea, and whose political and economic independence and territorial integrity should be guaranteed by international covenant.

XIV. A general association of nations must be formed under specific covenants for the purpose of affording mutual guarantees of political independence and territorial integrity to great and small states alike.

In regard to these essential rectifications of wrong and assertions of right we feel ourselves to be intimate partners of all the governments and peoples associated together against the Imperialists. We cannot be separated in interest or divided in purpose. We stand together until the end.

For such arrangements and covenants we are willing to fight and to continue to fight until they are achieved; but only because we wish the right to prevail and desire a just and stable peace such as can be secured only by removing the chief provocations to war, which this program does not remove. We have no jealousy of German greatness, and there is nothing in this program that impairs it. We grudge her no achievement or distinction of learning or of pacific enterprise such as have made her record very bright and very enviable. We do not wish to injure her or to block in any way her legitimate influence or power. We do not wish to fight her either with arms or with hostile arrangements of trade if she is willing to associate herself with us and the other peace-loving nations of the world in covenants of justice and law and fair dealing. We wish her only to accept a place of equality among the peoples of the world,—the new world in which we now live,—instead of a place of mastery.

Neither do we presume to suggest to her any alteration or modification of her institutions. But it is necessary, we must frankly say, and necessary as a preliminary to any intelligent dealings with her on our part, that we should know whom her spokesmen speak for when they speak to us, whether for the Reichstag majority or for the military party and the men whose creed is imperial domination.

We have spoken now, surely, in terms too concrete to admit of any further doubt or question. An evident principle runs through the whole program I have outlined. It is the principle of justice to all peoples and nationalities, and their right to live on equal terms of liberty and safety with one another, whether they be strong or weak. Unless this principle be made its foundation no part of the structure of international justice can stand. The people of the United States could act upon no other principle; and to the vindication of this principle they are ready to devote their lives, their honor, and everything that they possess. The moral climax of this the culminating and final war for human liberty has come, and they are ready to put their own strength, their own highest purpose, their own integrity and devotion to the test.

Roosevelt's Fireside Chat on the Bank Crisis (1933)

Commentary

On March 12, 1933, his ninth day in office, President Franklin D. Roosevelt (1882–1945) delivered the first of a series of radio addresses to the nation. They were quickly dubbed "fireside chats," because people supposedly gathered around the hearth to listen to the president speak.

In the four months between Roosevelt's election, in November 1932, and his inauguration, on March 4, 1933, the American banking system had collapsed. When a few banks went bankrupt, people everywhere quickly lost confidence in all banks and began withdrawing their savings in droves. The banks, whose business it was to lend out the money kept on deposit in personal accounts, did not have enough cash on hand to return to depositors the money they had placed in the banks. Nor could they quickly call in loans to businesses and individuals. The result was that more and more banks went under, until, by March 1933, thirty-eight governors had suspended all banking activity in their states.

On March 5, the day after he was sworn in as president, Roosevelt called a "bank holiday," ordering all banks closed for a few days. He did this on rather shaky authority, citing the Trading with the Enemy Act, a 1917 law passed during World War I (1914–1918) to allow the president to suspend business activities that benefited an enemy in wartime. If it was not entirely legal, it was nonetheless an appropriate course to take, for the Great Depression was, as Roosevelt said in his inaugural address, very much like an attack by a hostile enemy.

The bank holiday gave people time to cool off—and it gave Roosevelt time to send a draft of new legislation to Congress. On March 12, the day before the banks were scheduled to reopen, Roosevelt went on radio to speak directly to the people. The audience was estimated at 60 million people. His reassuring words (reproduced here as text and in an audio recording from the Franklin D. Roosevelt Library at Hyde Park, New York) convinced the overwhelming majority of his listeners that they could trust the banks. More important, Roosevelt convinced people they could trust the

government to support the banks. (Government insurance for individual deposits was still three months in the future.) When the banks reopened the next day, deposits exceeded withdrawals, surprising many and stabilizing the economy in the short term.

I want to talk for a few minutes with the people of the United States about banking—with the comparatively few who understand the mechanics of banking but more particularly with the overwhelming majority who use banks for the making of deposits and the drawing of checks. I want to tell you what has been done in the last few days, why it was done, and what the next steps are going to be. I recognize that the many proclamations from State Capitols and from Washington, the legislation, the Treasury regulations, etc., couched for the most part in banking and legal terms should be explained for the benefit of the average citizen. I owe this in particular because of the fortitude and good temper with which everybody has accepted the inconvenience and hardships of the banking holiday. I know that when you understand what we in Washington have been about I shall continue to have your cooperation as fully as I have had your sympathy and help during the past week.

First of all let me state the simple fact that when you deposit money in a bank the bank does not put the money into a safe deposit vault. It invests your money in many different forms of credit-bonds, commercial paper, mortgages and many other kinds of loans. In other words, the bank puts your money to work to keep the wheels of industry and of agriculture turning around. A comparatively small part of the money you put into the bank is kept in currency—an amount which in normal times is wholly sufficient to cover the cash needs of the average citizen. In other words the total amount of all the currency in the country is only a small fraction of the total deposits in all of the banks.

What, then, happened during the last few days of February and the first few days of March? Because of undermined confidence on the part of the public, there was a general rush by a large portion of our population to turn bank deposits into currency or gold. —A rush so great that the soundest banks could not get enough currency to meet the demand. The reason for this was that on the spur of the moment it was, of course, impossible to sell perfectly sound assets of a bank and convert them into cash except at panic prices far below their real value.

By the afternoon of March 3 scarcely a bank in the country was open to do business. Proclamations temporarily closing them in whose or in part had been issued by the Governors in almost all the states.

It was then that I issued the proclamation providing for the nation-wide bank holiday, and this was the first step in the Government's reconstruction of our financial and economic fabric.

The second step was the legislation promptly and patriotically passed by the Congress confirming my proclamation and broadening my powers so that it became possible in view of the requirement of time to entend [*sic*] the holiday and lift the ban of that holiday gradually. This law also gave authority to develop a program of rehabilitation of our banking facilities. I want to tell our citizens in every part of the Nation that the national Congress—Republicans and Democrats alike—showed by this action a devotion to public welfare and a realization of the emergency and the necessity for speed that it is difficult to match in our history.

The third stage has been the series of regulations permitting the banks to continue their functions to take care of the distribution of food and household necessities and the payment of payrolls.

This bank holiday while resulting in many cases in great inconvenience is affording us the opportunity to supply the currency necessary to meet the situation. No sound bank is a dollar worse off than it was when it closed its doors last Monday. Neither is any bank which may turn out not to be in a position for immediate opening. The new law allows the twelve Federal Reserve banks to issue additional currency on good assets and thus the banks which reopen will be able to meet every legitimate call. The new currency is being sent out by the Bureau of Engraving and Printing in large volume to every part of the country. It is sound currency because it is backed by actual, good assets.

As a result we start tomorrow, Monday, with the opening of banks in the twelve Federal Reserve bank cities—those banks which on first examination by the Treasury have already been found to be all right. This will be followed on Tuesday by the resumption of all their functions by banks already found to be sound in cities where there are recognized clearing houses. That means about 250 cities of the United States.

On Wednesday and succeeding days banks in smaller places all through the country will resume business, subject, of course, to the Government's physical ability to complete its survey. It is necessary that the reopening of banks be extended over a period in order to permit the banks to make applications for necessary loans, to obtain currency needed to meet their requirements and to enable the Government to make common sense checkups. Let me make it clear to you that if your bank does not open the first day you are by no means justified in believing that it will not open. A bank that opens on one of the subsequent days is in exactly the same status as the bank that opens tomorrow.

I know that many people are worrying about State banks not members of the Federal Reserve System. These banks can and will receive assistance from members banks and from the Reconstruction Finance Corporation. These state banks are following the same course as the national banks except that they get their licenses to resume business from the state authorities, and these authorities have been asked by the Secretary of the Treasury to permit their good banks to open up on the same schedule as the national banks. I am confident that the state banking departments will be as careful as the National Government in the policy relating to the opening of banks and will follow the same broad policy. It is possible that when the banks resume a very few people who have not recovered from their fear may again begin withdrawals. Let me make it clear that the banks will take care of all needs—and it is my belief that hoarding during the past week has become an exceedingly unfashionable pastime. It needs no prophet to tell you that when the people find that they can get their money—that they can get it when they want it for all legitimate purposes—the phantom of fear will soon be laid. People will again be glad to have their money where it will be safely taken care of and where they can use it conveniently at any time. I can assure you that it is safer to keep your money in a reopened bank than under the mattress.

The success of our whole great national program depends, of course, upon the cooperation of the public—on its intelligent support and use of a reliable system.

Remember that the essential accomplishment of the new legislation is that it makes it possible for banks more readily to convert their assets into cash than was the case before. More liberal provision has been made for banks to borrow on these assets at the Reserve Banks and more liberal provision has also been made for issuing currency on the security of those good assets. This currency is not fiat currency. It is issued only on adequate security—and every good bank has an abundance of such security.

One more point before I close. There will be, of course, some banks unable to reopen without being reorganized. The new law allows the Government to assist in making these reorganizations quickly and effectively and even allows the Government to subscribe to at least a part of new capital which may be required.

I hope you can see from this elemental recital of what your government is doing that there is nothing complex, or radical in the process.

We had a bad banking situation. Some of our bankers had shown themselves either incompetent or dishonest in their handling of the people's funds. They had used the money entrusted to them in speculations and unwise loans. This was of course not true in the vast majority of our banks but it was true in enough of them to shock the people for a time into a sense of insecurity and to put them into a frame of mind where they did not differentiate, but seemed to assume that the acts of a comparative few had tainted them all. It was the Government's job to straighten out this situation and do it as quickly as possible—and the job is being performed.

I do not promise you that every bank will be reopened or that individual losses will not be suffered, but there will be no losses that possibly could be avoided; and there would have been more and greater losses had we continued to drift. I can even promise you salvation for some at least of the sorely pressed banks. We shall be engaged not merely in reopening sound banks but in the creation of sound banks through reorganization. It has been wonderful to me to catch the note of confidence from all over the country. I can never be sufficiently grateful to the people for the loyal support they have given me in their acceptance of the judgment that has dictated our course, even though all of our processes may not have seemed clear to them.

After all there is an element in the readjustment of our financial system more important than currency, more important than gold, and that is the confidence of the people. Confidence and courage are the essentials of success in carrying out our plan. You people must have faith; you must not be stampeded by rumors or guesses. Let us unite in banishing fear. We have provided the machinery to restore our financial system; it is up to you to support and make it work.

It is your problem no less than it is mine. Together we cannot fail.

Franklin D. Roosevelt's First Inaugural Address (1933)

Commentary

President Franklin D. Roosevelt (1882–1945) delivered a powerful speech to a dispirited nation when he took office on March 4, 1933. His inaugural address sketched a vision of an active federal government that would reach beyond its historical limits to combat the crippling economic crisis of the Great Depression.

Roosevelt opened his address formally:

"I am certain that my fellow Americans expect that on my induction into the Presidency I will address them with a candor and a decision which the present situation of our Nation impels. This is preeminently the time to speak the truth, the whole truth, frankly and boldly. Nor need we shrink from honestly facing conditions in our country today. This great Nation will endure as it has endured, will revive and will prosper. So, first of all, let me assert my firm belief that the only thing we have to fear is fear itself, nameless, unreasoning, unjustified terror which paralyzes needed efforts to convert retreat into advance."

The latter part of his opening—"the only thing we have to fear is fear itself"—has become the very symbol of the combative spirit with which Roosevelt led the nation in the early days of his administration. However, in 1933 the phrase echoed out to the anxious crowd that had gathered to hear the new president. There was no applause or recognition from the people. In fact, it took some time for the cadences of Roosevelt's speech to produce a response from the audience, whose silence was followed by timid applause, and then, at length, by shouts of approval.

Incidentally, Roosevelt was the last president inaugurated in March. On March 2, 1932, one year before he took office, Congress passed legislation that became the Twentieth Amendment to the U.S. Constitution. That amendment, declared ratified on February 6, 1933, eliminated a "lame duck" congressional session (a winter session in which ousted legislators continue to hold their seats) and specified the beginning of the presidential term: January 20. The measure was a direct response to the depression. In that time of crisis, it was felt that the four-month period between national elections in November and the swearing in of newly elected representatives was simply too long.

I am certain that my fellow Americans expect that on my induction into the Presidency I will address them with a candor and a decision which the present situation of our Nation impels. This is preeminently the time to speak the truth, the whole truth, frankly and boldly. Nor need we shrink from honestly facing conditions in our country today. This great Nation will endure as it has endured, will revive and will prosper. So, first of all, let me assert my firm belief that the only thing we have to fear is fear itself, nameless, unreasoning, unjustified terror which paralyzes needed efforts to convert retreat into advance. In every dark hour of our national life a leadership of frankness and vigor has met with that understanding and support of the people themselves which is essential to victory. I am convinced that you will again give that support to leadership in these critical days.

In such a spirit on my part and on yours we face our common difficulties. They concern, thank God, only material things. Values have shrunken to fantastic levels; taxes have risen; our ability to pay has fallen; government of all kinds is faced by serious curtailment of income; the means of exchange are frozen in the currents of trade; the withered leaves of industrial enterprise lie on every side; farmers find no markets for their produce; the savings of many years in thousands of families are gone.

More important, a host of unemployed citizens face the grim problem of existence, and an equally great number toil with little return. Only a foolish optimist can deny the dark realities of the moment.

Yet our distress comes from no failure of substance. We are stricken by no plague of locusts. Compared with the perils which our forefathers conquered because they believed and were not afraid, we have still much to be thankful for. Nature still offers her bounty and human efforts have multiplied it. Plenty is at our doorstep, but a generous use of it languishes in the very sight of the supply. Primarily this is because the rulers of the exchange of mankind's goods have failed, through their own stubbornness and their own incompetence, have admitted their failure, and abdicated. Practices of the unscrupulous money changers stand indicted in the court of public opinion, rejected by the hearts and minds of men.

True they have tried, but their efforts have been cast in the pattern of an outworn tradition. Faced by failure of credit they have proposed only the lending of more money. Stripped of the lure of profit by which to induce our people to follow their false leadership, they have resorted to exhortations, pleading tearfully for restored confidence. They know only the rules of a generation of self-seekers. They have no vision, and when there is no vision the people perish.

The money changers have fled from their high seats in the temple of our civilization. We may now restore that temple to the ancient truths. The measure of the restoration lies in the extent to which we apply social values more noble than mere monetary profit.

Happiness lies not in the mere possession of money; it lies in the joy of achievement, in the thrill of creative effort. The joy and moral stimulation of work no longer must be forgotten in the mad chase of evanescent profits. These dark days will be worth all they cost us if they teach us that our true destiny is not to be ministered unto but to minister to ourselves and to our fellow men.

Recognition of the falsity of material wealth as the standard of success goes hand in hand with the abandonment of the false belief that public office and high political position are to be valued only by the standards of pride of place and personal profit; and there must be an end to a conduct in banking and in business which too often has given to a sacred trust the likeness of callous and selfish wrongdoing. Small wonder that confidence languishes, for it thrives only on honesty, on honor, on the sacredness of obligations, on faithful protection, on unselfish performance; without them it cannot live.

Restoration calls, however, not for changes in ethics alone. This Nation asks for action, and action now.

Our greatest primary task is to put people to work. This is no unsolvable problem if we face it wisely and courageously. It can be accomplished in part by direct recruiting by the Government itself, treating the task as we would treat the emergency of a war, but at the same time, through this employment, accomplishing greatly needed projects to stimulate and reorganize the use of our natural resources.

Hand in hand with this we must frankly recognize the overbalance of population in our industrial centers and, by engaging on a national scale in a redistribution, endeavor to provide a better use of the land for those best fitted for the land. The task can be helped by definite efforts to raise the values of agricultural products and with this the power to purchase the output of our cities. It can be helped by preventing realistically the tragedy of the growing loss through foreclosure of our small homes and our farms. It can be helped by insistence that the Federal, State, and local governments act forthwith on the demand that their cost be drastically reduced. It can be helped by the unifying of relief activities which today are often scattered, uneconomical, and unequal. It can be helped by national planning for and supervision of all forms of transportation and of communications and other utilities which have a definitely public character. There are many ways in which it can be helped, but it can never be helped merely by talking about it. We must act and act quickly.

Finally, in our progress toward a resumption of work we require two safeguards against a return of the evils of the old order; there must be a strict supervision of all banking and credits and investments; there must be an end to speculation with other people's money, and there must be provision for an adequate but sound currency.

There are the lines of attack. I shall presently urge upon a new Congress in special session detailed measures for their fulfillment, and I shall seek the immediate assistance of the several States.

Through this program of action we address ourselves to putting our own national house in order and making income balance outgo. Our international trade relations, though vastly important, are in point of time and necessity secondary to the establishment of a sound national economy. I favor as a practical policy the putting of first things first. I shall spare no effort to restore world trade by international economic readjustment, but the emergency at home cannot wait on that accomplishment.

The basic thought that guides these specific means of national recovery is not narrowly nationalistic. It is the insistence, as a first consideration, upon the interdependence of the various elements in all parts of the United States, a recognition of the old and permanently important manifestation of the American spirit of the pioneer. It is the way to recovery. It is the immediate way. It is the strongest assurance that the recovery will endure.

In the field of world policy I would dedicate this Nation to the policy of the good neighbor, the neighbor who resolutely respects himself and, because he does so, respects the rights of others, the neighbor who respects his obligations and respects the sanctity of his agreements in and with a world of neighbors.

If I read the temper of our people correctly, we now realize as we have never realized before our interdependence on each other; that we can not merely take but we must give as well; that if we are to go forward, we must move as a trained and loyal army willing to sacrifice for the good of a common discipline, because without such discipline no progress is made, no leadership becomes effective. We are, I know, ready and willing to submit our lives and property to such discipline, because it makes possible a leadership which aims at a larger good. This I propose to offer, pledging that the larger purposes will bind upon us all as a sacred obligation with a unity of duty hitherto evoked only in time of armed strife.

With this pledge taken, I assume unhesitatingly the leadership of this great army of our people dedicated to a disciplined attack upon our common problems.

Action in this image and to this end is feasible under the form of government which we have inherited from our ancestors. Our Constitution is so simple and practical that it is possible always to meet extraordinary needs by changes in emphasis and arrangement without loss of essential form. That is why our constitutional system has proved itself the most superbly enduring political mechanism the modern world has produced. It has met every stress of vast expansion of territory, of foreign wars, of bitter internal strife, of world relations.

It is to be hoped that the normal balance of executive and legislative authority may be wholly adequate to meet the unprecedented task before us. But it may be that an unprecedented demand and need for undelayed action may call for temporary departure from that normal balance of public procedure.

I am prepared under my constitutional duty to recommend the measures that a stricken nation in the midst of a stricken world may require. These measures, or such other measures as the Congress may build out of its experience and wisdom, I shall seek, within my constitutional authority, to bring to speedy adoption.

But in the event that the Congress shall fail to take one of these two courses, and in the event that the national emergency is still critical, I shall not evade the clear course of duty that will then confront me. I shall ask the Congress for the one remaining instrument to meet the crisis, broad Executive power to wage a war against the emergency, as great as the power that would be given to me if we were in fact invaded by a foreign foe.

For the trust reposed in me I will return the courage and the devotion that befit the time. I can do no less.

We face the arduous days that lie before us in the warm courage of the national unity; with the clear consciousness of seeking old and precious moral values; with the clean satisfaction that comes from the stern performance of duty by old and young alike. We aim at the assurance of a rounded and permanent national life.

We do not distrust the future of essential democracy. The people of the United States have not failed. In their need they have registered a mandate that they want direct, vigorous action. They have asked for discipline and direction under leadership. They have made me the present instrument of their wishes. In the spirit of the gift I take it.

In this dedication of a Nation we humbly ask the blessing of God. May He protect each and every one of us. May He guide me in the days to come.

Green Light Letter (1942)

Commentary

After Pearl Harbor, baseball's commissioner, Judge Kenesaw Mountain Landis (1866–1944), wrote to President Franklin D. Roosevelt asking for an opinion on whether or not to continue baseball for the duration of the war. Roosevelt's reply, known as the "Green Light Letter," provided baseball and other organized sports encouragement to continue to play. By 1944 more than 60 percent of 1941 baseball's starting major leaguers had joined the military. Most teams filled their rosters with younger and older players, with some former players coming out of retirement to participate. Keeping baseball and other sports active during the war helped provide a boost in morale for the American public.

January 16, 1942
My dear Judge:

Thanks you for yours of Jan. 14. As you will, of course, realize, the final decision about the baseball season must rest with you and the baseball club owners—so what I am going to say is solely a personal and not an official point of view.

I honestly feel that it would be best for the country to keep baseball going. There will be fewer people unemployed and everybody will work longer hours and harder than ever before.

And that means that they ought to have a chance for recreation and for taking their minds off their work even more than before.

Baseball provides a recreation which does not last over two hours or two hours and a half, and which can be got for very little cost. And, incidentally, I hope that night games can be extended because it gives an opportunity to the day shift to see a game occasionally.

As to the players themselves, I know you agree with me that individual players who are of active military or naval age should go, without question, into the services. Even if the actual quality of the teams is lowered by the greater use of older players, this will not dampen the popularity of the sport. Of course, if any individual has some particular aptitude in a trade or profession, he ought to serve the Government. That, however, is a matter which I know you can handle with complete justice.

Here is another way of looking at it—if 300 teams use 5,000 or 6,000 players, these players are a definite recreational asset to at least 20,000,000 of their fellow citizens—and that in my judgment is thoroughly worthwhile.

A

A. Philip Randolph Institute, **4:**147

ABC (American Broadcasting Company), **3:**90, **4:**187

Abenaki Indians, **1:**56, 122

Abolitionists, **2:1–3**
  Anthony, Susan B., **2:**11
  Douglass, Frederick, **2:**48–49
  emancipation, **2:**2
  Fourth of July, **1:**73
  free blacks, **2:**3–4
  history, **2:**159–160
  journalism, **2:**123
  music, **2:**118–119
  Quakers, **1:**167, 170, 171, **2:**1
  Stanton, Elizabeth Cady, **2:**163
  in states, **1:**178
  violence and nonviolence, **2:**1–2
  and woman's rights movement, **2:**187
  See also Slavery; Thirteenth Amendment

Abu Gharib prison abuse, **4:**214

Account of the Battle of Lexington, **1:**240

Acheson, Dean, **4:**8, 118–119, 120, 148, 194, 195

Acheson-Lilienthal Report, **4:**8

Achille Lauro hijacking incident, **4:**127, 189

ACLU. *See* American Civil Liberties Union (ACLU)

Act Concerning Aliens (1798), **1:**236
  See also Alien and Sedition Laws

Adams, Abigail, **1:1–2**, *2*, **1:**61–63, **1:**157

Adams, Charity, *3:204*

Adams, Charles, *3:40*

Adams, Eddie, *4:191*

Adams, John (composer), **4:**127

Adams, John (politician), **1:2–4**, *3*
  and Adams, Abigail, **1:**1, 2, 61–63
  Alien and Sedition Laws, **1:**4, **2:**164
  American Revolution, **1:**3
  in art, **1:**137
  and *Common Sense* (Paine), **1:**33, 35
  Declaration of Independence, **1:**3, 49
  diplomacy and leadership, **1:**3–4
  early life, **1:**3
  family life, **1:**61–63
  Federalist Party, **1:**66
  Fourth of July, **1:**72
  and Jefferson, Thomas, **1:**3, 4
  Massachusetts state constitution, **1:**178
  Quasi-War, **1:**146
  as Revolutionary icon, **1:**142
  slavery, **1:**170
  and Warren, Mercy Otis, **1:**197

Adams, John Quincy, **1:**125, 170, 195–196

Adams, Samuel, **1:**24, 43, 137, 167, 174, *174*

Addams, Jane, **3:1–2**, *2*
  disarmament and arms control, **3:**39
  dissent in World War I, **3:**42
  feminism, **3:**55
  nonviolence, **4:**145–146
  peace movements, **3:**137, 138
  women and World War I, **3:**202
  World War I, **3:**19
  See also Peace movements

"Address to the Nation on the War in Vietnam" (Nixon), **4:**256

Advertising and journalism, World War I, **3:**86

Advice to the Unemployed in the Great Depression, (Ford) **3:**246

Aerial photography, **3:**141, 142, **4:**27

Aerospace industry, **4:1–3**, *2*, 38, 39, 125
  See also Military-industrial complex; Space race

AFC (America First Committee), **3:**43, 63, *80*, 138, 212

Afghanistan invasion, **4:**3, 20, 28, 139, 157–158

AFL. *See* American Federation of Labor (AFL)

AFL-CIO, **4:**108

African Americans
  American Revolution, **1:**121–122, 143, 157–158, 167, 168, **2:**3
  antebellum era, **2:**3–4
  arts as weapon, **4:**10
  churches, mainstream, **4:**25
  Civil Rights movement, **4:**32–35, *33*
  Civil War and its aftermath, **2:**4–5
  Civil War music, **2:**118, 119
  Civil War troops, **2:**30
  Civil War veterans, **2:**30
  Civilian Conservation Corps, **3:**24
  conscription, World War II, **3:**34
  in Continental Army, **1:**168
  education, **2:**54, 55–56, 56, 70, *71*
  education, Civil War, **2:**55
  education prior to Civil War, **2:**54, 55
  family life, **2:**64

Page numbers in **bold** indicate the main article on a subject. Page numbers in *italics* indicate illustrations. Page numbers followed by *t* indicate tables. The number preceding the colon indicates the volume number, and the number after the colon indicates the page number. This index is sorted word by word.

W